SUNSHINE AND SHADOW

The author. From a portrait, 1943, by Baron Kurt Pantz

SUNSHINE AND SHADOW

Being the fourth book of an Autobiography

1930–1946

by

CECIL ROBERTS

HODDER AND STOUGHTON
LONDON SYDNEY AUCKLAND TORONTO

CONTENTS

5

ILLUSTRATIONS

ILLUSTRATIONS

Key to acknowledgments

1 Anthony
2 Ker Seymer
3 Paul Tanqueray
4 Harrod's
5 Cecil Beaton
6 Underwood and Underwood
7 G. W. Romer

PREFACE

The Growing Boy, the first volume of my autobiography, covered the years 1892–1908, which saw the reigns of Queen Victoria and Edward VII. British power was paramount. The Navy was supreme in the world. The Empire flourished. My second volume, *The Years of Promise*, covered the years 1908–1919. They witnessed the Titanic struggle with Germany that shook the world. My early manhood coincided with the close of this conflict. Privilege had been shaken, our wealth depleted, our youth decimated. My third volume, *The Bright Twenties*, dealt with the years 1920–1929. We had emerged into what seemed a promising dawn, soon to be clouded by political ineptitude and the threat of another world war.

Now in this fourth volume, *Sunshine and Shadow*, covering the years 1930–1946, I take up my story. I established myself as an author. I was buoyant in spirit. I acquired a country house I loved, where I entertained friends drawn from many circles. The first years were halycon. Fate seemed to smile on me. But I was never content to live in an ivory tower. I heard birds sing, I also heard menacing thunder and observed a darkening horizon. The growing Nazi threat clouded the day. There were repeated warnings from Churchill, ignored. I travelled in Germany and Italy, and what I saw perturbed me. I felt, with growing certainty, that without the support of the U.S.A., which we had alienated by the foolish repudiation of our war debt, with dire consequences such as the Neutrality Act, we could not survive. I had a wide knowledge of the United States, where I was known. I felt I could make a special contribution to winning American aid. The story of my effort is in the second half of this book, with the cost of it to me mentally, physically, financially.

Sunshine and Shadow presents a private and a public phase of sixteen years in which I experienced happiness, frustration and grief.

The writer of an autobiography suffers a handicap. He is open to the charge of egotism and immodesty if he blows the trumpet his biographer might sound. In fear of this he may do himself some injustice by too much repression. I hope I have maintained a proper balance. A crowded life of varied activity has taught me to shed all vanity. "Oh why should the spirit of mortal be proud?" I have tried to be just, under provocation, wherefore I was particularly gratified when a reviewer in *The Listener* observed of *The Bright Twenties*, "This is a zestful book, a paean of living, free of literary and other malice." I have tried not to depart from this standard.

This personal record covers a wide field on two continents, in which are mentioned many names, dates, and places. I may have committed errors, my task has not been easy. I kept no detailed records, save a few letters. I lost in the bombing of London the whole of my small pocket diaries up to 1939. Contemporaries I would have consulted have passed from the scene. The best of memories is not proof against errors in the flow of Time.

C. R.

CHAPTER ONE

The Titan of Oxford Street

I

When in the first hour of 1930 I started to walk to my rooms, having heard from the high terrace of my friend's Westminster apartment Big Ben toll out midnight, I indulged in the usual retrospect before turning to the blank page of a new year. The streets were almost empty, those long, London streets spaced with lamps and patrolled by policemen who, with their dark uniforms and stealthy tread, always seemed to match the black cats of London, also nocturnal patrollers. My way lay by Green Park to Hyde Park, black with leafless trees. The streets were silent chasms. The January night was cold, the air still.

I was thirty-seven years of age, two years past the half-way of the span allotted by the Psalmist. I was a little behind in my programme. It had been my intention to write an account of my journey, an autobiography, to be called *Half Way*, but the book that should have marked the completion of my thirty-five years was only three-parts written. The first resolution of this new year was to finish it before future events blurred the record. It might seem presumptuous to be writing one's life when only half-way through it, but mine had been no ordinary, placid journey. For a fatherless boy of fifteen it had not been an easy one but the flame of ambition had burned brightly within me. I had never taken no for an answer, endowed, despite a highly sensitive nature, with enough egotism to make me irrepressible. Desperate, as are many boys who find themselves in a prison instead of on a crusade, I defiantly quitted an office stool and became in turn a schoolmaster, a literary editor, a war correspondent, a civil servant, the editor of a newspaper, and now, finally, what I had always intended to be, an established author.

Nevertheless, I was still apprehensive about the future, despite the assets in hand. I had published eight novels, with gratifying success. "I must say that your name seems to be getting about nowadays quite a good deal," wrote Arnold Bennett. I was familiar with the Continent and the United States. A measure of fame opened doors that otherwise would have been firmly closed to me.

At thirty-seven one is no longer 'a young man of promise'. Verging on forty and middle-age, the promise should be crowned with achievement. I was still hoping for 'the big break', the seventh wave that carries one firmly to established success. The years had already brought their losses; an illness had put an end to my political ambitions; a frustrated love affair had left me scarred; and I had lost the one dearest to me in all the world. There was always the fear that my inspiration would run out and that, having arrived on the platform, before a large audience, I should have nothing to say. My friend, Sir Philip Gibbs, a veteran with forty books behind him, scoffed at my apprehension. "Something always happens to start one off," he said. He was right. I had just delivered to my publisher the manuscript of *Havana Bound*. One year ago I had sailed for Havana. A 'spookiness' about my cabin, and my refusal to stay in it, had drawn from the purser the story of its last occupant, a Cuban millionaire who in mid-Atlantic had disappeared out of it without leaving a clue. I began the novel in New York three months later, continued it in Venice and Warsaw, and had finished it just before Christmas.

And now? I was intermittently busy on *Half Way*, but the next novel, my tenth, where was that coming from? In the morning and in the evening I worried about it, rejecting a dozen propositions.

When I reached my apartment, and while I was putting my key in the lock, a young policeman passed. He halted to see if I was respectable, smiled, and said, "A happy New Year to you, sir!" I thanked him, reciprocated the wish, and, suddenly, asked him a question. "You must have seen a lot of odd things, Officer. Can you recall one that might make a plot for a story? I'm a dried-up novelist." He laughed. "I don't think I've anything of use to you, sir. A novelist! Funny that, sir. I've only met one before, and he was a drunk I had to remove at an Election Party at Selfridge's. Quite famous, they said, but he had had too much and got obstreperous. We put him in a taxi and sent him home." "Well, you won't have to do that for me. I've been to a party. I'm not drunk, and I'm home," I said, opening my door. "It's the New Year. What about a drink?" He grinned. "Thank you, sir, but I don't know as I should." "You spend much of your life dealing with people who do what they shouldn't?" He grinned again. "Well, sir——" and stepped inside.

I believe now that that young policeman was provided by Fate. The following morning I read, in the gossip column of my paper, that Lord Bective, son of the Marquess of Headfort and the ex-Gaiety chorus girl, Rosie Boote, was working in Selfridge's store in Oxford Street 'to gain experience'. Selfridge's. The policeman and the peer's son had twice evoked that name. Suddenly I knew I had found my story. There was a novel in Gordon Selfridge. He was one of the most astonishing figures in London. I had been his guest on one occasion, at a large party at Lansdowne House.

Gordon Selfridge was born at Ripon, Wisconsin, in 1857. His father died a year after he was born. His mother was a remarkable woman, beautiful and gracious. Her only child, he adored her all his life. She was a poorly paid teacher in a State school in neighbouring Jackson. He was an errand boy at the age of twelve, then worked in a store for $1.50 a week, later, in a bank as a junior clerk at $8 a week. The youthful Selfridge attracted the attention of Leonard Field, a cousin of Marshall Field, president of the flourishing Chicago store, Field, Leiter and Co. Marshall Field started the seventeen-year-old Selfridge at $10 a week. He sent home a quarter of this to his mother, saved fifty cents and lived on the remainder. He rose like a rocket, a terrific worker of genius. At the age of thirty-three he claimed a junior partnership. In 1904, at the age of forty-seven, he had amassed a fortune of £300,000, in present-day value some two million pounds.

During this time he had travelled in Europe and returned with ideas about store-keeping. He had married the girl he loved, at twenty-eight, and had a wedding ceremony that made history in Chicago. A devoted husband with a family of one son, and two daughters who married Russian and French noblemen, he remained his adored mother's son. Beautiful as old lace, she never left his side until her death. He always consulted her in his business moves. Selfridge was a good-looking man, sturdy but under height, which he strove to correct by wearing high-heeled boots. Something of a dandy, he was reserved in manner and speech. I had first seen him when, *de rigueur* in a black morning coat, wearing a glossy top hat, he made his morning tour of Selfridge's.

In 1904 he had astonished Marshall Field by tendering his resignation. It might be thought that a man of forty-seven, with £300,000 in hand, would be content to retire after thirty-five years of strenuous work. But this was not Selfridge's idea. In the next two years he bought and sold a Chicago business. Then in 1906 he left for London to make an astonishing conquest. He was now almost fifty. 'Madame', as his mother was always known, and his wife, went with him. No shop he saw suited him. He decided to build his own premises. He took a long lease on 42,000 sq. feet in Oxford Street. Later he doubled his premises. He began by clearing away the small buildings and built a grandiose store, with one hundred and thirty departments, a restaurant and a roof garden. The façade was magnificent, a long line of Corinthian columns rising above the ground floor, with an entrance that might have come from the Baths of Caracalla.

It took almost three years to get Selfridge's ready for business but when it opened its doors in March, 1909, there were crowds in front of the windows looking at the astonishing displays. Inside there was an enormous open floor revealing £100,000 worth of goods. The staff of eighteen hundred had been on the payroll for three months, rehearsing for this opening day. They were instructed to treat the customers as guests, to 'push' nothing, to be polite and give them the impression that they were always right.

From the first day Selfridge's store was a sensational success. Thousands streamed through its great bronze doors which had no name above them. Selfridge's had no need of a name-plate. Not a detail was missed. He wanted a simple telephone number. No 1 on the Gerrard exchange belonged to a doctor. Selfridge bought the number from him and arranged for a famous revue star—Teddy Gerrard—to sing a song with a line refrain 'One Gerrard'. Selfridge knew the value of press publicity. He spent £40,000 on advertising in the first year. He wrote all his own advertisements. He sent newspaper editors bouquets of flowers at Easter. The slogan was 'Wear something new for Easter'. He started a daily column in *The Times* and other newspapers, in the form of an essay with not a word of advertising in it. It made irresistible reading. For years everyone wanted to know who was this *Callisthenes* who signed them. Classical professors, famous authors, all were in turn credited with writing the articles. Clergymen based sermons on them. The mystery of the authorship was maintained for many years. Then Selfridge supplied some information. "Callisthenes lived about 360—328 B.C. He was related to Aristotle and travelled with Alexander the Great, recording his journeys. When Alexander became swollen-headed and claimed divine powers, Callisthenes denounced him. He died in prison. Here then is an excellent name to be given to one who, twenty centuries later, has the task of writing about a great enterprise." This explanation did not reveal anything. Ultimately it was divulged that the author of the articles was Selfridge himself.

The New Year policeman and the peer's son, recalling the name of Selfridge, planted in my mind the germ of a novel. I would base it on the life-story of this extraordinary man. To get realistic data I would work in his store. Two days later I asked to see Selfridge. He made a point of being accessible. In my letter I said that I had been his guest at one of his parties at Lansdowne House, the magnificent furnished house he rented from the Marquess of Lansdowne. I enclosed a copy of my latest book. At once I received an appointment. His office was on the top floor. It was not the usual office. It was elegantly furnished, with a rose in a vase on the desk. He told someone that the three greatest things in the world were 'a flower, a baby's smile, a sunrise'. He was sincere in this. Near the rose stood a small sand hour-glass. He gave no one more than fifteen minutes' time, which it measured. When the sand ran out you were out.

He was now a famous figure, a great host, a lavish spender, impassive, quietly elegant with a high stiff collar and a vest-slip. He wore rimless pince-nez. His white hair, long at the back, reminded me of Lloyd George, five years his junior. Selfridge was now seventy-two. He listened to me gravely. Yes, he would give me the facility I requested, to work in the store for two or three weeks. He made a stipulation that in no way I should imply that I had had any connection with the store or use the name Selfridge. It must remain a work of fiction. I thanked him. He summoned one of his assistants, explained my requirements, and bade me good-day. The sand had not run out in the hour-glass. I was handed over to one of the brains of the business, a man of about my age, who had been with him as an advertising specialist since 1914 and would be with him for twenty-two years. Some ten years after Selfridge died he wrote a book about his old chief, kindly and admiring in tone.*

In the middle of January I began my apprenticeship. After five days I moved down into the bargain basement. It was suggested I had thereby lowered myself, but I felt it presented a richer stratum of life. One day I received a two-shilling tip from a fat lady for being 'such an obliging young man'. I told her regretfully that I could not accept it as there was a firm rule that assistants may not take tips.

By the end of three weeks, from 8.30 to 6 p.m., I had gathered all I wanted. In the middle of February I left for Paris en route for Berlin, which I had visited briefly on my way from Poland last autumn. What I saw then intrigued me by its tense political atmosphere. A demagogue named Hitler was attracting attention. I postponed writing *Bargain Basement*, my chosen title, until I was in Paris again in November, but I was always thinking of it. Then in four months I wrote the novel. Instead of a peer's son I made a peer's daughter the heroine. The head of Marling's, as I called the store, said to her, to quote my novel—

> I shall start you at the very bottom, in all senses of the word. After you've been in the despatch room, I shall transfer you to the Bargain Basement. You must not feel dismayed. There is a lot of nonsense talked about the Basement. The air perhaps is not as good as it should be, though that's a matter of opinion. And perhaps the class of customer is not quite as good—though I have seen the Duchess of Runcorn there, searching for a sale line in silk stockings. From what I have seen of members of the aristocracy they will haggle over a shilling, and, having saved it, take a taxi to Claridge's for lunch. You'll learn a lot about humanity in the Basement.

The *Daily Mirror* had serialised my novel, *Pamela's Spring Song*. The editor wanted another serial from me. He offered an increased price of £750. I told him that I did not write for serialisation but he could see my next novel, which he did. He found it unsuitable. It was *Havana Bound*. Afterwards he regretted his decision. He asked for an option on the next. I astonished him by refusing. "If you tempt me to write with an eye on serialisation I shall ruin my work," I explained. I thought that was the end of the matter but six months

* *No Name on the Door: Memoirs of Gordon Selfridge*, A. H. Williams, C.B.E. (W. H. Allen, 1956).

16

later he asked if he could look at my next novel whose title he had seen in my publisher's preliminary list. I happened to have *Bargain Basement* in proof and let him look at it. He bought it overnight. He wanted to call it simply *At Selfridge's*. I told him the use of the name or any mention of the store was barred. "Why, Selfridge must be crazy. He's getting a 3,000,000 reader-publicity for nothing!" I agreed but told him I must honour my word. So the title remained *Bargain Basement*. There could be no doubt in anybody's mind that it was Selfridge's; it was the only great store in London with a bargain basement.

The serial was advertised all over London. As soon as it had finished serialisation the book came out and subscribed 20,000 copies. I asked my publishers to arrange a special display in Selfridge's windows and in their book department. To our astonishment Selfridge's declined making any display in their windows or in the book department. Had something I had written given offence to Gordon Selfridge? No, I was informed, but he didn't wish it to be thought Selfridge's was in collusion with any newspaper or publisher. Yet he sent roses to editors! The advertisement manager just looked blank, unable to find words. We were up against one of those quirks of character that afflict great men. When the book rapidly had a second printing, and Harrod's store displayed it, Selfridge's planned a special display and asked if I would attend and autograph copies! Years later one of Selfridge's directors, to whom I mentioned this odd behaviour over my novel, said, "I think I know what upset him. In it you make your store-owner a peer and then marry him to a widowed countess. He was very loyal to the memory of his wife and never contemplated a second marriage, though he did not lack offers. And the peerage you gave your tycoon must have irritated him. Despite the great impression he made on commercial life no official recognition was ever shown him, even after he took British citizenship in old age, like Henry James, on whom they conferred the Order of Merit. Yet he had a far greater impact on English life than James and gave employment to thousands. It was a scandal he was not given a knighthood, let alone a peerage, as Waring, the furniture-store owner. I am sure this omission ate into him. You unconsciously rubbed an open wound."

The end of the story is dismal. How did a man of almost puritanical

rectitude, a model husband and son, come to wreck himself on the
shoals of sex and gambling? He was over sixty when he fell into the
clutches of the notorious Gaby Deslys, the personification of blatant
sex, who had pulled a monarch, Manuel II of Portugal, off his throne
and now shook the throne of this monarch of industry. He danced
attention on a ruthless exploiter who sold her favours. The young
Guards' officers who hung round the stage door found that the
price of taking her out to supper was at least £50. The dazzled
victims stood in a queue. To great allure she added wit. The Archbishop of Canterbury denounced her flagrant appearances. Asked,
on leaving England, what she thought of the Archbishop's censure,
she replied, "Tell the old darling he shows too much leg!" After
setting her up in a Kensington house, Selfridge bought her expensive
jewellery in the Rue de la Paix. He let her ransack his store. By the
time their relations cooled she had extracted many thousands of
pounds from him. Then, in the mid-Twenties, a pair of more ruthless
harpies moved in, the Dolly Sisters, American vaudeville artists, born
in Hungary but reared in New York's East Side by immigrant Jewish
parents. They had made their debut in 1909 in the Ziegfeld Follies
and overnight became famous on Broadway and subsequently throughout Europe. Maurice Chevalier partnered them at the height of their
fame. They appeared at the parties at Lansdowne House. The
saxophones wailed, while upwards of three hundred guests danced
the Charleston and the Black Bottom, led by the Dolly Sisters,
glittering with diamonds.

Selfridge did not neglect his business but his weekends were
extended. His temper was sometimes frayed. He was spending over
£40,000 a year. His town house cost £5,000 p.a., a country house,
resplendent Highcliffe Castle, cost £3,000, a yacht cost £10,000 a
year, seldom used. He bought land for private building projects,
he gave costly parties. He lived up to the hilt. The store flourished
but there were recurrent credit crises. Now, in old age, he squandered
money on love affairs; worse, he took to reckless gambling at casinos.
The two Dolly Sisters, common in speech, humour and laughter,
but alluring, captured him. I never saw them in London, but it
chanced that in New York in October, 1924, I was the guest of the
Dutch Treat Club, a very popular journalists' weekly luncheon club.
When I had conferred on me a large plaster medal, the badge of

membership for distinguished guests, I was kissed on both cheeks by the Dolly Sisters, to loud applause.

Not caring for London, the Jennie twin retired, still in her thirties and took a villa at Fontainebleau, but she was restless and moved between Vichy, Deauville, Le Touquet, Cannes and Monte Carlo. She had Selfridge in tow. Encouraged, he followed her from place to place, travelling by his private aeroplane at weekends. He foresaw its future when Louis Blériot made aviation history by crossing the English Channel on July 25, 1909, in a small monoplane. Selfridge went straight to the aerodrome and within an hour bought the rights to exhibit the plane at Selfridge's. It drew enormous crowds. From that day he was a flying fan. When Jennie, in Fontainebleau, expressed a desire for ice-cream he had it flown to her daily. His cheque book bled with her demands, cars, clothes, furs, jewels, and anything she fancied in his store. Worse, at Le Touquet and Deauville, she led him to the gaming tables. Soon he was converted into an insensate gambler. Jennie took his gains and he covered her losses. To this wild expenditure he added the cost of parties in France of a vulgar lavishness never seen at Lansdowne House. Some wondered, seeing the white-haired old man sitting apart from all the riot engendered by the raffish Jennie, whether it was frustration, not sex, that held him a victim. Even so, every Monday he was back in his office, austere, efficient, planning new moves. What his gambling losses were no one knew, but in eight years he spent £1,800,000. The attachment cooled in the early Thirties. Jennie finally ended in poverty in Hollywood where, in 1947, she committed suicide. Her sister Rosie lived on to be seventy-seven, dying in 1970.

The Company ran into difficulties. A trade boom had ended. Selfridge had to borrow from private financiers and banks. A vulgar company promoter, Jimmy White, who ended a suicide, somehow hypnotised Selfridge. He formed for him a £3,000,000 Gordon Selfridge Trust which was immediately oversubscribed. Its first move was disastrous. It took over William Whiteley's famous store, nearly insolvent. Its shareholders were cajoled into the take-over by Selfridge recklessly guaranteeing them a dividend of twenty per cent. It became a millstone round his neck. He was seventy when he made this plunge. His fortunes from that day took a downward path. Soon, with his high personal expenditure, he was in difficulties.

He had a gambling debt of £100,000 and was pressed for payment. His private fortune had almost vanished. The directors became nervous, the banks involved pressed Selfridge. By 1940, in a time of war shortages and restrictions, the Board felt it must act. They removed Selfridge from control, sorrowfully, since they retained a deep admiration of the Titan who had created their fortunes. At eighty-three, Selfridge, divested of authority, was given the empty title of President—with a salary of £2,000 a year. His debt to the Company was £118,000. They waived this. The office with the rose and the hour-glass saw him no more. But he could not wholly leave the scene. He moved with dignity to an office they gave him across Oxford Street, from where he could look at the Olympian façade of his great creation, but he was not called in to Board Meetings. His £2,000 a year proved inadequate for his household expenses. No Rolls-Royce now carried him to his Putney Heath home. He queued up for a bus in Oxford Street before the blackout and the raids came. The office was a useless pretence. Then in his ninetieth year, he came no more. One May day in 1947, unheeded, the forgotten Titan was carried to rest in a Hampshire churchyard, there to join his wife and his mother.

> Men are we, and must grieve when even the shade
> Of that which once was great is pass'd away.

II

My time in Selfridge's Bargain Basement, my notes of this lively experience made, I left for Paris, en route to Berlin. I spent three weeks in Paris towards the end of February, the guest of my friend Norman Fuller, an ex-R.F.C. officer and a director of the Paris office of the Anglo-Persian Oil Company. He had just moved into an apartment at Auteuil, overlooking the Seine. From my window and its balcony I had a magnificent view down the river towards the Pont Mirabeau, of the dome of the Invalides, and the Eiffel Tower. Among my fellow guests was a somewhat shy man, my senior. I was destined to begin there a friendship that endured for over forty years. He was the Hon. Seddon Cripps, the eldest son of Lord Parmoor, the Privy Councillor and British representative on the League of Nations, who had married one of the three remarkable Potter sisters, of whom one was a life-partner in that formidable Fabian pair, the Sidney Webbs, the brains of the rising Labour Party. My friend Seddon had a younger brother, Stafford Cripps, later Chancellor of the Exchequer and a stormy petrel of the Labour Party. A greater contrast to the quiescent Seddon could not be imagined than Stafford Cripps, puritanical, aggressive to the verge of crankiness, whom I had once on a public occasion dubbed 'an unburnt Savonarola'. Seddon was always loyally mute about his brother. At the time of our meeting he was the Bursar of Queen's College, Oxford. Beautifully lodged there, quietly hospitable, his friendship enriched my life. I was soon to be almost a neighbour, doubly so, for the cottage I acquired that summer was just below the Parmoor estate, and only half an hour's drive from Oxford.

In the middle of March I left for Berlin. "Why Berlin, it is desolate!" said my friend. "It is the storm centre of Europe," I replied, "I am anxious to see what will happen there." Many of my friends wondered why I, an author, should concern myself with the political and economic state of Europe. But I have always believed that life is larger than literature. Some forty years later *The Times*, reviewing the first volume of this Autobiography, pertinently observed, "The story of the world is part of his own story."

In the few days I had spent in Berlin the previous year I was aware of a malaise in the body politic. It did not require any great percipience to sense the gathering of a storm, based partly on despair, partly on a sentiment of revenge. The Allies were planning for the peace they were going to enjoy. The Germans had no reason for wasting time on an ideal new world. They had been limited by the Versailles Treaty to an army of one hundred thousand men. As early as 1922 General von Seeckt had his plan to wreck that signed obligation. He kept a secret German staff alive. Meanwhile another unofficial army was forming under Hitler and Röhm; it began politically, basing itself on hatred of the Jews. They offered a patriotic version of German resurgence under a swastika banner soon to wave over the marching Nazi storm-troopers. Their prophet was a man of evil genius, the thwarted Adolf Hitler, coming out of a prison where he had written the new German Bible *Mein Kampf*. In the 1930 September Election his party, the National Socialist (NAZI), surprised everybody by taking a hundred and seven seats from the moderates.

The previous year they had had only twelve in the Reichstag. Their programme was denunciation of the Versailles Treaty and the creation of a military state. In September, 1929, I asked a young German what were the Nazis. He replied, "Oh, they're a bunch of arrogant misfits led by a ranter called Hitler, who's financed by Hugenberg and the industrial gangsters who are afraid of communism."

III

When I arrived in Berlin in the middle of March, 1930, Germany was just coming out of an economic blizzard that had struck it. The Wall Street crash of the previous October, with hundreds of bank failures, had stopped the flow of loose, speculation money from across the Atlantic. Poverty was widespread, the number of unemployed was above five millions. The German public was utterly demoralised. I had been recommended to a modest hotel. It was clean, comfortable. I was there a week before I discovered I was living in a brothel! The couples that appeared in the breakfast room seemed oddly assorted. There was a continuous going up and down the staircase of young women, youths and men. The arrivals had no baggage. It was all very orderly and decorous. Then I observed there was a payment down for the one-night rooms. There were no bills, weekly or otherwise. Before the war the hotel had had an excellent reputation, and had been patronised by friends of mine. I moved. Many of the first-class hotels were out of business. The Adlon Hotel was packed. There was a new hotel-de-luxe, expensive. I took a room for my short stay. Evidently it was a war profiteers' paradise. All the servants were smartly uniformed. There was a line of twelve page-boys, gold-epauletted, white-gloved, all of a size, drilled like guardsmen. Max Bauer, a German journalist to whom I had a letter of introduction, lunched with me and said, "They're part of the room service."

He offered to show me the night-life. Our first call was a very smart bar filled with expensively gowned young women. They were languid in movement and had roving eyes. Some of them were jewelled, with elaborate head-dresses. Two of them left their bar stools and came over to our table. We ordered drinks. They were slim, beautiful, and, it would seem, witty, for my friend laughed a lot. I could not follow their German. They were clearly disappointed when we left. "We'll slip these boys a couple of dollars each, they're probably hungry." Boys? I had the clue then to something about them. They were too svelte, too permissive. My 'girl' said something, smiled and slipped the dollar bills into her corsage. "Now, I'll show you the counterpart," said my companion, calling a taxi. We arrived at a café, dimly lit. It was noisy and full of young men and girls. A gramophone blared, the air was heavy with smoke. We pushed our way up to the bar. A stocky young man with black curls gave place for me, and when I proceeded to drink surprised me by saying "Cheerio!" He spoke good English. He told me his mother was Irish. He offered me a cigarette and introduced his companion, a delicate-looking youth in a green corduroy suit, with a bright yellow tie. He seemed pleased to display his English. "My dad was a prisoner in England, at Reading. He liked it," he said. I then became aware that the young man wore four rings on his right hand and the corduroy youth wore small earrings. Nearly all these young men were women. I enquired about the 'tough' with a square-cropped head, wearing a brown jersey, smoking a cigar, and obviously popular. "She's a well-known wrestler—lesbian. There's a sprinkling of them here." "You must go, dear?" he-she cried as we moved away. We continued our tour.

"If you like being beaten—here's your chance," said Bauer as we came to another bar. There was nothing unusual about the place, a dreary room with people sitting at tables, some with no drink, some playing cards. The men looked like truck drivers or labourers, hefty and stupid, the women heavy and blowsy. Someone was playing a zither. We stood in the doorway. "You take your pick. They go home with you and beat you. For a higher fee you can beat them. Now let's go to an elegant scene," said my guide re-entering the taxi. We drew up in front of a large hotel, walked through the lounge into a ball-room brilliantly lit. An orchestra played on a dais bright with flowers. The waiters were in evening dress. The company was elegantly attired, and of all ages. Some of the women were extremely beautiful. Everything seemed decorous. I noticed that all the tables around the dance floor had telephones with large number cards. Many of the girls were sitting alone. "You make your choice, telephone her table and ask her if she would like to dance.

If she accepts, you go over, buy her a drink and take her on the floor. If you dance with her and don't take her out you must give her five dollars." "And the tariff if one does?" I asked. "You must fix that—thirty dollars up. There's a nice girl I know, at table nineteen, with a friend. Let's dance!" He rang table nineteen and got an answering smile. We took the floor with them. My partner, pretty, about twenty, was an excellent dancer. She said she was an out-of-work ballerina. During our second dance she was hailed by a young officer in the Reichswehr uniform. He joined our table for a drink. When we left the girls were obviously disappointed. "I suppose that lad in uniform is her lover?" I commented. "Hans? Oh, no, her brother! He's a ski champion kept by an ambassador's wife."

It was past midnight. "A few more dives?" I agreed. "Now I'll try your stomach." He stopped the taxi at the end of a dark street full of cheap cafés. "That café's got boys of fifteen—homeless, most of them." Two pale thin boys in leather shorts ogled us as we passed. "Now—here's the *Bart-Palast*". He pushed open a door. It was a dim room with long tables with diced red and white covers. A very fat man with a beard down to his waist was delivering beer mugs to the customers. The air was thick with smoke. We sat down. I wondered why I had been brought here. I then noticed that everyone was bearded. There were elderly men with white beards, and young men with brown and red beards. One with a beard covering his chest was combing it ostentatiously. "Don't laugh, they are very serious. The bearded come here to date one another. The man in the corner with the grey beard is a famous professor of archaeology who excavates in Persia," said Max. We drank and left. Two of them bowed gravely as we went out.

My friend escorted me to my hotel. "If you want to investigate further, on Saturday night there is Dr. Magnus Hirschfeld's famous ball. He is the great authority on sexual inversion. He has a clinic, a great library on the subject, and he has written many treatises, among them *Sexuelle Zwischenstufen. Das männliche Weib und der weibliche Mann*—which is a classic on the inverts we saw in our first two bars. He is campaigning for a charter on sexual freedom. At his Saturday night balls over two hundred male homosexuals dance to a band on the upper floor and a similar number of lesbians on the lower. In the interval they join up and listen to a lecture on inversion, and pass resolutions demanding abolition of repressive laws. Hirschfeld's books are on sale at a stall. Everyone is very serious, polite and well-behaved. The police watch the proceedings considerately. Hirschfeld is taken quite seriously by some. His standard work in three volumes *Sexualpathologie. Ein Lesebuch fur Ärzte und Studierende* is used as a text book at Berlin University."

"Is Berlin the great centre for perversion?" I asked, as we sat in my room. "They don't use that word—inversion, *zwischenstufen* is politer!" replied Max, smiling. "No. I don't think there's more inversion here than in other capitals of the world. But there's been a breakdown of all morality, financial as well as social. Many persons are quite ruined—there's a seventeen per cent suicide rate—out of work, hungry, in despair. Many sell themselves for a few marks— women, men, girls, youths, schoolboys and psychopaths. Not all, of course. There's a hard core that won't admit defeat—a military element. They vow that Germany shall rise again. We're cheating you on the military restrictions—I am speaking as a Liberal. There's von Seeckt, there's Hitler, whose National Socialists grow in power every day. He attracts the youth, the best elements, virile, moral, dedicated, in whom the flame of patriotism still burns. For Germany won't go on like this. We are coming out of our demoralisation."

Three days later on a Sunday morning Max rang me. If I was free he would take me to a *Wellenbad* at the end of the Kurfürsten-damm. It was a swimming pool where a water-polo team practised. "You'll meet some youths there, athletes. Most of them are Brown-shirts. I want you to meet Ernst Ritter, very intelligent. He's been a year in a London bank, speaks fluent English. He's very opinionated and downright."

The Kurfürstendamm was a long wide avenue, bright with modern shops and cafés. We came to the baths. There was a long swimming pool under a glass roof. A machine installed at one end changed the water and created waves so that we had the impression of swimming in the sea. The pool was quiescent when we arrived at our cabins. Two teams were playing water-polo. As this was a private session for men only the swimmers were naked. Presently the polo game ended. The machine began to agitate the water and we all dived in. All of these youths were of good physique. They might have come from a frieze of the Parthenon. Presently I was introduced in the

25

water to Ernst Ritter. He was crop-headed, bronzed, sturdily
built. I was not surprised to learn he was a fine athlete, about
twenty-five years of age. On leaving the pool, wrapping ourselves in towels, we went and drank coffee. He was somewhat
reticent at first, appraising me with his blue eyes. I remarked on his
excellent English. "We had a Scotch nannie until the war took her
home. And I was a year with the Deutsche Bank in London," he
said. I asked if he liked London. "Very much—but I was under a
cloud. You don't like us. You think we started the war and now
you're trying to throttle us. Your Lloyd George cried 'Hang the
Kaiser' and 'Make Germany pay'. He wasn't able to do either!" He
said this with a charming smile, smoothing a bare leg. I let the
remark go. He worked in a Berlin bank but he had just completed
three months' training with the Reichswehr, as a cadet officer. He was
transferring to the S.A., Hitler's storm-troopers. He wanted to give
up banking and be a professional soldier, but at present it was not
posssible. "We can't expand because of the Disarmament Clauses
in the Versailles Treaty. We shall finish all that when we've got rid of
Brüning." Brüning had just become Chancellor. "You don't like
Brüning?" "No—he's the old gang. He wants to put a Hohenzollern
on a restored throne. We've finished wih the Hohenzollerns. We want
new leaders." I asked if he had anyone in mind. "Yes, there's only
one man, our Führer, Adolf Hitler. He should be the Chancellor."
He embarked on a fervent description of the new movement, the
National Socialist Party led by Hitler. He had just been in Munich
and had heard him speak. He had met Röhm, commandant of the
storm-troopers. His eyes shone as he spoke.

It was one o'clock. The bath was closing. "Well?" asked Max as
I came out of my cabin, "I hope Ernst didn't offend you?" "Not at
all, I like his honesty. Let's ask him to lunch," I replied. Unfortunately he could not accept, he was meeting his fiancée. But he accepted
for dinner that evening. We parted cordially. As we left I was surprised to see that all these youths were dressed in brown shirts,
wearing red, white and black swastika armbands, leather top-boots
and peaked caps. When we parted at the door young Ritter shook
my hand firmly and, looking straight into my eyes, said, smiling, "You
English are backing the wrong horse. Your allies are no good. France
is rotten to the core, America's corrupt with gold, Russia is diseased

with communism. Together, England and Germany, of pure Anglo-Saxon blood, could put Europe on its feet." He smiled with his blue eyes, saluted, and left.

"Now you've met a real Nazi. What do you think of him?" asked Max as we went to lunch. I did not reply at once. Then I said, "I like him. He's got faith, he's honest and healthy. Germany's more likely to revive with fellows like that than with the sickly misfits we saw in those bars and *dielen*." Max agreed with me. I now realised he had deliberately taken me to a nest of Nazis. "Are you a Brown-shirt?" I asked. "Yes," he replied. "We take over the bath on Sunday mornings."

That afternoon I went to tea at the apartment of an Englishman, Christopher Wood, a well-to-do young man who was studying art. A number of his friends were present, mostly English, with a few Germans. I happened to mention my meeting with the young Nazis. There was an immediate explosion. "What a set of silly louts, got up in brown shirts, stamping their boots and bawling the Horst-Wessel *lied*!" exclaimed one of the company. He turned to our host. "Have you heard that at the Nürnberger Diele last night they walked in and beat up the fairies?" The general opinion was that Hitler was the crack-pot leader of a splinter party. But was he? I thought of the fervour, the healthy vigour of Ernst Ritter and his companions. They might have been a cohort of the young Alexander. There was something dedicated about them. The more I saw of Ernst and his companions the more I was impressed. They all swore they had no war-like intentions. Communism was the great enemy. It had infiltrated Germany, a cancer in the body politic. I was not the only Englishman at that time impressed with these young men. Even that turbulent iconoclast, Wyndham Lewis, was enthralled by the blue-eyed, disciplined Brownshirt *hoplites* of a new Germany. The German cesspool had to be cleaned. Like myself, he was quickly disillusioned by subsequent events. But at this stage I admired young Ernst; there was an unselfishness, a nobility of shining dedication, qualities Hitler was to profit by, and corrupt.

I was fortunate in finding in Berlin my host of Budapest, Baron Wolfner. He knew the city intimately and had wide social contacts. It was he who took me to call on the daughter of Field-Marshal Hindenburg, now, at eighty-two, the President of the German

Republic. Within two years he would be compelled to call in Hitler as Chancellor. "That man for Chancellor!" he growled, on first seeing him, "I'll make him a postmaster and he can lick stamps with my head on them!" The President's daughter was a very stout lady, formidable but gracious, whom some wit had nicknamed 'The Hindenburg Line' after her father's famous war-front.

IV

After a visit of three weeks the time came for departure. Max Bauer and Ernst Ritter accompanied me to the station. Yes, I would come again next year, I replied, in answer to their entreaties. It was not to be next year, however, but four years later, when everything would be changed and most illusions about Hitler and his cohorts would be shattered. My chief purpose in coming to Berlin this time had been to see the museums and in particular the famous Altar of Pergamon in the Kaiser Frederick Museum. Last year in brief transit from Warsaw I had not been able to fulfil my desire. It was temporarily closed. Now I saw it, a very rewarding experience. Fifty years earlier a German had discovered and excavated the ruins of the great temple King Eumenes II, of the Attalid Dynasty, had erected on the Acropolis of Pergamon, Asia Minor, in 180 B.C., to celebrate his victories. An enlightened monarch, he had made Pergamon one of the most important and beautiful of all Greek cities. It was an early example of town-planning, with a magnificent hill-side theatre, a school of sculpture and a great library that rivalled that of Alexandria under the Ptolemies. The famous sculptures, now in Berlin, had come from the great altar of Zeus. Splendidly displayed, the figures of Greeks and Barbarians fighting rivalled in importance, and surpassed in quantity and size, the Parthenon sculptures in the British Museum. The richness and mastery of execution were stupendous. There was a vast frieze, with figures in high relief representing the battle of the Gods and the Giants, which had decorated the temple, celebrating Eumenes' victory over the Gauls.

I had another interest in this monument from Pergamon. Many years after my visit to the museum I fulfilled another ambition. The author's calling is founded on the paper which constitutes his books. His ancient predecessor faced great material difficulties. In the beginning his writing material was papyrus, made from the pith of a water plant that grew in the Nile. The Ptolemies built up their great Alexandrian libraries on papyrus scrolls. When King Eumenes created his library at Pergamon he excited the envy and anger of Ptolemy Epiphanes (203–182 B.C.). The Egyptian king placed an embargo on the export of papyrus. It seemed a deadly blow to the growth of his rival's library but Eumenes was not thwarted. He reverted to vellum or parchment, made from the dressing of goat and sheep skins, *carta pergamena*. The book was born. When the German archaeologists excavated the library on the Acropolis they found it consisted of four rooms, in which had been housed 200,000 volumes. On my seventy-fifth birthday, thirty-seven years after my visit to the Pergamon Museum, I walked among the ruins of King Eumenes' great library with my old friend, George Maddocks, a superlative linguist, who spoke Turkish. It was this great library that Antony had given to Cleopatra. The magnificent Pergamon Museum disappeared during the Second World War when the Russians occupied Berlin. It is now completely restored.

CHAPTER TWO

Pilgrim Cottage

I

I was back in London early in April in time to fill two speaking engagements, one at the Lyceum Club, the other at the Whitefriars Club, a Fleet Street group of journalists who held a monthly luncheon. I was bracketed with R. C. Sheriff to respond to the toast of Literature. I regard his play *Journey's End* as the finest that had come out of the First World War, a dramatic counterpart that matched Remarque's novel *All Quiet on the Western Front*. I rather startled the company by saying that I feared these warnings in the play and the book looked like being in vain. Our Government was cutting down the defence forces, it was preparing to vacate our Egyptian base, as vital to our Mediterranean line and the passage to India as Gibraltar. I had just returned from Germany. All was not so quiet on that front. I had found a very truculent mood among the young Germans. They were cheating us on the disarmament clauses and creating the nucleus of a future army. I was listened to politely but clearly I was off-course in terms of a response to Literature. On leaving, Sheriff said to me, "I hope you're wrong but I fear you may be right—the poor, silly human race!"

In the middle of May I took over the weekly book page of the *Sphere* which Clement Shorter had made famous for many years. For this I received nine pounds a week. I maintained it for four years, reviewing three or four books weekly. It was not the money that attracted me nor the prestige of taking over Shorter's page, nor the many new books that enlarged my library. It was the retort it gave me. When in 1923 my first novel *Scissors* appeared, Shorter reviewed it, giving me the whole page. But its success irritated him. A pundit, assiduously courted, like Bennett and Gosse, he sometimes showed

30

his claws. Reviewing my book favourably, he wrote—"Surely recognition never came to young men of our earlier generation in the way that it comes today. I do not know of any writer who made much noise in the world before he was thirty. But nowadays young writers can get a public at almost any age. The younger generation has all the luck." It seems I should have waited and written a more mature novel. I was too young for so much success. There had been Dickens, of course, but Shorter did not think I should prove another Dickens. "We all have one novel in us, and perhaps this is to be Mr. Roberts's one effort in this department." I should not have worried over that ominous forecast. When forty-seven years later I gave a little lunch to celebrate the survival of this first novel, now in its twenty-first edition, it had twenty-three companions. There was irony in the fact that within five years of his complaint about the young having too much luck, I was occupying his book page!

Throughout the summer of 1930 I was busy writing my autobiography *Half Way*. I spoke at two public dinners and expressed my concern about the international situation and the Government's feeble handling of it under the verbose Ramsay MacDonald. From time to time Churchill, now out of office, voiced his dismay at our intention to draw out of Egypt and India. Wrapped in a *dhoti*, and looking like an amiable vulture, Gandhi toured England, where he confounded everybody by his gobbledegook. MacDonald found himself in a morass, unable to balance the Budget. No one bothered about what was happening in Germany. In despair Churchill returned to Chartwell, busy making money, which he greatly needed. He had finished the final volume of *The World Crisis*, 'The Eastern Front', which brought him an immediate £3,000. His enormous royalty of 33⅓ per cent sent his publisher, Thornton Butterworth, into bankruptcy. In the spring he went off to Cannes with his paintbox, for a respite. Always public-minded, Churchill emerged from time to time to admonish the Government. He sounded the tocsin again in his Romanes Address. But no one listened to him, no one cared.

In the second week of July, on the day that *Havana Bound* appeared, I motored with a friend to Oxford to lunch at Queen's College. Just after leaving Henley-on-Thames we had a puncture. While my friend changed the tyre I noticed a stile with a path leading

up the field. Afflicted all my life with 'round-the-corneritis' I went
over the stile and up the hill to see what might be on the other side.
There, nestling, were the tiled roofs of a cluster of cottages, their
gardens gay with summer flowers. There was a delightful little bay-
windowed inn, eighteenth century. Farther down the lane there
appeared, above a thick hedge, a dormer-windowed cottage. On its
green gate I read in white gothic letters, *Pilgrim Cottage*. I could just
see over the gate. What I saw was a low, red-tiled cottage with three
dormers, a yew-tree, an apple-tree, with a well and bucket underneath. The cottage, smothered in white roses, was in the centre of a
smooth, circular lawn bordered by deep flowerbeds. There was a
complete silence as it sat there in the afternoon sun. It looked as
enchanting as the castle of the Sleeping Beauty. I noticed that the
birds were walking on the lawn with the utmost confidence. Was
there anyone living there? I then saw that the simple green gate,
mantled with a mauve clematis, was padlocked. The owner must be
away.

I walked all round the thick hedge but could not get a full view of
the cottage in the centre, except for a chimney-stack, white-washed.
There was one spot where the bottom of the hedge was thin, almost a
hole. I stooped down but masses of phlox obscured the view. I thrust
my head in. The hawthorn hedge caught my jacket. It was almost as
easy to go forward as back. Shameless, I enlarged the hole, went
through, and found myself standing up on the other side of the hedge.
I had a new view of the cottage. There was a second chimney-stack.
On the north side the tiled roof went straight down to the lawn.
'Straight' was hardly the word, for it billowed like a wave. It was
overhung by a gnarled apple-tree. The east wing of the cottage had
black and white timbering. I thrust through the flower bed and stood
on the lawn, green and smooth as a billiard table. I circumnavigated
on grass the whole cottage. The garden had a large horse-chestnut
tree, seven apple-trees, and at another corner four tall, Lombardy
poplars. At the back of the chimney-stack there was a brick protuber-
ance overgrown with creepers and dwarf cypresses. It was a bake-
oven. At the east end of the cottage, almost obscuring the black and
white timbering, spread a fan-shaped vine. On this side of the garden
rose a high rustic trellis smothered with crimson roses, American
Pillar, and Dorothy Perkins in full bloom. Under an old russet apple-

Pilgrim Cottage

Pilgrim Cottage—east

tree was the last thing needed for a complete picture of country felicity, an old well with roofed windlass and bucket. The cottage door was shaded by a rustic porch covered with clematis. There was an elegant brass knocker, polished, on the dark brown door. I knocked, quite uselessly, for there was no one there. It might have been a deserted cottage except that everything was perfectly kept. There was a loving gardener somewhere. I stepped over a flower bed and peered in through a window. It was too dark to see anything clearly but the room was furnished.

I had to leave, I was keeping my friend waiting. I went back through the hole, breathless and excited. At the end of the lane, at the inn door, stood a burly man in his shirt-sleeves. He was the landlord of the Golden Ball. I asked him who was living in Pilgrim Cottage. "No one at present, sir. The gentleman who owned it died recently. It belongs to his son, who's in Burma, they say." I asked if it was to let or for sale. "I couldn't say, sir, there's only Thomas who comes once a week to do the garden. You might enquire at Simmons, the agents in Henley. A gem, ain't it?" I agreed, thanked him, hurried up the lane, down the field and over the stile. My friend stood by the car. "Where on earth—" he began. I cut him short and reported my discovery. "I want to get the key of the cottage at the agent's in Henley. If it's to let, I'll take it." "But we'll be late in Oxford!" he protested.

Being amiable, he turned the car and drove down the Fairmile, a wide sunny avenue bordered with magnificent elms, back to Henley, but he made one remark. "I've heard about you wanting a villa in Italy and now you've suddenly gone rustic!"

The word 'suddenly' was not apposite. For some time I had had something on my mind, a reproof I had suffered three years ago in Florida. I had been taken to see an old lady, widow of an English settler. Apologising for her garden, a noble effort in a sub-tropical climate, she remarked, "Of course this must seem a poor thing after yours." I told her I hadn't a garden. She stopped in her walk and fixed me with an eagle eye. "You haven't a garden! Then why are you an Englishman?" she cried. That reproof still echoed in my mind.

The agent proved to be an obliging but unenthusiastic fellow. Yes, the cottage was to let, furnished. "No linen or other things." The owner was a young man with an oil company in Burma. He hadn't been home since his father died eight months ago. The rent was three pounds a week plus the one-day gardener, eight shillings. There's no gas or electricity—or sewage—a cesspool. I expect it's damp, but the roof's sound." He gave me the key. We went back to Lower Assendon, as the cluster of a dozen cottages was called. We unlocked the gate and the door. The place smelt musty. The oak-beamed ceiling was low. There was a dining-room with a large open fireplace and dog-grate, a smaller room, and a larger sitting-room. Up a narrow stair-case we found a bathroom, and three small bedrooms, all built into the roof, with dormer windows. In the largest bedroom there was a radiator. This, and the bathroom and some of the furniture caused me to say, "I'll bet the owner was an American." The four-posted mahogany couch downstairs was a New England piece. My friend scoffed. "I can't see an American living here. They want a bathroom to every bedroom, and radiators everywhere." A few minutes later a framed inscription in gothic lettering settled the question. It was poor verse but with warm sentiment.

> In a lovely English hamlet some three hundred years ago,
> Elizabethan craftsmen wrought, as they so well know how,
> With oak and adze, with brick and lime,
> And flints mixed in like a crazy quilt,
> Nigh Pick Purse Lane and Asser's Don
> Twixt Henley Town and Stonor Park, a cosy chimney cot they
> built.
> About that time from an English port a Pilgrim ventured daringly
> To seek religious freedom in the New World oversea,
> Now a homeward-flown descendant of that self-same Pilgrim
> dwells,
> 'Midst flowers and birds and sheltering hills
> In peace and sweet security, within these mellowed walls.

"There you are!—an American descended from a Pilgrim Father," I said. We looked out. From the windows there was an enchanting view.

I took Pilgrim Cottage until Christmas for three pounds a week, the tenancy to begin at once. I found, up the lane, a woman to come in, an ex-cook, fat, willing. Cooking was by a paraffin stove, a contraption called a 'Florence'. The oil-lamp was an Aladdin, but the kitchen boiler was unromantically named a 'Beeston'. That summer my friends flocked down by car from London. It was a convenient rendezvous for sons at Oxford. Sometimes, somehow, there were six of us sleeping there at weekends. I deserted London except for public engagements.

Little by little the history of the cottage was unfolded. I learned a lot of history, romantic if not wholly accurate. There had originally been two cottages. My eighty-year-old gardener had been born in one of them. His mother had kept a village store there. One day I asked him where he had thrown the hedge-clippings. He said, "On the Roman Road." When I asked where that was, he replied, "This 'ere lane, sir. It was on the Oxford Road when I was a boy. It's a very hysterical road. Julius Caesar marched along here with his soldiers. My grandfather said that once upon a time a Mr. Chaucer, a poet, and a bit bawdy too, used to come by here on his way to Ewelme, to see his son and grand-daughter."

The old fellow was not wholly wrong. There had been a Roman camp at Dorchester near Oxford, and Chaucer's grand-daughter, Alice, Duchess of Suffolk, was buried in Ewelme Church, as was her father, Thomas. "She lies under an alabaster canopy, as proud as can be, sir, with a coronet on 'er head, the Garter on her arm, and her skellinton underneath." She had married first, the Earl of Salisbury, killed at Orleans in 1428, and secondly, the Duke of Suffolk, who was murdered. Her father, Sir Thomas, died in 1434. My gardener also informed me that King Charles I had crossed my garden, going from Oxford to Hambleden over the hill. All his information came from his father and grandfather. It was astonishing how near and real it all was to them. They had not read about the Roman Road, Chaucer and Charles I. It was history conveyed by word of mouth from generation to generation.

My old gardener was correct in saying that the king had crossed within a few yards of my cottage. This was corroborated by the fact that a bridle path passing my garden, which went up through Henley Park, was still called 'King Charles's Way'. It had led him to Hambleden Manor where he spent the night of April 27, 1646, having come from Oxford. He rode on horseback, disguised as a groom to John Ashburnham and Dr. Hudson. He was attempting to join Prince Rupert at Colnbrook. He had to avoid Henley, in the hands of the Parliamentarians. He must have seen my chimney-stack and red-tiled roof exactly as I saw them now.

I was somewhat doubtful about my gardener's assertion that young William Shakespeare went by the cottage, going from his home in Henley Street, Stratford-upon-Avon, to London, seeking a job. It is possible, for during some roof repairs a beam was found in the older part cut with initials and the date 1564. Shakespeare was born that year. It may, of course, have been a re-used beam.

I was for long nervous about my curving roof. The tiles were pegged on. When I had it examined an architect assured me it would last another three hundred years. It never leaked. The old well under the apple-tree was our joy. One day, as my guests and I drank the water, revelling in its purity, there was wild semaphoring behind the kitchen window from Mrs. Barefield, our worthy. I went in to learn what perturbed her. "Oh, sir, you mustn't drink that water—the sink and the bath water runs into it!" A 'moderniser' caused the death of that splendid old well. The constant inflow weakened the brick lining. One day the well collapsed with an ominous rumble. It had to be filled in, thirty feet of it.

What delight we had through those summer and autumn days! The beech trees on the hills turned gold, the apples reddened on the bough; the martins blackened the telegraph wires when gathering for their flight south. We stored the apples. A log fire blazed in the grate and as the evenings drew in we lit the Aladdin lamp, which served a dual purpose. It filled the room with a golden glow and warmed it.

I finished my autobiography *Half Way*. In December, 1930, I was leaving for Cannes and my tenancy was ending. By now the cottage had wound its tendrils round my heart and it saddened me to think of leaving it, and losing it.

I had learned a great deal about the late owner. It seems he had not occupied it for more than two years. The presiding ghost was that of an American lady, Mrs. Anne Holt, an elderly widow. It was she who had bought the two almost derelict cottages, turned them into one, put in a bath and a solitary bedroom radiator. She had also made the garden. Mrs. Barefield had worked for her. She was a very tall American woman with silver hair. She must have banged her head on the low doorways, I suggested. "Oh no, sir! She allus kept her 'at on in the 'ouse." From another source I learned more about her. She was born in Syracuse, N.Y., and her mother, a Bostonian, claimed descent from a Pilgrim Father. Some years previously an elderly

British Consul-General in New York, Mr. Carlisle Taylor, had cast his spell over her. When he returned to England the enamoured lady followed him, and, somewhat to his embarrassment, settled near Henley, where he had chosen to end his days. She bought the cottages, called the conversion Pilgrim Cottage, nostalgically, and doubtless wrote the verses we found in it. There was a sad impediment in this love affair. The ex-Consul had a wife, the inmate of a private asylum. No scandal attached itself to dignified Mrs. Holt and her beloved ex-Consul. Two or three times a week he came to lunch or tea. They walked in the garden, both passionate gardeners. Childless, a widow, Mrs. Holt lived in the cottage for six years, then one June night she died in her sleep. She left the cottage to the ex-Consul. By the irony of Fate his wife died within a year. He was free too late. He moved into the cottage, and lived there for two years. One morning he, too, was found dead in bed. The cottage passed to his only son in Burma. It had been empty ever since. The roses the frustrated elderly lovers had planted kept fragrant their memory. Later, looking at some of the books on a shelf, I learned a little more about Carlisle Taylor. He had written a book—*The Life of Admiral Mahan*. The American admiral had won fame with a three-volume work *The Influence of Sea Power upon History* which became a classic. So my cottage had housed an author! The biography was well written.

Before I left for Cannes in December, 1930, I asked the house agent if he thought the present owner would sell the cottage. He made enquiries and reported that he would. We began leisurely negotiations. My host in Cannes was old Lord Trent, more widely known as Jesse Boot. His was a great success story. A fatherless boy, he had built up the vast Boots Cash Chemist's business. Now a multi-millionaire, his munificence towards his native city seemed unbounded. He provided the site for its university, which he endowed generously. On his seventieth birthday in 1920 I saw him made an Honorary Freeman of Nottingham. He used the occasion for giving the city a quarter of a million pounds for various purposes to mark 'a long and happy life'. He was, at that ceremony, a gallant but sad figure. He was completely paralysed and confined to a wheelchair. He retired to Jersey and had a winter home in Cannes. Now eighty, blind and deaf, he made the journey south to Cannes on an invalid's stretcher. At Springland, his villa, he never came out of his room.

37

His devoted wife organised large house parties. One by one the guests were invited up to the invalid's room, reached through corridors massed with flowers. The bedroom was shuttered and dark. Sir Jesse, as we all still called him, could not bear the daylight. He lay there flat on his back, clad all in white. You shouted at him through an ear-trumpet. He was fed through a spout. "Isn't it lovely here! I hope you're enjoying yourself," he would say in a loud, cracked voice because he could not hear himself. You were allowed a few minutes by watchful Lady Trent. I always came out of the room with tears in my eyes.

The great villa was run with a lavishness commensurate with our host's wealth. There were chauffeured cars for excursions in the hills. There were cabins for bathing reserved at Eden Roc. On Christmas Day a famous Russian Cossack Choir, thirty strong, was engaged to sing for us. The food and wines were superb, and, naturally, the guests at large lunches and dinners, cosmopolitan, were in their most amiable mood. But for most of us there was a ghost at the feast, that white-clad fate-imprisoned figure upstairs.

Nothing could be more serene than life in this luxurious villa above Cannes. One of the guests was Sir Sydney Nettleton, a distinguished retired Chief Justice of Cyprus. I had arguments with him and other guests over the international outlook. They thought me an alarmist. For nine months now, since my return from Berlin, I had become increasingly worried by events in Germany. I kept up a correspondence with Max Bauer. His ardent friend Ernst Ritter had now become a full S.A. officer and was on the staff of Röhm. He too wrote to me. These letters had the same tenor. Hitler had rallied the youth of Germany and would build a new Jerusalem. But events did not endorse this view. The Nazis, denouncing the Versailles Treaty, gained a hundred and seven seats in the Reichstag. Hitler's claims became increasingly violent. In England there was complete indifference to what was brewing in Germany. The attacks on the Jews were deplored but shrugged off. In the House of Commons the Labour Government whittled down our defence forces, abetted by the Conservatives who were also climbing on the Peace wagon. Ramsay MacDonald sank deeper and deeper in an economic morass. One man alone raised his voice, Churchill. He was out of the Government, he was out of favour with his party over Suez and India. One evening, returning from a public dinner where, a guest speaker, I had been listened to with cool apathy, I sat down and wrote a long letter to Churchill, outlining a policy, political and social, that I thought would halt our decline. I believed there were young men in the country who would follow his lead. He wrote back from Chartwell on December 20, 1930:

> Dear Cecil Roberts,
> Although I view with the greatest sympathy all the kind of schemes about which you write to me, I have not the life and strength to give to them the time they require.
> Yours sincerely,
> Winston Churchill.

In retrospect that is a remarkable letter. He was then fifty-six. Some ten years later, after continuous attacks on a supine Government presided over by Chamberlain, he became Prime Minister in England's darkest hour. Sixteen years later, at the age of seventy-two, he was the acknowledged architect of victory, the saviour of our civilisation. The life and strength had somehow been given to him.

Meanwhile, I worked. On my way from London to the Riviera I had tarried in Paris for a couple of weeks, staying with my hospitable friend Norman Fuller. There, one night at two a.m., I awoke, and the whole theme of *Bargain Basement*, long deferred, because the data I had collected did not shape itself into a coherent form, was clear in my mind. I got up and wrote until breakfast. Like a train the story gathered speed. I continued to work at Springland. A robbery on the Blue Train I had taken was a gift from heaven. I rose every morning at dawn, which was often magnificent coming up out of an indigo sea. I had a room with a bay window opening on to a balcony. Pyjama-clad, writing at a black and gold buhl table, I was hardly aware of the servant who brought in my breakfast. I worked until noon, then dressed and joined the gathering house party. When I returned to London early in January I had half the novel written.

On the last day of the old year, returning from a gala evening at Eden Roc Hotel in celebration of the New Year of 1931, I sat down at the desk in my bedroom and made the annual audit for my diary. It had been a year of great industry. I had saved £2,000. My 'Author's Contingency Fund', for the grey years, when my creative capacity would be diminished and my vogue gone, was growing. A problem arose. How much should I give to others less fortunate ? I settled for the Old Testament rule. I gave away at least ten per cent of my net income, and never missed it, such is habit.

On New Year's Day, 1931, I went on to Monte Carlo. Somerset Maugham invited me to lunch at the Villa Mauresque at Cap Ferrat. At that time I did not know him well. I had met him at my friend Fuller's house in Paris and I had not found him *simpatico*. He seemed grim and abrupt, and I was a little in awe of his position in the world of letters. He occupied a large white villa on a hill amid olive groves, overlooking the long harbour of Villefranche. There was a view of Mont Boron which hid Nice. The villa had been built by a retired bishop, who had served in North Africa. It was Moorish in style. Over the stone portal Maugham had placed a carving, beehive form. It had been a device of his father's against the evil eye. 'Willie', as we all called him, had adopted this emblem and it appeared on the covers of all his books.

He certainly lived in state. A butler opened the door. After crossing a marble entrance hall I was shown into a long bright salon. It had a wide open fireplace of Arles stone. The room was furnished in a modern style with fine rugs. Books filled gothic alcoves, all the colours being bright. Paintings of the Impressionist School decorated the walls.

Willie rose to greet me. He had two guests, young Leigh, the lyric writer, and Mrs. Ivor Back, wife of a surgeon. Slim, beautiful, intense, she was famed for her wit and common sense, which had an earthy quality. Also present was the tall, angular, square-headed Gerald Haxton. An American, over the years he had become Willie's intimate friend, travelling companion and astute man of affairs. It was he who compelled Willie to write every morning, all the morning. Many liked him, a few detested him. Shrewd, the faithful watchdog, everything appertaining to the novelist's interests was settled by Gerald.

Maugham, short of stature, neat, had a thin, downward-curving mouth. With his sallow parchment skin and cool eyes there was something saurian about him. It was almost impossible for any of his compelling stories to have a happy ending. Of his first book, *Liza of Lambeth*, *Vanity Fair* said, 'An unpleasant unhealthy novel'. Throughout life his works kept the same key. He had also a habit of unkindly caricaturing his friends and hosts, as he did to poor Hugh Walpole in *Cakes and Ale*. He had many libel actions.

40

In life I found him pleasanter than the characters he created. The cordiality of his manner towards me contradicted the general opinion that he was acid and austere. He had a beautiful voice and accent but was troubled with a stammer that impeded his conversation. Some years later when we spoke at public functions in New York I was astonished to find that on the platform his stammer wholly disappeared. He was fluent and easy as a public speaker. Willie was now a man of fifty-six years of age, with smooth greying hair and a dark close-cropped moustache. When not talking or smiling his face had a legal severity. In appearance he could well have assumed his brother's role of Lord Chancellor.

Presently we went in to lunch. It was excellent, served in a round dining-room that had good modern paintings. The conversation was lively, often provoked by Barbara Back, who had a teasing way with Willie. He asked me about my reviewing for the *Sphere*. "Now don't tell me you read those books through!" he said. I assured him I did. "Your last book had two errors of fact, one of place and five misprints. I listed them on the end page. I'll send you them, if you like," I said.

After coffee we went round the grounds. These were extensive. There was a tennis court (he was a passionate tennis-player), a pergola, an orangery, and a garden planned on terraces. On this hill-side, facing the sea, he had built a marble swimming pool. He owned, to protect him, a piece of land on the promontory. There were four gardeners and six servants. Apart from the house there was his study built on the roof. It had no window at one end, thus shutting out the distracting beauty of the view but in the west wall there was a window of painted glass. It was a picture of Eve, holding an apple, the work of Gauguin. It had been brought from a Tahiti house where the artist had painted it during convalescence. As I left the Villa Mauresque, the sunset tinged the white walls of the villa, picking it out in a roseate glow against the cool blue sky and the dark background of pines and olive trees.

Some years later Willie told me a story about his piece of land on the Cap Ferrat peninsula. He was asked if he would receive an official deputation on a very private matter. Mystified, he agreed. On the appointed day eight gentlemen arrived at the villa. Four of them were in uniform, a rear-admiral with his attaché, a general with his attaché.

The Préfet du Département, the Mayor of Nice, and two Government officials, were in informal morning dress, with top hats and gloves. There was considerable humming and hawing after they had been received, but at last the Préfet explained the reason of their presence. They were sure Monsieur Maugham would be sympathetic to their proposal, as he had shown himself always to be a great lover of France. It was this: owing to the grave international situation France was taking stock of her defences. Monsieur Maugham possessed a piece of land that happened to be of strategic value. They had come to ask if he would agree to having a gun mounted there. It would be discreetly placed and would not in any way damage his property.

Much relieved, for the nature of the deputation had suggested something serious, perhaps a strategic road, Willie said there could not be any question of his acquiescence. He was only too happy to render any service to a country so hospitable. An air of general relief, of amity, spread over the deputation. After a pause it was the turn of one of the officials. Very tactfully he came to the point. How much would M'sieur Maugham require for compensation? "Why, messieurs, nothing, nothing at all. I am only too happy to be of service to you in any way," replied Maugham. This statement was received with gestures of appreciation. *Vive L'Entente Cordiale!* Then the butler brought in drinks. After a time the deputation, with handshaking and bowing, left, in a glow of general satisfaction. Monsieur Maugham would receive the official proposal in due course.

Weeks went by, months, and nothing further happened. Finally Willie made an enquiry of the Mayor. They would not place the gun there after all. "Ah, Monsieur Maugham, you made a great mistake. You were too generous in offering the site for nothing. They thought there must be a catch in it!"

While I was in France I learned that Hutchinson, the publishers, had made an offer for *Half Way*. As my own publishers had recently had *Havana Bound* and would soon have another novel, *Bargain Basement*, I thought it prudent not to crowd one list. This was a non-fiction work. At the last moment I added a dedication to my mother. She would now never see it but she had heard it for I had read it to her within a few minutes of writing it.

I have not sung for you
One word of all the tribute I would pay:
But oh, if you knew
The things that crowd in my heart at the thought of you,
Then might you say
'To me belongs the song of songs'.

One never knows where the printed word will travel, or for how long. Thirty years after writing these lines I happened to be in the Brevoort Hotel, in New York, speaking at a meeting of the Poetry Society. Afterwards one of the members suggested we should adjourn to the bar. It was crowded. A middle-aged woman slipped off a stool and came up to me. She was blowsy in appearance and fuddled with drink, her eyes half-closed. "Aren't you Cecil Roberts?" she asked, huskily. Reluctantly I said I was. "I recognise you from your *Half Way* jacket," she said, then slowly and accurately she began to recite —'I have not sung for you . . .' When she had finished and before I could say anything she turned and went back to her stool. I followed her and thanked her. I shall never know who she was, or her fate. I still see her raddled face.

I arrived home from the Riviera at the end of February with *Bargain Basement* finished. The *Daily Mirror* bought the serial rights. I learned that *Havana Bound* was in its fourth edition. The economic crisis dominated the political scene. The next Budget would reveal a deficiency of a hundred million pounds. The Labour Party floundered desperately. Young, promising Oswald Mosley deserted it to found the New Party. It had a positive policy. Harold Nicolson, Yeats-Brown and I were attracted by it.

I had hesitated about buying my first property but the smile of fortune encouraged me. Last August, while living in the cottage I had taken a New York editor to see it. Little Mrs. Meloney Brown edited the weekly magazine of the *New York Herald Tribune*. She was pale and frail as an autumn leaf. I had often written for her magazine. When I opened the gate on our arrival, she stood still for a few moments. "Oh!—it's unbelievable! And to think an American woman created it!" I told her I was considering whether to buy it. She asked what the price was. I told her. "Ridiculous! Of course you'll buy it! I'll commission four articles now—all about the cottage and its surroundings. It must have a lot of history." So I went ahead

43

and bought Pilgrim Cottage. The price was ridiculous. I was in paradise for £750. As with all buyers of old property I embarked on improvements that eventually cost me three times the purchase price.

On a bright day in May in a room on the upper floor of an office in Clifford Street, where the roar of Bond Street traffic was faint, a solicitor rustled papers on his desk, asked me to sign my name, then put my finger on a certain spot and repeat the words 'I deliver this as my act and deed', whereupon a young man in Burma received £750 and I received treasure in the Chilterns. I left the office carrying one of those long envelopes in which solicitors like to put long deeds. In the course of years I was to have a score of such envelopes holding property deeds, but none ever gave me the pleasure of this first one. The envelope was not only long, it was fat. It contained a series of deeds, written in parchment by long-dead hands, certainly by quill pens, conveyance on conveyance, that carried one back to the seventeenth century. One day yet another conveyance would alienate the cottage from me. But that was many years distant. In the meantime I was to know in Pilgrim Cottage the happiest and saddest years of my long life; sunshine and shadow.

II

In that same month *Half Way* appeared. It was an autobiography. I gave it that title because it was the story of my life up to the age of thirty-five. The miracle of medical science has since moved the halfway mark to forty. At that time it was considered presumptuous for a man of thirty-five to write his autobiography. It was assumed that at such an age he had achieved little, seen little and he should modestly keep his mouth shut until the shadow of senility fell upon him. "What!" exclaimed Sir Sidney Low, the retired editor of a London newspaper, "Why, I haven't begun mine yet and I'm seventy!" He had been at the centre of political history for a lifetime. I pointed out that fate had rapidly filled my life with events. I had been in a War Ministry with Churchill, a war correspondent with the Navy, the Air Force, the Army, and on the Western Front. I had been in the victorious march to the Rhine, the editor of a daily newspaper and a parliamentary candidate. I had published nine novels and made three lecture tours across America. On two continents I had become acquainted with a number of famous men in politics, art, science, journalism and literature. These had all been kind and encouraging to an ambitious young man. The book succeeded beyond all my expectations. Within three months it was reprinted five times. So here I was, my journey, half-way, recorded. I should have to travel another thirty-five years before I could start to recount the whole way. It seemed to me, then, a very remote chance.

Through June, July and August the cottage was renovated. I added a garage, and converted the larder under the long-falling roof into a housekeeper's bedroom. This left me three upstairs bedrooms. The large bedroom had a trap door floor. "That's the coffin-chute. We all of us came down that way," said old Thomas. He had another odd explanation. A patch of the wall by the sitting-room fireplace exuded a white salty powder. We scraped and painted but it always returned. "Ye'll never get rid of it. When this was a shop they put bacon flitches there—it's been sucking in salt for over a hundred years. Taste it!" he said, wetting a finger and taking off some powder. I wetted a finger and tasted. It was pure salt.

Before I took possession the furniture was put up for sale. The auction was held on a hot June day on the lawn. How demented can people become at an auction? Before I realised what had happened, all the gardening tools, lawn-mower, roller, hose, spades, shears, were gone. When Thomas arrived the next day he had no tools, not a spade, fork or shears. I had to drive into town and buy a set. What hurt him most was the loss of five dozen assorted flower pots. All that I had bought at the sale was a French travelling clock in a leather case. Had it come with Mrs. Holt from America, having twice crossed the Atlantic? It cost me £5. When I sold it forty years later it brought me £200. The chief bait was a Chippendale chair. I had passed uncomfortable evenings in it. It may have been a thing of beauty but it was never a joy to sit in. But it was Chippendale and the name, printed in enlarged black letters in the catalogue, went to the heads of a number of grey-haired women. They came with the light of battle in their eyes. For some unknown reason two pairs of coloured bed sheets, a bilious green and a revolting pink, sent them into a frenzy of possession. They went for twice the price of new ones.

In July *Bargain Basement* was published having finished its run in the *Daily Mirror*. The treatment it received at Selfridge's, already described, gave me a shock. It was soon reprinting, four times in its first year. An early English film enterprise, the Gainsborough Company, formed by a young man of some genius, Michael Balcon, bought the film rights of my book for £500. Prices for British productions were poor in those days but the subject was essentially English. When a year later the producer and his script-writers visited me at the cottage with the scenario I was horrified by the travesty of the book. I expressed myself so forcibly that they never made the film. It was an error on my part, as I learned later from James Hilton. "If you take their money you must keep your mouth shut. Prostitutes have no rights."

The improvements at Pilgrim Cottage were badly behind schedule. There was no possibility of my moving in at the end of July. They were still mixing mortar on the lawn. I decided to go to Venice, a visit that was almost an annual fixture, where many of my friends gathered. At home the political situation was disastrous. The pound had fallen. The Ramsay MacDonald Labour Government had collapsed. I travelled up the Rhine Valley with a friend, then on to Venice which was in a whirl of seasonal excitement. The rich Americans had rented palaces and were giving extravagant parties. The impoverished Venetian patricians retreated into their attics or to their country villas, happy to earn dollars. The Duff Coopers were in Venice. Suddenly he rushed home, hoping to get office in the reshuffling of the Government, now a Coalition with MacDonald heading it and Baldwin as Lord President. Duff Cooper picked up a Financial Secretaryship at the War Office. Lady Diana remained on in Venice. Count Robilant had let his Palazzo Mocenigo on the Grand Canal, with its memories of Byron, to the wealthy, dynamic millionairess, Mrs. Corrigan. She collected guests from indigent royalties down. When Duff Cooper departed she insisted on Lady Diana coming to stay. She gives us an inimitable picture of the scene in her diary *The Light of Common Day*.

> Laura Corrigan had that year married the Adriatic. I got lured to the Palazzo Mocenigo and never regretted it . . . I dined last night and my plate was pyramided with birthday presents, including a really noble cigarette case from Laura. It's a modern fairy tale, with everything that Beauty wants in her new palace—

twenty backgammon boards, rare friandises. Placards on all the bedroom doors warn you to tip the servants at your peril, and you must not pay for drinks at the Grand Hotel or Lido bar.

From the palazzo's balcony I saw the vivid pageantry of the annual regatta and one day I was speeded out to a luncheon party given on two fishing boats tethered off the Excelsior Lido pier, with guitar music under the great russet sails and the waiters disguised as Venetian fishermen. Our host was wealthy Charles Bestegui who lived in the fabulous Palazzo Labia, where a previous occupant, my friend Neil McEachern, uncovered a Tiepolo fresco, and thereby made it impossible to buy the palazzo, for it was then declared a national monument.

Early in September I returned to London. At last Pilgrim Cottage was ready for occupation. At the end of September I gave up my London rooms and moved the furniture there. This done, I spent the weekend with a friend in his near-by home at Lane End. I now had to find a housekeeper. A fellow guest that weekend was a young Frenchman, twenty-one, who had been working at the Grosvenor Hotel in order to learn English. He was about to return home to do his military service. Vivacious, warm-hearted, intelligent, he had made many friends in England. His name was Louis Tissier, born in the Côte d'Or. The next day I had to go to the cottage in order to pay the gardener and give him instructions. I asked young Tissier if he would like to go with me and see the place. He was delighted. On arrival he went round and round it. "It is Hans Andersen and Fontaine! I would wish to live here for ever!" he exclaimed. It was a late October afternoon. A red sunset was burning through the beech woods. The air was chill. Inside, I lit the Aladdin lamp. The charwoman had made up a log fire. I put a match to it, the flames leapt up the wide chimney. These and the soft lamplight made a picture of utter cosiness. Tissier touched the oak beams overhead. He opened the iron door of the bake-oven in the back of the fireplace, he examined the alcove where the jug of mulled ale had been kept warm. His face shone with delight. He sat down in a winged armchair. "*Ravissant, ravissant!*" he murmured, running a finger over the tapestry cover. "What fortune for you! What books to write! I would never, never leave!" "You must come and visit me," I said. "When do you leave for your military service ?" "Next week. But I do not have to leave, not for a year if I wish," he replied. I then did an impulsive thing, touched by his youthful enthusiasm. "Would you like to come here for a year ? You could make yourself useful, in the garden, collecting guests at the station, improving my French," I added. He jumped up, excited. "*Merveilleux! Merveilleux!* We work here. I type your manuscript!" "Can you type ?" I asked. "Yes, I type at the Grosvenor. My English is not yet all good but it would have to be good soon!" I laughed. "A moment," I said, leaving him. I went to the winebin and came back with a bottle of Rüdesheimer and two glasses. I filled them. "Here's to our agreement. I've engaged a French secretary," I said, raising my glass. "*Oh merveilleux! Merveilleux!*" he responded, touching my glass. When the fire had died we locked up the cottage and motored back to Lane End. We would return on Monday.

III

Our first necessity was a housekeeper. Three of them were tragedies. After six months of misfits I was recommended by a local lady to put an advertisement in the *Reading Mercury*. It produced fifty-four replies. I interviewed seven and chose a buxom, forty-ish spinster, Ethel Stratford. God in His bounty had given me a treasure. She was with me until her too-early death. If I said, fearfully, there were going to be seven for lunch, or twelve for tea, she would say, "Oh, how lovely!" She liked people. She adored the cottage. She was a good cook. I found she disliked cleaning shoes, so Louis cleaned his own, and when guests were in the house he was up betimes and did theirs. She loved flowers and her bowl arrangements were master-pieces. The kitchen casement window looked out over the well and the russet apple-tree. She once said, "I've the most beautiful kitchen window in the world." As there was no back door she did her shopping through it. I paid her £1 a week.

We began to have guests. Our first, according to my Visitors' Book, were Sir Philip and Lady Gibbs and their son Anthony. They signed their names at the head of the first page on October 14, 1931. Nothing pleased me more than to entertain my former war-correspondent colleague. He was a noble soul, a Sir Galahad, and greatly enriched my life. He was slight and thin. His wife was tall and managerial. She took a science degree at over fifty. She had a passion for changing homes. I entered ten new addresses in twenty years. She was extremely hospitable and I was in and out of their town and country houses as long as they lived.

I will add a word about my guest book, which was to receive some remarkable names, some famous ones, some tragic, including twenty killed, five suicides and one murderer. One year in Venice I discovered a bookbinder who asserted he was a descendant of a family that had bound books for the Aldine Press (Aldus Manutius, 1449–1515) and the Doges. It was an exciting shop with hand-made Venetian papers in all colours, stamped with lions, crocodiles, fleur-de-lys, etc. He was an expert bookbinder. I had manuscripts and first editions bound with Venetian end-papers. I found there one day a delightful volume of hand-made paper, vellum-bound, with deckled edges. He asked me what I would like on the spine, and rashly I said, "Poems by Cecil Roberts." My muse had been dead for two years. I thought it might revive her. But for a time the book remained blank. For five years it stood mocking me on my bookshelf. On entering Pilgrim Cottage I used it for a guest book, writing on the title page 'My Friends are My Poems'.

The cottage had inhabitants other than human. On my mantelpiece stood a small bottle with a dead mouse in it. When friends asked about this macabre ornament I told them it was my LL.D degree. We had only been in the cottage a few weeks when I became aware of mice scurrying in the roof. I bought a wooden box-mousetrap, baited it and set it there. I forgot about it and then after a week went to look. I was horrified to find a mouse, which had been starving in the trap. I filled a bucket and drowned the mouse. The deed has haunted me for the rest of my life. It was a field mouse. Why didn't I release it in the field opposite and let it enjoy its life? I murdered it. So no more ghastly traps were set. I ignored an odd scampering above. In 1927 Washington and Jefferson College, in the U.S.A. conferred an honorary LL.D. on me after I had made the Commencement Address. I received a parchment scroll. The carton containing this I put in the bottom drawer of my writing desk. Five years afterwards, during a clearance, I picked up the carton. Something rattled in it. I shook it and out came a mouse, petrified. Of the parchment only a few nibbled inches remained. The mouse had consumed it and had been killed by the arsenic with which vellum is dressed. As there was no method of extracting my degree from the mouse's stomach I therefore bottled the petrified container. The story of my mouse degree delighted the President of the College who sent me another scroll.

To this history of the mouse I will add that of the bird, a later occupant. It was a French bird, small, of beautiful blue plumage. It sang prodigiously in its golden cage, filling the cottage with its morning salute. It had come from Paris, a present from Louis. Often I took its cage up to the landing where I hung it outside the guest bedroom. This room had a little sliding window looking on to the landing which I had made in order to give a current of air through the tiny room, and also to afford a vista, through the dormer window opposite, of the hill-side and the beech woods. My guest, awakened by bird-song, looked out and saw my bird. Its song ended, he tried to encourage it, with a tweet-tweet, to sing again. It remained silent, observing him with beady eyes. Something in those fixed eyes awoke suspicion and the hoax was unmasked. It was a mechanical bird, with moving head, beak and tail. A key under the cage provided a series of warblings that could be made continuous or intermittent. One of my guests was very testy when he found he had been hoaxed, others were delighted.

Little by little we learned local lore and history. Mr. Harris, the keeper of the Golden Ball at the end of the lane, was a storehouse. The inn, eighteenth-century, had a delightful bay window that jutted out into the lane. The Golden Ball, signified by a golden ball that hung on a sign, shone gaily in the sun with its red tiles and white-washed walls. Harris was a retired sergeant with Indian service. I had been examining the inn and a large circular space in front of it, now a kitchen-garden, and learned it was formerly the site of an old coach-yard where the coaches came in for a change of horses. The incoming mail coach from Aylesbury to Henley, the 'Tantivy' (red), the 'Magnet' (blue), from Cheltenham, the 'Alert' from Oxford, and the Gloucester and Stroud mails, all called. "No wonder Tom King and Dick Turpin hung about here," observed Harris. Dick Turpin, the highwayman, hero of the ballad of my boyhood, who made the famous ride to York, why should he leave the Great North Road to ride past my garden? I expressed my suspicion. "Well, sir, he was born in Essex and worked all round London. He knew every inch of the Chilterns. He'd places to 'dive' in when it got too hot for him. Come inside and have a look, sir, I'll show you one of his boltholes," said Harris. I followed him. The ostlers' taproom was now a living-room but in the old days it communicated with the parlour for the gentry. Between the rooms there was a thick chimney-stack. As usual with these old chimneys there was a bend in it, completely hidden by wall boarding. To my surprise Harris opened a cupboard door, revealing a narrow passage to a place above. There was space in the bend for a man to stand and through a slit peer down on the occupants of the bar. On making enquiries I found that King and Turpin had 'worked' the Oxford and Watlington roads.

IV

In that first month at Pilgrim Cottage the interior peace was invaded by news of the troubled outside world. I was never able to detach myself wholly, the latent politician in me had not been exorcised by my tragic collapse nine years earlier as a parliamentary candidate. I had watched Oswald Mosley form his New Party, to fail dismally at a General Election. The skies of the world were glowering. Germany threw her sinister shadow, to which no one paid attention. In September the long-attenuated death-pangs of the League of Nations, already shaken by Mussolini in his Corfu invasion, suffered another graver rebuff. In the month of our departure from the gold standard and the fall of the pound, Japan, defying the League, invaded Manchuria, Chinese territory. She denied that it was any affair of the League's although many of its members asked for an economic boycott. Japan laughed, remembering Corfu. When six months later a League commission reported that Manchuria should be restored to China she laughed again and set up a puppet regime. Even Churchill was nervous about any action. "I do not think that the League of Nations would be well advised to have a quarrel with Japan. . . . On one side Japan sees the dark menace of Soviet Russia, on the other, the chaos of China, four or five provinces of which are now being tortured under communist rule." To fears of Russia Churchill added his growing fears of Germany. For the moment his public warnings were intermittent. He was busy at Chartwell finishing *The World Crisis*. The sixth volume of this great survey, 'The Eastern Front', appeared among my books for review. Observing that the Titanic struggle of the Russians on the Eastern Front had received only meagre attention, since naturally we were obsessed with that on the Western, he set out to chronicle that vast and grim drama. Much of it covered the death-grapple of Austria with her Italian, Serbian and Russian foes. It was a deeply moving story of the crash of the great Austro-Hungarian Empire.

It happened that I was already interested in her tragic downfall. In 1928 I had been in Vienna where I had seen harrowing evidence of the cost of defeat—poverty, hunger, ruined businesses and homes, a once resplendent, gay capital, the setting of a brilliant court, now shabby and torn with political faction. Its proud, feckless and arrogant aristocracy had been utterly shattered. I had left, en route, via the Dolomites, for Venice in September of that year and broken my journey at the little Tyrolean town of Kitzbühel. There I stayed in Schloss Kaps, the property of the Lamberg family. Like other aristocratic Austrian families it faced necessitous days. The enterprising Countess, with a young son and two daughters, had turned her ancestral *schloss* into a pension. Earlier I had been at Cortina. In the Dolomites I had stopped on a slope of Monte Tofana, and there, solitary, amid the firs, was a military cemetery. To my surprise I discovered that the rows of headstones all bore the names of Austrian soldiers, though I was standing on Italian soil, on territory taken from Austria. To the pathos of early death was added the irony that these lads were now sleeping on alien soil. For three years I carried the memory of that lonely cemetery, of Schloss Kaps and ruined Austria in my mind. Now in Churchill's book my own experience fitted into the vast drama of the Eastern Front. I had found my theme and was fired by it. In the warm lamplight of my cottage in the Chilterns, between November 22 and December 22, 1931, I wrote *Spears Against Us*. Everything was conducive to creation, the low-raftered room, the glowing log fire, the deep silence of the country night. I wrote the novel lying on a couch, an old chintz-covered roll-end sofa on which my mother had spent the last years of her life. It had come out of the Duchess of Newcastle's boudoir, at a sale of the effects of Clumber House, in Sherwood Forest, before its demolition. The shade of my mother apart, I envisaged that of a forgotten duchess in her lingerie. The young Gladstone often visited Clumber and might have talked to her as she lay on it.

The top of a three-ply tea chest rested on my knees as a desk when I wrote in French *cahiers* (Papeterie St. Philippe-du-Roule) that I bought in Paris. Each held 25,000 words, so that I knew how I was getting on. I wrote from eight to ten, when Ethel came in with the tea tray before retiring. The lovely odour of burning wood mingled with that of Earl Grey tea mixture. At ten thirty I began work again, often till long past midnight. Near me, in the wing chair sat Louis. From time to time he hunted up a reference, a word-spelling, consulted maps or fetched books I required from my shelves. With a gift for map-reading and French and German, a born encyclopaedia-hunter, he was an excellent amanuensis. He insisted before retiring that I should read what I had written. There through a month of cosy nights, in that raftered lamplit room, the novel was written. I arranged for publication the following February. Though convinced it was possibly the best novel I had written, I was nervous about it. It was miles apart from its predecessor *Bargain Basement*, a light entertainment with a note of comedy. *Spears Against Us* was based on grim history, a study of the destruction of a proud nation. In the fall of the house of Edelstein the dark tragedy of defeat was lit only by vain heroism in the death-grapple among the mountains of the Austro-Italian frontier.

Soon after the novel appeared I received a letter from a young British officer, a member of a Hatton Garden diamond firm, who had fought with our Italian allies on the Austrian front. My hero, Karl Edelstein, the young heir of Schloss Edelstein, had fallen at Monte Tofana, not far distant from his Kitzbühel home. My correspondent enclosed some weather-stained photographs in his letter. One day he had come across the body of a young Austrian officer. "Someone had rifled his pockets and strewn the photographs in the grass around his dead body. Somehow it seemed a little horrible to have his private treasures so publicly displayed. I collected them and have kept them ever since 1918. Why, I could not say." There was a 'Karl' in one of the photographs, taken on what might be the terrace of a *schloss*. He was surrounded, presumably, by his mother, and two sisters—Anna and Paula, as in my novel.

The coincidence pointed out by my correspondent did not end

there. This young Karl had been killed within a few miles of Monte Tofana, where my Karl had fallen and, from the date on a postcard he had received from home, his death must have been within a week of the date on which I had ended the life of Karl Edelstein. Still more incredible, the address from which the postcard had been sent was within a dozen miles of the valley where I had placed my Schloss Edelstein! The other photographs in the letter might have been used as illustrations of my book, so perfectly did they fit the text. "I met another Karl, too," said my correspondent, "in our front line—a prisoner, English public school, very fair, very English-looking. We chatted for about five minutes before he walked out of my life, to return today as Karl Edelstein in your story."

I had created the Edelstein family from my imagination. I have frequently been asked whether I had any experience of the fighting on the Austrian Front described in my novel. I had none at all, and my knowledge of it was confined to a close study of all the military text books, to the Austrian and Italian official reports, and the maps of each area over which I pored until every track was familiar to my mind, so that I could have led a detachment of soldiers, like my Major Oberbach at Malersteig. Some years after the publication of my novel I was again motoring through Cortina, via Schluderbach and the great Gross Glockner range. My chauffeur was an Austrian ex-soldier who had fought in this district. He was greatly astonished by my recognition of the various scenes of battle. I knew each footpath, each tunnel, each gun-emplacement and the lines of trenches on the mountain face. Nothing would convince him that I had not been a spy or soldier with the invading Italian army, that I had never seen this honeycombed battleground before. Did I imagine my story, or in the intensity of concentration is there evoked a higher intelligence that uses one as a receptive instrument? It is a question one cannot answer. There are times when one's belief in the finite self is rudely shaken.

There was another letter, apropos my novel, that gave me particular pleasure. It came from Sir Gerald du Maurier, at that time the most famous actor-manager in London.

I have to thank you for the following reason [he wrote]. I have been ill in bed, and am still. My wife asked me if I had ever read a book called *Spears Against Us*. I hadn't but I have now, and I think it's a real corker. I loved every member of those two adorable families. I had one rather like them myself in those days, but they have all gone west.

Soon afterwards Sir Gerald died. He was the son of Punch's famous artist and author of *Trilby*, George du Maurier, and he enjoyed a long period of success in the West End as a highly sensitive actor. Sir Gerald du Maurier was the father of Daphne du Maurier, the novelist.

Early in February, on the eve of the publication of my novel, I had a weekend visitor who was riding on a tide of success with a book that carried him to fame and fortune. This was the author of *Magnolia Street*, Louis Golding. Some years previous there had appeared at various literary gatherings where I had spoken, a little swarthy and stocky Jew. He was always ambitious to make a contribution to any discussion. He spoke well. He cultivated my acquaintance as a successful author. Always ready to encourage an eager young writer striving for recognition, I responded to his overtures. Hearing his personal history I admired his spirit. He had come up the hard way. His parents were Russian Jews who had escaped from a pogrom. They settled in a poor Jewish quarter in Manchester. Their son Louis won a scholarship to Manchester Grammar School, and then to Queen's College, Oxford. On graduating he moved to London where he lived in a grim Paddington bed-sitting room. At the time that I met him he had published a couple of books of verse and one novel which, well received, had little success. He was having a grim struggle to live. Years later he said, "You dazzled me. You seemed to have everything, aristocratic birth, good looks, a wonderful gift of speech, tremendous success with your books. And you were kind with it all and not puffed up." I denied the aristocratic birth but I could never shake that obsession. He was inimical to 'county' folk. Even in later prosperous years he had communist sympathies. He was not alone, there were dozens of fellow travellers. It was a fashion among the young *literati*. We had fierce arguments. "You, with your county background, riding to hounds, living in halls and manor houses!" In vain I told him I had never ridden to hounds, or lived in a manor house, that I had been born in a provincial city and started life on an office stool at sixteen, earning eight shillings a week. I think his *idée fixe* came from my late father's crested ring, almost the only gold he

55

had ever inherited, and from having seen me in public debate with young Lord David Cecil, who had just published a successful biography of Cowper. Perversely, he imagined a blood relationship between the two Cecils!

By sheer hard work and talent Louis kept his head above water, but his novels never earned the advance payments on them. One day in 1931 he came to consult me. He was in great distress. He had submitted to his publisher a new novel, his eighth. He knew it was the finest thing he had ever written, his heart's blood had gone into it but the publisher said that it was much too long and insisted on drastic cutting. He had tears in his eyes when he told me this. It would ruin his book. I suggested sending it to another publisher. "I can't. I've drawn the £150 advance, and spent it," he replied. Would I read it and say whether he was right? I agreed to. Somehow all my life I have been a proof-reader to authors, to Lord Birkenhead, Sir Thomas Beecham, John Betjeman, Philip Gibbs, James Hilton, Montgomery Hyde, Leonide Massine, Charles Morgan, etc.; the list is a long one and the pleasure was mine. I was somewhat dismayed by the bulk of the typed manuscript Golding gave me, but once I had begun it I could not put it down. He was right, it was his masterpiece, it would be an outrage to cut it. It was the story of Jewish families living in a Manchester back street named Magnolia Street. He was heartened by my opinion, but what could he do? He owed his publisher £150. "That is no problem," I said. "I will lend you £150. But it won't be necessary. Take the book to Gollancz. He's a Jewish publisher. He'll jump at it. With his advance you can refund the £150." Gollancz took *Magnolia Street*. Its success was immediate and overwhelming.

Golding arrived at the cottage for the weekend bringing me a copy of his book, inscribed for 'One pilgrim to another, in Pilgrim Cottage, affectionately, Feb. 6, 1932.' He was exhausted by the overwhelming success of his book after years of hard struggle. He was now thirty-six and had earned enough to be comfortable, after having lodged in a dingy little bed-sitting-room in Paddington. We reckoned that he would make at least £10,000. From all sources it might be £40,000 or £50,000, with serial rights, film rights and possibly a play which he contemplated making from it. We were amused and disgusted by the general fawning of critics and editors who formerly had dismissed or ignored his work. Our hopes were not wholly fulfilled. No film rights were bought and the play he produced failed. Even so, he made enough money with which to buy a house in select Hamilton Terrace, St. John's Wood, to entertain and to travel, and, with forward contracts, never to have financial worries again. Alas, he died suddenly, aged sixty.

At the time of Golding's visit I had just received advance copies of *Spears Against Us*. He read it all that evening and took it to bed with him. In the morning, at breakfast, he said, "If I know anything you've got a winner also. I'm deeply moved by it." His prophecy was fulfilled. It was reprinted twenty times in the next seventeen years. When the *Bookseller* issued its list of the winter's best sellers I found myself named along with Golding's *Magnolia Street*, Galsworthy's *Maid in Waiting*, Charles Morgan's *The Fountain* and Aldous Huxley's *Brave New World*. I could not help wondering how many of us would stay the course. Today I am the lone survivor, at eighty.

I received, as do all writers with a 'hit', a large mail. It was all part of the excitement of climbing the ladder. Three letters gave me particular pleasure. One was from an unknown young novelist, one of whose early books I had reviewed. "It is almost too dangerous in these days for one writer to praise the work of another but still I feel I must write to say how much I liked and enjoyed your novel, both as a novel and also because I happen to like the Austrians. I was in Vienna for a time after the War." The writer was James Hilton, who burst into world fame within eighteen months with *Goodbye Mr. Chips*.

CHAPTER THREE

Fripp, Lady Warwick, D'Annunzio

I

Spears Against Us launched, I now took a deep breath and sat back. I felt like a schoolboy who had done well in the High Jump on Sports Day. Expectantly, they would move the bar higher and higher. I was somewhat scared. I waited two years before I wrote a successor, despite my publisher's plea. This had been my first novel with a historical basis. In later years I dealt with the dramas of the Second World War, the disastrous Crete campaign (*So Immortal a Flower*), the costly battle for Monte Cassino (*Eight for Eternity*) and with nineteenth-century Rome (*The Remarkable Young Man*). All these novels entailed immense research.

We had guests in February and March. One of them was a German, Dr. Theodore Auer, a Secretary at the German Embassy in London, whom I had met in Paris. I was still intensely interested in events in Germany. I had kept up a correspondence with Max Bauer and Ernst Ritter. They sang the praises and recorded the victories of the Führer. When I quoted from their letters, Auer looked at me quietly. "They are silly young men. Hitler will lead us into trouble," he said very quietly. I had surmised he was not sympathetic towards the Nazis. This was the first time he had openly expressed his opinion. He was at the Embassy from 1930 to 1934, when he was sent to Paris. He had great difficulty in hiding his dislike of his Nazi masters and was apprehensive of what might happen to him if war broke out. His lack of enthusiasm for the regime appears to have been detected. His many English friends parted with him sadly, wondering if they would ever see him again. Thirty years were to elapse before I had news of him, in the most singular manner. In 1962 I made a cruise round the world. We briefly visited Ceylon. Just as our ship was about to sail from Colombo, Lady Corea, wife of an official who had called on friends, departing for shore, came up and gave me a note. It was from Dr. Theodore Auer, now German Ambassador to Ceylon! Too late he had heard I was on board and had scribbled a note to me. Subsequently I learned what had happened to him. On the outbreak of war in 1939 he was called back to Berlin. We feared he had fallen a victim to the Nazis' ruthless extermination of their critics. And now to my ship came this piece of paper on which he had scribbled 'Greetings from Teddy Auer, German Ambassador to Ceylon'. After his return to Berlin he was sent as Consul-General to Morocco where he stayed until the British-American attack and invasion. Back in Berlin he was arrested one day and made a political prisoner on remand, from July, 1943 to May, 1945. He was interned in the Berlin-Plötzensee prison, one of the places of execution of those involved in the abortive coup led by young Graf von Stauffenberg. "They must all be hanged like cattle!" cried Hitler. The condemned men were herded into a room in which meat hooks hung from the ceiling. They were hung up on the hooks, a noose of piano wire round their necks. A movie camera recorded the scene as they dangled and strangled. The developed film, as ordered, was rushed to Hitler so that he could view it the same evening.

Auer awaited death for almost two years in this notorious prison. He was liberated in May, 1945, by the Russian Red Army, only to be arrested by the Russian Secret Police. For seven years, 1945–1952, he was the prisoner of the Russian Occupation Army and, later, of the Communist East German authorities. In July, 1952, he was liberated. After a period of convalescence, he reported at the German Foreign Office. In March, 1956, he was appointed West German Ambassador to Ceylon, his last post before retirement. Such was the history of my guest at Pilgrim Cottage in February, 1932.

At the end of May, Louis Tissier left for his military service. His departure was a great loss for me. He had endeared himself to all my friends with his joyous nature and his utter unselfishness. I think he loved Pilgrim Cottage more ardently than I did. One of his enthusiasms was characteristic. He had developed a passion for Woolworth's Stores. There was one in Henley. He was always there, enticed by the items he could buy for sixpence. The assistants all knew 'the

French Boy' and it was characteristic that before departure he went and said goodbye to all of them. He sadly packed and I motored him to Victoria Station. Ethel was in tears. His term of service was twelve months, when he would return to Pilgrim Cottage. We had not discussed his return. It was taken for granted that this was his home. He was delighted when he discovered he was posted to Caen. "That's where your William the Conqueror came from, so in a way it's part of England. One day I shall follow him over the Channel!" he wrote.

I did not have to wait a year to see him. Within six months he had a week's leave. He crossed on a night boat and was at the cottage for breakfast. He flung his arms round each of the four poplar trees and kissed them. "Home, Sweet Home!" he sang. He had learned the tune from an old musical box I possessed.

The morning before his leave he had had a harrowing experience. They had been called at dawn and marched into the Grand Place. In the centre there was a guillotine. A crowd had collected. It was the soldiers' duty to hold it back around the scaffold. Presently a hefty, red-headed youth appeared, under guard, in a white shirt that had been cut away at the neck where his hair had been shaved. When he had mounted the scaffold he shouted obscenities at the crowd and struggled with his guards. He kicked the prayer-book out of the hands of the chaplain. Screaming, he was forced down on the plank, to which he was firmly strapped. It then slid forward and the heavy steel knife came noiselessly down. The severed head jumped and nearly missed the basket. The force of his blood was so great that it splashed some of the soldiers below, one of whom fainted. Then the soldiers were marched back to the barracks for breakfast. "Incredible! Barbaric! Are we civilised? Are we the country of Degas and Proust?" exclaimed Louis.

Only six days, and he was gone again. "*Mon cher*, six months with sweaty peasants, vile food, straw beds, and *Vive La France*, and then I am a human being again. *Vive Pilgrim Cottage!*" he cried, embracing me before entering the train.

I was now hard at work finishing a new book, not a novel this time, but the life of a surgeon I had never known or seen. One day I received a letter from a Lady Fripp. She had read *Half Way*. It had evoked a desire that I should write her late husband's life. He was Sir Alfred Fripp, a famous surgeon and a popular figure in London's social life. There were several reasons why I did not wish to undertake the work. I had no professional knowledge, his life had been lived in an era that was not yet history, it would entail immense labour and I should be under the scrutiny of those who knew Fripp; nor could I believe that the book would have a remunerative sale. Since all these reasons did not deter Lady Fripp from asking me to undertake the work, I told her it was a commission she would find too expensive. What would be my fee, she asked. I said five hundred pounds, thinking that would end the proposition. To my dismay she thought it was most reasonable. I then made a stipulation. I would not write her husband's life if I had to consult any of the family. I could not write for a committee. She must accept the book as I wrote it, the decision to publish resting with her. All these conditions were accepted. When I left the house in Portland Place I was perturbed at having committed myself. Sir Alfred had kept copious diaries, medical and social. These and all his letters would be at my disposal.

One day two large trunks arrived at Pilgrim Cottage. They contained forty-one closely written diaries, hundreds of letters, medical case sheets and photographs. There was no room for all these in my cottage. I kept the trunks in the garage. I began to read the material. The diaries started with a student's notes, proceeded to his first professional case, then to the intimate details of his honeymoon. As I read on and on I became fascinated by his story. He had been skyrocketed into fame and fortune before starting to practise. It took me three months to read through all this material. Having digested this I spent six months writing the biography. All this time I rarely consulted Lady Fripp and then only about the inclusion or omission of certain incidents and passages. After delivering the manuscript to her there was a long silence. Then one day I was asked to lunch. I went expecting trouble. Almost at once Lady Fripp said, "We are all delighted with the book. In some ways you know my husband better than I did." Thanking me, she gave me a cheque for the copyright. I had arrived at a stage where any publisher would take almost anything from me, but I advised her to accept a low royalty as the book would not have a large sale. I was wrong. It had three printings in six months.

Fripp had a fairy godmother from birth. He was tall, the good-looking son of an artist. He was endowed with great personal charm and a zest for living. His godfather was the Rev. John Dalton, of Trinity College, Cambridge, who was tutor to H.R.H. Prince Albert Edward, Duke of Clarence, son of Edward the Prince of Wales and Princess Alexandra. One July morning in 1884 Fripp met the Prince at his godfather's breakfast table. A little later they met again when the Prince dined with his tutor. The two young men after dinner had a tête-à-tête that lasted two hours and they parted on cordial terms. That seemed the end of the friendship, for Fripp was a student at Guy's Hospital Medical School, and the Prince was going into the army. But fate willed otherwise.

Young Fripp had just qualified as a surgeon at Guy's and was still studying there when he secured a holiday appointment with a Dr. Jalland, at York, who was professionally attached to the 10th Hussars at the barracks. Dr. Jalland took him, as a locum-tenens, on an introductory round before he left for his holiday. Thus it happened that six years after their meeting at Cambridge Fripp again met Prince Albert. It seemed Jalland had been in attendance but now satisfied that his royal patient was recovered, he went off on holiday. The Prince moved from his barracks into the Royal Hotel at Scarborough. There, one Monday morning, he fell ill again and young Fripp was hastily summoned.

> You would be amused [Fripp wrote to his father] to see me dancing attendance on H.R.H. He sent for me yesterday to Scarborough. I put him to bed at once as he had a sharp attack of fever ... Don't mention H.R.H.'s illness outside our house as the Prince of Wales particularly wants it not to get into the papers. He is afraid the public will get the impression his son is a chronic invalid.

But it was not a fever that afflicted the young man. Fripp's prescriptions, which he had had returned from the chemist and filed, revealed the nature of the trouble. It was the return of an attack of gonorrhoea which was thought to be cured. He had gone on board a steam yacht at Scarborough and drank champagne. For the next three weeks Fripp was in daily attendance on the Prince. Meanwhile there was alarm at Court. Who was this young man attending the heir-presumptive? The Prince of Wales sent his trusted physician to 'vet' the doctor. The report was good. The patient recovered. Jalland returned from holiday, and paid his locum-tenens nineteen guineas.

But instead of taking the train next day to London, Fripp took one at midnight to Edinburgh, en route to Mar Lodge, seat of the Duke and Duchess of Fife, where he was a fellow-guest with the Prince. What he had expected had not happened, he was not discarded. He was now in possession of a medical secret and was taken into the royal circle. The friendship between doctor and patient had become a firm one. Fripp was not only a promising young surgeon, he had great personal charm and natural gaiety. At Mar Lodge he met the Prince and Princess of Wales. Prince Albert confided in Fripp about a love affair. He had his eye on Princess May of Teck. Fripp attended some of the guests. At first he had been boarded out at the Fife Arms, soon he was moved into Mar Lodge. What a different world it was from the Out-Patients' Department at Guy's, the destitution, disease, and hopelessness of many who had little to live for. But he kept his head remarkably well. The royal house party moved on to Abergeldie Castle, the Prince of Wales's seat. The Prince took stock of him and, impressed, asked him to accompany his son on an official visit to Wales, as equerry and medical attendant. One day at Abergeldie he was having a bath when the Prince of Wales sent for him. He was kept waiting and then was ushered into the presence of Queen Victoria. She put him at ease at once, chatted about water-colour painting, knowing his father's eminence in that art, and about the health of the Duke of Clarence.

After his return to London Fripp was not forgotten. The young Prince gave him a black pearl pin, and paid a bill for medical attention. In December, 1891, the announcement was made of the Duke's engagement to Princess May of Teck. A month later came a shattering blow. Prince Albert died within three days, of double pneumonia. But it was not the end of royal favours. The Prince of Wales did not forget him. Within five years he was appointed surgeon-in-ordinary. The following year, aged thirty-two, he married Margaret Haywood, aged eighteen. She was beautiful and an heiress. Her father bought the couple a house in Portland Place. In that house they lived for the whole of their happy, eventful lives.

There was one very black day in the life of Sir Alfred Fripp. On June 14, 1902, ten days before King Edward's coronation, Fripp was hastily summoned by Lord Victor Crichton, one of the equerries. The King had been taken ill at Aldershot. They left at once for Waterloo, to take a special train, but as they were about to leave a telegram was handed to Crichton countermanding the journey as the King was better. Fripp wrote in his diary, "I should not have acted upon the telegram which was not sent by a professional man, and which cancelled the request of my professional colleague, Sir Francis Laking." So he returned home, and waited, while sensational rumours filled the air. He waited for ten days in some anxiety. As Surgeon-in-Ordinary he felt certain he would be kept informed. On June 24 he went to see the coronation decorations at the Abbey as the guest of Lord Esher. As he crossed Parliament Square he heard a policeman say to an enquiring American "Bless my soul, there won't be any Coronation, the King's being operated on at this moment." Dumbfounded, on his way home Fripp saw the newspaper posters announcing an operation, performed by Sir Frederick Treves, Sergeant-Surgeon to the King. Treves had taken a special train to Sandringham and performed the operation without informing his colleague. A feud ensued between the two surgeons which reached the ears of the King, who warned them that if they did not stop it he would dismiss both of them. It was the first setback suffered by Fripp in a triumphant career. In that year he wrote in his diary, in red ink, "*Aug. 23, 1902.* I handled today four millionaires, Crocker, Beit, Astor, and the sister of Pierpont Morgan." His career at Guy's Hospital was in the ascendant, he became third Assistant Surgeon. He was adored by the patients there. "His face was a lifeboat," wrote one of them, gratefully. An ardent 'first nighter', the bosom friend of Beerbohm Tree, he often went from the theatre to the operating table, or vice versa. His last two operations in 1902 were on Captain Holford, owner of the magnificent Dorchester House in Park Lane, and on the Duchess of Sutherland, at Stafford House. He visited South Africa with a hospital unit, scathingly denounced the medical breakdown there during the war, and emerged triumphant before a Commission of Enquiry. A knighthood followed. He was thirty-eight.

As I read through Fripp's diaries I became aware that they contained explosive material. Some of those mentioned were living. There was also the sanctity of the confidence a patient reposes in his doctor. The records were sometimes humorous, tragic and sensational. It was tantalising material for a biographer and many of my nights were troubled pondering over what I could keep in or leave

Pilgrim Cottage—dining-room

Pilgrim Cottage—sitting-room

out. There was the case of the astonishing Countess of Warwick, the great social beauty who was for some time King Edward's mistress, his 'Darling Daisy'. Fripp was much entertained by her too and went frequently to the famous house parties at Warwick Castle. A diary entry runs—"Jan. 12, 1896, at Warwick Castle. Awfully nice. Slept in Cardinal Wolsey's bed. Valet 5/–. Coachman 2/6."

Among Fripp's papers I found one, dated Warwick Castle, May 10, 1910, just after King Edward's death.

My dear Sir Alfred,
    We had such a nice little party for you (Lord Kitchener and Admiral Sir E. Seymour) but on reflection think it best to have no party this weekend before the funeral. Are you disengaged 21st to come for a few days? We should love it. I am so sad and I am sure you are feeling it also. And I *do* want to talk to you about *Everything*. I have a tiny house, the White House, Tite St., Chelsea (Whistler's old studio, and next door to Sargent). I go there this evening. Will you write there to say if you could come to talk *any* time—evenings best, I suppose. I shall be there till Saturday anyhow.
                    Yours ever sincerely, Frances Warwick.

Did they discuss *Everything*? I imagine not.

Among the Fripp collection of correspondence there was a small bundle of letters tied up with a blue ribbon. Examining these I found they were written from various addresses—Balmoral, Marlborough House, Sandringham. Some of them opened 'My darling Daisy,' and their tone was that of an ardent lover. They were signed and in the handwriting of King Edward VII, then Prince of Wales. They were treasure-trove but useless. For many reasons they could not be printed or quoted from. Their copyright belonged now to King George V. Moreover, the recipient and owner, Frances, Countess of Warwick, was living, a beautiful old lady of seventy. The question uppermost in my mind was how did they come to be in the possession of Fripp? A few days later, on a bright May day, Lady Fripp came to lunch at my cottage with her son, then at Eton. I asked if she could tell me how Sir Alfred came to possess these letters. She did not know, and suggested I should ask Lady Warwick, and give them back to her. So I wrote explaining how I came to have the letters and asked if I might see her. She answered she would be very glad to see me. On the day appointed I called on her, and was shown into the drawing-room by the butler. She was still, at seventy, a very beautiful woman, but very stout. She had a smooth pink skin, beautiful eyes and hair, and she wore a scarf of tulle round her neck and a long string of pearls. She was regal in every line of her. A Borzoi hound rose with her. She put out a white jewelled hand for me to take. There was a twinkle in her eyes when she said, "Tell me, Mr. Roberts, is it biography or blackmail?" I laughed and said it was purely biography. When we were seated I passed the packet of letters to her. "Dear me, dear me! I had forgotten all about them!" she exclaimed, running her fingers over the envelope. She withdrew three of the letters and read them. Her little taunt of blackmail rather shook me. It was a sinister word to come from her lips, even in banter. Some thirty years later I learned there was a special significance in her use of the word. In one of the letters there was a rather cryptic reference to Lady Rosslyn. I asked if she knew what the King referred to. "Oh, that's my darling mother! You must ask her. She'd love to see you. She loves visitors!" My mind worked quickly. Lady Warwick was seventy, her mother then must be nearing ninety. "She's ninety and has all her faculties!" she said. Lady Warwick counted the letters, six in all. "I suppose they are my property?" she asked. "Yes," I replied, "Lady Fripp wishes to return them to you". "How kind of her!" commented Lady Warwick. "Well, I will tell you how Sir Alfred came to possess them. I suppose you are too young to know what a commotion there was when just before the coronation King Edward was struck down with appendicitis. There was some trouble because Sir Frederick Treves kept the operation to himself and did not call in Sir Alfred to assist. The King's illness seemed to create a fashion, a multitude of loyal appendixes became inflamed! And dear Sir Alfred—did you know him, what a charming, clever man!—was in great demand. He operated on my mother, on John Jacob Astor, on Mrs. Georgie Keppel, on Mr. Crocker, on others. He once told me that he did ten private operations and twenty-six hospital ones in ten days. I suppose to be in the fashion, I had to have it! Just before my operation I gave the packet of letters to Sir Alfred saying, that if it went wrong he must promise to give them to the King with his own hand. All went well, and in the excitement it seems both of us forgot about the letters! Thank you so very much, dear Mr. Roberts. I must write to Lady Fripp."

A remarkable lovely woman but at that time I did not know how remarkable. There were a lot of rumours about her. She had become a Socialist and was almost bankrupt. She had been one of the greatest hostesses of her era, dispensing lavish hospitality at stately Warwick Castle.

An heiress at fifteen, with £30,000 a year, and incredibly beautiful, Queen Victoria wished her to marry Prince Leopold, but instead Miss Maynard married the equerry, young Lord Brooke, son and heir of the Earl of Warwick. The Prince of Wales signed the marriage register. In due course, as Countess of Warwick, she reigned at historic Warwick Castle, giving sensational house parties. Conjugal faithfulness does not seem to have prevailed in her circle of high society. She became the mistress of Lord Charles Beresford. Her husband was accused of having assaulted the famous Elinor Glyn, novelist and red-haired beauty, in the gardens of Warwick Castle. Ten years after marriage, the Prince of Wales replaced Lord Charles Beresford as her lover. She was a slim thirty, he a stout fifty. He wrote her a number of passionate love letters. "God bless my own adored little Daisy Wife . . . Forever yours, Your only Love," etc. Later the avowal was broken. After nine years he transferred his affection to Mrs. George Keppel, among others.

Lady Warwick's madly lavish entertaining began to erode her fortune. She became financially embarrassed. She was hauled into court for debt. One of her friends was the amiable millionaire Arthur du Cros, M.P. for Hastings and Chairman of the Dunlop Rubber Company. He lent her £16,000 at three per cent. But she fell into arrears and when he pressed for payment she said she would soon be able to repay, she was disposing of some two hundred valuable letters. Alarmed, du Cros went to see the Countess. It was 1914, four years after the death of King Edward. Her plan was a simple one. She would demand £100,000 of King George V, or she would publish the letters in her autobiography. The notorious Frank Harris in Paris, a man of some literary genius but a natural blackguard who had had to leave England, was offering, claiming an agent's fee of £5,000, the American rights of her proposed book. It was at this stage during her attempt to blackmail King George that Arthur du Cros became involved. He feared that these letters might rock the monarchy. The letters of the late King Edward were not only love letters but they were full of comments on Court personalities and affairs of State. Their indiscretions were more than those of an amorous married man to a married woman well-known as a gossip. The well-meaning Arthur du Cros undertook to approach the Palace authorities in the hope they might make an offer for the letters. Frank Harris must be driven off the scene. He therefore approached Lord Stamfordham, King George's secretary, with a view to a direct deal. He was anxious to be seen as the well-meaning friend of both parties. The Hon. Charles Russell, the King's solicitor, played him like a salmon.

Meanwhile, the Palace authorities resorted to legal action, which had a note of illegality. With the greatest secrecy King George obtained, in the judge's private chambers, an injunction prohibiting the publication of the letters. The Great War had begun and regulations under the Defence of the Realm Act, recently promulgated, made this possible. King Edward's name did not appear in any of the documents. Later it was ordered that all the documents in the case should be destroyed and all affidavits should be taken off the Court files. This display of monarchal power smacked of the times of Charles I, but no one challenged this assertion of royal privilege since blackmail was threatened. By July, 1915, the Countess of Warwick was utterly defeated. Had she not chosen so august a figure she might have appeared in dock and have drawn a prison sentence. As it was nothing of the case appeared in the public records. Lady Warwick's solicitor was persuaded to hand over to King George the menacing letters. As for du Cros, the result was dismal. His service to the Crown was not rewarded as he hoped. The King's solicitor was created a baronet. Worse, under a threat, Lady Warwick enforced du Cros to settle her debts to the tune of £48,000, so that with the £16,000, plus interest she owed him, he lost in all nearly £70,000. She was socially ruined but that did not distress her. She became a Socialist, patroness of the Labour M.P., Will Thorne, and on her death in 1939, aged seventy-eight, she left her only property, Eastern Lodge, in pawn, to the Trades Union Council. Of her great fortune only £37,000 remained. King Edward's letters deposited by her with Fripp were intimate but not amatory.

The Lady Warwick letters were not the only sensational material that I had to handle with discretion. There was the strange case of Admiral Sir Reginald Tyrwhitt. During the First World War Fripp was appointed Consulting-Surgeon to the Grand Fleet. He refused the rank of Rear-Admiral or to wear uniform. His headquarters was the hospital ship *Sheelah*, Admiral Beatty's private yacht, which he lent to the Admiralty and maintained at his cost. In the years before the war Fripp had met, on the Duke of Sutherland's yacht, a brilliant young naval officer, Commander Tyrwhitt. Events now brought them together and Fripp was often Admiral Tyrwhitt's guest on his flagship. The strain in the North Sea was terrific, with gales, mines and submarines. Men broke down under it. "One night," wrote Fripp in his diary, "having succeeded in dodging Tyrwhitt's hospitable desire to give me his bunk and sleep himself in his cabin on the foretop, I withdrew to my room and was feeling sleepy when there was a tap at the door and in came the Flag Lieutenant. 'Can I speak to you, sir?' he asked. 'Yes, of course,' I answered. 'What is it?' 'Well, sir,' said the nervous young man, 'it's a dead secret. I have no right to do it, and if it became known I am done for in the Service.' I looked at his frank face. 'Never mind, fire away, my boy,' I answered. 'Nothing you say to me shall be given away.' 'Well, sir, I want to tell you because you are the only person who can prevent what may be a serious catastrophe. It's about our Admiral. He's not the man he was. We all adore him and I, who am with him more than anybody else, admire him most of all, and that is why I want to protect him and his reputation. He's working far too hard. He won't let any of his staff take any responsibility. He even has the telephone at his bedside, and at all hours of the night, if we are in harbour, he's called up by the Admiralty or the Grand Fleet, with the result he's not been getting anything like his proper sleep. The other day he drew up a plan in regard to the action of certain units which could have resulted in disaster. Obviously his brain is overworked or he would never have done it. As you know, sir, he's a very obstinate man, and like so many deaf men, deafest of all when people want to convert him. However, with the greatest difficulty we managed to get him to alter the orders, just in time. Now, as I say, nobody but you, sir, can take the necessary action, because you're not in uniform. If he does have a breakdown the only possible service course is for a medical board to examine him, and he might be shifted from his command. So I've come to you, sir. We want to save him from a breakdown.' 'Enough, young man,' I said, 'your secret shall be kept. Leave it to me,' I said. The next morning I travelled to London by the earliest train and went straight to the Admiralty and saw my old friend, Reginald Hall, the Director of Naval Intelligence. I swore him to secrecy, which was not difficult since we knew each other. He said, 'Can you wait five minutes while I go upstairs and see the First Lord?' When he came down he said, 'It's all right, Tyrwhitt's packing his traps. He's been given a month's leave of absence and told to go and fish in Scotland.' As I walked out of the Admiralty, I reflected that I could not have achieved this, and indeed would not have been approached by that devoted young fellow, if I had been wearing the uniform of Rear-Admiral, as the Admiralty desired."

Here was an excellent story for my book, but the difficulty was that Admiral Sir Reginald Tyrwhitt was still alive, and on active service. I pondered what I should do. I decided to set up in proof Fripp's account and send it to the Admiral for his comment. I expected an explosion. His reply was polite but emphatic. Down the side of Fripp's account he had written, "I think this is rubbish and certainly untrue." His letter accompanied my proof sheet.

Admiralty House, Chatham.
2 Sept., 1932.

Dear Sir,

Thank you for your letter and the enclosed proof, which I have read very carefully. Sir Alfred Fripp was a great friend of mine and I was one of his greatest admirers. I of course cannot contradict anything he has written but it is indeed news to me that I was on the point of going off my head in the War. I consulted Fripp once during the War as I had some slight internal trouble but apart from that I never had a day's sickness. For the whole period, as far as I know, I was as fit as a fiddle. My secretary, who has been with me for 21 years, and who knows me better than I know myself, has no recollection of any orders I gave being cancelled because they were dangerous, and he surely would have known as all my orders went straight to him. There may be truth in the part about going on leave, as it is true I had no leave at all until 1918. I was sent for by Admiral Wemyss (the 1st Sea Lord) in Feb. 1918 to be asked if I had had any leave during the war. I replied 'No.' He said, 'I should like you to go on a month's leave forthwith and suggested the Riviera, to which I strongly objected. I said if you insist on my going on leave I will go to Scotland to fish but not now. I'll go in April, which I did and to corroborate this—the Italians had their greatest disaster about 3 days after I arrived at Kelso and I was nearly recalled by the Admiralty in consequence. I went for 14 days and got an extension of 7 days later on. I think it is quite likely that Fripp did mention the fact that I had not been on leave to Admiral Hall, who was a great friend of us both, and he very probably mentioned it to the First Sea Lord.

I am sorry to spoil a good yarn but you can hardly expect me to acquiesce in the announcement that I was practically off my head during the whole of the war and I must request that you will therefore refrain from publishing a story which I am quite certain is untrue or is a gross exaggeration.

Yours sincerely,
Reginald Tyrwhitt.

Now here were two honourable men with a warm regard for each other, and one said that what the other had written was quite untrue. In the face of this letter I had no alternative but to write to the Admiral and assure him that nothing of this would appear in my book. But my own view was that Fripp had told the truth, too many facts agreed, and my view was confirmed by a second letter from the Admiral, which came a few days later.

Dear Roberts,
Many thanks for your letter and for the cancellation of the story. I have thought about it since I wrote and incidentally, it was quite impossible for the Flag Lieutenant to have known (in advance) of my proposed undertaking. The strictest secrecy was invariably observed in all these matters and no orders ever issued until just before sailing. I think Sir Alfred was responsible for my going on leave and worked that through Sir R. Hall. Again many thanks.

I had been eager to retain a good story but I could not use it without corroboration from the Admiral. He killed it. As he remarked —"You can hardly expect me to acquiesce in the announcement that I was practically off my head during the war."

Some years later I met an officer who had served in his squadron and he said, involuntarily, when talking of those days, "Our old man nearly went crackers. He kept seeing submarines in the harbour and had us scurrying out while they cleaned them up. We never found one."

Admiral Tyrwhitt had a long and distinguished career after the War, as Senior Naval Officer at Gibraltar, then in command 3rd

Light Cruiser Squadron, then Commander-in-Chief, China Station, then Admiral Superintendent of H.M. Dockyard, Rosyth, and then at Chatham. In 1918 he was created a baronet, thanked by Parliament and granted £10,000.

Fripp died aged sixty-four, worn out. One day, January 13, 1930, he asked a colleague at Guy's to look at him. He went home, entered his study, wrote on a slip of paper which he hid away—"My number is up, I must go." He went to his summer home at Lulworth with his family. He confessed to being tired. He died within six weeks. Hundreds of letters and telegrams poured in from all parts of the world, from rich and poor, eminent and humble, to whom he had been the bringer of hope and the releaser from pain. St. Martin-in-the-Fields could not hold all those who came to the memorial service.

II

I worked indoors and out that summer. By now Ethel was accustomed to my writing habits. I wrote for about twelve hours a day. Sometimes I did not go to bed until four o'clock in the morning, if the flow was good. At other times I broke off to go round the garden. In May it was enchanting with pink apple blossoms, golden forsythia, laburnum, daffodils and violets under the windows and the first white roses covering the face of the cottage. I postponed my work and motored to spend three days with Lady Fripp at the house Lutyens had built for them on the edge of the Cove, in order that I might describe it. Also that summer I fulfilled a number of speaking engagements. In May I spoke at a luncheon at Grosvenor House that was given in honour of Miss Radclyffe Hall, author of *The Well of Loneliness*. Christina Foyle, the daughter of the owner of Foyle's Bookshop, when a girl still at school, had the bright idea to give monthly lunches at which the reading public could meet, see, and hear the eminent persons of the day. Through the years the Foyle Lunch grew into almost a national institution at whose meetings were seen every celebrity in the world of literature, art, music, science, the theatre and politics. On our seventieth birthdays, in 1962 and 1969, both myself and Noël Coward were given complimentary lunches. In 1971 Christina Foyle celebrated the five-hundredth lunch. She had started with small afternoon teas at their bookshop where Hall Caine,

Conan Doyle, John Drinkwater, etc., were star guests. These were so popular that youthful Christina began to hold monthly lunches at the Holborn Restaurant. Success had emboldened her to take the next step. When she went in 1930 to see the banquet manager at Grosvenor House, in order to take the ballroom for upwards of five hundred guests, he was astonished to find himself dealing with a mere girl.

Her lunch in 1932 for Miss Radclyffe Hall was sensational. The ball-room was crammed to overflowing. "You came along to the luncheon and proposed the toast of Literature", she wrote. "I found it very hard to persuade people to associate themselves with Radclyffe Hall in those difficult days." She succeeded in obtaining a famous surgeon of the day, Sir Arbuthnot Lane, to take the chair, and Sheila Kaye-Smith, then a prominent novelist, to respond to the toast I proposed.

It is difficult today to comprehend the furore that Radclyffe Hall's novel provoked, with its restrained study of lesbianism. Oscar Wilde's name was still banned in polite society. He was a bold person who used the word 'homosexual', or revealed that he knew anything about such a condition. At the time of the appearance of *The Well of Loneliness* there was a popular journalist named James Douglas. A sensation-monger, he set himself up as a moral arbiter. He had a nose for dirt like a hound for truffles. He violently attacked the book in the *Sunday Express*. As a result of his article, urging prohibition of the book, the nervous publishers wrote to the Home Secretary, who advised its withdrawal. The following month a Paris firm issued an English edition and exported copies to England. The Home Office by banning action provoked the importation of 'indecent' literature. It created a clandestine traffic in *Ulysses, Lady Chatterley's Lover*, etc. These books were seized by the Customs on the Home Secretary's order. In 1928 Miss Hall was prosecuted under the Obscene Publications Act, 1857, which gave a magistrate power to order the destruction of offending books. In Court my friend Norman Birkett appeared for Miss Radclyffe Hall. "I felt there was no word of obscenity in the book, well-written, from the first page to the last, and to call it an obscene book was a dreadful misuse of language," he said. The proceedings were a travesty of justice. For the defence, Birkett called Desmond McCarthy, one of the leading critics of the day. Sir Chartres Biron, the magistrate, refused to let him give evidence, or allow the authoress herself, and thirty-eight others, including Julian Huxley. The magistrate's order for the destruction of the book was upheld by the Quarter Sessions whose chairman described it as 'most dangerous and corrupting'. The effect of this prosecution was to establish the fame of its author, and of the book. In Paris it appeared in every bookshop window. It was translated into eleven languages. A Court in U.S.A., after a trial promoted by a 'purity' crank, gave full sanction for publication. It sold forthwith a million copies, and fourteen years later enjoyed an annual sale of over 100,000 copies.

Radclyffe Hall was a beautiful woman with somewhat austere features, wealthy, a fine horsewoman. She affected masculine attire, a tailor-made jacket and shirt, and stiff collar. She wore a black Spanish sombrero and her conduct was dignified. She made no secret of her relationship with her friend, Lady Troubridge. The singular English law did not prosecute feminine homosexuality, though, with the assistance of *agents provocateurs*, it encouraged the blackmail of male homosexuals. The Wolfenden Report, and a plaque on Oscar Wilde's house in Tite Street, were thirty years off.

At the Foyle lunch the 'sisterhood' was very much in evidence, with cropped heads, stiff collars and tailored jackets. Males seemed in a minority. There was a high-ranking police officer on my left, in uniform, bemedalled. After lunch he smoked a cigar. Only when he rose to speak did I discover that the officer wore a skirt and was a woman, a distinguished Commandant of the Women's Police Corps. On rising to propose the toast of Literature, after surveying the company I remarked that, a mere male, I rose 'from a deep well of loneliness'. It proved an hilarious incident for one of Miss Foyle's most successful luncheons. In my speech I said I did not think I should live to see the day when Miss Hall, who had then been prosecuted in British police courts, would be honoured here, with a famous medical chairman on her left and a female police officer on her right, and I was very glad to pay tribute to one who had not only made a distinguished contribution to our literature but had striven fearlessly for freedom of thought and expression. Sir Arbuthnot Lane, speaking from the chair, said Miss Hall had drawn one of the most distinguished audiences he had ever seen, despite all that had been said against her. How faint these landmarks seem today but whose establishment then called for courage and tenacity!

74

III

That summer I indulged in a property deal. The Fawley Court estate at Henley came on the market. I bought the lodge-keeper's cottage, situated on King Charles's Way, at the edge of the deer park, and the Old Forge cottage, high up at Fawley. Both these properties were inhabited, the former by an old estate gamekeeper, eighty, the latter by an old blacksmith, aged eighty-one. The Old Forge was superbly situated with a view over the Thames valley, the Round Tower at Windsor Castle visible on the horizon. In the cottage dwelt an attractive pair, the blacksmith and his devoted wife of seventy-seven. It became a pleasant excursion for me and my guests to visit the village blacksmith's. The old lady was an avid reader and I generally arrived with a book. In winter Louis and I walked through the dusk of the short afternoon, the keen wind in our faces on that high ridge. The cottage door opened in eager welcome, the hob fire was poked, the cat turned out of the easy chair, the lamp lit and tea laid on the table. The blacksmith's grandfather's chair had been given him in celebration of fifty years of bell-ringing in the church. On the high mantelpiece stood the photograph of a youth, twenty, their only son, killed in the last fortnight of the Great War. After tea came the home-made wine. It made us sing all the way home. They were very happy when they learned I had bought their cottage and would be their landlord. In June I attended the celebration of their golden wedding.

That summer I had a ludicrous experience. The owner of Phyllis Court, a Regency house, by Henley Bridge, had converted it into a riverside club. He was extremely hospitable and I was fortunate in having such a neighbour. I lunched there on the opening day of Henley Regatta. Evan Morgan (Lord Tredegar) rushed up to me. "You must come up to my box. I've got André Maurois with me. He wants to meet you!" he cried. I felt this was rather strange as I knew André Maurois, but I followed Evan up on to the Grand Stand. His guests were Sir John Lavery with his beautiful wife, whose face had been modelled on the Irish coinage, Baroness d'Erlanger, and a young man who was introduced to me as André Maurois. He certainly was not Maurois. Later, I tactfully questioned the bogus author, who became embarrassed and drew me aside. "This is terrible! Lord Tredegar persists in introducing me as André Maurois. I am not André Maurois. I am Paul Morand!" said the author of *Ouvert La Nuit*.

Walking across the great lawn during the tea interval I commented to Sir John on the roses that lined the brick embankment built by Cromwell, from which to bombard the Royalists up the river. "Lloyd George always has marvellous roses," said Sir John. "I remarked on them one day when I was painting his portrait. The Prime Minister's eyes twinkled as he said, 'Yes, I get wonderful manure from the barracks at Aldershot. It's the only good thing I've ever had from the Army!'"

I was now able to accept some social engagements. One day I lunched with a fellow novelist, Muriel Hine, who loved giving lunches in her Chelsea home, a place full of sunshine and beautiful china. I found there Eva Moore, wife of H. V. Esmond, the dramatist, in whose plays they acted together. She was the mother of Jill Esmond, the wife of a young actor, Laurence Olivier, who has a son with the singular name of Tarquin. Another guest was adorable little Adeline Genée. She had founded the Royal Academy of Dancing. Danish, she made her first appearance aged ten. She came to London at nineteen, and retired in 1914, having been for eighteen years *première danseuse* at the Empire ballets. Born at Aarhus, Denmark, in 1878, she was now fifty-four, a little piece of Copenhagen china. She would hardly believe me when I told her I had been in Aarhus. "I never meet anyone who has ever heard of it, let alone been in it!" she exclaimed. I went from that lunch to have tea with Laura Knight, A.R.A. We both had early Nottingham associations. Honours were beginning to snow upon her, D.B.E., in 1929, LL.D. of St. Andrews in 1931, R.A. in 1934. She was a downright little woman with a large Bohemian circle of friends. You found in her Maida Vale studio people drawn from every phase of life, T. E. Lawrence, G. B. Shaw, W. H. Davies the poet, Alfred Munnings the animal painter, Augustus John, Karsavina the ballerina, and Mills the circus impresario, who, like Diaghilev, had given her the *entrée* to their productions. I visited her until the year of her death. It was singular that she and Adeline Genée died in the same year, 1970, both 92, and both Dames of the British Empire.

That August there came to me the idea of writing a novel based on Pilgrim Cottage. The germ of it had been present in my mind for some time. One morning I had turned over some notes made during a visit to Moscow three years earlier. They had been made in a notebook I had bought in Venice, in 1929. Out of Venice and Moscow my story took birth. In the year in which I had lodged in the Pensione Smith in the Torre dell' Orologio on the Piazza at Venice, I had been accosted on the staircase by a pretty young English girl. She asked if she could speak to me privately. Not wishing to take her into my bedroom we went to have a drink in a café below. She was very nervous but presently she asked if I could lend her ten pounds. She had run up a bill with Frau Smith, who had been kind, but was pressing for payment.

Little by little I learned her story. She was only eighteen, an orphan, living with an aunt in London, but very unhappy. Her aunt drank. She had been at a French seminary at Tours for six months. On the train to Paris she had met a young Frenchman, touring with a ballet company. He had enticed her to join the company, promising her a career as a ballerina. For five months they had toured in France, Germany, Austria and Italy. In Trieste the company went bankrupt and dispersed. She came with her lover to Venice en route to Paris. Here, a month ago, he had abandoned her. Was she telling me the truth? She answered my questions without hesitation. She had written to her aunt twice, on postcards, saying she had joined a theatrical company and was happy. Yes, she and Louis had lived together. They were very much in love. He said that when things improved and they were back in Paris, he would marry her. But a girl in the company told her he was married. He denied this. No, she was not expecting a child. There was something simple and straightforward about her. She had written to her aunt for money, and had had no answer yet. She had written to a cousin, again no answer. She lacked the fare to go home.

I made her an offer. I would pay her bill and see her off on a train to London. The next day I took her to the station and bought her a ticket. She would repay me when she got home. I put no store on that. Her aunt did not sound sympathetic. As I waited for the train to leave a handsome German youth, in *lederhosen*, breathlessly appeared. He came from the Pensione Smith. He had just heard she was leaving.

He loved her. He was in tears. He would marry her one day, if she would wait. He was still at the university. What a scene, these two impassioned children! I stood aside, like an old uncle. The train drew out. All the way back, in a mixture of German and English he poured out the story of his love. How long had he known her? *Zwei Wochen. Wunderschön! Wunderschön!* Life would never be the same again.

Two weeks later I had a surprise. I received a money order for fifteen pounds. All was well. Her aunt was glad to have her home. and I had my story. Venice, Moscow, a wayward ballerina, a pair of young lovers in Pilgrim Cottage, but an English not a German lover. By the end of August I had written the first hundred pages of *Pilgrim Cottage.*

I had promised to join some friends at Riva on Lake Garda early in September and to go thence to Venice. En route from Riva I planned to call on Gabriele D'Annunzio at the Villa Vittoriale at Cargnacco. I had been his guest there in 1923. He had invited me to return but nine years had passed and I had not done so. My introduction to him had been singular, as was everything connected with the poet. In Venice I had known a Signora de Blaas, mother of 'Lulu', the portrait painter. D'Annunzio was a friend of the family. He had often come from his *palazzo* on the Grand Canal to dine with them. One day, shortly after Italy had entered the First World War, he arrived with a fish in a bucket. "I'm joining the Air Force. I shall do unparalled deeds, I may fall. This is goodbye. You know that the fish is the holy emblem of Christians—you see it engraved in all the catacombs. So I have given to this fish the safeguarding of my soul. You must keep it for me until I return." Nothing he said surprised them. But keeping the fish was a problem. Finally, they put it in a small tin bath, so that it would have room to swim. They placed the bath in a spare lavatory. Then one day the Austrians bombed Venice. They just missed the *palazzo*, which rocked. The fish, alarmed by the agitated water, leapt out, landed in the lavatory pan and disappeared forever. D'Annunzio never asked for his 'soul'. Happily he had forgotten all about it.

It was Signora de Blaas who gave me a letter of introduction to D'Annunzio, a recluse. The Villa Vittoriale was a warren, consisting of a dark congeries of rooms, heavily carpeted, a seraglio perfumed with sandalwood, heated, and crammed with the most bizarre objects.

After he had seized Fiume with his three hundred *Arditi* volunteers, to stop it going to Yugoslavia, the Italian Navy bombarded his head-quarters and he was driven out. Though defeated, he was a national hero. He had lost an eye in the war and had dropped propaganda leaflets over Vienna from his plane. He retreated to the Villa Vit-toriale, as he called it. When I visited him in 1923 he was something of a problem for the Italian Government. Mussolini, a little afraid of him as a popular figure, visited him and created him Prince of Monte Nevoso. He was always in financial difficulties. Early in his career he had had to flee to France because of debts in Italy. He settled at Arcachon on the Atlantic coast. Threatened by more debts, on the outbreak of war he returned to Italy. He played a flamboyant and heroic role. He was a world-famous figure. His books were read, his plays performed, but the income proved inadequate to sustain his princely style of living.

During the war the Italian Government had sequestrated a villa at Cargnacco above Lake Garda, the property of a German archaeo-logist, Heinrich Thöde. The Government let D'Annunzio occupy it. He refused to leave it. He turned the villa into a show-piece. When I went there he had obtained the prow of the *Puglia*, an Italian destroyer that had been engaged at Spalato in July, 1920. He had mounted it on the hill-side. He decorated the grounds with all manner of war memorials, mostly to his *Arditi*, and on a masthead above the prow he flew flags commemorating the historic events of his tenure of his 'kingdom' of Fiume. Four great mastiffs guarded his gate. He had ceremonial manners. Sixty-three, he was a very bald little man who would have been ugly but for his vital eyes. Was he a genius or a poseur? Both, I thought. One heard all kinds of stories about the women he enchanted but his great romance had been with Eleonora Duse, whom he cruelly satirised in *Il Fuoco*, one of his best novels.

During my twenty hours at the villa I never saw a woman there. What I saw was a truckload of old books arrive, brought from a derelict monastery. He went through these, I learned, searching for obsolete words, to bring them back into the language. I was housed in the dependence. We had two sessions of talk before and after dinner. Talk is not the word to describe what was a monologue, delivered in such rapid French that I lost half of it. He was aggrieved that he was not better known in England. Could I do something about it? Why had he no British public, and why were his plays not performed? He raised his hands in protest. The next morning he escorted me through the grounds. There was a small temple lined with black velvet. On a plinth within he uncovered a pair of beautifully sculptured hands. They were Duse's. He contemplated them in silence and then veiled them. We went out into the bright morning, not a word said; was this an act of contrition? He had a passion for roses and told me he had planted a thousand trees and would plant more. When, on departure, he ceremoniously saw me off, my car was filled with them. I carried away a signed volume of his plays and a large autographed photo. I was destined never to see him again. When arriving in Riva in 1932, I telephoned the villa, I was invited to lunch the following Friday. Two days later, I was informed by his secretary that the maestro had had a bad attack of asthma and was too ill to receive visitors.

In 1950 I came to know a Jewish author living in the hills near San Remo, who had translated some of D'Annunzio's books into German and knew the poet well. He told me a singular story about the Villa Vittoriale. After the war the widow of Herr Thöde, a Swede, claimed back the property. D'Annunzio refused to surrender it, stating he had bought it from the Italian Government. She started litigation. D'Annunzio invited her to visit him and see if things could not be settled amicably. He put her up in the local inn, and invited her to dinner. On returning she was violently ill, vomiting all night. Certain that he had tried to poison her, she fled the next morning. She never obtained her property but years later she had her revenge. The thing D'Annunzio coveted most was the Nobel Prize. He set in motion proceedings for his name to be considered. Hearing of this, Frau Thöde acquainted the selection committee with the facts concerning her villa. She killed all chances of D'Annunzio getting the prize. The Villa Vittoriale is now a shrine that may outlast his works, for he created a legend. I recall him with some warmth. He was hospitable and courteous, and unforgettable. It was like being in the wing of a theatre. He dramatised every moment.

As I motored through Gargnano, after leaving Riva, I thought of D. H. Lawrence, who had eloped there twenty years earlier with Mrs. Frieda Weekley. In the Villa Igea, down by the shore, he wrote his novel *Sons and Lovers* which put him on the threshold of fame. They paid sixty-six shillings a month for a five-roomed furnished apartment and an orchard full of peach-trees. Lawrence had burned his boats, and with only fifty pounds in hand had walked over the Italian frontier with Frieda, the Nottingham professor's wife.

On my arrival in Venice I took up my quarters in the Pensione Seguso, having a great welcome from the three sisters and their cat, Moses. Just around the corner were the newly married septua-genarians, Grace and Riccardo Nobili. In appearance he was as noble as his name. The adoring Grace would emerge with a large straw sombrero to protect him from sunstroke as he sat painting in the garden. Only five minutes' walk along the Zattere by the Giudecca Canal stood the Palazzo Clary, the property of Prince Clary, who lived there, dispossessed of his great estate and castle of Teplitz in the former Bohemia, where once, a guest, the nineteen-year-old Chopin had played for an earlier prince and princess. Prince Alphonse Clary let off the first floor to the old Duchess of Canevaro, a relation, widow of an admiral. I used to go in the Twenties, and have tea with the old lady. She loved to talk of London, where her young husband had been a naval attaché. Possessed of a beautiful voice, she had sung duets with Adelina Patti for Queen Victoria. As a girl she had been taught to play the piano by Liszt and the score he had marked for her was on the music rack. In the long salon hung family portraits. There was a little card tucked into the frame of each, 'so they shall know to whom they go when I am dead'. After tea there was a familiar cere-mony. A white-jacketed young footman took a huge macaw out of its cage and advanced to the duchess who gave it a lump of sugar. Then the youth opened the long windows of the balcony. He spread a rug over the balustrade and the parrot took his exercise along it. He spread his great blue wings against the sunset and began to screech madly, tormented by children on the pavement below. When the noise got too raucous the duchess rang a bell and said to the servant, "Bring in the wicked Beppo!" As he was taken back to the cage she shook an admonishing finger. I never knew why Beppo was called 'wicked' until some thirty years later when, meeting Prince Clary for the first time, I asked him about his late tenant. He told me that the parrot had been acquired by Admiral Canevaro in a shop in Malta. It had formerly belonged to a British sailor. In the course of time it acquired some

Italian naval words. One day, when the British Fleet paid a visit to Venice, Admiral the Duke of Edinburgh, Queen Victoria's son, went to lunch with the Carnevaros. After lunch, seeing the parrot in the cage, His Royal Highness said to it in English, "Polly, Polly, pretty Polly!" The parrot retorted, remembering his native tongue, "Bugger off!" It seemed that when Beppo was put out on the *palazzo* balcony he used the most frightful Italian words, to the delight of the children below who provoked him. Hence, "Bring in the wicked Beppo!"

Just off the Zattere there was the Palazzo Catecumeni. It was a low rambling eighteenth-century palace, in a very dilapidated condition. It had a vast garden behind. In this palace the Duke of Rutland's family had stayed in 1912. Among the guests was Prime Minister Asquith. It was here that young Prince Clary, a dashing Austrian cavalry officer, taught Lady Victoria and her sister, Lady Diana Manners, to dance Viennese waltzes. On one occasion, for a party, they dressed up Mr. Asquith as a Doge of Venice.

I missed one friend in Venice this year, Neil McEachern, who had lived in the Palazzo Labia, off the Grand Canal. He left it to make a fabulous garden at the Villa Taranto on Lake Maggiore. The baroque Venetian palace had been built for Prince Labia, a war profiteer who got himself ennobled in 1645. It was famous for its frescoes of the life of Antony and Cleopatra. The palace had fallen into a derelict state when McEachern took a lease of it and uncovered the frescoes hidden under the whitewash. Their disclosure resulted in the palace being made a national monument. McEachern was irritated by the restrictions of the Fascist authorities. On surrendering his lease the Palazzo Labia returned to the family. The Prince Labia carried on the restoration from 1931 to 1936.

The Prince died in 1936 and the palace was empty until in 1948 Don Carlos de Beistegui, a Mexican millionaire, bought it. He spent three years and £1,000,000 restoring and furnishing it. Then, on September 3, 1951, he gave a sensational house-warming ball attended by fifteen hundred guests in fancy dress. One felt one was back in the Venice of Guardi and Casanova, except for the big, carpeted, floating platform for the gondolas, with arriving guests, ablaze in the Kleig lights of the cinema operators. It was, indeed, a return to the old days of the original Labias, who seemed to have been vulgarly ostentatious. They gave dinners on gold plate that afterwards was thrown out of the windows into the Canal. But, below the water, nets were placed so that all the gold plate was retrieved after the guests had departed. It was said that on this occasion Prince Labia cried—"*Le abbia, o non le abbia, sono sempre Labia!*—Whether I have it or whether I haven't, I shall always be Labia." In 1964 Beistegui sold the palace which passed into the hands of the Italian Radio Corporation, who have completely restored it. Neil McEachern had never entertained on the Beistegui scale but I missed his dinner parties and entertainments given against the background of Tiepolo's joyous frescoes.

I spent three delightful weeks in Venice working each morning on *Pilgrim Cottage*, sitting under a peach-tree in the Nobili's garden, with the sound of a fountain whose water fell from a lion's mouth into a basin.

When I arrived back in England the autumn tints were in the Chiltern woods around me. During my vacation I had kept up my book reviews for the *Sphere*. One week there was an exciting discovery. Duff Cooper had published a biography of Talleyrand. I felt certain it was a masterpiece. Full of admiration, I wrote to tell him so. He answered

90 Gower Street, W.C.
Sept. 29, 1932.

Dear Mr. Cecil Roberts,
A writer of books yourself you will understand the delight that your letter has given me, being the first quite independent comment I have received on my first publication. If my book is as good as you think, I am indeed a happy man. I know that you are not too easily pleased nor too lavish of praise and I can therefore only hope that you are as right as you usually are.
Yours sincerely,
Duff Cooper.

I did not foresee that one day, during the Second World War, we should be associated when he became the unhappy Minister of Information, the predecessor of the dynamic Brendan Bracken. The year before his death, at sixty-three, he published an excellent autobiography, *Old Men Forget*. In a sense *Talleyrand* was a product of defeat, as was *The World Crisis* by Churchill. Both authors, politicians, losing office, had retreated to the country to write, the latter to Chartwell, the former to a summer home at Bognor.

IV

In October I took a London *pied-à-terre* at 50 Eaton Terrace. I had the first-floor drawing-room with two windows in this small three-storey house. The street was quiet, near Eaton Square, and borrowed something of its aristocratic tone, being part of the West-minster estate. One was surprised by the presence of a public house, the Duke of Wellington. Possibly it was allowed there to accommodate, in more affluent days, the butlers and footmen of the surrounding houses. The head of the Duke of Wellington on the sign gave it an air. Just round the corner, in Gerald Road, I had Noël Coward for a neighbour. To me the most notable house near by was 99 Eaton Place. Here had lived Mrs. Sartoris, niece of Gainsborough's 'Mrs. Siddons', and sister of Fanny Kemble. It was in her drawing-room that Chopin gave his first public recital in London, on the afternoon of June 23, 1848. He was unwell, and played in a subdued manner, but with great charm. He died the next year.

In the nineteen-thirties I could park my car and leave it out all night opposite No. 50. The long street had not a dozen cars in it. It took me one hour to motor between Pilgrim Cottage and Eaton Terrace. In Cliveden Place lived my colleague, Sir Philip Gibbs. I was in and out of their house all the time they lived there, which was not long, for they seemed to change houses every two years. My next-door neighbour I never knew. The brassplate on his door said 'Dr. Quackenbos'. I always regretted I was never able to say, "I have just been to see Dr. Quackenbos." How Dickens would have loved that name! Later I wondered what had happened to the poor doctor. In 1942 a bomb obliterated the houses and with them a stationer's shop on the corner. The little, untidy shop was kept by two timid sisters, who thanked you fervently whether you spent £2 or 2d. Now on this site an elegant pseudo-Regency house has arisen. No. 50 was just spared, but so badly damaged that it had to be evacuated. Thieves broke in and stole the furniture, including some of mine. One loss was irreparable, a mahogany secretaire that held my father's papers, and twenty of my pocket diaries, which caused me endless trouble when I came to write *The Growing Boy*, and *The Years of Promise*, etc. My landlady and her daughter fled to Bath and never came back, I being in America. It was in this pleasant little house, through the winter of 1932-3, that I wrote much of *Pilgrim Cottage*. In November my biography of Alfred Fripp appeared. It had been a great effort both of organisation, and of selection, since many of those who provided the richest stories were still living.

On a beautiful starry night, towards midnight of the last day of the year 1932, after a long session at my desk in Pilgrim Cottage, I put down my pen. I went into the garden and walked on the lawn round the old house. The windows glowed golden from the light within. I had had a happy year, in fair health. I wondered if the new year would equal it. Perhaps it was too much to hope since we are mortal playthings of fate. A slice of a silver moon shone through the branches of a poplar tree. A passing motorist's headlights caught my white chimney pots in a brief noose of light; then darkness and silence, save for a bird stirring. I went indoors and, as was my habit, made in my diary the year's audit. I had earned £3,786. It seemed a lot of money but up the valley there was a stockbroker who made, he told me, some £2,000 a month and I had a barrister friend who had made £40,000 that year. Even so, I would not have changed places with them. I was happy doing just what I had always wanted to do.

CHAPTER FOUR

Rumbold, Rintelen, Two Gondoliers

I

The year 1933 opened ominously. On January 30 Hitler became the German Chancellor, with a Nazi Cabinet. I had a letter from Ernst Ritter in Berlin. "The German people have come to their senses and despite the machinations of the Jews Germany will again be respected." He wrote six pages of triumphant Nazi news. There followed a mass of literature acclaiming the Führer as the Messiah of a new era. The feeble President Hindenburg was pushed into the background. I replied coolly. I was beginning to tire of this propaganda, but I did not stop his reports. It was useful to have a finger on the Nazi pulse. Why he should seek to influence me I did not know. Perhaps, he thought, as an author I moulded public opinion.

At home no one took much notice of Hitler's rise to power, but when in February the Reichstag was set on fire and a witless Dutch youth was accused of arson, suspicion of Nazi methods grew. A disarmament plan put forth by Britain failed. Hitler insisted that his storm-troopers should not be counted in the total army strength under the revised Treaty clauses. In April the anti-Jewish measures became violent. Jews were removed from national and civic positions. A boycott began of all Jewish businesses and professions. Uniformed Nazi louts began to beat up the Jews in public. The communists in Germany had been eliminated. The spring election brought forth a sinister propagandist, Dr. Goebbels, and a ruthless swashbuckler, Goering. Hitler took over the Reichstag with seventeen and a half million votes, and his majority gave him complete emergency powers as Chancellor for four years. Democratic government in Germany was dead. The MacDonald-Baldwin Government seemed quite indifferent to what was happening. We were the fifth in air-power in

86

Europe. Churchill's protests went unheeded, the Government was hell-bent on peace at any cost. We were more concerned with getting out of India than over Hitler's reconstruction of the German army. A set of youths in the Oxford Union gave him an encouraging push. Led by Professor Joad, they passed a shameful resolution 'That this House will not fight for King and Country'. In a few years many of them would redeem their folly by giving their lives for England.

I was in a state of deep despair. Churchill, in the role of Cassandra, grew daily more unpopular, and unheeded. Out of office, he had time for literary work. He was busy at Chartwell on his monumental *Marlborough*. By the end of the year the Government, financially desperate, with nearly three million unemployed, committed the supreme folly of suspending interest payment on the American debt. It was a small sum, thirty-five million pounds, as against the money we threw away in various subsidies. At a Henley-on-Thames Conservative meeting a jackass M.P. gloated over the debt cancellation. "Why give money to those bloated Americans who didn't win the war? Think of the number of motor cars, with benefit to our industry and ourselves, we can buy with that money!" he cried. I rose and asked how he would feel, as a property owner, if his tenants repudiated their rents, and bought themselves Ford cars instead? I was indignantly shouted down. His lordship in the chair said I was out of order, to loud applause. That repudiated chicken came home to roost within six years in the form of the Neutrality Act which, with its 'cash and carry' clause, cost us hundreds of millions of pounds. As a result, on the outbreak of war, $2,500,000,000 of British-held American securities were forcibly taken over by the Bank of England to pay for munitions, etc. But in 1933 the 'Hate America' boom was as popular as the 'Love America' boom ten years later when America again came to our assistance in the Second World War. At dinners and cocktail parties, and at meetings where I spoke, I was regarded as mentally unbalanced on the subject of America and Germany.

Superficially the social scene was gay. I was in full creative flood, cosily housed and, as an author, currently very successful. Certainly I was fortunate in my friends. At one end of Eaton Square lived Harry Brodie, to whose savoir-faire I owed so much since coming to London. The Brodie home was ever open to me. Equally near to me were Sir Philip and Lady Gibbs. I never knew a man sweeter in character, with a greater Christian humility, and to the very end of his eighty-two years he had unconquerable optimism and faith in his fellow men. I, perhaps unduly pessimistic about the human race, had many collisions with him. He believed ardently in the League of Nations, he was compassionate in spirit. In essence, he was a Sir Galahad.

I was frequently at his table. It was there I first met Lord Robert Cecil, Field-Marshal Smuts, J. B. Priestley, Anthony Eden, Cicely Hamilton, H. G. Wells, Ramsay MacDonald and Wickham Steed. His interests embraced public affairs as well as literature. At the beginning of the year he had a strange bird at his table, the errant son of Stanley Baldwin. Oliver, in his perverse twenties, was a communist, wearing a red tie and a beard. He had the effrontery to stand for and win a seat as a Labour M.P. in the very heart of his father's domain. At dinner that evening he was opinionated to a point of rudeness. He exhibited no noteworthy intelligence. Later a Labour Government sent him off, as the second Lord Baldwin of Bewdley, to be the Governor of the Leeward Islands. At least he was remote from mischief. How different were Lord Robert Cecil, polite but firm, Jan Smuts, whose words had a legal balance, and J. B. Priestley, whose Yorkshire downrightness challenged specious nonsense.

Among my friends who entertained lavishly was the remarkable Mrs. Elrington Grierson. In her seventies, she had a passion for giving parties and lunches. Warm-hearted, ebullient, she lived in a large house in Prince's Gate. Bohemian, slightly eccentric in dress and spasmodic in domestic arrangements, she was assisted by a widowed daughter, Mrs. Haig, who kept a quiet watchful eye on things. For the parties forty would be invited and sixty would come, to Mrs. Grierson's delight. Some four years after I had known her the servant problem drove her out of the house in Prince's Gate, with its sixteen rooms, to a flat at 81 Piccadilly. It was on the first floor. The long drawing-room windows overlooked Piccadilly and Green Park. When I remarked on the noise of traffic to Mrs. Haig, she replied, "Oh, it doesn't worry mother. She loves to sit by the window and see all the red buses go by!"

One day in February, 1933, I arrived somewhat early for one of her large lunch parties and was shown into the drawing-room. It was empty but presently a little old gentleman, somewhat timid in manner, was shown in. "I'm early?" he asked. "I'm not good at judging distances in London." "You don't live here?" I said. He smiled quietly at me. "Alas, no, I wish I could, but I can't!" he replied. "Why can't you?" I asked. Again he smiled. "I can't because I've a house in Wiltshire." "Can't you sell it?" "No—it's full of heirlooms," he replied, sadly. Further questions were prevented by the arrival of other guests, and the fluttering entrance of my hostess. When we were seated at lunch I noticed that the old gentleman was in the seat of honour. "Tell me," I said to Mrs. Haig, "who's that old gentleman seated on the right of your mother?" "Oh, that's Lord Nelson of Trafalgar!" she replied. I looked and marvelled. What a name to throw when asked who you were. "I'm Lord Nelson of Trafalgar!" Instead, all I had heard in our brief conversation was "I wish I could, but I can't!" The house full of heirlooms was now explained. He was Thomas Horatio, fourth Earl Nelson, of Trafalgar House, in Wiltshire. He was in receipt of a State pension of £5,000 a year by virtue of the fact that he was the descendant of Lord Nelson's sister Susanna, Mrs. Bolton, whose son assumed the name of Nelson, as the second Earl, and to whom Trafalgar House and the pension in perpetuity had been given by a grateful country. Recently a Labour Government has cancelled the pension, and our Lord Nelson, a bachelor, who had no direct heir, would be the last to receive it.

It was always impossible to foretell what would happen in the Elrington Grierson home. There had been an occasion in the Prince's Gate mansion when the postman had delivered the wrong letters. Mrs. Grierson was wandering around in her nightgown and slippers, her hair in curlers. She snatched the letters out of the box, opened the door and pursued the postman down Prince's Gate, oblivious of astonished spectators. I was once a member of her party for the opera. We arrived, six of us, at Covent Garden, where our hostess discovered she had forgotten the tickets. There was a commotion. No one knew the numbers of the stalls. The curtain was about to go up. Mrs. Grierson went up to the manager. "Have you an empty box?" "No, madam, only the royal box," he answered. "Then put us in it until the chauffeur comes back with the tickets," she commanded, and she unhooked a string of pearls. "There's my security!" she said, thrusting it into the astonished man's hand. We were given a box. The chauffeur returned with the tickets and in between acts we moved into our stalls.

Mrs. Grierson owned a large house at Maidenhead with a lawn going down to the river. I was invited over one evening to dinner, at 7.30 p.m. At 8.30 still no dinner appeared. At 9 p.m. Mrs. Grierson, reminded by her daughter, became aware that dinner was late. She rang the bell, which an ancient butler, hired for the occasion, answered. "Where's dinner?" asked Mrs. Grierson. The old man's voice trembled. "There won't be no dinner, ma'am. Your cook's drunk on the floor, and my missus can't cope." We were all taken to Skindle's Hotel over the bridge. The previous year, on a hot August day, Pilgrim Cottage had been the scene of a comedy. I had asked Mrs. Grierson, her daughter and a house guest, gentle little Richard Pryce, the novelist and dramatist, to tea. They arrived bringing with them Tiny, Mrs. Grierson's rat-like chihuahua which she adored. It was one of the sacred breed of toy dogs of the Aztecs. Noble families are said to have kept upwards of a hundred, each with its attendant slave. Mrs. Grierson certainly was a slave to Tiny. We were happily having tea in the garden when Tiny appeared. He had a blood-red mouth, belly and legs. He looked as if he had just come up from Hell. Mrs. Grierson gave a shriek, picked him up and pressed him to her bosom, ruining her white summer dress. The dog had been in the house sniffing about. Tiny must have been on the hearthstone of the dining-room fireplace which had been coated earlier with a Venetian-red wash, still wet. Ethel took blood-red Tiny and washed him but could do nothing with Mrs. Elrington Grierson's dress. Like my tea party, it was ruined. For a month it was her favourite story, told with great verve.

II

It was in this year that I first dined with the glamorous Rosita Forbes at her house in Great Cumberland Place. We had met frequently on public platforms and in talks and debates at literary societies. She had made her name, still young, as an intrepid traveller. Her books had a wide sale. It always puzzled me how a person so delicate in form and feature could have endured the hardships of deserts and jungles. She always looked as if she had just come from

Elizabeth Arden's instead of Timbuctoo. She had a silent colonel-husband who adored her. The house in Cumberland Place was famous for its iron banister of leaping leopards, also for an enormous black bed in which she wrote. Her guests were usually drawn from the eminent or the gifted. There was never a dull moment. It was around this time that I attacked, in the Daily Express, a play by Somerset Maugham, For Services Rendered. It was a good play but its theme was vicious, in tune with the defeatism of the period. It presented a soldier in retirement, a V.C. of proven courage but wholly despicable in character. My article made a sensation. The Express asked me to review, with candour, half a dozen plays. At the conclusion the editor offered me the post of dramatic critic at £1,000 p.a. I declined the offer, as did Michael Arlen, in turn. It would have been interesting and enjoyable but I had no desire to be tied to 'first nights' and the Fleet Street rush.

It was a period of offers. In the same week a Commander Rich, a retired naval officer, having found a wealthy backer, decided to go into publishing. He had had plenty of experience with the firm of Hutchinson. He invited me to a cocktail party in Upper Brook Street, which I remember vividly because along came Compton MacKenzie just from the Law Courts where the Government was prosecuting him under the Defence of the Realm Act for disclosing, it alleged, secrets obtained in his role of an official correspondent. It was a disgraceful and vicious proceeding. He looked very tired after a gruelling day in court. Commander Rich asked me to lunch with him at the Savoy Grill. When a publisher invites an author to lunch at the Savoy there is usually something he wants. I was not wrong in this anticipation. He wanted me to write a life of Admiral Lord Beatty, for which he had got authorisation. Again I declined. The Fripp life had been a great labour. I did not want any Tyrwhitt episodes, nor had I any professional qualification for the task. I had got out of the medical noose very well. I would not risk a naval one. Moreover, I was saving myself for the next jump. I was the favourite filly in the Hodder stable and Percy Hodder-Williams, its dynamic director, was eager to lead me out to the starting post with Pilgrim Cottage, now half-written.

At the end of January I went to Edinburgh, Dundee and Aberdeen to lecture for the English Association. That experience had two comic highpoints. In Edinburgh I stayed in a leading hotel and learned with amazement that the bedrooms had only electric fires, 'shilling-in-the-slot'. I was given a vast, icy room with a gothic fireplace. Before I went out I put money in the slot and turned on the fire so that when I returned after my lecture the room would be warm. But four hours later it was still icy. I therefore decided to move the fire to the bedside, undress in front of it and jump into bed. I discovered that the fire, now with one salmon pink bar showing, was chained to the fireplace. I had brought with me a heavy sable fur coat with a deep astrakhan collar, bought from an impoverished Grand Duke who committed suicide after giving a party with the money. Putting the fur coat over my pyjamas I got into bed. In the morning I rang for the maid to prepare my bath. On entering and seeing in the bed a man buried in an astrakhan collar, she almost had hysterics. Possibly she thought the Russians had invaded Edinburgh. There had been a legend, during the First World War, that the Russians from the Arctic had passed through Edinburgh on their way to the Western Front. And here was a wild Russian in bed in his sables. She recovered and turned on my bath, not with a tap but with a crankshaft. There was a roar of boiling water filling the very large marble, mahogany-surrounded, bath, but when I sat down in it my posterior was chilled by the still icy marble.

Hearing that Aberdeen was the Granite City, I took no risk. I wrote to my host, Professor Jack, asking if I might have a fire in my bedroom. He nobly responded. When I went to my room there was a colossal fire blazing half-way up the chimney. The room was so hot that I had to open the window. Even when the fire died I could not sleep for the heat and discarded one blanket after another. When I went down to breakfast, feeling boiled, the professor asked if I had been warm enough. I assured him I had. I saw a glint in his eye when he said, "You should have been. One of the hot pipes of the University runs through the room!"

On my return from Scotland warm-hearted Mrs. Grierson had a dinner party and afterwards we went to see a verse drama, *Richard of Bordeaux*. The youthful lead was John Gielgud. A friend took me to his dressing-room. I seldom like actors in their dressing-rooms. They are often *en pose*. Nothing could have exceeded Gielgud's natural and simple manner, something he has retained down the years. The next day, on the invitation of Sir Edward Iliffe, I addressed the London Chamber of Commerce and was heard with some incredulity. We were so safe in the skilful hands of Messrs. Mac-Donald and Baldwin. For this was, as Churchill observed, "one of those awful periods which occur in our history, when the noble British nation seems to fall from its high estate, frothing pious platitudes while foemen forge their arms."

At the end of February I finished *Pilgrim Cottage*, seven months' incessant work. In the middle of April Louis Tissier arrived, his military service ended. He was free, and exuberantly healthy. He did not know that I was making plans for his future. He arrived just in time to join my Easter house party. One member of it was a stranger to us all. He soon demonstrated a capacity for annoying everybody. I was soon aware that, acting on an impulse, I had got a strange fish in my net. Just before Good Friday, I was at a sherry party at Queen's College, Oxford. Among the company were some undergraduates and I found myself talking to a youth who informed me he had just published a novel called *Little Victims*. His name was Rumbold. "It's created a stink and I've been 'sent to Coventry'. They can't bear to have a genius in their midst. Look what they did to Shelley!" he exclaimed. I asked what they had done to him. They had debagged him and thrown him in the fountain at 'The House' (Christ Church), Father Knox had banned him from the Mass. He was a Roman Catholic. I saw he was under a strain, probably neurotic, but there was something attractive about him. He had a vibrant personality. When I asked two other youths about him, one said, "He's crazy! Keep away from him." I began to feel sorry for the branded youth. After leaving Queen's College I did some shopping and in the Broad met young Rumbold. I enquired if he would be in Oxford over Easter. "Yes—I've nowhere to go and no one wants me." I asked whether he would like to lunch at my cottage on Good Friday. He eagerly accepted and then, on impulse, I asked him if he would care to spend the Easter weekend with my small house party. "How very kind. I should love it. Do you mean it?" he exclaimed. I invited him to come on Thursday evening until Tuesday.

He arrived at six o'clock and his first request was extraordinary. "Can I have a hot bath? I don't want to smell of that filthy Oxford!" When he came downstairs he presented me with a copy of his novel,

Little Victims, for which I thanked him. There were six of us at dinner. Before retiring he had upset everybody. He had a habit of saying "Do you think so?" and then proceeded to contradict one. "Where did you find that young pup?" asked my friend Duncan MacPherson. I explained that he had had a bad time at Christ Church and I felt sorry for him. "I don't wonder he's not popular!" said Duncan. "What conceit!"

On Good Friday morning while I was cutting flowers Louis came across the lawn to me. He had a book in his hand. He was very agitated and his eyes blazed. He opened *Little Victims*, with the author's inscription, 'To Cecil Roberts, showing him how to write a novel. Richard Rumbold.' I laughed. "He insults you! He is monstrous! He must go!" exclaimed Louis, vehemently, all his loyalty affronted. "I think you should make yourself nice to him, Louis," I said. "He's having a difficult time. He's by no means a fool." Louis snorted. "Very well, since you say, I'll make charm for him!" he declared, going off. That evening I took my house party to dinner at Sir Edward Iliffe's at Yattendon. I was somewhat apprehensive about Rumbold, but he behaved beautifully. Assisted by his good looks and boyish eagerness he was quite a success. On Saturday morning he came down to breakfast in bright yellow silk pyjamas and a Chinese gold-dragon dressing-gown. He was still in his pyjamas when two of my lady friends called. They were enchanted with him. "What a lamb!" said one of them on departing. Lamb was not the word I would have chosen.

Over the weekend the weather was gloriously hot. On Sunday morning, with newspapers, we went up on to the sunbathing platform. Suddenly there was an explosion. Richard shook one of the newspapers violently. "There goes my filthy father stealing my publicity!" he cried. Startled, we asked what he meant. It seemed that his father, reading an adverse review of *Little Victims*, had written a letter disclaiming any responsibility for the book. It was certainly an odd letter for a father to write. By now we were becoming more amused than annoyed. Little by little I learned something of his history. He had had a rich, eccentric and kind grandfather whose odd behaviour had made him one of the bizarre figures of Victorian Brighton. A son of this eccentric, who had bought kneeling mats for charwomen and safety spectacles for road-menders, was Richard

94

Rumbold's father. He became an army captain although he had wished to join the Navy. Handsome, domineering and rich, he bought a boat and spent his days navigating the waterways of France. His wife, mother of Richard and his sister Rosemary, went out of her mind and committed suicide, throwing herself in the Seine. The children were sent off to relatives. With such a background, and perhaps an hereditary taint—his sister committed suicide later—the surroundings of young Richard had not been normal. His mother was a Roman Catholic and although the Rumbolds were an Anglican family Richard had been brought up in her faith. He was sent to a Catholic preparatory school. What he wrote about the school in *Little Victims* created such an uproar that Father Knox refused him Communion, something he never got over. It created a life-long hostility to Rome. "I have been trying to recover my religious faith in the hope of getting some help from it. But it is extremely uphill work, bringing also numerous conflicts, particularly in relation to one's sensuous life," he wrote to a friend.

On Tuesday my guests departed, except Richard who asked if he might stay over until the next day. An odd thing had happened, he had become almost popular. We had treated him like a spoilt child and had refused to challenge his preposterous statements. He had made a complete conquest of my housekeeper, going into the kitchen and having long talks with her. I was astonished to find him there on Monday afternoon wiping the dishes. Even Louis thawed. "I think him nice boy but peacock." "Peacock?" I queried. "Yes, he likes to show his feathers and scream."

The day after Rumbold left he wrote me a letter of thanks. "You are wonderfully kind. Louis is a pet and Ethel a darling. I hope I wasn't too awful." Two weeks later I dined with him in his rooms at Christ Church. Then, in town, I lunched with him as he wanted me to meet his cousin, William Plomer, the poet. And then in the way of things he went out of my life. One day in 1945 I read in the *Spectator* an excellent article by him on night-bombing over Germany. I wrote to congratulate him, happy to learn he had survived the massacre of youth. Then in July, 1946, after my return from America, he rang up asking if he could visit me. Two days later he came with his devoted companion of many adventures, Hilda Young. He had not greatly changed. Tall, good-looking, eager, he was about to leave on a North

95

African safari. He would see me when he returned. They left after a happy visit. I was never to see him again.

Later, I learned some details of what had happened to him in the past thirteen years. On the outbreak of war he joined the R.A.F. in which he became a sergeant-pilot. He was engaged in bombing operations over Germany. Later he applied to join Fighter Command and trained in North Wales. Again the mad streak in him showed up. One day he flew his plane under the Menai Straits Bridge. He was court-martialled, grounded for three months, deprived of his rank, and sent to another station to do manual labour. He had had one tubercular attack, and now had another and was discharged from the R.A.F. as physically unfit, and went into a sanatorium for a time. He published an autobiographical book, *My Father's Son*. It frankly told the story of his father's behaviour towards his mother, driving her to suicide, and of his own stormy relationship. It is a remarkable book, but painful, and he was strongly criticised for publishing it. It was his second and last book. He had also collaborated with Lady Margaret Stewart, second daughter of the seventh Marquess of Londonderry, in a biography of Antoine de St. Exupéry, the French airman and pilot. Lady Margaret was an extraordinary woman, a war correspondent during the Second World War and an ardent air pilot. She had travelled all over the world. Richard had made motor-caravan safaris with her. But his master passion was writing. Here he suffered frustration. In his diary he confessed, "I am now more than ever convinced there is no great book in me." He wandered about the world. There were relapses that had taken him to the psychiatrist's couch, to a mental home, to a sanatorium for consumptives. A religious quest never ceased. He went to North Africa, Ceylon, Japan, spiritually restless. After Humanism and Buddhism he found Zen and entered a monastery at Kyoto. He was now forty-three. He stayed there two months and then began his wanderings again with his devoted companion, Mrs. Hilda Young. In 1961 they arrived in Palermo, Sicily, staying at the Hotel des Palmes. During March he was working on a book, trying to write the elusive masterpiece. Mrs. Young, who acted as his amanuensis, was typing for him when, suddenly, he walked into an adjacent room. He did not return. A few minutes later she learned that his body had been found on the street below.

Pilgrim Cottage—study

Louis Tissier

Henley Regatta.
The author, Sir
John Lavery,
Paul Morand,
Lady Lavery,
Baroness
d'Erlanger

It was singular how our paths had crossed. In February, 1961, I was in Palermo. This time, unhappily, I did not go to the Hotel des Palmes as formerly. I did not know Richard was in Palermo. I did not hear of his death until six weeks later when I met his friend, Archibald Colquhoun, in Rome. He had just won some fame as the translator of *The Leopard,* a novel by a Sicilian prince, discovered posthumously, that made a sensation. Colquhoun was with Richard at the time of his death and to him fell the task of dealing with the Italian authorities. Aware of the endless formalities that would be encountered in exporting the body of a foreigner, he discovered a British merchant ship in harbour, sailing for England. He arranged with the captain to smuggle the body on board. So Rumbold, aged forty-eight, was taken back to England and buried in the family grave, fulfilling the wish expressed in his will.

Twelve months later, in the course of a world cruise, I was in Japan and visited Kyoto. A young American was eking out a living as a guide for a travel agency. He told me he had spent three years in a Zen monastery there. He described some of its strange inhabitants. There was an Englishman, a clever, very odd fellow, consumptive, named Rumbold who—"Richard Rumbold?" I asked, interrupting him. "Yea, that's the name, a bit crazy, like all of us, but a nice guy. I was sorry when he left. Wonder what happened to him—you know him?" I told him that he had died in Palermo.

Rumbold had kept a diary, 1932–60. Three years after his death his second cousin, William Plomer, wrote an introduction to a selection of the entries which he had edited.* It is a strange, moving diary of a complex, tortured spirit. Plomer's introduction is in the nature of an epitaph that gives a just esimate of the ill-starred youth who came to my cottage at Easter 1933. He wrote:

> I myself knew Richard for nearly a quarter of a century. I found him in face of his recurrent troubles, a courageous and exceptionally honest man, warmly affectionate and unembittered. Not one line in the papers he left and nothing I have heard about him, whether in his lifetime or after his death, has made

A Message in Code: The Diary of Richard Rumbold (Weidenfeld and Nicolson, 1964).

me think otherwise. His courage and honesty light up the evidence of his lifelong battle to overcome his troubles and fulfil himself as a person and as a writer.

At the beginning of May I left for Paris to stay with my friend Fuller. He had moved from his apartment overlooking the Seine, but my regret for this change vanished on seeing his new abode, a fine villa in the Avenue Théophile Gautier which had been a former Polish Minister's home. There was a purpose in my visit. I had to arrange the future of my secretary, Louis Tissier. Returned from the army, he would have been well content to stay with me in Pilgrim Cottage. Much as I would have liked this I felt that it would be selfish to retain him. I could not offer him any kind of career. My friend in Paris, an important official with the Anglo-Persian Oil Company, offered him a post in the business. It was a weight off my mind but it was going to be a wrench for both of us. I passed a delightful, gay fortnight in Paris. The la Rochefoucaulds were as hospitable as ever and I had to resist strongly the invitation to stay with them. I felt closer than ever in spirit with Armand's beautiful mother, the Duchess de Doudeauville. I was in and out of their home in the Rue de Varenne and we made delightful excursions. Paris is never so intoxicating as in the spring, when the young leaves are out in the Bois and the flower beds of the Louvre are in virginal bloom. For good measure it happened that Somerset Maugham was there. Despite his Dantean grimness he was always a good host. My visit was also enlivened by the flamboyant Evan Morgan, installed at the Hotel Lancaster. One night, under a full moon, he took the Comtesse Villeneuve, Lady Louis Mountbatten and myself driving through the Bois de Boulogne in a twin-horsed landau after dining at the Pré Catalan. I thought of a line from Alfred de Musset's *La Nuit de Mai*—

> *La fleur de l'églantier sent ses bourgeons éclore,*
> *Le printemps nait ce soir; les vents vont s'embrasser.*

I had to be home at the end of May to debate with Lord David Cecil, who had recently won recognition with his first biography, *The Stricken Deer*, at the Writers Club, on the theme 'That modern writing lacks imagination', one of those foolish subjects that desperate secretaries evolve.

III

Shortly after my return I had a visitor even more extraordinary than Richard Rumbold. One day in my club I was introduced to Captain Fritz von Rintelen, a German ex-naval officer. Later, I invited him down to my cottage. He was the author of *The Dark Invader*. His extraordinary book had an enormous success. It was the story of Rintelen's adventures as Germany's leading spy in U.S.A. during the First World War. A godson of the Kaiser, a member of a well-known Baltic landed family, he had been for two years a lieutenant in the Imperial Navy. He then took up a banking career in New York. He had a wonderful command of English. He was popular and moved in the best social circles. On the outbreak of the war he was recalled to the German Navy and served in a cruiser, achieving the rank of captain. Later, he was selected for a special mission in the U.S.A. England and France were buying munitions there which were shipped to Europe. The Germans sank all the munition-carrying ships they could, at considerable cost to themselves in lost submarines. Someone had a bright idea. This was the cigar-bomb. It was a small tube containing sulphuric acid at one end with picric acid at the other. The latter ate through a partition and produced an explosion. It was inexpensive and deadly. The plan was to place these 'cigars' in munition factories and in the ships carrying munitions. The cigars in the ships would explode when two or three days out at sea. Working under Franz von Papen, Naval Attaché at the German Embassy in Washington, Rintelen posed as a Swiss business man. He was extraordinarily successful. It was a sinister business, murder on the high seas, and murder on land, for he planted his cigar bombs in the munitions workshops of the U.S.A., a neutral country. Captain von Rintelen had no doubt that he was patriotically serving his country. After all, those munitions, if they reached their destination, were for the purpose of killing German soldiers, brave men who happened to be enemies. If he blew up factories, trains and ships, killing civilians as well as sailors, he was only ahead of his time. The bombing of open towns with the massacre of their populations would come later. Hiroshima was only a few decades away. So Captain von Rintelen had no compunction about his mission.

It was Admiral Reginald Hall of Naval Intelligence in Whitehall who tracked down von Rintelen. He succeeded in solving the German cipher code and soon was reading Berlin's instructions to their agent. If he denounced him Rintelen might get away before the American Government, neutral, took action, and proof might be difficult. So the Admiral set an ingenious trap. He sent a message in the German code, purporting to come from Berlin, instructing von Rintelen to return, for consultation. He was to travel home in a Dutch ship, the *Noordam*, using a Swiss 'business name', E. V. Gaché. The ship arrived at the Downs and underwent the inspection imposed on all ships bound for neutral European ports. A naval inspection officer picked off 'Herr Gaché' who protested in vain that he was a Swiss commercial traveller in leather goods, returning home with a large order book. Under prolonged questioning he saw the game was up and Captain von Rintelen joined other German officer prisoners at Castle Donington Hall. Here he might have stayed safely but when America came into the war she asked for von Rintelen, to stand trial for spying and murderous sabotage. He was tried and, lucky to escape the electric chair, was sentenced to fifteen years' imprisonment with hard labour.

It would seem that Admiral Hall's conscience was not easy. He had trapped the fellow but he had handed his prisoner over to the Americans. His later relations with von Rintelen were as singular as they were magnanimous. When the war ended Rintelen's sentence was commuted. He returned to Germany. He tried to replan his life, but he was not happy in the new Hitlerian Germany and after some years he came to England and got into contact with Admiral Hall.

> My dear Rintelen, (wrote Sir Reginald)
> I wish to tell you today that I have the greatest sympathy for you. I know that you have suffered more than a man should be called on to suffer, and I am full of admiration for the manner in which you have retained your balance of mind and your courage. That the fortune of war made it my job to bring so many disasters on you is my sorrow, and if by anything I can do I can in some manner assist you to get peace and happiness, I shall feel happy myself.

He followed up his promise. Thus it was that one day von Rintelen arrived with a manuscript in the newly opened office of an enterprising young Canadian, Lovat Dickson, who had courageously set himself up as a publisher. Admiral Hall had sent him, and offered to write a preface to the book. Dickson at once saw he had a winner. He re-christened the book, the story of von Rintelen's American mission, *The Dark Invader*. It had a great success. It went through edition after edition and for a time its author was greatly in demand as a lecturer, an engaging ex-spy with a somewhat sinister aura. Admiral Hall showed him much kindness.

When von Rintelen first visited me at Pilgrim Cottage in May, 1933, in the first flush of success, I found him an intensely interesting person. When he was last my guest, in 1938, his vogue had waned somewhat and I imagined he was finding life a little difficult. He lived in a working man's hostel near Euston Station. Then came the Second World War and I saw and heard no more of him. I was away in the United States, with the British Mission, throughout the war and he was out of mind. It was not until Lovat Dickson sent me his autobiography *The House of Words*, in 1963, that I had news of Rintelen. His end was pathetic and I felt, as his publisher felt, that it was something of a reproach that we had not enquired about him after he had been engulfed, a downright anti-Nazi, in the second war. I join with my friend Dickson in his *mea culpa*.

Captain von Rintelen was found dead on South Kensington Underground railway station at 7 a.m. on a winter's morning in 1946. Clutched in his hand was a workman's ticket. He was on his way to his daily work as a jobbing gardener when a fatal attack of coronary thrombosis seized him; and there in the early morning light, on a District Railway platform, the captain, who had been the Kaiser's godson—and my first successful author—parted with his life. The evidence of my failure of character was that I did not know until after he died that Rintelen was in London, much less that he had fallen on hard times and was working as a labourer. I had left him behind in my upward flight, with never a thought as to what became of him, though he had helped me to launch myself as a publisher. This was ingratitude. I had not thought of him for years until I read the sad details of his death in a London evening paper.

The day following von Rintelen's first visit Louis and I were in Oxford. We lunched with Seddon Cripps at high table in Queen's College. Louis' comment on the dons was unforgettable—"What a lot of wisdom wrapped up in old parchment!"

On the first of June I presented Louis with an advance copy of *Pilgrim Cottage*. It carried a dedication, '*À mon cher ami, Louis Tissier, souvenir de Pilgrim Cottage*'. When he turned the page and read it there were tears in his eyes. He pressed the book to him and said softly, "*Il vivera toujours dans mon coeur!*" A week later he left for his new post in Paris. We had had a week of wonderful June weather. On his last day I let him go alone round the garden after he had returned from saying goodbye at Woolworth's. He tried to be gay but I knew he was heavy-hearted. It could never be the same again for this place had been his home.

One day there was a commotion at Pilgrim Cottage. Out of a van descended six men, with cameras and measuring tapes. My dynamic publisher, Percy Hodder-Williams, had had an idea. When *Pilgrim Cottage* was published he would have a large scale model in a window of Harrod's Store in the Brompton Road. The men were busy all the morning, taking photos from every angle. They even went up on to the sunbathing platform from which there was a view of the wavy, old tiled roof. "What size is it going to be?" I asked, watching them measuring and drawing. "Twenty feet long, sir!" "Goodness gracious! Will it go in the window?" "Yes, sir, we've got the measurement of their furniture window."

They departed. They planted a seed in my mind that germinated. I took one of my French exercise books and wrote on the front page *Gone Rustic*. It would be an account of how I found the cottage and of the life I lived in it. The day *Pilgrim Cottage* was published I gave a talk at Harrod's, to coincide with the large model in their window. It was so large and real that I felt I could have walked into it and sat down at my desk. There it was, the door open, the porch, clematis-covered, roses growing round the dormer windows. Was I really in Knightsbridge or the Chilterns? There was a large crowd before the window. It never lessened and the police complained of obstruction, but the model was on show for a week. It was fun to join the crowd and hear the comments, flattering or adverse. "I wouldn't live in that place as a gift! You'd always be banging your head!" exclaimed a burly man to his wife. "I'll bet its damp—that's how the roof gets them twists—Elizabethan arthritis in the beams!" "I'll bet he sits in it with an umbrella up for the leaks!" It was hard to hear my nest so maligned. The head-banging criticism was correct. Those Tudor inhabitants must have been small. For a time I, six-foot tall, con-cussed myself on the low door lintels. After two months of repeated concussion I had all the lintels raised. But the remark about the roof leaking was libellous. It never once leaked. Since the cottage was built before nails were used every tile was held on the curving oak laths by wooden pegs. When I first went up into the roof to look my heart almost stopped. You could see daylight everywhere, but miraculously it never leaked though every lath had 'arthritis' which gave the roof 'a permanent wave' another Elizabeth (Arden) could have envied. Mostly the viewers at Harrod's were complimentary and envious. "I call that a dream! I wonder if it's a fake—it's sheer Hans Andersen," said one. "That's my idea of heaven, to live snug like that, a merry widow!" "Why, a widow?" "So your husband can't change his mind and want something new!" "They're taking it to America," said a man near me.—"A millionaire's bought it, and's going to rebuild it. This is the model." For a moment panic seized me at the thought. Then another voice said, "Oh, I'd love to live in it if only for a week." It was a middle-aged woman, neatly shabby, family-worn. "Yes, and just listen to things grow," said her com-panion, who gripped a faded parasol, in a housework-shiney hand. They moved away. 'Listen to things grow'—what a phrase! It was like seeing a bed of tulips open in the pavement. And I then realised how truly fortunate I was. In my early years life had not been easy for me, but in the battle I had won some slight security. By virtue of my pen I had gained a passport to interesting society, to travel, to devote my life to writing. Also, I had my own quiet corner of the earth in which to live.

Pilgrim Cottage was reprinted six times in twelve months. It was in the American best seller lists. *Gone Rustic*, which appeared the follow-ing April, was reprinted five times. It was success at a price. The books must have been read all over the world, judging from my mail. In a thoughtless moment I had given the name of my cottage to the novel. My retreat was invaded. There were lines of cars in the lane. Tourists jumped up to look over the hedge. They rattled the gate. Some were charming, some obstreperous. They felt that having borrowed my books at a library they were entitled to walk all over the cottage. Two women sneaked in and went upstairs. Louis heard footsteps overhead. He went up and caught them in my bedroom, turning down the sheets to see if they were linen! I returned one day to find a family of five, picnic basket open, lunching in my porch. They seemed surprised that I objected. But many were delightful. One day my garden gate opened and a woman stood there having got out of a car. She was holding what looked like a large dog. I then saw that she held a deformed woman, a hunchback, shrivelled. I insisted on carrying her round the garden and into the house. The poor little woman, about fifty, was well-read. When I put her in my big arm-chair, keeping them for tea, her feet did not touch the ground. Nine months later, while abroad, Ethel informed me that a large parcel had arrived. It was a most beautiful patchwork silk quilt, the work of my deformed visitor.

Then, in an odd manner, the Allinghams came into my life. One hot July afternoon I was sunning myself on my platform which over-looked the lane. I heard a car drive up, and a voice say, "Tony, don't. He won't like it. He's probably very disagreeable." I raised myself up and saw a small open car with a girl and a youth in it. The latter was standing up in the car with a camera. They were startled by seeing a half-naked man appear over the parapet above and a voice—"I assure you I am not at all disagreeable, and if you'd like to come in and take photos, do!" I went down to meet them. They were a breath-taking pair, she, delicate and lovely as a rose, all sunshine, he, obviously her brother, a handsome lad with a mane of golden hair. I see them now, vivid, intoxicated with life, no shadow of their dark destiny upon them. They were Ann and Anthony Allingham, twenty-one and fifteen, grandchildren of William Allingham, the Victorian poet of 'The Fairies'.

> Four ducks on a pond,
> A grass-bank beyond,
> A blue sky of Spring,
> White clouds on the wing:
> What a little thing
> To remember for years—
> To remember with tears.

When C. K. Scott-Moncrieff made his inspired translation of Proust's *À l'ombre des jeunes filles en fleurs* he took for its title the first line of one of Allingham's lyrics, 'Within a budding grove'. Allingham married, at fifty, the artist Helen Patterson. It was their grandson,

Anthony who, knowing my passion for Venice, brought me one day a painting by her of the Gesuati Church, which was only a few yards from my lodging on the Zattere.

The Allinghams lived at Pinkneys Green, Berks, father, mother, Tony, Pat and Ann. Soon I was part of the family. The father, an engineer, was tall and energetic, the mother, lovely, had a gossamer frailty. They lived in sunshine, infectiously happy. I often teased Tony with his theme—'Mummy, Dad, Ann and Pat'. "And how's Mummy, Dad, Ann and Pat ?" I would ask. In a sense they were my show-piece. Here was an English family at its best, in a beautiful home facing the Green.

That June there was a naval occasion. I was invited to address the Portsmouth Brotherhood, a gathering of a thousand ratings in a vast chapel under a blanket of tobacco smoke. The Brotherhood had been conceived by the Commander-in-Chief, Portsmouth, Sir Arthur Waistell, to provide Sunday afternoon entertainment for the men of the Navy. On arrival at Portsmouth I was taken first to view Nelson's flagship *Victory*. It was undergoing repairs and the officer gave me a small piece of oak from one of the old timbers. It had been at Trafalgar, I had not. Sometimes, in summer, it kept open the door of my cottage. A lovely young visitor held it in her hand for a moment and then kissed it. "I can't see why that piece of old oak should be luckier than I am," I complained. She took the hint and kissed me. "That's what they call 'the Nelson touch'," I said, gratefully.

From the *Victory* we went to the *Iron Duke* for drinks. I could hardly believe it when I heard that this was the same *Iron Duke* in which at Scapa Flow I had talked with Admiral Jellicoe a few days before the Battle of Jutland in 1916. We could not know, this bright Sunday morning, that a few years hence, in October, 1939, the German Luftwaffe would straddle the *Iron Duke* with bombs in a daring raid on Scapa Flow, and that she would have to be beached to prevent her sinking. Now all was bright and happy on board. Commander Figgins apologised for receiving me in 'plus fours', he was just leaving for a game of golf. He was a brisk, handsome fellow, the first man to have reached the rank of commander from the lower deck, and destined to become an admiral.

In the packed auditorium my chairman was the Commander-in-Chief. My subject was 'These United States' and I took the audience with me on a lecture tour. I stayed that night at the George Hotel, later bombed out of existence. It was the hotel where Nelson had slept. There was a plaque on his bedroom door. Passing it, I noticed an elegant pair of lady's shoes outside. I could not resist leaving my visiting card in one of them, with 'Lady Hamilton, I presume', written on it. Years later at a dinner party I sat beside a lady who said she had found my card in her shoe at the George Hotel. She was Lady Brooke, the Ranee of Sarawak.

IV

I was in Venice again that August and had my old quarters in the little house on the Zattere where Ezra Pound had once been my neighbour. One day on a side canal my attention was arrested by two children, a girl and a boy, rowing a boat, fore and aft, with the motion of professional gondoliers. They looked about twelve years of age, the girl dressed in a kilt, the boy in shorts. Blonde, bronzed, they were a beautiful pair with sheer poetry in their movements. They managed their boat with the greatest dexterity along the crowded canal, and then at a corner they disappeared. Two days later I saw them again. This time the tawny boy was on the poop, rowing, while the girl sat with a Sealyham dog in her lap. I knew the dog belonged to the British Consul. Lunching at the Consulate the next Sunday I asked who were the children who took out his dog, and what nationality. They were Scotch, Bevis and Lucien Reid. Their father was an artist and they lived in a small apartment off one of the Rios. "Those kids can match any gondolier and they swim like otters," said the Consul. "I don't know how the Reids scrape a living here, but nothing daunts them. The children are beautifully brought up."

Of course Grace Nobili knew them. "I'll ask them to tea and you shall meet them." And so one day on the Fondamenta Bonlini, in their garden with its tinkling fountain and the campanile of San Trovaso cutting the blue sky, I met the Reid family, to the enrichment of my life.

I had now two faithful courtiers. They rowed me here, they rowed me there. Their knowledge of Venice was intimate. We spent hours on the lagoon, we bathed on lonely stretches of the Lido. They seemed to know everybody. Thus it was I came to know Princess Aspasia of Greece, widow of King Alexander. Her small daughter, Alexandra, was their friend and they played in the great walled garden looking south down the lagoon. Its name 'Giardino Eden' fitted the scene, for it was a paradise that had been created, with a summer villa, by a Mr. and Mrs. Eden, who had occupied the Palazzo Barbarigo on the Grand Canal. The Garden of Eden was really an island tethered to the Giudecca by an arched *ponte*. On one side of the garden rose a vista of the great dome of the Church of the Redentore with its twin bell towers.

At this time there was also another small boy who joined their games in the garden, young Derek Mond, whose father and mother, Lord and Lady Melchett, sometimes occupied the guest house. The children swam and rowed over the lagoon that lay around the great garden with its fountain and pergolas. A blood-red sunset burnished the water at eventide adding a crimson glow to the long brick retaining wall. How little we knew what would befall! Within a decade both Lucien and Derek would be soldiers in the Second World War. Alexandra would marry Peter, the ex-King of Jugoslavia, and Bevis would be a lieutenant in the A.T.S., with the British Army in North Africa.

A visit down the long lagoon one day gave me a new novel. The Nobilis had a friend, the Countess Bevilacqua-Meehan, who owned an old island-fortress just off the Lido at Alberoni. Solid, built to defend Venice against the Genoese, it was octagonal in shape, from which its name Ottagono was devised. The Countess had married an American, Charles Meehan, an employee in the American Consulate in Venice. They were poor but happy, with a family growing up, and to ease their situation, the Countess turned the fortress on the lagoon into a pension. There, on a hot August day, we visited them. The sailing boat that had collected us at Alberoni, on the Lido, had carried us in twenty minutes across to the fortress. We landed on a tiny jetty and went through a massive opening into the octagonal fortress. Its walls were about twelve feet thick. A number of rooms looked on the lagoon, low, arched, cool. Some had been powder stores, etc. When we went through the thick walls we came to a large gardèn with a well, but no view. This was an internal world, sunk in the concave centre of the fort. All around was the circular parapet. It provided a promenade of endless vistas over the long lagoon, the Lido and the Adriatic Sea. The old fortress was a paradise of light and silence. It was teatime when we arrived. There was a white-haired old lady presiding over the teapot. I thought at first she was the Countess's mother but she was a guest in this pension. I learned that she was an American, turned eighty, from Princeton, New Jersey, a spinster named Miss Marie Waite Fox. When I asked her how long she had been travelling, she said about two years. She had fallen ill in Venice and hearing of this retreat had come to it and had recovered. "It's heaven, no noise, no telephone, no relatives bothering you—absolute peace. And I'm wonderfully looked after." She told me of the alarm of her relations, with whom she lived, when she announced she was sailing for Europe. Alone, turned eighty, it was her first Atlantic crossing. The family protested but in vain. "And here I am—do you like your tea weak or strong, Mr. Roberts?"

There were other guests but Miss Fox was a person apart. We walked round the ramparts. The sun began to fall and burnish the lagoon. "Sometimes I think I am living in the heart of an opal," she said. She showed me her room, a former powder store. She had a portable typewriter.

We sailed from Ottagono on a crimson flood. "Isn't it unique?" asked Grace Nobili, "I knew you would like it." She could not know then how much I liked it. I had got my next novel—an old lady, living with her married son, hears on the extension telephone her grand-daughter Sylvia talking to her beau. "Sure we'll travel when she pops off—I can do what I like with my share of it. The dear old thing must throw in her hand soon!" There was a male laugh at the other end of the telephone. Mrs. Ethel B. Silving, as I call her in my novel, books a passage to England to start the Grand Tour. When she announces this the family is up in arms at the idea. But she goes. In time she arrives in Venice, and there she discovers Ottagono, the fortress-retreat. Her life there, the lives of the guests who came there, old Mrs. Silving with a typewriter, it all began to take shape in my mind as we sailed home up the lagoon. When the steamer arrived back in Venice and I parted from the Nobilis, they asked me if I had enjoyed myself. I replied, "You've given me my next novel. I shall call it *The Guests Arrive* and I shall dedicate it to you!"

There was a singular sequel to this excursion. Six years later I received a letter, written in pencil, in large letters, from Miss Marie Waite Fox in New Jersey, U.S.A.

A review of your new book *They Wanted to Live*, revived an impulse to write to you. I am looking forward to the pleasure of reading it or rather of having it read to me, for my eyesight is nearly gone, I should not be writing this letter but I've a trick of doing as I please, even at the age of eighty-seven. Do you remember Ottagono, that picturesque, once fortified little island near Venice where, in 1933, you drank innumerable cups of tea poured out by a little American old lady? My good friend the Countess Bevilacqua-Meehan, with whom I spent two summers there, told me that I had been given the honour of being the original of one of the characters in your books. It was with great interest that I read *The Guests Arrive* and *Victoria Four-Thirty*. I make my bow to Mrs. Silving. She is far my superior. I feel a kinship to the lady and send you my gratitude. Your people are so real and alive.

I acknowledged the letter and thanked her for having given me a plot. And then I forgot about her. But the sequel had a sequel. In the very hot June of 1942, I gave a talk on a New York radio. When I finished I was called to the telephone. It was the grandniece of Miss Fox. The old lady had heard me and sent her love. So again I wrote to her. Her reply this time was in even larger pencil letters.

Yes, I am ninety. I should have gone long ago but there seemed always to be some little odds and ends for me to finish. Mine has been a busy and full life—work, play, travel, friendship, love. I do not fear the future—'Underneath the Everlasting Arms'—Writing is too difficult. I am very blind. A slight stroke has crippled my right hand and my left is none too adequate. It takes both hands to guide my pencil. Radio is my solace— I can hear news, travel, criticism. Sorry, but TOO HOT. Marie Waite Fox.

After a week of peerless sunshine but too much scirocco I thought I would have some mountain air and went off to Zell-am-See in the Tyrol to join some friends. For six days it steadily rained. I am a sun-flower, not a hydrangea, and I wilted, so I hurried back to Venice to see a superb performance of *Romeo and Juliet*, with Italians in the cast. It was performed with enormous zest in the open air, the setting being the little arched bridge and Corte San Travaso near the Nobilis' house. One evening I hired three hungry young *'wander-vögels'* with guitars and good voices and put them in a gondola, with special instructions. It was a night with a full moon. As we dined, a party of ten, al fresco in my host's garden, voices were heard singing by the water gate. We listened, in amazement, except myself, in the plot. When my host opened the grill-gate there was the gondola with the *'wandervögels'* in white shirts and *lederhosen*, strumming their guitars and singing *Lieder* and folksongs. They were bidden in, were wined, and sang to us till past midnight.

When the time came to leave Venice, my exit was made in state. I arrived at the station with my two young gondoliers, Bevis and Lucien. They would be there waiting for me when I returned next year. I did not go straight home. Sending my baggage forward to Lucerne I got out of the train at Airolo where it plunges into the tunnels of the great San Gothard range. I had gone through them so often that I now decided to walk over the summit via Andermatt down to Flüelen on Lake Lucerne. I satisfied my curiosity about that barren, grim upland. But I had an unpleasant little adventure. I had sent my portmanteau forward by train to Lucerne. It was a long walk down from the St. Gothard towards the lake. I arrived in the evening at Altdorf where I decided to spend the night. One of the first things I noticed was an advertisement for a circus that was due to give a performance that very evening. I have always found circuses irresistible, and this being a foreign one had a special attraction. The performance began at 8 p.m. When I went to the circus I was still wearing my shorts. The circus was in the open air and sitting there I felt my exposed knees getting very cold. The show was excellent, and a 'local' turn, this being Altdorf, was a William Tell act. A small boy was put up against a dummy tree and his father shot an arrow, splitting the apple on his head. It was a terrifying act. Later I learned that the arrow was magnetised, flew to a plate and a trick apple was split by pulling a string. What some people have to do to earn a living! The next morning when I got out of bed the pain in my lately exposed knees was quite excruciating. Possibly I had got a chill on tired knee-muscles. Five days elapsed before I could walk normally. I took the train to Lucerne.

On arriving home the political situation was appalling. I grew more and more to despair of our political ineptitude. The lazy complacency of Ramsay MacDonald and Baldwin in face of the darkening scene in Germany and Italy filled me with apprehension. There was a widespread mood in the country of peace at any price. I watched Churchill's futile battle in the House of Commons. He opposed giving up our vital bases in Egypt, which might lose us the control of the Mediterranean and the Suez Canal. He opposed giving up India, which would result in internecine quarrels and the slaughter of millions. I did not feel that the elegant Anthony Eden had the requisite toughness. In reaction I began to admire the resolute mood of Oswald Mosley, who had left the uncertain ranks of the Coalition to form the echelons of a new patriotic party. I had had a long talk with him in my club and was impressed by his forceful personality. I was not alone in this. Harold Nicolson, also unhappy about the national drift, had joined Mosley's party. My friend Yeats-Brown, the author of the widely successful *Bengal Lancer*, now editing *Everyman*, was also in the Mosley camp and repeatedly urged me to join the British Fascists. I had no liking of fascists, aware of the arrogance of their *credo*, but my discontent with our rulers made me susceptible to alternatives. But I marked time, unhappy and undetermined.

V

One day in October I was invited to a small dinner party at the Cavalry Club in Piccadilly, arranged by Yeats-Brown, to enable a few friends to meet Oswald Mosley who would address them. I found myself in a mixed company, very few of whom I knew, but there were some well-known persons, among them the poet-critic J. C. Squire, editor of the influential *London Mercury*. Others were political candidates, barristers, business directors. They were mostly in the middle-forties united by one thing, their present discontent. Unhappily the 'star' of the dinner was missing, Mosley was ill. After dinner the chairman called on some of us to speak. I learned that not one of us was in the Mosley Party: it was a missionary meeting. Our contributions made, we then adjourned to a large room at the back of the club, to find an audience gathered. We were to be addressed by the secretary of the party. He was a thin, pale, intense man, extremely eloquent. I do not believe that Robespierre at the height of his power in the French Revolution ever addressed his followers with more venomous passion. I found him horrifying. He was loudly applauded. I did not know who the man was, his name conveyed nothing to me but the effect of his tirade was to kill any thought of belonging to a party that harboured such a man. I hurried out of the hall. Going down the steps into Piccadilly I was accosted by Squire, who complimented me on my speech. I asked him what he thought of the meeting. "I'd sooner take rat poison than join up with a fellow like that. I don't like Baldwin or Ramsay but damn it all, I'm an Englishman. Who the hell is that reptile anyhow?"

My next political meeting was very different. How dignified, sweetly reasonable, and endearingly young! I was invited to address the Eton College Political Society and answer questions afterwards. My theme was the present European outlook. I faced an audience of well-bred and very serious youths. As is often the case with the privileged young, I found an air of liberalism, almost Leftish, and altruistic in tone. These future prime ministers, ambassadors and governors were unanimous about one thing. Their god was Anthony Eden; as a corollary most of them were fervent believers in the League of Nations whose principles Eden was just then vigorously defending. I soon ran my head against the wall. I deeply shocked them when I proceeded to demolish the Geneva bastion. They listened very politely, but when question time followed they came at me like hornets. They were very intelligent, those boys, and I found myself hard pressed. To my crime of obtuseness I added sacrilege. I had not bowed down to the peerless Anthony.

I dined later with the Provost, Mr. (later Sir) Henry Marten. As we walked across to his room I remarked that I feared I had shocked my young audience. "You've certainly rattled them, and given them something to think about. They're a bit starry-eyed, which is admirable, I think. In what you said I'm much in agreement. Anyhow, it was an enjoyable occasion," he observed.

The evening after my Eton College talk I dined with Sir Philip Gibbs. He wholly approved of those boys. This was a dinner party in which he found himself in a minority. It consisted of Cosmo Hamilton, his half-brother, Yeats-Brown and Father Woodlock, S.J. of Farm Street. Poor Philip, passionately pro-League, had a hard time, attacked by his brother, Yeats-Brown and myself. Father Woodlock, very mild, sat on the sideline. The next day Germany walked out of the League, underlining all we had said. I read the news as I turned off the Strand into Robert Street, Adelphi, to lunch with two Anglican clergy, the Bishop of London and the Rev. C. B. Mortlock, seventy-five years and forty years old respectively. I had first met the latter at the Dean of Windsor's, a fellow guest in the Deanery at Windsor Castle. We formed a friendship and Mortlock was frequently my guest at Pilgrim Cottage. Now he was my host in his own flat at No. 1 Robert Street, just under the eyrie flat that James Barrie had occupied. Mortlock was an enigma to many. Though he wore a clerical collar his heart was in Fleet Street. He was knowledgeable in many spheres and wrote for various papers as a critic of the ballet, stage, art, archaeology and ecclesiastical history. Sometimes he wrote leaders for the *Daily Telegraph*. He was a kind of liaison officer of the world of affairs and of the Church. At this time he had no 'living', no set church duties. His connections were wide and often surprising. Soon after this lunch he became the Vicar of Epping. The size of the vicarage bewildered him, a bachelor. I contributed to its furnishing a round mahogany table which gave him the greatest pleasure. It would hold eight comfortably and the names of those who sat around it would prove a remarkable list of persons eminent in many spheres. One of these was Jacob Epstein, the sculptor, who lived in his parish. They became great friends. Epstein gave him his massive statue, '*Ecce Homo*', considered outrageous and rejected by the authorities who had commissioned it. It weighed nine tons and was ten feet high. Mortlock defended the work and tried to get it erected outside St. Paul's but, mercifully, failed. Eventually it found a home in Battersea Park, not without opposition. Epstein's 'Rima' frightened the birds in Hyde Park, they said. '*Ecce Homo*' certainly frightened some Christians.

After eleven years at Epping, Mortlock was given a living in the City. He was made the rector of St. Vedast's, in Foster Lane, near St. Paul's, a Wren church rebuilt at what many considered an outrageous expenditure for a church that had almost no congregation. Mortlock found himself housed in a commodious and stately new rectory, opening on to a paved court. It was all his heart could desire, particularly his London heart, for it was within a few steps of Fleet Street. In addition he had a charming country retreat provided by the Church. He was made a canon and treasurer of Chichester Cathedral, again near to a theatrical enterprise. Had he lived long enough no doubt he would have been closely associated with the productions in the new repertory theatre. I found him, on visiting Chichester, in one of a row of delightful little cottages, bordering the precincts, that housed various canons and clerics.

In 1960 he visited Nubia to inspect the antiquities of Abu Simbel, then threatened by the new dam. He went, aged seventy-two, as the archaeological correspondent of the *Daily Telegraph*. Nine months later he called on me in Rome. He had visited the old City of Jerusalem and inspected the excavations of the British School as a member of the suite of the Archbishop of Canterbury. He was present at the historic meeting between Pope John and the Archbishop. In 1963 he knew an hour of triumph at St. Vedast's when he held the annual service for the Royal Ballet Company, which Princess Margaret attended as President. His sense of humour failed him when I quipped that he should have appeared in a ballet called *The Clerical Hat*, with a corps of choirboys selling newspapers.

At the time that I lunched with him, on a sunny November day in 1933, the guest of honour was the Bishop of London, the Rt. Honourable the Rt. Reverend Dr. Winnington Ingram. He was a prominent figure in London's life and *persona grata* in royal circles. He was knighted, he was a Privy Councillor, a bachelor, an author of more than twenty books. He had worked in London for fifty years and lived in the stately Fulham Palace. He had a lovely life and he enjoyed and adorned it. A smile always hovered on the thin mouth of his ascetic face. He was now, at seventy-five, a beautiful old man, white-haired, tall, slim. He ably graced the State functions at St. Paul's. There was present another friend of mine, J. B. Firth, an assistant editor of the *Daily Telegraph*, who would be immensely proud one day that his son, a former Winchester master, would be the Master of the Temple.

The conversation might have been churchy. Actually, it was wholly worldly, of the ballet, the stage, Epstein's latest shocker, and the plan for the demolition and reconstruction of the Adelphi with its threat to my host's home.

In October I had a guest, my host in Budapest, Baron János

Wolfner. He was a passionate Anglo-Hungarian. He always took the same lodgings in Curzon Street, and the same valet returned. He stored three trunks of clothes at Harrod's, and every year he added to them in Savile Row. He lived lavishly, entertained regally, dressed flawlessly, wore a monocle, and might have played 'The wicked Baron'. I had helped him to fulfil his great ambition, to be a member of a good London club. I got him, through my infallible Harry Brodie, elected to the Reform Club. When he died, twenty-five years later, in exile in London, after terrible vicissitudes and torture in a Nazi prison, he left generous bequests to the club servants. He was a wonderful host in Hungary to the visiting English. He was thoughtful and kind. But he was now worried by events in Germany and Austria. He had Jewish blood. As a precaution he had stored money in a St. James's Street bank. I asked him why he did not make his home in England, and become naturalised. He screwed in his monocle and looked hard at me. "I am a Hungarian, and proud of my country. We must challenge the barbarians," he said.

At the beginning of December I finished *Gone Rustic*. I cleared the deck for the novel *The Guests Arrive*, with which I was still in a state of gestation.

Two days before Christmas Louis arrived at the cottage from Paris, like a homing bird. He brought with him a dozen of the French exercise books I liked to write in. "What are you going to put in them?" he asked. I replied, "I'm going to write about an old lady, an American, whom I met in a fortress on the lagoon at Venice. She escaped from her relatives, took a world tour and settled there with her typewriter."

That morning we walked up through the beechwoods to Fawley, to take Christmas presents to the old village blacksmith and his wife. Mrs. Harman insisted on our drinking some home-made wine. We joined her husband who was sitting in the sun with two neighbours, he eighty-four, John Rixon eighty-one, Charlie Sharp eighty-six, a merry octogenarian trio.

We walked home downhill all the way for lunch in the cottage, where four guests awaited us. It was a crisp morning, golden leaves still on the trees. Mrs. Harman's wine made us sing all the way. "I think, my dear Cecil, there is no life better than this," said Louis, "And I hope when we are eighty we too will sit in the sun at Christmas." I was turned forty and he was twenty-four but I didn't spoil the idea. Ethel met us on the garden path, beaming. "There's six arrived and you said four for lunch! But it doesn't matter," she said. Bless her, it never did matter. She loved people.

I made my annual summary for the year. I was still climbing, working harder than ever. But there had been a stern warning from my doctor. I was running down the batteries, he said. I fear I took little notice of him. One morning, on rising, the mirror gave me a shock. My lips had blown up like a Hottentot's. I rushed to Harley Street. Dear, robust Fergusson Hannay gave me a 'shot'. The lips went down like a punctured tyre. He laughed. "Now you will behave yourself!" he said. "The next time it will be a swollen head." "I've got one already," I retorted. "I don't wonder," said Hannay, "I see your publisher's advertising the fifth edition of *Pilgrim Cottage* in five months. Give yourself a rest." I made a promise, and broke it. In the last year I had written half a million words and given eighteen lectures.

VI

By the end of 1933 my cottage had welcomed a great number of my author friends, the famous, and the unknown, for I liked to help those who had not yet arrived but showed much promise. My guest book carried the signatures of Humbert Wolfe, Philip Gibbs, Louis Golding, Charles Morgan, Alec' Waugh, Phyllis Bentley, Robert Nichols, Mrs. Belloc Lowndes, Richard Rumbold, Gilbert Frankau, James Hilton, and many ardent young aspirants from near-by Oxford. There was a youth soon to prove the brightest in the nest. Handsome, nineteen, he won my heart by saying he had a beautiful mother who was a great admirer of my books. Might he take me to see her? So one day we went to his home in South Kensington. He had not exaggerated, she was beautiful indeed, with a rose-cream complexion, blonde hair and sunlit eyes. Little by little my new friend revealed his ambition. He wanted to be a playwright, but he came of a family of distinguished diplomats. So, with such excellent family credentials, he was to study for the Foreign Office entrance examination. His grandfather, Sir William, a great jurist and linguist, had built up Punjab University, established the Sikh College at Amritsar, and been an M.P. His father, in the diplomatic service, had been British High Commissioner at Constantinople, among various posts. It was, therefore, folly for this youngster, with this tradition behind him, to risk all for the hazardous calling of authorship. "Go into the Diplomatic Service. It will give you plenty of leisure in which to write. It's sheer folly for you to gamble with your future by scribbling," I said. He took no notice of my advice. When he got to Oxford he joined the O.U.D.S. He made brief appearances in *Hassan,* in *Romeo and Juliet* and then, in 1932, in *Faustus,* in which I saw him. He had for an acting colleague the young Angus Wilson, who played one of the Deadly Sins. While at Oxford my friend deliberately went wild. "I intend to be 'sent down' in order not to become a diplomat, and to write plays," he told me. He succeeded. He was 'sent down' by the Proctors for having females in licensed lodgings after hours. The females were Meriel Forbes (later Lady Richardson), Barbara Hoffe, and Douggie Byng, the famed entertainer, dressed in one of his roles as 'Minnie, a messy old mermaid'.

How soon I was going to eat my words of warning! In the first week of the New Year, 1934, he sent me tickets for a play to be produced at the Comedy Theatre, called *First Episode,* written in collaboration with an Oxford friend. It was well received but had little success. The second episode in his career as dramatist was two years later, when, sole author, he produced his play *French Without Tears.* Terence Rattigan had stepped overnight into fame. When I left the Criterion Theatre on that first night it had been made clear that he had an infallible sense of the theatre. *French Without Tears* was no flash in the pan. It ran and ran, and then came *While The Sun Shines.* Both played a thousand performances. His *Flare Path* ran eighteen months. *The Winslow Boy* ran for fifteen months, *Love in Idleness,* two years. On he went, success after success. How woefully wrong I had been! He was only twenty-four when he soared into fame with *French Without Tears.*

There is an echo of my doleful warning in its dialogue. One of the characters, the Hon. Alan Howard, son of an ambassador, studying at a French crammer's, has written a novel. He says he will quit his studies to write. His friend Kenneth protests. "You must be mad, Alan. I mean even if you want to write you could still do it in the Diplomatic. What would His Excellency say?" "His Excellency,"

replied Alan, "says he doesn't mind me choosing my own career—
but provided always it's the one chosen for me."

Playwriting seems to have been in his blood from birth. His first
attempt was at eleven. And he will continue to the end. He has told us
why. "My ambition is to write one great play before I die."

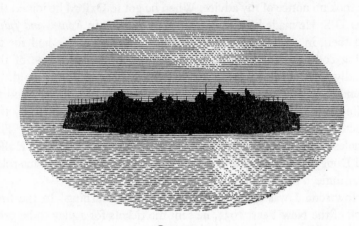

Ottagono

CHAPTER FIVE

European Journey

I

On New Year's Eve I was at my desk writing. The curtains were drawn, Louis kept putting logs on the fire. I was still writing when he stood up and said, "Listen!" He opened a casement window and with the cold air in came the sound of bells. They were announcing the New Year, 1934. I put down my pen and we went out into the garden. Little more than a mile away, by Henley Bridge, rose the square tower of the church. In its belfry the bells were joyously ringing. The sound came over the beechwoods in Henley Park, along the Fairmile, into our little hamlet encased in the valley. There were stars but no moon, my poplars black against the sky. The cottage was aglow with lights. One shone in the garden-level window of my housekeeper's room. From the lawn I shouted my New Year's wishes and she cheerfully responded.

The dead year had been a good one for me. My twelfth novel, *Pilgrim Cottage*, had been successfully launched. There had been a rewarding visit to Venice with the excursion to the lagoon fortress that had provided material for its successor. To my garland of friendships I had added a lovely flower. A friend, giving a lunch in Soho had introduced me to the young Marchesa Nadja Malacrida. She was not foreign as her name sounded, she was indeed wholly English, the niece of Lord and Lady Cowdray, married to a tall young Italian working as a journalist in London, the Marchese Pietro Malacrida. She was a woman of quite surpassing beauty, and many talents, much admired and popular in the young West End set. She had black smooth hair, a lovely oval face with vivacious eyes, and her figure was exquisite. She was radiant with life and I accounted myself fortunate that, admiring my work, she should wish to know me. The Malacridas had a house in Upper Grosvenor Street where they entertained friends of the social, literary and theatrical worlds. It was at one of their parties, often held in the Florentine *settecento* library they had created, that I met Humbert Wolfe, the poet, Sir Shane Leslie, notable for his wit, and his kilt, the beautiful and astonishing Rosita Forbes, just in from a desert, a jungle or a tropical island, vivid as a bird of paradise, and worldly-wise Gilbert Frankau, the novelist, famous for *Peter Jackson, Cigar Merchant* and the best satirical poem since Byron, *One of Us*. You never knew who you would meet there, Generals, Royal Academicians, diplomats, members of the B.B.C., Air Marshals, etc. Nadja Malacrida had her own achievements. She had published a novel and a book of poems. Possessing a beautiful voice, she read over the B.B.C. She was a fine horsewoman, trained at her uncle's Cowdray Park, the home of polo. She was also one of the first women to gain a flying pilot's certificate. In the library her beauty seemed to have been gathered up in a large painting by Ettore Tito, à la Botticelli's *Primavera*. In short, enjoyment of her friendship was an enrichment of life. "She makes my heart tremble," said Louis, on first meeting her. In the background of this cosmopolitan setting was her handsome husband, Pietro.

During the last year I had been much in and out of the homes of Philip Gibbs, and Lord Iliffe. Nor must I forget Mrs. Young, the eccentric vicar's wife up at Fawley Rectory, living in a large Georgian house in a state of unimaginable disorder. She was a Baskerville, daughter of a colonel famed for his lurid language on and off the Bench. Once, calling on octogenarian Mrs. Baskerville, I was sent up to the schoolroom to have tea with 'the boys', to find there her two bachelor sons, sixty and sixty-two respectively. One of them wrote a history of monastic life that became a classic. The Rev. Capel Young of Fawley, the double of President Roosevelt, had been a chaplain at the British Embassy in St. Petersburg, from which he brought fabulous and horrific stories, such as a 'bag' at a nobleman's shoot, 640 partridges and 38 peasants. "You mean pheasants?" I queried. "Not at all—peasants, the 'guns' were drunk with vodka and shot down thirty-eight beaters who were taken off in trucks, dead and wounded." When the Rev. Capel Young died his widow retreated to a tiny house in Henley High Street. The place looked like a junk shop, carpets unrolled, a tin hip-bath on the grand piano, empty birdcages on the tables, two Charles II spaniels bedded on a Brussels tapestry. She wore a gardener's green apron over her white nightgown, her head in papercurls. "I'm not straight yet," she said. She never had been straight, a genius of disorder. Behind her was a large photograph of her in court dress, at a royal ball in St. Petersburg. She had an infectious zest for life, though wheezy with bronchitis. She insisted on giving me a marble 'Column of Phocas', a model of the one excavated by a Duchess of Devonshire in the Roman Forum, brought back by her Baskerville great-grandfather from the Grand Tour.

Another neighbour, at Phyllis Court, was Captain Roy Finlay. He had inherited the large Regency house with splendid lawns bordering the Thames, copper beeches, a long river-wall, covered with roses in summer, a Grand Stand looking up the course, and over the winning post near-by Henley Bridge. At Regatta-time the lawns were crowded by members, the ladies in lovely summer frocks, a band playing under an elm-tree. The festivities closed with a ball, a scene of youth and beauty. Finlay lived in an upstairs suite and always kept a good table. In the subsequent four decades Henley withered away as a social event and a preserve of the Public Schools and the Universities. The tennis championships at Wimbledon killed it. The houseboats gay with flowers vanished, as also the punts; the motorcar and the outboard-engine wrote Henley's death-warrant. But the loveliness of the setting is almost indestructible. The bridge, the towered church, the old inn and the silver river create an exquisite scene.

There was another hospitable home that I always visited with delight. This was Munstead House, near Godalming, my friend Timmy Jekyll's home. It was presided over by his remarkable mother, Lady Jekyll, and stood for all that was best in England in a regime that would soon vanish. It was a large commodious house, set in beautiful grounds, with a great lawn, cedars and beeches. Some persons found Lady Jekyll formidable. Perhaps they were cowed by her prodigious energy and talents. She was a daughter of William Graham, sometime Liberal M.P. for Glasgow, and a friend of Gladstone and John Bright. He had a splendid art collection, particularly of the Italian schools. Some of these paintings now graced Munstead House. Lady Jekyll, a Dame of the British Empire, had had a wide experience. Her late husband had been private secretary to two Lord

Lieutenants of Ireland (1885–6 and 1892–5), and an acting secretary at the British Embassy in Paris. Her own career was formidable. She served with countless committees, societies and Orders, a Lady of Grace, a Lady of Justice, Visitor to a Borstal institute for girls, governor of a county school, a county magistrate. Above all she was a wonderful hostess, no detail overlooked, and entertained some of the most famous figures of the Edwardian and Georgian eras. Lytton Strachey, a cynic where most people were concerned, fell under her spell. "When she appeared life was entranced and intensified," he wrote. She had a son and two daughters, Timmy, Pamela, who married Reginald McKenna, Chancellor of the Exchequer in the famous Asquith Cabinet, and Barbara, first married to Francis McLaren, Lord Aberconway's son, killed flying in the First World War, by whom she had two sons, Martin and Guy, and then to Colonel Freyberg, V.C., the Dardanelles hero. To her other gifts Timmy's mother added that of being a gourmet. Her table was renowned, and she published a cookery book.

In this house of beauty, warmth and intellectual zest, where one morning J. M. Barrie had come down to breakfast and announced that he had got an idea for a new play, about a little boy who would not grow up (Peter Pan), there was another remarkable figure, Howes, the elderly butler. His benign presence made him one of the family assets. He had served it since he was twelve. He was as efficient with the cantankerous old as with the undisciplined young. "Howes thinks . . ." a member of the family would say, and what Howes thought, went. His smile was a benediction. Not a detail for your pleasure was missed. In the winter months he amused himself by making flower pictures out of clippings from gardeners' catalogues. They were works of art in their kind. When he presented me with a framed copy of one of these works I knew I had been taken into the family. The whole house had a pot-pourri odour and charm. My bedroom was sheer delight. It had a carved Florentine bed with canopy and backcloth. Lying in bed, an Italian primitive on the wall, I felt like Carpaccio's St. Ursula in that famous bedroom of the princess on pilgrimage with her thousand maidens. In summer, when I went up to dress for dinner, the sound of cawing rooks came in from the trees across the lawn.

Over the road were the house and garden of Munstead Wood that

Timmy's aunt, Gertrude Jekyll, had made world famous. When I first visited Munstead House she was a half-blind old lady, nearing ninety, a recluse. On her death in 1932 Timmy inherited his aunt's property and later went to live in the house.

Gertrude Jekyll's sister, married to Frederic Eden, lived for forty years in the Palazzo Barbarigo in Venice. They created the 'Garden of Eden' on the Giudecca, which Princess Aspasia of Greece later acquired. Gardening seemed to run in the Jekyll blood. With Gertrude it was a gift akin to genius. In 1876 she had acquired twenty acres on Munstead Heath and began to plan her garden. She met a young man of twenty, a student of architecture, named Edwin Lutyens. She commissioned him to build a small studio house. She lived in this house called the Hut. Soon they were planning a larger house, Munstead Wood. She sought advice from Ruskin about building it. There was an upper gallery, oak-floored, that was like a quarter-deck. Lutyens' penchant for high chimney-stacks and tremendous sloping tiled roofs was thus early demonstrated. With its thick walls, embrasured lattice windows and giant beams it was almost a fortress in the wood. Despite the great gallery, staircase, and almost medieval kitchen, there was not a bathroom in the house; until her death, aged ninety-three, she scorned such nonsense.

There was a long white-washed room that was her workshop. She could do anything with her hands. Alexandra, Princess of Wales, ordered some repoussé work, and Gertrude carved a fireplace for the Duke of Westminster at Eaton. There was a demand for her cushions decorated with white whalebone. All over the United Kingdom, and abroad, she was commissioned to design gardens. I found my own garden had been planted with 'Munstead dwarf lavender'. When Lutyens, now the famous Sir Edwin, made a model of Government House at Delhi, she modelled the small trees for it. Meanwhile, her fame as a gardener spread over the world, as also her gardening books. She received the Royal Horticultural Society's Victoria Medal. Almost blind for the last quarter of her long life, she was the Great Panjandrum of Gardens. Even her gardening boots became revered relics. Sir William Nicholson did a painting of them, now in the Tate Gallery. For fifty-four years she laboured in that monastic house. She did photography, botany, grafting, made decorative use of woods, metals, embroidery and allied needle crafts. She loved music and had musical friends such as Dame Ethel Smyth and Sir Henry Wood, the conductor.

When Timmy inherited the house and moved in, it was like invading the holy of holies with all the relics of a life's work around. He could not maintain the gardens as she had done, with four gardeners, but he was knowledgeable and worthy of his inheritance. After a time he found the large house and all the gardens unworkable and moved into Lutyens' firstling, the Hut. I stayed with him frequently in both houses. He lived to be eighty and died there. Munstead House, Munstead Wood, Munstead Hut, like Gertrude Jekyll's lavender, the names produce a fragrance in my memory.

As the bells rang in 1934, I wondered if another year could be as full of happiness and achievement as the past had been. Indoors again, in the warm glow of the lamplit, low-raftered room we drank to the New Year, and went up to bed.

II

On the morrow when Louis had to return to Paris we motored up to London through a thick fog. I had to speak at a dinner that evening. I had in my pocket a letter from Ernst Ritter extolling Hitler. My growing detestation of the Führer and our own supine indifference coloured my speech. "You don't think it's as bad as that?" asked a friend on leaving. "Worse—the Nazi juggernaut begins to move," I replied. When I wrote to Ritter I was tactful. He had read a report of one of Mosley's speeches and praised it. I made no adverse comment. I was playing Ritter, a window I kept open on the German scene.

Back in the cottage I finished *Gone Rustic*, sent it off to the typist and cleared the deck for *The Guests Arrive*. A few days later I went to town for Terence Rattigan's *First Episode*. The next day I read that Germany had made a ten-year Non-Aggression Pact with Poland, a country they would wipe out within six years. At a cocktail party at the Malacridas', people seemed to think it would take the heat out of the Polish Corridor question and ensure peace. Home again, in the wintry cosiness of my cottage, I buried myself in the opening chapter of *The Guests Arrive*, set in the fortress-pension on the summer-bright Venetian lagoon. Outside my window on a bird-table covered with snow, the starlings, blackbirds and a robin cleared the platter. I missed the two house-martins, Messrs. Fortnum and Mason, that ran along the ridge of the roof. They derived their names from two elegant youths clad in black tail-coats who took orders at the exclusive grocery store in Piccadilly. One day one of these young gentlemen called on me. He wanted to see his 'namesake', but my house-martins now were somewhere in the sunny south.

For Easter I had the cottage full. Louis came on the Good Friday. On Easter Monday there were sixteen for tea, Ethel beaming, after which Louis sorrowfully departed for Paris. I returned to writing *The Guests Arrive*. *Gone Rustic* was in its fourth edition. But the pace was too exhausting. I gave up the *Sphere* book page. I had engaged to accompany Sir Philip Gibbs in May on a European tour. He had been commissioned to write a book about the political situation. It was while working hard to finish my new novel that I was surprised one April day by the sudden advent of a friend, Sir Harold Bowden, bringing with him the girl who had given me such delight and torment ten years ago. At the moment that the garden gate opened and they entered, I was mowing the lawn. I stood still, my heart seemed to stop. There, smiling and alluring as ever, was Myra.* I had last seen her in Washington seven years ago when all my hopes had been shattered. She was now the wife of a diplomat, a social figure in Washington. She had not changed, it seemed. Impulsive as ever, without a word, she came up, flung her arms about me and, all sweaty as I was, kissed me. "Now say you are glad to see me!" she cried. The miracle of her loveliness was still about her. At last I found some words. "But what a paradise!" she cried, linking my arm and standing still as she surveyed the rose-covered cottage. "No wonder you've deserted America!" I looked in her eyes, unfathomable as always. "Who deserted who?" I asked. She hugged my arm and made no reply. We began the tour of the garden. Obviously my friend enjoyed the situation he had created. Then we went in to tea. Towards six they departed. She was leaving for Paris, she would be back in August. I told her I should be away, in Venice, *our* Venice of all places.

I finished *The Guests Arrive* in the first week of May, it had almost written itself. The day before I left for Paris to join Philip Gibbs I ordered electric light to be put into the cottage. The Aladdin lamps,

* *The Bright Twenties*, Ch. 9, IV.

lovely as they were, created too much work. I was glad to be away while the work was done. I should have trembled with fear at the threatened damage. The estimate was £50. When I returned I found the job had been excellently done. I congratulated the contractor. He looked rueful. "Had I known, it would have been £100. I had to buy my men new tools. They couldn't get through the oak-beams. They're just iron!" he said.

In Paris, after a few days with the la Rochefoucaulds, I joined Philip Gibbs and his friend, Capt. Edgar Lander, who would illustrate his book. Lander was an ex-officer of the Fusiliers. In battle he had lost his right hand and had learned to draw with his left. Gibbs called Lander and myself 'the chorus of my wanderings', anonymously quoting us from time to time. He wrote an amusing description of me.

> He is, in appearance, a strange attractive combination of Lord Robert Cecil as a young man and that great genius, Grock, in his noble moods. Temperamental, excitable and nervy, he has a child-like quality of responding to every impression. He's well-known as a novelist, poet, and I've inflicted great agonies upon him by claiming the literary copyright of all things seen and heard on this journey. There were moments when he found this condition intolerable. Looking back on the journey, I have a sense of guiltiness in having thwarted his genius. We joined him in Paris and dragged him down from the society of French dukes and other aristocrats to our social level, which was strictly limited to second-class hostelries and ordinary folk.

I had indeed undertaken not to write about our journey. It was his job exclusively. To travel with him was a joy. We knew each other affectionately, ex-war correspondents together. I forgave him the comparison with the hairless Grock, a comedian of surpassing genius, mollified by the Robert Cecil. In views we were diametrically opposed. He was an unquenchable, sentimental optimist. He believed in a bright new world. I, a realist, had no such hopes. I saw humanity steadily walking to perdition. The conflict of views was greatest when we came to Geneva after journeying from Paris through the enchantment of spring in Moret, Sens, where they showed us the robes once worn by its bishop, Thomas-à-Becket, Auxerre, Avallon, Vézeley, Semur, Autun, the very poetry of names in landscape. In Geneva we stayed in an hotel on the Quai du Mont Blanc, already filled with delegates to the final futile sittings of the Disarmament Conference. There we met Anthony Eden, handsome, a fashion-plate, who represented the British Government as Lord Privy Seal. He had been round Europe, trying to sell to Hitler, Mussolini and Barthou a new peace plan now that the famous Locarno Treaty, which had won a K.G. for Sir Austen Chamberlain, in a mood of euphoria, had failed. But Eden for all his skill and eloquence had served a collapsed soufflé. The delegates were now trying to find a face-saving formula to hearten the pacifists at home.

In this city of airy nonsense they were building the temple of peace, a home for the League of Nations, already the size of Versailles. The larger its failures, the larger its halls, the numbers of its officials and secretaries. It was already the house of two hundred typists. We went out to look at it. Great derricks were swinging blocks of stone in the air full of white dust from cement-mixers. New annexes sprawled along the hill overlooking the Lake. A horde of bronzed, half-naked labourers were building the House of Dreams. My companion saw in it the living soul of World Peace. I saw in it only a corpse stuffed with illusions. Gibbs talked to the workmen. "No, monsieur, we're not building the Palais des Nations. We're building a hospital for the wounded in the next war!" He spat on the ground and looked at my friend with mocking eyes. His words raised a chorus of hilarious assent among the workmen. "And I say we're building a barracks for the Germans to occupy when they march this way!" declared a giant covered in white dust. "That's right! That's right!" chorused his fellows. "You think the Germans are preparing for war?" I asked, provocatively. "Monsieur, we know they are! Can't everyone see? The air will be full of planes dropping bombs. Herr Hitler will follow in his motor car. The bands will play *Deutschland über Alles*. Those who don't *Heil* Hitler will be shot at dawn. We shall have to learn the goose-step!" He provoked a chorus of grinning assent. They had mistaken the three of us for delegates to the Disarmament Conference. They leaned over their spades, delighted to pull our legs. Poor Philip, he hid his dismay. Lander and I were confirmed in our pessimism.

All this took place amid the cranes and cement-mixers, on May 16, 1934. On May 16, 1970, exactly thirty-six years later, I was in Geneva and went with a companion to look at the corpse that cannot get buried. I was astonished to see the Palais des Nations still spreading across the hillside above the lake. The giant was adding new annexes. There was a forest of derricks and cranes, hordes of navvies among the cement-mixers. For 2.50 Swiss francs there was a tour of the palace. In the beautiful avenues surrounding it there were hundreds of parked cars of officials. What do they all do? They were doing whatever it was, at great public expense, under a multitude of high-sounding names. "Is it still the House of Two Hundred Typists?" I enquired of the man at the ticket office. "Monsieur, of Four Hundred!" he replied. As I went down the hill past the Botanical Gardens to lunch by the lake, I recalled the towering skyscraper of the equally futile New York headquarters of the United Nations, where the delegates talked and talked, some of them without paying their subscriptions.

When in 1934 I opened the wardrobe in my hotel bedroom I was surprised to find nine suits hanging there. I reported this to the hotel manager. "Oh, yes, they belong to your countryman, Monsieur Arthur Henderson. You have his room. We sometimes let it when he is away. He likes to keep it for when he comes." I knew 'Uncle Arthur' as they called him, the popular Labour Cabinet Minister. The room had a beautiful view over the lake, with the roseate evening glow of Mont Blanc in the distance.

We went on into Germany. We found no comfort there. Everyone assured us that Germany had no intention under Hitler of making war. Everything we saw told us that it had. In Frankfurt we encountered a Hitler Youth Day. Hundreds of sturdy youths in shorts and vests, bronzed, exultantly vigorous, marched in well-disciplined platoons. They were beautiful to observe, radiant with physical ardour. In a great square they massed and in one voice, arms upraised, shouted, "I swear unbreakable troth to Adolf Hitler and unbounded obedience to him and his appointed leaders." It was overpowering in its unanimity. I could not help contrasting these healthy youths with the ill-clad, half-fed lads I had seen selling their bodies in the *lokals* of Berlin four years earlier. This was indeed a renaissance, one of Hitler's miracles. But no alert observer could remain indifferent to this forging of a powerful weapon by the Nazis, who daily increased their grip, with violence and propaganda, on private freedom. The Jews were being pillaged and hunted. *"Heil der Führer!"* was the

Marchesa Nadja Malacrida

Judy Campbell

The author at Nassau

At Florian's Café, Venice. Mrs. Valentine Fleming, Amaryllis Fleming,
Princesses Isabel and Ariel Faucigny-Lucinge

hourly cry. While they talked peace they prepared for war. The Hitler *Jugend* had bombing practice. Air-raid shelters were built—against attack by whom? The Russians, the French, they responded. Everywhere there were drums, and flags blazing with the swastika. It was amazing what nonsense they talked. In Ulm a banner across the street declared, "The German People must become a Nation of Flyers." In the market place there was a large aerial torpedo, painted with the swastika. Elsewhere posters declared, "One People, One Danger, One Defence." Danger from whom, defence from what? Again you could get no answers. "Who helps the German Air Force, helps Germany." I recalled a warning of Churchill's, fallen on deaf ears, only two months ago. "Our planes are obsolescent . . . As we go to and fro in this peaceful country with its decent ordinary people going about their business under free conditions, it is startling and fearful to realise that we are no longer safe in our island home." I saw the truth of that all over Germany with its emphasis on the aeroplane. Everywhere the Germans were friendly, smiling, eager to assure us of their peaceful intentions. Everywhere we saw they were building a sinister war machine.

In Stuttgart we found under the railway station a large air-raid shelter. There was not one in France or England. A huge dummy bomb stood on a stand at a traffic crossing, while smiling boys, in the dapper black topboots of the Hitler *Jugend*, rattled collecting boxes, raising money 'to make Germany air-safe'. One boy, a fair-haired cherub, smiled and saluted. He cried *Danke schön* when Gibbs and I dropped coins in his box. He then pinned little Luftwaffe metal badges on our jackets. I asked him who he thought was going to bomb them. "We must be prepared, we must be air-minded. *Ein Volk, Ein Reich, Ein Führer*," replied the future blaster of Warsaw, Rotterdam and Coventry, parrot-wise. Our chauffeur, an ex-admiral of the Russian Imperial Navy, refused a badge. After the defeat of the White Army he and his wife had reached Constantinople, then begged their way to Paris, where he became a taxi-driver and, later, worked for the hire-car agency we patronised. He had obtained French citizenship. He looked at us disapprovingly. "Civil aviation! Messieurs, they're collecting to make planes to bomb us!" Rebuked, we took off our badges.

I had advised Ernst Ritter of our advent in Munich. A staff

captain of Röhm's S.A., he was working in the Brown House, the
Nazi headquarters. It was guarded by storm-troopers in helmets. We
called on him there and had a warm welcome. Very handsome in his
uniform of Röhm's elite corps, he introduced us to other officials. He
was eager to do anything he could for us. Gibbs expressed a desire to
see one of the Youth Labour Camps. Of course. He introduced an
older officer who was an *Oberfeldmeister*, in what was called the
Arbeitsdienst. He was a monocled aristocrat, a baron, educated at
Oxford and Heidelberg. He had good manners and excellent English.
The next morning he called for us in a large staff car. During the
drive to the Labour Camp at Förstenried, ten miles outside Munich,
we plied him with questions, some of them critical. He always had an
answer and was very amiable even when he sensed an air of opposition. We came to a camp of about three hundred boys. With surprise
we learned that we had arrived during the 'rest hour' in the early
afternoon. All the youths had to lie on their beds for an hour after
the morning's work and lunch. They lay in bunks over each other.
The environment was spartan. A bugle blew and the whole camp
came to life. Quickly three hundred half naked, bronzed lads were
lined up in ranks. They were fine physical specimens. I thought of
the Greek Hoplites who, with Leonidas, had fallen at Thermopylae,
and of the Spartans who fell, shield to shield, in a blood bond. We
were conducted from platoon to platoon. It was very democratic,
mostly unemployed street lads, factory lads, peasants, but also some
university students. All were compelled to do six months' service in
the Labour Camp. They rose at 5.30, took a shower, ran and drilled,
bootless and naked. There was a hospital. "But very few beds are
used. The boys are all in top form." They marched with spades as
their work-symbol but I learned they also had gun practice. They did
six hours' work, could go out from six to nine, and were free from
Saturday afternoon to Sunday night. When I spoke of them as
Spartans, our guide solemnly said, "Yes—but not wholly. They are
not homosexual. We encourage them to have girls." I asked about
religious instruction. Cardinal Faulhaber of Munich was anti-Nazi
and risked arrest. He had protested angrily because Corpus Christi
religious processions had been prohibited. His Catholic boys were not
permitted to march with banners. He had said to them, massed in
front of the cathedral, "Your flags have been forbidden but you have

come without them. We have lost our liberty, but you have not lost your faith." Knowing of this, I asked a question. For the first time the *Oberfeldmeister* lost his urbanity. "No, we do not teach religion here. We do not encourage it. The cardinals and priests are playing politics, the old guard. The Pope doesn't rule here—let him mind his own business."

I found Philip Gibbs, a Catholic, troubled by this. Lander was caustic. "Liberty—what do these bloody Nazis know about liberty? Look what they're doing to the Jews!" Before we left the boys sang for us some marching songs. Their pure massed voices, with the German inborn talent for *lieder*-singing, their unity and freshness, I found deeply moving. As we left they waved and smiled. "Beautiful!" exclaimed Lander, "But *der Führer*'s going to destroy Europe with them." "Oh, I don't think the Germans want war. Everyone we talk with is against it," said Philip, an obstinate optimist, with a bright faith in humanity. The natural sweetness in him was always buoyant above the evil in the world.

On our last night in Munich we invited Ritter and the *Oberfeldmeister* to dine. The latter brought with him a portfolio. He was an amateur artist and Lander was impressed by his work. He surprised us by saying he had been a prisoner in Yorkshire during the First World War. He had a sister who lived in New York. Under the warmth of wine he became confidential. He was a doubtful Nazi! He did not believe the young men in the Party had the experience to run the nation. Ritter dissented. But they were united in their firm belief that the Nazi Party and the Führer were not out for war. "Then why all this drilling and marching?" asked Gibbs. The *Oberfeldmeister* waved a hand deprecatingly. "Discipline and patriotism are the antidotes to Germany's demoralised youth. You know how low we sank after defeat. And besides, we are never easy about France and Russia. They might combine to attack." When we said we thought this an impossibility, he said, "You English are a happy people. You have no land-frontiers a thousand miles long on each side of you. We must always be prepared."

The evening went very pleasantly. We dropped politics and talked of art, music, literature, in which both of them were well versed. We parted very cordially on the night of June 2.

Following the night of the 29th, Hitler, afraid of Röhm's growing

power, flew in at dawn the next day, put leaders of the S.A. in the
Brown House under arrest, and pounced on Röhm and his chief
officers in the chalet at Wiessee. Röhm, in a Munich prison cell, was
given a revolver to shoot himself. Refusing, he was riddled with
bullets. His men were executed all that afternoon. Squad after squad
of Brownshirts faced Hitler's firing parties. The massacre went on. At
intervals the executioners had to be relieved, breaking under the
strain. Volley after volley shook the prison yard. Many of the victims,
under the illusion that an anti-Nazi *putsch* had gained control, fell
shouting *Heil Hitler!* By sundown Hitler was the supreme leader,
having shed himself of his old comrades. All Germany was cowed.
There had been a similar massacre in Berlin. I believe Ernst Ritter,
and the lover of art, the *Oberfeldmeister*, were shot. I was never able
to obtain news of them. Two letters to Ritter were unanswered.

We had left Munich on the morning of June 3. Twenty-seven days
after our departure, Munich was a stricken city of blood and massacre.
The number 'liquidated' was never known. The estimate ran from
four to seven thousand.

Later I received news from various correspondents of mine in
Germany that filled in the story of the Munich massacre. My Berlin
friend, Max Bauer, who had a passionate love of music, often went to
Munich, for the opera there. He knew Dr. Willi Schmidt, a gifted
cellist who acted as the music critic of the *Münchner Neueste Nach-
richten*. Ten days after the massacre Bauer was in Munich and called
on his friend. His apartment was closed. His enquiry for the Schmidts
produced a horrifying tale. Dr. Schmidt had never had anything to do
with politics. He was a quiet, happily married man whose only
interests were music and writing criticisms for his paper. On the
evening preceding Hitler's coup, the door bell rang. He was playing
his cello. His three children with his wife were in another room. Frau
Schmidt went to the door and was confronted with four S.S. men
holding revolvers. Without a word they walked into the sitting-room,
seized Schmidt and, despite protests, hurried him out into a van in
the street. After the terrible shock his wife went to the police who
knew nothing about the incident, and were not willing to make any
enquiries. Two days later a coffin was delivered to the apartment and
Frau Schmidt was warned not to open it. In the evening after she had
buried her husband, two S.S. men called. They told her they had

arrested and shot the wrong Schmidt. They brought her compensation money, which she refused. A few hours later Himmler rang up, ordered her to take the money and keep quiet. She again refused and soon after was ceremoniously called on by Hoess, later the notorious commandant of the camp at Auschwitz, where four million Jews, brought there in freight cars from all over Germany, Poland and Hungary, were exterminated. He told Frau Schmidt that they deeply regretted the error. They had awarded her a pension. She could regard her husband as a martyr in a great cause. The S.A. storm-troopers (*Sturm Abteilung*), in brown uniforms, and the S.S. (*Schutz Staffeln*), in black, would jointly fire a volley over her husband's grave. She refused to countenance the 'honour'. Such was one incident of that event known as 'The Night of the Long Knives'.

The day after Hitler returned to Berlin, he gave a tea-party at the Chancellery, formerly the Radziwill palace where Chopin had played for his princely host, and where my hostess at Lançut in 1929, Countess Potocka, née Radziwill, had been born. Later, Hitler harangued the Reichstag, justifying his action, and received from Marshal Hindenburg, President of the German Republic, a letter commending him for his 'determined action and gallant intervention which had nipped treason in the bud'. It is probable that this letter was concocted, for in July, 1934, Hindenburg was senile, and died three weeks later.

III

I arrived back in England on June 8 and before going down to Pilgrim Cottage was persuaded by Yeats-Brown to attend a great rally at Olympia of the British Union of Fascists which would be addressed by Oswald Mosley. I was reluctant to go as I wanted to get home but I am glad I went. It was an astonishing affair. A pseudo-Nazi air prevailed. The Blackshirts were massed in the hall. Mosley, accompanied by his bodyguard, walked down through them amid the salutes of his army, up to the platform where he was spotlighted. The whole thing was Hitlerian. Interrupters were violently evicted. Any lingering hopes I had about Mosley's crusade for the revival of the national spirit were dispelled. He harangued his blackshirted cohorts

for over an hour and a half. We were politically sick, but I preferred
Baldwin's ineptitude to Mosley's brazen parade of power.

On reaching Pilgrim Cottage I wrote out a report of what I had
seen in Germany and sent it to Winston Churchill. He maintained a
private bureau of information at Chartwell. July saw the Nazi
attempt to seize Vienna. Austria was marked for doom. The attempt
collapsed but little Dollfuss was shot in his Chancellery and left to
bleed to death on a couch.

CHAPTER SIX

Tragedy

I

Throughout July I prepared for a Greek tour. I was due to leave from Venice in a ship chartered by the Hellenic Travellers Club, on a cruise among the Greek Islands and up the Dardanelles to Constantinople. I had been engaged as one of the lecturers on board. These included Arnold Lunn, Father Martindale, S.J., Douglas Woodruff, Canon Wigram and two Oxford dons.

Early that month I had been invited by Pietro and Nadja Malacrida to a lunch they gave in their house in Upper Grosvenor Street. It was, as always with their parties, a delightful occasion. The guests included the Marquess and Marchioness of Milford Haven. He had been a friend since we had first met in May, 1916, in his ship H.M.S. *New Zealand* at Rosyth, just before his marriage. There was also Marie Tempest, who was still delighting audiences with her arch piquancy. She had made an art of pouring tea in a stage drawing-room scene. Others present included Lionel Fielden, old Lord Queenborough and handsome Humbert Wolfe, the poet-civil-servant, very much in love with our hostess—and who was not?

This summer Pietro and Nadja had come to lunch at my cottage for the first time. They fell in love with the place so I invited them to come again, for Henley Regatta. Sitting in the garden Nadja suddenly exclaimed, "Oh, if only I could spend weeks here. It would be heaven! How can you bear to leave it!" People often talk like that in a state of momentary enthusiasm, but country life soon bores them, they are town sparrows. Was Nadja one of these? I suspected it.

I was always unhappy that my cottage should be empty for two whole summer months. It could give much pleasure to others. In the

135

garden the roses, gladiolis, hollyhocks and dahlias would bloom unseen and the apples redden on the boughs unplucked. This year I had lent it to friends for August who would bring their own servant, and Ethel could take a holiday, returning at the end of the month, but there was the waste of the following month. Impulsively, I offered the cottage to Nadja for September. She was incredulous. "Do you really mean it?" she asked. I assured her that I did. So it was all settled, and Ethel would look after them.

This July month was hectic. I finished the proofs of my Venetian novel *The Guests Arrive*. I went to the wedding of Lord Trent's grand-daughter when she married young Willoughby Norman, grandson of handsome old Lord Aberconway, who wintered at his peninsula-sited Château de La Garoupe at Cap d'Antibes. His mother, Lady Norman, an almost fabulous character, was a dear friend of mine. I made repeated visits to the Château after she inherited it. Following the wedding at St. Margaret's there was a reception at the Aberconway house in Belgrave Square. Young Norman was destined to preside over the vast Boots Drug business when Jesse Boot's only son, the second Lord Trent, died. Forty-eight hours before the wedding I was at Bradfield College for the Greek play. These plays, superbly presented, were always the purest joy. The leafy outdoor amphitheatre is unsurpassed; neither the theatre of Herodes Atticus at Athens nor the vast amphitheatre at Epidauros is superior in beauty, for Bradfield has a vernal loveliness these others lack. This year there was a Cassandra of fifteen, in the *Agamemnon* of Aeschylus, who froze our marrows.

In the middle of July I was again at Munstead House. This visit was memorable for two things. I now had my first sight of Munstead Wood and the celebrated garden which Timmy had inherited from his aunt, Gertrude Jekyll. And it was now that I met the famous Colonel Freyberg, V.C., born in New Zealand, the second husband of Timmy's sister, Barbara. Freyberg had won fame overnight with his swimming exploit on a Gallipoli beach. To call him brave was insufficient. He did not know the nature of fear. He had been nine times wounded, six times mentioned in dispatches. When James Barrie gave his famous Rectorial Address at St. Andrew's University, he chose 'Courage' for his theme, and had its inspirer, Freyberg, sitting on the platform with him. He had become a legend in another way. He was one of the small group, all doomed to fall except Freyberg, who had buried Rupert Brooke on the island of Skyros at midnight on April 23, 1915, under a clouded moon. Freyberg had helped to dig the grave. "We lined it with flowers and set a wreath of olives on the coffin. Freyberg, Oc, Charles Lister and I stayed behind and covered the grave with great pieces of white marble," wrote Denis Browne to Edward Marsh. In a second letter he gives us another glimpse of Freyberg. "We have just come back from a little demonstration close to the shore and Freyberg has just gone off on a fire-lighting expedition—swimming. We are all anxious about him. He has been wonderful these last few days. He loved and understood Rupert intuitively in spite of the differences in their temperaments; and last night, when we were making the grave, he was as gentle as a woman, and as strong as a giant."

At the time when I first met Freyberg he seemed to have come to the end of his army career, having suffered a terrible blow. He had been given a command of the British Army in India, with headquarters in Calcutta, a fitting crown to his career. He went for a medical check-up, when it was found that his heart would not stand a hot climate. This eventually entailed his going on the retired list. He was now finding employment for himself by building houses on land they possessed near Haslemere. He took Timmy and myself to look at one. I felt the sadness of it all. Freyberg was a well-built man, slender, very quiet in mien, with a slight air of melancholy, I thought. His hopes were now concentrated on his small son, Paul. But his distinguished career had not closed. Before he left the Army he requested that, if a war came, he should be eligible for a training job at home. When war came, in September, 1939, he went to Salisbury Plain, re-joining the Army, and a year later was appointed to command the New Zealand Expeditionary Force.

My visit to Munstead House was at the time of ominous rumours concerning Mussolini. His success over the Greek frontier delimitation imbroglio, followed by the brutal bombardment of Corfu and his defiance of the League of Nations, had whetted his appetite. There were rumours that he had designs on Abyssinia but these were dismissed as negligible. Italy had never forgotten her humiliation when in 1896 she had been ignominiously defeated at Adowa by what had been regarded as a mere native rabble. This was something to be avenged. Mussolini was building up his navy in the Mediterranean, which he would make *Mare Nostrum*.

A discussion arose at Lady Jekyll's table on the world situation. I expressed my alarm at Baldwin's flabbiness, his indifference to all the portents, his rejection of Churchill's persistent attacks charging him with neglect of Britain's defences. I recounted what I had seen these last years in Germany and Italy. I found all my fears pooh-poohed by Freyberg. Italy? She could be knocked out in five hours by our Navy! I could not accept this. I told him that Italy had built up a navy that was now a considerable force. He laughed. I told him that at Spezia I had seen the enormous increase in her naval establishment, that I had seen in Venice the ferryboats, plying between the Zattere and the Giudecca, crowded with workers making munitions in old factories. We ranked below the Italians in air-power. I had discovered that on the island of Pantelleria, off Tunisia, a prison for anti-Fascists, a blockhouse had been constructed in the channel of the passage to Egypt and the eastern Mediterranean. This, in conjunction with Sicilian bases, was a threat to our vital shipping. (In the subsequent war, at a critical phase, we were forced to make a long and costly detour via the Cape of South Africa owing to the Italian naval and air strength in the Mediterranean. At Leros, off the coast of Asia Minor, they had created a harbour and a fortified submarine base that would play a dominant role in the subjugation of the Aegean Islands. Later, in our attempts to take Leros and Cos we suffered heavy losses.

While in America I had read an article, illustrated, about the fast motorboats, carrying two torpedoes, which Italy was building in large numbers. For what? Freyberg denied that any such small vessel was capable of carrying two torpedoes. "You believe what you read in an American magazine? Good God!" he exclaimed. I told him of the submarine-frogmen who were being trained. He scoffed. He trampled on Timmy's arguments. The discussion became somewhat acrimonious. Lady Jekyll tactfully changed the subject. Out in the hall Timmy was indignant. "You can't argue with him. He knows it all!" he exclaimed. I replied, "You must remember he's an experienced professional soldier who thinks we're a pair of half-witted highbrows. He reflects the views of the War Office and the Cabinet. He's one of the Ostrich Party and has distinguished companions."

In the drawing-room where we gathered later I offered to send

Freyberg the American magazine in which the new torpedo-boats were described. "Thank you," he said, coolly. I sent it, marked. Did he learn later, in December, 1941, that Prince Borghese led undersea riders who attached time-bombs underneath H.M.S. *Queen Elizabeth* and H.M.S. *Valiant*, in Alexandria harbour, putting them out of commission and thereby eliminating our Mediterranean Battle Fleet? It was ironical that on the shores of the Mediterranean Freyberg should suffer his worst rebuffs when the war came. He gallantly commanded the New Zealand Forces in Crete, from which he was driven by the Germans. He was in the costly, frustrating siege of Monte Cassino, whose monastery was needlessly destroyed, thus giving the Germans the right to invest the ruins. After the war Freyberg was raised to the peerage. He became a popular Governor of New Zealand, his native soil, and died the Lieutenant-Governor of Windsor Castle.

Soon after my visit to Munstead, Baldwin, nettled by Churchill, announced an increase in the size of the Air Force. It was something at last. When Hindenburg, aged eighty-seven, died, total power had fallen into Hitler's hands. Again Churchill warned Parliament of the German menace. The House shrugged its shoulders. He had become a bore on the subject of defence. The Labour Party opposed all estimates for increasing the Forces.

At the end of July the Malacridas gave another lunch in their Upper Grosvenor Street home. There was the usual interesting company representing politics, art, literature and the stage. I lingered behind in order to discuss the final arrangements for Nadja's occupancy of my cottage. All details completed, I departed around three o'clock. "You're a dear, I want to kiss you," she said. I accepted her accolade and went into the street. I did not know that I should never see her again.

Five days before my departure for Venice a shadow fell on my home. In June I had lectured at the Royal Air Force College at Cranwell. One of the cadets, Patrick Southby, told me that he lived at Oxford. Might he come one day and see me? I invited him to lunch. Aged twenty, my guests liked him, he had grace of mind and body. Then, during his leave, I invited him for the weekend. Mrs. Bingham, the wife of the American Ambassador said she had two

debutantes staying with her who longed to see my cottage. I asked
her to bring them to lunch. To meet her I also asked Madame
d'Hautpoul, the aunt of my neighbour Lord Camoys, of Stonor Park.
She was a close friend of Queen Mary and the royal family. The
grounds of her home, Turville Grange, above me on Turville Heath,
had trees planted by her royal guests to commemorate their visits. For
young company I commandeered Tony Allingham and Patrick
Southby, so that the debutantes should have two beaux for company.
It was a great success. On Monday, soon after lunch, Patrick departed
on his motor-cycle for his home at Oxford, twenty miles distant. As he
mounted his roaring machine he said, thanking me, "Can I come
again? You know all my friends envy me knowing you and Pilgrim
Cottage!" and with that he rode off.

At eight o'clock that evening the telephone rang. It was Mrs.
Southby asking me if Patrick was there. He had said he would be
home for supper. Surprised, I told her that he had left five hours ago.
The next morning I was called again by Patrick's sister. She informed
me that last night, very late, his body had been found lying in a ditch.
Apparently his machine had skidded and struck a telegraph pole. I
left the cottage for Venice and the Greek cruise with the shadow of
this tragedy over it.

II

On arrival at Venice I was met by my faithful escorts, Lucien and
Bevis Reid, with their inseparable friend the British Consul's white
Sealyham dog. Lucien deftly manœuvred his boat to the quayside
and I embarked. I knew every inch of this journey down the Grand
Canal and across to my old lodgings on the Zattere. Later, I rented a
little Venetian house, 390 Dursoduro, by the Rio Torresella, for my
return from the Greek cruise. It had a walled-in courtyard, a garden
fountain, and open marble stairs, covered with a vine, which led to an
upper floor with three bedrooms, dining-room, kitchen and bath.
There was a garden-level salon. All this and heaven too for eight
hundred lire a month! (£10).

After three days in Venice I embarked, rowed to our cruise ship off
the Salute by my young gondoliers, whose skill and beauty drew the
eyes of my fellow-travellers. There were then no 'package tourists'.

It was not yet the era of the 'fourteen days, nine ports', on the very restricted allowance of the Bank of England, following our winning a war. Englishmen in 1934 were still affluent abroad and respected by foreigners. Our cruise was no ordinary holiday jaunt. It was a serious excursion to Greece by persons who knew what they were looking at, for many of our company were classical scholars who, like Browning's Grammarian, could have 'settled *Hoti*'s business'. Some of them had saved hard for this momentous excursion. Many of the women were unabashed bluestockings, spectacled, weighed down with classical commentaries and dictionaries. There was enough learning on board to have sunk us over the Plimsoll Line. Two of our lecturers were classical scholars. Their standing was part of the allure of this somewhat expensive cruise. To lighten the itinerary there were some non-classical excursions, to Ragusa (Dubrovnik), to the Dardanelles, with tantalising vistas of the battlefields of Gallipoli and Troy, and, briefly, to Constantinople.

Our chief lecturer, Canon Wigram, was a remarkable character, a portly little man, fluent in exposition. His passionate enthusiasm for things Hellenic often turned him into something of a votary, addicted to the ancient 'Mysteries', so that at times he seemed to forget he was a canon of the Anglican Church. There were moments of eloquence when some of us feared that he might carry off our learned ladies in a bacchanal-rout terminating in priapic rites. He was also apt to arouse an element of suspense, of a different kind. He wore the flimsiest shantung trousers enveloping an ample stomach. The belt holding them up often slipped below his perimeter. Lost in classical exposition, he seemed oblivious to the peril that he might suddenly become debagged. There was a moment, one hot August morning, as the audience sat around at Eleusis, while he coyly expounded the Eleusinian mysteries, when he retrieved his falling trousers in the very nick of time. Some apprehensive ladies had quickly lowered their sunshades. He was deeply versed in his subject, with a gift of vivid exposition. He enjoyed an unrivalled popularity as a lecturer. On landing at Constantinople, a scene and subject that we expected would be quite outside his field, the Canon proved to be an astonishingly well-equipped guide. Very familiar with the scene, he startled us by speaking Turkish. His knowledge of Constantinople came from having been a member of the Archbishop of Canterbury's Mission to the Assyrian Christians in Turkish Kurdistan. His learning was formidable if odd. He had published a work on *The Separation of the Monophysites*. He was intimate with the nature of Bacchic orgies. His familiarity with Turkish came from having been a prisoner in Turkey in the First World War.

Not only was the Church of England somewhat eclipsed by the ancient gods of Greece, we became aware of a strong Roman Catholic aura. Arnold Lunn, our genial director, a champion skier and author, had become a convert to the Catholic Faith. This probably accounted for the presence of two other eminent Catholics, Father Martindale, S.J., and Douglas Woodruff, late editor of the Catholic journal, *The Tablet*. The old gods and the new were thus ably represented. My own contribution as a lecturer was a light one. My subject was Ragusa (Dubrovnik), our last port of call. Its history, largely Venetian, was within my range.

On the outward journey down the Adriatic our first call was Corfu, whose story is an amalgam of Greek, Venetian, French and British rule. Its most vivid recent experience had been Mussolini's outrageous show of power during the Albanian-Greek frontier incident, when an Italian member of a delimitation mission had been murdered. Mussolini, taking abrupt action, had bombarded Corfu's citadel, killing some of its occupants. He occupied the town as a preliminary to the financial blackmail of Greece and of the impotent Council of Ambassadors, to whom the nervous League had referred the case.

The cost of our cruise was such that youth was almost absent from the passenger list, but there was a small group of undergraduates travelling steerage and achieving a maximum excitement. Among these there was a tall, blond lad from Trinity College, Cambridge, Peter Kemp. Well-informed, eager, he became my particular companion on the more strenuous excursions, such as that at Santorin, the ancient Thera, a volcano-island south of Crete, still trembling from an old eruption. In its inner pool, filling the old crater, there was a small volcano still active, a heart of red fire in the dark blue pool. At Santorin the Egyptian Ptolemies had based their navy. From the rim-crater town we took an arduous ride to the deserted mountain-top gymnasium. Here the youth of the Dorian world had competed for the crown of Beauty. Long-haired, naked, they were too disciplined by the hoplite's drill to resemble the filthy hippies of our twentieth century. There were erotic inscriptions in the ancient gymnasium, tributes to competing youths, which Canon Wigram declined to translate. Observing the phallic images, he murmured, "This place would have pleased D. H. Lawrence."

The island made an intense impression on me, and within six months of this visit I wrote my next novel, *Volcano*, set in this place whose blasted cone was rimmed with white houses and domed churches. At the close of the visit our ship, which could find no anchorage, so deep was that inner sea, sailed out through the precipitous jaws of the riven volcano into the sunset over the Aegean. Homeward bound, there came again the heart-lifting moment when the Acropolis, crowning Athens, came into view. With Peter Kemp I chose the hour of the violet sunset to mount the Sacred Way. The Parthenon in the dusk and silence possessed us, an enchantment of golden marble in which still beat the heart that had sent a current of Hellenic civilisation coursing down the centuries. Our guide-map marked a spot called 'The Cave of Pan'. We took with us a bottle of wine and there, in revolt against the proselytism permeating our cruise ship, we made a libation to the Great God Pan, swearing he was not dead. Below us Athens burned in the evening glow. Above us, on the plateau of the Acropolis, the caryatids of the Erectheum stood wrapped in centuries of silence. They seemed to approve our gesture. Then back down the Sacred Way we went towards the noisy city, happy in our foolishness.

A year later Peter Kemp, now graduated from Cambridge with an Honours degree in Classics and Law, ardent as ever, had found a new adventure. He was off to Spain to fight in the Spanish Civil War, at first with the Carlist Cavalry and later in the Spanish Foreign Legion, rising from the ranks to lieutenant. He was four times wounded, once seriously, resulting in a smashed jaw. He wrote articles and news reports for the British Press. On his departure to join the Army I gave him my blessing, and a typewriter. He returned home in 1939, having been awarded the Spanish Cruz de Guerra and the Cruz del Merito, and mentioned in dispatches. The Second World War added an even more eventful chapter to his saga. He served throughout in the commandos and in the Special Operations Executive. In August, 1943, he was parachuted into Albania, spending eight months there and in

Montenegro, organising resistance and guerilla warfare in the mountains. In December, 1944, he changed his field of operations and was parachuted into Poland, now a Nazi inferno, and worked with the Polish underground, and there, in 1945, he fell into the hands of the Russians, who imprisoned him.

This would seem enough adventure for any young man of twenty-nine. But not so for Peter Kemp. Released, he was parachuted into Siam just before the end of the Japanese war. After this, until January, 1946, he commanded a chain of intelligence missions along the north-east Siam-Indochina frontier and saw the beginning of the Viet Minh rebellion. His area of operations comprised some fifty thousand square miles, with over two hundred and fifty miles of frontier. His duties included giving help to the French colonial forces. He had a price of £500 put on his head by the Viet Minh. The next stage of this astonishing career was peaceful but spectacular. From February to June, 1946, he commanded, now a lieutenant-colonel, the Advanced Allied Mission to Bali and Lambok, liberating these islands from the Japanese. He was Military Governor of both islands and, later, political adviser to the Dutch commander in Bali. With a D.S.O. and mention in dispatches, he was demobilised in October, 1946. Only thirty, his adventurous blood had not cooled. In 1956 the Hungarian revolution broke out and *The Tablet* commissioned him as a correspondent. He was in Hungary throughout the Russian repression. After five weeks the triumphant Russians compelled the Ministry of the Interior to expel him. He crossed the Austrian frontier, escaping arrest by only a few minutes.

I knew nothing of these achievements. I often wondered what his fate had been. In March, 1951, I was sitting on the terrace of the Rock Hotel at Gibraltar, overlooking the Straits, where I had taken refuge after crossing the Atlantic in a hurricane that nearly sank my Italian liner from New York, when I heard my name called. Turning, I saw Peter Kemp,* unchanged except for a damaged jaw, a legacy of the Spanish period. We greeted each other exuberantly and he introduced me to his wife. They were living in Algeciras and had

---

* Lt.-Col. Peter Kemp, D.S.O. Born 1916, son of the late Sir Norman Kemp, ex-Chief Justice of Bombay. Educated Wellington College and Trinity, Cambridge. Author of *Mine was the Trouble*—memoirs of the Spanish war—*No Colours or Crest*—the European war—*Alms for Oblivion*.

come over to Gibraltar for the day. I now heard the story of his adventures. After the war he lived in Italy throughout 1947, a representative of Miles Aircraft, Ltd. Then tragedy struck him down. He developed tuberculosis and spent the whole of 1948 in a Swiss sanatorium. Recovering, in 1949 he joined the Foreign Office, and served in Rome until May, 1950, when another attack of tuberculosis caused him to return home. He remained in a sanatorium at Midhurst until the following autumn. Cured, he settled in Algeciras, with its beneficial climate. I was glad to see him looking so well and happy. On parting we made a resolution not to let so long a gap of time occur again, but in the wayward nature of things another eighteen years had elapsed when, in 1969, I encountered him, unchanged in his eager and ever-youthful self, at a Knightsbridge cocktail party given by Prince and Princess of Pless. In the interim years he had turned author and travelled in south-east Asia, covering Formosa, the Philippines, Borneo, Thailand, Laos, Malaysia, Indonesia and Vietnam. Such was the history of that pleasant youth who, with the Hellenic Cruise in 1934, had drunk with me on the Acropolis a libation to Pan.

On September 1, ending our cruise, we arrived at Dubrovnik, where I gave my lecture. Three days later we were back in Venice.

My two young gondoliers collected me and took me to the little house I had rented. I invited Timmy Jekyll to stay with me and also sent for Louis Tissier in Paris. Since he could not have his summer holiday at Pilgrim Cottage I felt Venice would compensate him. It was his first visit. For ten days he was in a state of ecstasy. Meanwhile, I was involved in a singular episode. Among the passengers on our cruise there was a Mrs. Valentine Fleming, with her little red-haired, adopted daughter, Amaryllis. I had not met Mrs. Fleming before but I knew something about her. She had married Major Valentine Fleming, killed in the First World War, and was a widow with four sons over whom she exercised a loving but firm control. The eldest son, Peter, aged twenty-seven, had already distinguished himself as an explorer and writer. A younger son, Ian, was a dashing youth who, just down from Eton and studying for the Diplomatic Service, had, with his handsome looks, dazzled the Austrian girls of Kitzbühel, where he was at a crammer's. It was there that I met him, destined to be the creator of the James Bond saga that brought him fame and fortune.*

Mrs. Fleming knew of me as an author living at Pilgrim Cottage, near Joyce Grove, the house of her mother-in-law, Mrs. Robert Fleming. We naturally sought each other's company. She was a delightful companion, beautiful, a gifted amateur violinist. She lived in the Chelsea house where Constable had had his studio. She entertained artists and musicians, among them Augustus John, Epstein and Thomas Beecham.

One morning as we sat on deck, our ship nearing Rhodes, she asked me if I knew Greys Court, near Henley-on-Thames. I knew it quite well, having often lunched there with its owner. It was an Elizabethan mansion of considerable history, well-situated high above me, with wide views of the Chiltern Hills, an impressive grey Tudor pile with a gabled façade. It had once been part of a feudal castle and its fortifications could still be traced. From A.D. 1191 to 1216 it belonged to Walter de Grey, Archbishop of York in the reign of Edward III. A Lord de Grey had fortified and crenellated it in 1348. Four of the old towers were now in various states of ruin with walls four feet thick. The house had been granted, after confiscation, to another Lord de Grey by Henry VIII at an annual rent of a red rose at midsummer. Later, Greys Court fell into the possession of Sir Francis Knollys, in the time of Queen Elizabeth. He built the Queen's Gate for her visit. There still existed in the line of the curtain-wall the large stables and barn in which, at the time of the Civil War, Cromwell's soldiers had kept their horses. For anyone who wanted a well-sited, historic, gabled mansion, it was a tempting proposition but it would cost a considerable sum in restoration and modernisation. The mansion was now in the market at what seemed a knockdown price, £17,000. Mrs. Fleming coveted it. "But if I make a bid for it," she said, "they'll keep up the price. The Henley agents imagine all the Flemings are millionaires. I want it very much. Will you act for me and bid for it in your name?" I was somewhat startled by her suggestion but I agreed to do so. Cables and letters passed between the agents in Henley and myself in Greece and Venice. I bid £10,000. They countered with £15,000. I felt we could get it for £11,000 or £12,000.

* See *The Bright Twenties*, Ch. 15, IV.

146

Mrs. Fleming stayed on in Venice for some time. Louis and I lunched with her at the Excelsior Lido Hotel. She met my friends at my little house. The Nobilis entertained her at their home, *Domus Amicorum*, and gave a party for the publication of *The Guests Arrive*, which I had dedicated to them. We made excursions to Murano and Padua, taking Amaryllis, Bevis and Lucien with us. Mrs. Fleming commissioned Lucien's father to paint a miniature of Amaryllis. Prince and Princess Faucigny-Lucinge were in Venice with their two little daughters, Isabel and Ariel, nine and eight. Poor little Ariel. She was killed by an automobile outside the Carlton Hotel at Cannes, before her parents' eyes. Some years later her mother died after an accident during the Second World War. She was riding pillion on a motor-cycle. A wire stretched across the road by the Germans struck her fatally. But these tragedies had not touched them when we laughed and ate ices at Florian's and made excursions on the canals and lagoons.

The history of little Amaryllis was a happier one. When she was eleven she decided to become a cellist. At fourteen Mrs. Fleming bought her a Ruggieri viola. She studied at the Royal College of Music and made her professional debut with the Hallé Orchestra. After that she won fame as an artist playing with the leading orchestras. In 1970, at New College, Oxford, she appeared in the string trio, her creation, known as the Fleming Trio.

One night in Venice I had an experience that has never faded from my memory. I had dined with old Sir Hubert Miller in his little house decorated with cherubs, *putti*, crowned Virgins, saints, crimson damask hangings and all the rococo trimmings expressive of his ardent Anglo-Catholicism. ("Why doesn't the old boy go right over ?" asked Timmy.) Sir Hubert kept a good table. His menage consisted of a gondolier, who 'waited', and his wife Maria, the fat jolly cook. It was nearly one o'clock in the morning when the guests departed. I walked alone down the long, narrow Merceria. On emerging into the Piazza San Marco I was astonished to see at the far end of that great square rows of little lights, which proved to be the illuminated stands of an orchestra. Behind these some fifty persons were grouped, all sombrely dressed, a choir. I had not recovered from my surprise when I heard the orchestra begin to play. I halted and took a chair outside Florian's Café. The rest of the Piazza was completely deserted.

When the choir sang waves of glorious sound rolled through the long, empty arcades. There was a pause. Presently a sturdy little man stood forth, wearing a beret and a scarf. He unwound the scarf, awaiting the beat of the conductor. Then a tenor voice of the purest silver rose in the night air. After a few notes I realised that he was singing, to the soft accompaniment of the orchestra, an aria from Verdi's Requiem Mass. I sat entranced. Here was a full performance, with no audience, of Verdi's masterpiece. Nowhere else in the world could this work have found such a marvellous auditorium.

After three-quarters of an hour the performance ended. The musicians began to pack their instruments. On my way home I learned from one of them that this was a rehearsal for a public performance in the Piazza on the following evening. The singer, the tenor in the beret, whose pure notes had soared up to the stars, was Gigli, the greatest living tenor of the day.

One day, before lunching with Mrs. Fleming at the Excelsior Hotel, I had a close-up of Mussolini giving one of his exhibitions of vitality. He had undressed somewhere in the hotel and came down, clad in a bathing costume, through the lounge. Short, stocky, with black eyes in a bullet head, he walked quickly through the lounge towards the terrace, between lines of applauding Italians crying *"Duce! Duce!"* Unresponding, grim, he strutted on down to the beach. He went straight into the sea and vigorously swam out beyond the pier, followed by a boat-load of camera and Press men. To the disappointment of the crowd he did not come back but went off down shore, being picked up later, and henceforth invisible. That night, attending a performance at the Fenice Theatre, he came out on the balcony and addressed the vociferous crowd. The oration was in his typical manner, aggressive, and bombastic. He was at the peak of his prestige, only eleven years from his countrymen's bullets at Dongo and a shameful hanging of his body, upside down, in a Milan square.

III

My news from England was good. *The Guests Arrive* was in its third printing within a month of publication. One morning Timmy, beaming, informed me that Russia had joined the League of Nations.

148

I found nothing for optimism. She would do little but frustrate its policies. And I had lost all faith in it, anyhow.

Meanwhile I was receiving letters from Nadja Malacrida in Pilgrim Cottage. They were written in violet ink, in a large legible hand.

I've been here a week and I still gaze with wonder and surprise every time I open the garden door—am I making you hideously homesick? I can't help it for I want you to know how utterly happy I am here and how grateful, grateful beyond all words, I am to you for this delicious fairytale existence.

A second letter came a few days later.

Pilgrim Cottage, Sunday night . . . an apple has just fallen outside the window, a doleful cow is mooing her unrest, from the distance comes the sound of home-going motorists in a faint hum, and reminds me that there really is a world outside the garden of your almost too-good-to-be-true cottage. I've been here a week and I still gasp with wonder. I'm having a delightful time among your books . . . Good night to you, and a million blessings for this happy time.

Another letter with the Henley postmark also arrived. It was from the estate agents. They would accept £13,000 for Greys Court. I stuck to my £10,000 bid. Excitement had been added to our bargaining by little Amaryllis who, during an excursion to Padua, had put her small hand on the shrine of St. Anthony and made a wish. She kept it secret but we guessed what it was. "We shall get Greys Court," said Mrs. Fleming. "St. Anthony never fails!"

On September 20th came another letter from Nadja.

It's past my 'Half-Way' now and already the return to London and all that town life entails looms gloomily before me. But it has been the greatest delight, this month down here, and so much have Peter and I fallen in love with this part of the country that we are scouring the neighbourhood for a small place of our own. So you may have us as neighbours yet! The apples on the 'red' tree are almost gone; you will still see your russets on the bough. I am not a bit surprised you love your place. And your house-keeper, of course, is a joy. Bless her! She has made me so comfortable. After which I must say good night and au revoir.

It looked as if I was going to have three very pleasant new neighbours, the Malacridas and Mrs. Fleming, who had just left Venice for London. I was certain that if I wrote the agent, withdrawing, and Mrs. Fleming appeared with a cheque for £11,000 the place would be hers, and Amaryllis's request of St. Anthony would be fulfilled.

A few days later, as I was sunning myself on my Venetian balcony, plucking sun-warmed figs from a tree below, the postman came. One letter was from Nadja.

> You have been so very kind that you will probably not be surprised to learn that, like Oliver Twist, I am asking for more. You are the direct cause of our falling in love with this part of the world, and with one particular house in it, and Peter has today made an offer for the Greys Court property . . .

I stopped reading, stunned. It must be a fantasy. After a few moments I read on.

> If you are not returning until October 8 could we trespass on your amazing hospitality until the 4th or 5th? This will help Peter enormously as he is living in a maelstrom of architects, builders, land agents, surveyors and what not. Do you know Greys? It is all so exciting that I have a sort of feeling that if one wants a thing sufficiently one sometimes gets it . . . I hope this will catch you before you leave.

Louis was packing to return to Paris. I went into his bedroom and handed him the letter. He read it. *"Incroyable!"* he exclaimed. Timmy in turn found it incredible. What on earth were the Henley agents thinking, with offers coming from someone in Pilgrim Cottage, and also from its owner in the Mediterranean! Obviously, very puzzled, they had kept their mouths shut. I wrote at once to Nadja explaining my position. They, and Mrs. Fleming, must fight it out without me.

My Venetian tenancy came to an end. On October 1 my young gondoliers rowed me to the station. Under the Rialto bridge I photographed Lucien on the poop of our boat, rowing me like a professional gondolier, Bevis at the prow. It was a wrench to leave my Venetian house and these delectable children. I broke my journey in Turin, and after three days I left for Paris where Louis met me. In the car on the way to Norman Fuller's, where I was halting en route for London, Louis seemed grave and quiet. Were there any letters for me? "Yes, here, quite a pile." I opened them. One, with the familiar violet ink was from Nadja Malacrida. I read it aloud to Louis.

Pilgrim Cottage, Oct. 1.

. . . It is certainly the most amazing coincidence, and we were not less flabbergasted by your letter than you were by mine. But I am very much afraid we shall not get the place, for this morning we were informed that someone else had just made an offer far larger than ours, and I imagine your Mrs. Fleming will get the prize. I am so desperately in love with Greys that I am heartbroken. I adore it, its possibilities, and its country. And this when, as the agents say, Greys has been spurned and neglected for years! I was quite decided that I was going to live at Greys for the rest of my life . . . I send this to Paris and look forward to seeing you very soon. Your garden is looking exquisite in its early autumn finery, and awaits you eagerly. And there are still some trees with their apple harvest on them. And its warm and mellow and kindly and altogether beautiful. Welcome back whenever you come and may the ghost of my happiness haunt you just a little in the future.

There was a silence when I finished reading, and a curious expression on Louis's face. He passed a copy of yesterday's London *Times* to me and pointed to a bold headline. I read—

CAR'S CRASH OVER EMBANKMENT. MARCHESA MALACRIDA KILLED

The Marchesa Malacrida was killed yesterday when her car which she was driving, skidded, crashed through a fence, and plunged down a forty-foot bank on the hill just above Henley bridge. The groundsman of a near-by cricket ground saw the car turn over as it fell down the bank. He ran to the scene and found the Marchesa a few yards from the wrecked car. She was dead. The road at the bottom of the bank was littered with suitcases and hatboxes. The car was going up the hill when it mounted the path at the side of the road, tore through the fencing and fell down onto a lower road. A spaniel which was in the car, ran away when the crash occurred, and was found later, terrified but uninjured. The Marchesa, who was thirty-five, a niece of the late Annie, Lady Cowdray, was on her way back to London after a stay at Pilgrim Cottage, the property of Mr. Cecil Roberts, the author.

It was now October 5. That night I could not sleep. The last sentence in Nadja's letter rang in my head. In retrospect it seemed almost a vale—"May the ghost of my happiness haunt you just a little in the future."

The next morning I decided to hurry home but learned over the telephone that Nadja would be buried that noon in the little hillside cemetery whose cypresses were visible from my cottage. My housekeeper, Ethel, had been the last to speak to the Marchesa. She drove off down the lane in her large, open Isotta-Fraschini car, waving goodbye, Amy, her spaniel, at her side, the luggage behind. Within five minutes she was dead. How? The coroner could find no answer. She was a skilled motorist. No mechanical defect was found in the automobile. Had an insect stung her, impairing her sight momentarily, had the spaniel in some way distracted her? The mystery was never solved.

IV

It was a heavenly October morning with gold tints in the woods around the cottage when I reached home. I went at once across the road to her grave piled with flowers. A few days later Peter Malacrida came. He told me of a conversation with Nadja. One day as they were crossing the field from Greys Court they came to a crest of the hill where suddenly the cypresses of the cemetery below became visible. "I love this valley. I'd like to be buried there," said Nadja, lightly. Too soon her wish had been fulfilled.

A few weeks later Peter Malacrida brought me a bundle of letters that had passed between them. When separated they wrote to each other every day. In August, before coming to the cottage, they had both been touring separately on the Continent; Nadja with her parents, Peter with his. In all some forty letters were exchanged, sent from the different places they visited. I read them, and it occurred to me that, collected, they would make a fine memorial. So they were published in a volume I called *Finale*. Nadja's last letter to Peter had been written on August 23, from Arras, just before they were united in Pilgrim Cottage. "Oh dear, dear lover of mine, this separation has taught me a lot of things. Don't let us ever, not even for a passing moment, get on each other's nerves again. Real love is too precious to be wasted. In a few hours, my beloved, and until my last breath, yours, and only yours, Nadja."

V

In Paris a telegram had awaited me. It was from Mrs. Fleming. She had bought Greys Court for £11,000. She restored it thoroughly. The next year, when the work had been completed, she took me over the house before lunch and then showed me another restoration. She had splendidly converted the barn and stables into a separate establishment, with a large studio, specially for her son Peter, of whose growing fame as a writer she was very proud. I remarked how pleased he must be. She stood still and looked at me, then said, controlling her voice, "Pleased? Pleased? It's all been for nothing! He'll never come here now. He's just married Celia Johnson, the actress." There was nothing I could say. We returned to the house.

After a few years she tired of the loneliness of Greys Court and sold it.

VI

Within a week of my return to Pilgrim Cottage there came ominous news from Marseilles. King Alexander of Yugoslavia was assassinated while driving in an open carriage together with M. Barthou, the French Foreign Minister, who had gone to receive him. The King's son Peter, aged eleven, at a preparatory school in England, succeeded to the throne, under a Regent. One day I was to play a singular role in the life of this boy-king, who actually reigned for only a month. He was destined to live an impoverished, unhappy life until he died in California, aged forty-seven. The story of my part in his history is for a later time, adding to the fantastic events that have encompassed my life. Unconsciously, I was to be the cause of his marriage.

I was now hard at work on a second country book to follow *Gone Rustic* which, published in the spring, had dealt with my life in Pilgrim Cottage. Its successor, *Gone Rambling*, went farther afield, covering much local history and legend, including the famous trial of poor Miss Blandy of Henley who, in the eighteenth century, poisoned her father on behalf of an aristocratic rapscallion lover. Condemned, she was publicly hanged in Oxford. Her last words, as she ascended the ladder were, "Gentlemen, do not hang me high for the sake of decency." Meanwhile, I succeeded Harold Nicolson as the 'star' critic of the *Daily Telegraph*. He had left for the U.S.A. commissioned to write the Life of Dwight Morrow, one-time U.S. ambassador to Mexico. A rich man, he was the father-in-law of Charles Lindbergh, the youthful airman who had flown the Atlantic, solo, in 1927. Now a national hero, Lindbergh had suffered the tragedy of having his infant son kidnapped and murdered. My weekly book review for the *Daily Telegraph* covered two columns, for which I received £15 as against Nicolson's £20. I wrote it with zest.

I seemed on the top of the world with *Gone Rustic* running neck and neck with *The Guests Arrive*, both already in a fifth printing, but I suppressed any feelings of elation. Literary success is a horse that can throw one at any moment. About this time my mind was increasingly troubled by the knowledge that we were sliding into a war of Germany's making. Considering all the reports of its rapidly growing army, based on the secret plan of Von Seeckt, creator of the Reichswehr, and of the enormous growth of its air-arm, I could not understand how so many highly placed politicians at home remained contemptuous of this blatant revival of German military might, which had engulfed the world in the First World War. "Why do you English think we are preparing for war? We are only restoring our self-respect," said one of the aides at the German Embassy, whom I met at lunch one day. "We shall help to stabilise Europe. We've just signed a ten-year Non-Aggression Pact with Poland, despite the Corridor." Within six years Germany had begun the Second World War by massacring Poland. The United States, alarmed by secret reports from inside Germany, warned the British Government of the grave menace of her rapidly growing air-arm. It took as little notice of this as of Churchill's repeated warnings. Some of my friends began to think I was a little mental on the subject. It certainly clouded my life in these days of my expanding success.

Christmas came and I had my usual house party. Somehow we housed six persons. To attend my party Louis sat up all night on the Channel boat in order to arrive for breakfast. He was happy with his work in the Anglo-Persian Oil office in Paris. "But, *mon cher*, though my head's there, my heart's here." He brought me that Christmas the mechanical singing bird.

At the end of 1934 I made my usual summary. I had published *Gone Rustic* and *The Guests Arrive*. To these I would now add *Gone Rambling*, finished in these last days of December. In addition there had been the *Sphere* and *Daily Telegraph* book reviews. All told, I had written half a million words, omitting fifty thousand I must have erased. In addition there had been over a dozen lectures and the Hellenic cruise. Everything interested me. When a magazine asked me, for a symposium, what I thought was the best kind of life, I replied, "To be in a continuous state of intellectual excitement." I have not changed that opinion in sixty years. Everything interested me. My friends were astonished that I read *The Economist* as well as the *Classical Quarterly*. I also read *The Times*, with growing irritation. It had an editor, Geoffrey Dawson, a Baldwinite and an appeaser, who saw no danger in Germany and admired Hitler.

One morning in December I received a letter that gave me pleasure. It was from young Lord Birkenhead. "I have just read *The Guests Arrive* and want to tell you how excellent I thought it was. I haven't enjoyed a novel so much for a long time. I hope you are well and that we shall meet again soon. Why not come as my guest at The Odd Volumes ?" I had read for Birkenhead the proofs of the *Life* of his father. It revealed a gift that would be fulfilled in future years. Writing was in the blood. His sister, Lady Eleanor Smith in her day won considerable success as a novelist.

At each year's end it had amused me to look at myself as a private company, running a literary business, with a little more candour than that exhibited by many company chairmen, who annually advertise their achievements in the Press, always announcing an increase in profits. In the past year my income was £4,300, my expenditure, which covered gifts, cottage, a *pied-à-terre* in London, a car, service, travel, came to £1,800. The surplus went into the 'Author's Contingency Fund' against the day when a writer's income shrinks, from lessened industry, invention, loss of vogue, or the incalculable mutability of life. At the end of his working days an author receives no pension from his publisher. I read with envy how one director who, when his company wished to get rid of him, received a tax-free compensation of £33,000, and of another who was given 'a golden handshake' of £100,000. No publisher would do that for an author in his decline, whatever the company profits.

On the last evening of December I heard the bells of Henley church begin to ring in the New Year of 1935, as I had heard them ring in the year 1934. This time I was alone. I went out into the garden. The air was sharp, the heavens cloudy. I walked round the cottage on the springy turf in the intermittent moonlight. As the bells rang distantly I could not refrain from a retrospect of the dead year. It had brought me much success. At forty-two I seemed established but this past year had been darkened by tragedy. I grieved for two friends, one, a lad of twenty, one, beautiful Nadja Malacrida, thirty-five; no more to walk in this garden they had known.

CHAPTER SEVEN

Neighbours and Visitors

I

In the New Year, 1935, I took a bold step and signed an agreement for four new novels. On the day that I signed the new contract I dined with Gilbert Frankau, then a fashionable novelist. Just after leaving Eton he had written the best satirical long poem since Byron, *One of Us*. The son of a Jewish diamond merchant, he was a prolific writer and *bon vivant*. He lived in a slice of a house in Basil Street, Knightsbridge, and exuded bonhomie. He was now, aged fifty, living with his third wife, Susan, as pretty and almost as young as his daughter Pamela, by his first wife. He kept a good table. Once a week he hunted in Leicestershire. That evening he gave me a copy of his new novel, *Three Englishmen*, which was having a considerable success. He told me he always made and spent £4,000 a year. There were two other guests and we had a delightful evening.

His daughter Pamela aspired to be a novelist. Attractive, but with a strong face and tense in manner, she said to me, "All that really matters is being in love and that's a form of torture." She experienced this, poor girl. She had a frantic love affair with Humbert Wolfe, then married, which ended disastrously. Returning with her on the same liner from America in 1947 she told me that she had married an American army officer, by whom she had a baby that died and was buried in California. In 1949 she struck success with the novel she had described to me, *The Willow Cabin*. She became a public figure, entered politics and then died, at fifty-two after a long and painful illness, endured with great courage. Shortly before the end she wrote a farewell message. "I give praise to Almighty God for the gift of life. I thank my lovers, my friends, my acquaintances and my benefactors for helping to make it such a beautiful adventure." It was rewarding to have known her.

Frankau told me he could never write his autobiography having two wives living, and his best reminiscences would not be printable. He gave us a sample that evening. When a rabbi wanted to circumcise him his father refused to let him be 'mutilated'. One day in a Saigon night-club a German colonel called him a dirty Jew. Frankau bet the German £5 that he was not a Jew. Getting one of the girls to be a stakeholder, he retired behind a screen with her. In a few moments she popped her head over the screen and shouted, "Colonel, you've lost. He's a Christian!"

The next weekend I spent at Yattendon Court, near Newbury, the guest of the ever-hospitable Iliffes. Tod, as he was affectionately called, had built himself a large mansion, in Tudor style, standing on an eminence overlooking the Berkshire Hills, with a park skilfully landscaped. The house always gave me great pleasure. Well-sited, it had space and dignity, with long terraces and fine vistas. In the grounds my host, a first-class tennis player, a President of the Lawn Tennis Association, had built a large, covered tennis court with a spectators' gallery and an indoor, heated swimming pool. I should not have been surprised to find a theatre, for this many-gifted man was interested in the drama. For many years he was chairman of the trustees of the Shakespeare Memorial Theatre, and a leading figure at the Stratford-on-Avon Birthday Festival. It was a miracle that he found time to do so much, so calmly. He managed the large family publishing business, was a joint proprietor of the *Daily Telegraph*, a director of Allied Newspapers, of the Amalgamated Press, and two insurance companies. He was also President of the Association of British Chambers of Commerce. With all this he never showed the slightest sense of pressure. He was now fifty-seven years of age, most happily married to his boyhood love, Charlotte, with two sons and a daughter. I had first met him in 1917 when we were both serving in the Ministry of Munitions under Winston Churchill. We began there a cherished friendship that was to last forty-three years until his death in 1960, aged eighty-three. His wife, Charlotte, was modest to a point of self-effacement. A good musician, Tod had built for her, hidden behind the oak panelling of the large hall, an organ that she had to be induced to play if anyone was around. Tod farmed many acres, a serious enterprise, and had his model estate office in the beautiful village of Yattendon, where for many years Robert Bridges, the Poet Laureate, had made his home.

Such was the mansion, Yattendon Court, to which I was a frequent visitor down the years. In the Thirties, living in the vicinity at Pilgrim Cottage, I was often bidden over, and this constant hospitality included my guests. Tod was a tall, good-looking man with tousled greyish hair, and eyes that had a twinkle. His manner was so easy and genial that it was difficult to believe he carried heavy and varied responsibilities.

It was the custom for guests to breakfast in their rooms and very often he came to mine and talked at length, confidentially. He had touched life in so many phases that his talk was always rewarding. Amused, paternal, he never patronised me. When I arrived on this January day of 1935, I found a house party of about a dozen persons. A fire blazed in the great hall which had a fine Vernet painting, a harbour scene. An open room off the hall had an oriel window over-looking the terrace, the valley, the distant rising hill-side. If the party was small, we lunched or took tea there. Somehow it always seemed flooded with light and gaiety. On arriving I found my host, now Lord Iliffe, had a first touch of gout. He said it was a punishment for not drinking a gallon of water a day. Perhaps the cause was tension. He had just settled a newspaper war with Lord Rothermere.

After dinner, in the library, I got involved in a long discussion on the European situation. I said that if we did not get rid of Baldwin and Ramsay MacDonald they would bring us to disaster with their *laissez-faire* over defence. My host smiled, amused by my intensity. "Now—now, you intellectuals are all so gloomy about the future, especially about Germany," he said. A tall, dark, very handsome young man agreed with him. He assured me that the country was in safe hands. Mr. Baldwin was very alert, very capable. I discovered that my fellow-guest was Captain Alec Cunningham-Reid, a political careerist, smooth, polished. He had married the grand-daughter of the Jewish financier, Sir Ernest Cassel, Edward VII's friend. She had brought with her a dot of a million pounds. Her sister had married Lord Louis Mountbatten.

Cunningham-Reid, with a good war record (Royal Flying Corps, Dispatches, D.F.C.) a Parliamentary Private Secretary, a good shot, tennis player and skier, might well be considered Cabinet material in a Conservative Government. He did not think Germany was aggressive. Hitler had brought a healthy discipline to his country. We needed discipline too. By Monday morning he must have collected a few facts about me. Before leaving he was very affable. "I assure you you are quite wrong about Baldwin. We are not asleep!" he said. He asked for my address. Perhaps I would come to lunch one day? Did I know Baldwin? Well, he would arrange to have me meet him.

I admired his charming manner, quick mind, sartorial elegance. He drove away with his wife in a grey Rolls-Royce, chauffeur and maid sitting in the back. I followed in my little Austin Seven. They seemed an enviable pair. But fate plays tricks with us. He did not reach Cabinet rank. There was an unpleasant divorce case. He married again quickly and did not improve his status with a second divorce.

On returning home I found a visiting card awaiting me. It bore the name of Mrs. Robert Fleming. I much regretted missing her for I knew of her as a remarkable character who lived in the large family mansion, Joyce Grove, up at Nettlebed. Before I could return the call I saw, one afternoon, a large car draw up at my gate. By now I was getting used to 'cottage fans'. One never knew what sort of a surprise was in store. But winter callers were rarer than those the summer season brought from all parts of the globe. Ethel was about to serve tea when a chauffeur came down the path and enquired if I was in. He said his mistress, Mrs. Fleming, was in the car. I went out at once and found there a trim old lady, rather beautiful and very alert. I invited her in to tea and thus started a friendship that lasted until her death. She was a widow, her husband, Robert Fleming, having died, aged eighty-seven. He had had a remarkable career. Born in Dundee in 1845, the son of humble parents, he left school at fourteen and was employed as a clerk by a firm of Dundee jute merchants. Wishing to expand their interests they sent young Fleming, aged twenty-five, to the U.S.A. to look for opportunities in making investments. Shrewd, he recommended investing in railways, then a rapidly expanding business. His firm became one of the first subscribers to the new Union Pacific Railroad. In 1873 Fleming founded in Dundee the Scottish Investment Trust. He was then only twenty-eight years of age and might be regarded as the initiator of the investment trust. When he died in 1932, a very successful merchant banker, he left his

Lucien and Bevis Reid

Lucien, my gondolier, by the
Rialto, Venice

Richard Rumbold

Lucien,
aged
twenty-two

widow three million pounds, a town house in Grosvenor Square, a large shoot in Scotland, and Joyce Grove, the roomy country mansion which he had built at Nettlebed amid the Chiltern Woods. It was his sprightly little widow, looking very young for her eighty-four years, who had now called on me. "I read and love your books and want to know you as a neighbour," she said. She told me that that morning she had played eighteen holes on the Huntercombe Golf Course near us! I was not therefore astonished when I learned, later, that on her seventieth birthday she had stalked and bagged two stags in the family 100,000-acre deer forest in Argyllshire.

Mrs. Fleming was the mother of two sons, and two daughters. One son, Valentine, had had a remarkable career. He had rowed in the Eton Eight, been a Member of Parliament and by his marriage with the beautiful Miss Evelyn St. Croix Rose had four sons, two of whom, Peter and Ian, were to win fame as authors. Their father did not live to see this. Brilliant, handsome, he was killed in the First World War, aged thirty-five. Winston Churchill, who had been a guest at his shooting parties, wrote an obituary notice for *The Times*. His son, Ian, framed and hung the holograph tribute in his bedroom. Old Mrs. Fleming alluded with pride to her other grandson, Peter, who had published a book *Brazilian Adventure* and whose articles from the Far East, on his travels there, were appearing in *The Times*. She was surprised when I told her that I had met her grandson Ian in Kitzbühel in 1928, and also her daughter-in-law on a Greek cruise last summer. I said nothing about my connection with the Greys Court purchase. Mothers-in-law often do not appreciate the enterprises of their daughters-in-law.

I was soon to learn what a hospitable heart Mrs. Fleming possessed. She loved to entertain and the long table in the dining-room at Joyce Grove was often filled with guests of all ages. It was still an era of servants and generous living. Whenever I had guests at Pilgrim Cottage of some achievement and fame she always gave them a warm welcome. Her zest for life was boundless.

II

Throughout January I had worried over the theme of my next novel. Day and night, I turned over a story in my mind. I had been deeply impressed with that astonishing volcanic island of Santorin, which we had visited on our Hellenic cruise. I read up its history and studied its archaeology. I became obsessed with Santorin. My house-keeper complained that I did not know what she had asked me or what I was eating. I motored into Oxford and ransacked the Bodleian for information. I was restrained only by my *Daily Telegraph* reviews from returning, in the depth of winter, to the island, where I had spent only eight hours the previous August. And then fate dealt me a good card.

One day I went to lunch at Wadham College, Oxford. There was a party of seven. One of them was an old Frenchman visiting Oxford for a conference. What kind of a conference? An archaeological con-ference. He was a retired professor. Had he ever dug? Oh yes, with the French mission at Mycenae, Greece. Had he ever heard of Santorin? *Mais oui!* When he was a student he had excavated there with a mission. I could hardly contain my excitement. He promised to send me some literature on Santorin. The good professor sent me two volumes, one of them, *Mission scientifique à l'île Santorin*. When they arrived I read them in a fever of excitement from 6 p.m. to 4 a.m. They gave me all the information I wanted. Four days later I began *Volcano* and finished it in ten weeks.

The script had just come back from the typist when I received a request from the editor of the *Daily Mirror* for a serial. I sent him *Volcano*. He took it at once, running it through July. But he did not like my title and changed it to *Felicity Island*. I kept *Volcano* for the book. It proved to be Felicity Island in every sense and the story has had some thirty-seven years of life, and still marches on.

My work on *Volcano* was interrupted by two public engagements. Young Christina Foyle had made a great success of her literary lunches held at the Grosvenor House Hotel. She produced celebrities for an audience of three or four hundred and these lunches, each month, were always interesting and lively. For the third time I took the chair for her, a function I was to repeat often during the next thirty-five years. My other engagement was at the Metropole Hotel. My friend Holbrook Jackson was a gifted man of letters who wrote *The Eighteen-Nineties*. His chef-d'œuvre was the stupendous *Anatomy of Bibliography*. He had edited *T.P.s Weekly* and *The New Age* and was the founder and editor of *To-Day*, gathering about him the younger generation, who owed much to his encouragement. He very ably combined letters with business. He was the Editorial Director of The National Trade Press, and a renowned typographer. He did not receive the recognition that was due to him. He never penetrated the inner clique that organises literary reputations. He was thought to be offensively competent.

Jackson asked me to be a speaker at the annual banquet of the National Furnishing Trades Association, a gathering of some three hundred influential businessmen, dour and practical. It was a very different audience from that of the literary societies I usually addressed but I enjoyed variety. I was well aware that probably not one of them had ever heard of me or read a line I had written. Jackson asked me to reply to the toast of 'The Year 1935', and speak on American affairs, of which I had special experience. I agreed to do this, but I scrapped my intended speech, irritated by the complacency and political obtuseness of a previous speaker, a Parliamentary Under-Secretary, who predicted a rosy and prosperous future in phrases of the utmost banality. I proceeded to make an attack on the Government and Baldwin's evasiveness in face of the growing Nazi menace. It took the audience by surprise, as also my chairman, Holbrook Jackson. On leaving he said, "My God, you've shattered us! They've gone home almost paralysed—and it was supposed to be a convivial gathering! Where did you get all those facts? I can see ruins all around me!"*

A few days before a weekend at Munstead House, Eric Gillett gave me lunch at the Ivy Restaurant. It was then a fashionable rendezvous of writers, painters and actors. I saw there Noël Coward, Ivor Novello, as charming as he was handsome, John Betjeman, and the Freybergs with their sons, Martin and Guy McLaren and young Paul. Again at the Munstead house party I enjoyed the flawless hospitality of Lady Jekyll.

In the first week of March the Nazi menace grew. The Saar went back to Germany. Nine days later Hitler repudiated the disarmament

---

* When, eleven years later, I referred to this occasion in my book *And So To America*, Holbrook Jackson wrote to me, "I was pleased to see the reference to the great speech you gave at the Metropole Hotel in 1935 when you forecasted so many things which then seemed incredible. Those who heard you still talk about it."

clauses of the Versailles Treaty. It was an empty formality. He had ignored them for five years. Then, defiant, he announced conscription and the formation of the Luftwaffe. Alarmed at last, Britain, France and Italy met at Stresa to establish a common front. It was a piece of cynicism on the part of Italy. She was covertly preparing for her Abyssinian adventure.

At the end of the month James Hilton and his wife were my week-end guests. I had singled out his first novel *Catherine Herself*, published in 1930, when he was twenty-one, and we had become warm friends. He had followed this with three excellent novels, and recognition came in 1933 with his fifth novel, *Lost Horizon*, which was awarded the Hawthornden Prize. Despite good notices it had a disappointing sale. Then, suddenly, fame and fortune came next year in one overwhelming wave, with *Goodbye, Mr. Chips*. Fame is often a haphazard thing. Many just miss it. It is rarely won by mere effort or merit. It often springs from a curious sequence of events that we call luck. Hilton had written *Goodbye, Mr. Chips*, he told me, in four foggy November days. My publishers, owners of the *British Weekly*, wanted a story for their Christmas issue. A member of the firm, Leonard Cutts, a neighbour of Hilton, suggested he should write one for them, three thousand words in length. The tempting price offered was £15. When Hilton delivered the story Hodders were at first dismayed. It was not a Christmas story but a school one, and it was eighteen thousand words long! The story was so good, however, that rather than let it go they decided to print it as an inset of the paper. So it appeared on December 7, 1933. It was liked by readers but made no stir. Like its predecessor, *Lost Horizon*, it contained a seed of immortality, for these two novels gave birth to two names that have passed into the English language, Shangri-La and Mr. Chips. When President Roosevelt wished to keep secret the bases from which American bombers flew to Japan, he placed them in 'Shangri-La'.

A little disappointed by the reception of the story, but with unbounded faith in it, the publishers decided to offer it to Ellery Sedgwick, the American editor of the renowned *Atlantic Monthly*. Again, though Sedgwick admired it, the story was of an awkward length, moreover, it infringed an editorial rule, never to publish anything that had appeared elsewhere. So it was almost rejected, but on consideration it seemed too good a story to be lost. It appeared therefore in the June, 1934 issue.

And now the imp of luck played a card. In the U.S.A. Alexander Woollcott, the boisterous radio broadcaster, went on the air and told his vast audience that he had just read a story, a masterpiece, as good as anything written by de Maupassant. The sales of the *Atlantic Monthly* soared and it was decided to issue the story in book form. It had a tremendous reception. Hodder and Stoughton followed with an English edition in October, 1934. The American success was repeated. James Hilton was made, aged twenty-five. On the March day in 1935 when he and his wife came to stay with me the book had already brought him in £30,000. There was a large sum to follow for the film rights. He had written five novels in four years and now with a story that took four days to write he had won world fame and a fortune. It was partly autobiographical. His father was a retired schoolmaster and Mr. Chips was an amalgam of Hilton's father, of his classical master at Leys School, Cambridge, and of himself.

For this first visit of James and his wife to my cottage I gave a tea-party, inviting my neighbours, the Marquise d'Hautpoul, Lord and Lady Rathcreedan, Mrs. Robert Fleming and others. The next day Mrs. Fleming gave for them one of her large lunches at Joyce Grove. Modest, my 'lion' was a great success. On their return home I received a letter of thanks—"After our really delightful weekend there is no sincerer tribute that I can pay to it than to tell you that today I have written over 7,000 words of a new novel! I hope you have beaten this record. It just shows what Oxfordshire air will do, plus County visiting. We both of us had a good time." We had had long talks walking round the garden on financial as well as literary subjects. He was now beginning to have considerable money to invest and tantalising offers were coming in from America. He felt he should visit the U.S.A. "Go, and return quickly or it will destroy you," I said. "It's no atmosphere for Mr. Chips in real life." My words were to prove tragically true.

Early in June I went to Liverpool to propose the toast of 'The Immortal Memory' at the annual convention of the Dickens Fellowship. It resulted in my reading the Lesson next day in Liverpool Cathedral, on the invitation of the Dean. In 1916 I had watched that cathedral growing, walking to and from my newspaper office, never thinking that one day I should occupy its pulpit. Meanwhile the political atmosphere grew heavier. Baldwin formed a new Government, with Samuel Hoare as Foreign Secretary, Eden being sent to Geneva to organise the League against Mussolini's increasing threat to Abyssinia. In forming his Cabinet Baldwin deliberately ignored Churchill.

After the Liverpool visit I was the weekend guest, with Tony Allingham, of Evan Morgan, now Viscount Tredegar, at Tredegar House. We motored there on a glorious June day via the Wye Valley and Tintern Abbey. Tredegar was an impressive Inigo Jones house. It stood behind a pair of magnificent iron gates, but one went in by a different entrance. When I asked Evan who came in by the front gates he replied—"Only the true heir to the throne of England, the Crown Prince Rupprecht of Bavaria, who has Stuart blood. When he visited us we opened the ceremonial gates. When King Edward VII came here he asked why the front gates were not opened for him. My father told him the reason. The King just grunted. He may, of course, have thought the Tredegars a little mad!"*

Tredegar was crammed with pictures, tapestries, statues, silver and, most valuable of all, servants. Tony and I had beautiful rooms reached by a fine Grinling Gibbons staircase. We were two of fourteen guests. Among these were Viscount and Viscountess Massereene and Ferrard. She was a famous beauty. Their son, John, also there, was a good-looking, very tall youth. Other guests were Princess Hohenlohe, Lady Victoria Haig, the Field-Marshal's daughter, Mrs. Guinness, Olga Lynn, and H. A. Vachell the novelist. As a boy I had wept over his Harrow School novel, *The Hill*. He had also been successful in the theatre. He lived in a beautiful manor house at Widcombe near Bath that had in its forecourt a fountain by Sansovino. He was a connoisseur. Conversation kept us up until 2 a.m., the first night, the subject being Renaissance bronzes, on which Evan was also well-informed.

On the Sunday afternoon we were taken to the zoo in the grounds, fulfilling our host's passion for animals and birds. There was an aviary of rare birds, ibis, cranes, storks, toucans, parrots, pelicans and vultures. In the enclosure by the lake there was a boxing kangaroo.

* See also *The Bright Twenties*, Ch. 4, IV.

Evan invited us to take it on, but no one ventured, rumour saying that a former guest had been carried out on a stretcher! The agent told me that it cost £3,000 a year to feed these creatures.

That morning while our host had conducted some of his guests to church in Newport, I wandered in the park. At the gates I encountered an unemployed miner. He told me he had no work and could not feed his wife and four children. There were 20,000 miners out of work at Newport. I don't think he was exaggerating. Much of the Tredegar wealth came from a levy of sixpence on every truck of coal that passed on a railway line running across the estate. Despite this Evan, when standing for Parliament, had announced he was in favour of the abolition of coal royalties. I gave the miner something, he had not begged. His story depressed me all day.

Evan returned from a church parade at Newport where, as an honorary colonel, he had reviewed the Glamorganshire Yeomanry. He brought back with him the Roman Catholic Bishop, with two attendant priests. There were twenty-four guests for lunch at the long table. The silver was magnificent. Vachell said the Paul Lamerie vase in front of me was priceless. The pats of butter bore the Tredegar coronet. It seemed all out of proportion to me, a glasshouse of pleasure in which most of the guests twittered like budgerigars, all feathery gossip. This was the stuff of the French Revolution, I thought. Our Revolution, in the next thirty years, was to be as ruthless, though bloodless.

Evan, gay, attentive to every detail, was a perfect host, assisted by an excellent secretary-hostess and an agent. We departed on Monday morning with bouquets of flowers in our cars. When we arrived back at Pinkneys Court, the Allingham home, we found the family packed up and ready to leave. They had sold their house. But Mummy, Dad, Ann, Pat and Tony were in no way tearful. They had bought a smaller house near by.

The next day I was the guest speaker of the Gryphon Club at Trinity College, Oxford. It was one of those small clubs that undergraduates delight in. Our young host entertained us in his rooms, delightfully grave, and nervous. The next day I left for Durham to speak at an Education Conference. I was home for Henley Regatta. That week I entertained Lovat Dickson and his wife. He was the publisher of von Rintelen's *The Dark Invader*. Other guests were the

Allinghams and Canon Mortlock. On Saturday there were sixteen for tea in the garden. The weather was halcyon. I apologised to Ethel. "Oh, it's lovely! Let them all come," she exclaimed. One of my guests sounded an ominous note amid all this gaiety. He was an army captain just back from Abyssinia. He said the Italians would insist on war. They had everything ready. Djibouti was crammed with munitions.

III

On August 1 I again welcomed James Hilton and his wife. I was leaving for Salzburg and had lent them my cottage. I suppressed a memory evoked by their coming. It was almost a year ago that I had lent it to the Malacridas.

After a few days in Salzburg I left with Timmy and Tony on a brief tour of the Dolomites, which gave us two days in Venice before returning. There was a purpose in my Venetian visit. Lucien's parents were concerned about his schooling. He was now fourteen, attending the Liceo Marco Polo in Venice. It offered no curriculum for a future life in England. I would gladly have adopted him but he had devoted parents. We felt that his future called for an English schooling. The family had only an artist's frail, uncertain income. I had discussed Lucien's future with my friend Norman Fuller, who told me that after four years at a public school he could place him with the Anglo-Persian Oil Company, where he would have a promising career. Always generous, he offered a contribution towards the school fees. I therefore went ahead and during my brief call in Venice made a proposition. I would give Lucien four years at an English school and undertake to send him home twice a year, at Christmas and in the summer, so that the family ties should not be broken. His parents accepted my offer. Lucien was elated at the thought of an English school, the only shadow being the separation from his sister. They had grown up together, inseparable in all things. This achieved, I left Venice, happy in my mind. It was agreed that Lucien should come to me in mid-September.

Back in England I found I had overlooked one thing. I had not realised that a school would not accept a boy who had been educated with a foreign curriculum. After two weeks, in desperation, I appealed to the Provost of Eton, who had entertained me when I had lectured there. But Eton had a tremendous waiting list. The Provost did help, however. He was one of the Governors of the Imperial Service College across the river. It was Rudyard Kipling's old school and had figured in his *Stalky & Co.* He spoke with the headmaster and it was arranged for Lucien to enter the next week. I came away with a long list of things a boy needs at school. We spent a hectic day shopping in London. Then, while Lucien blissfully slept, Ethel and I sat up until a late hour stamping towels, underwear, shirts, collars, etc., with his initials and number.

On my return from Austria I had found awaiting me an American edition of *Goodbye Mr. Chips.* In it was written—"To Cecil from James Hilton after a lovely time at Pilgrim Cottage where the idea came for a new book." I thanked him. He replied:

> We really had a wonderful time at the cottage and my only regret was that we couldn't get away for a longer spell. Even as it was, the change was delightful and really recuperating, and as we had a car we were able to tour round a bit and see the countryside. We also had a lively time talking politics at the Golden Ball. And, as you can imagine, we were wonderfully looked after by Ethel. I seem likely to have a busy autumn, though not yet quite fixed as to dates. I am so very glad you liked the limited edition of *Mr. Chips,* which has been greedily snapped up by American collectors and now stands at a premium. I like to think of it in such good company as it will be on the shelves of Pilgrim Cottage.

That autumn he left for Hollywood on a scenario contract.

When I went to sign copies of my novel my publishers had cheering news. It had had a fifteen thousand subscription before publication. *Pilgrim Cottage* was in its eighth printing, *The Guests Arrive,* its seventh, *Gone Rustic,* its sixth, *Gone Rambling,* its fourth. It all made me a little apprehensive, I felt something must go wrong soon.

Harold Nicolson was returning from the U.S.A. and would resume the *Daily Telegraph* reviewing for which I had been his locum-tenens. I decided to give myself a long rest as I was in the doctor's hands much of the time. There was nothing in my head for a new book. So I lazed, picked apples, mowed the lawn and happily pottered. All this surprised my old gardener who was used to seeing me at my desk for long hours. "Don't he get dizzy?" he had asked Ethel.

In mid-September Louis arrived from Paris for his annual holiday. I had an idea to build a small garden-house between the populars and to make a flat roof for sunbathing. We got busy at once, bought concrete and bricks and ordered a French window. We worked frantically, getting up at 7 a.m., and bricklaying until dusk. One October afternoon while I was up a ladder Louis came out of the house looking very grave. "I've just heard on the radio the Italians have marched into Abyssinia," he said.

So Mussolini had carried out his threat, defying everybody. On that morning, October 3, at 5 a.m., without any declaration of war, General de Bono's troops had crossed the Eritrea frontier. It was not a surprise to anyone. For months Mussolini had been sending munitions and troopships down through Suez.

Whipped up by Eden, the League invoked sanctions against Italy by fifty votes to one. The word *Sanzioni* became a rallying cry of the Italians. Ironically, it was Italy that had pressed for Abyssinia's admission to the League in 1923 when England had then opposed it on grounds of her tyranny and slavery. "Italy will meet sanctions with discipline, with pugnacity and sacrifice," Mussolini cried. On September 12 England had made a vain gesture. She moved H.M.S. *Hood* and *Renown* to Gibraltar. Mussolini laughed, with reason. He believed England was soft, recalled the Joad 'won't fight for King and country' resolution at Oxford in 1933, and the Peace Ballot. Why did not Britain, with her Fleet based on Alexandria, close the Suez Canal? It would have stopped Mussolini's aggression. "You've lost your guts. You won't do it," said a candid Italian friend. We did not do it.

The British Admiralty knew no such action was possible. The Commander-in-Chief of the Mediterranean Fleet, Admiral Fisher, had reported that it lacked the necessary ammunition and anti-aircraft to defend itself against the Italian Air Force, now one of the best equipped in the world. It possessed bombers, and single-wing fighters able to deliver torpedo attacks. We had no aircraft carriers to send to the Mediterranean, no fighters which could operate even from French bases, had they been available. The Admiralty knew that aircraft with torpedoes could sink a battleship in a few minutes. Malta was highly vulnerable. Our Mediterranean Fleet was weaker than the Italian. It had only half its strength in carriers and destroyers. The

British battleships in Alexandria were menaced by the Italian submarine and motorboat suicide squads, as I had pointed out earlier to Freyberg. Mussolini, knowing all this, safely went ahead.

On October 1, Baldwin, in a speech to the Peace Society at the Guildhall, had said, "I give you my word there will be no great armaments." Mussolini took him at his word. "Baldwin has an administration more disastrous than any in our history!" cried Churchill.

In December there emerged the Hoare-Laval proposal to give large slices of Abyssinia to Italy. England and France boiled over with indignation. Sir Samuel Hoare, Foreign Secretary, skating in Switzerland, fell and broke his nose. It seemed symbolic. He was driven to resign. Mussolini won his war and made the midget king of Italy an Emperor. Sanctions, half-heartedly applied, failed. Oil supplies to Italy had not been stopped.

The League had suffered a mortal blow. Nevertheless it soon added a wing to its headquarters and engaged more typists. We had emerged deeply discredited, earning the hatred of Italy and the contempt of Germany, whom she would soon embrace.

The day that Louis, coming into the garden, had brought me news of Italy's aggression was the first anniversary of the death of Nadja Malacrida. I had just corrected the proofs of her letters for the memorial volume, *Finale*. The next day, after lunching with Sir Philip Gibbs, Louis left for Paris, called-up for three weeks of extra military service. I motored home. It was an autumn day, the beech-woods all golden. The sunset faded from crimson to emerald. Down the Fairmile with its yellowing elms one saw the flag flying on the tower of Henley Church.* I went indoors to a log fire, tea and toast. I purposely did not turn on the light, and watched the fire flickering on the walls and beams. It lit my Van Dyck painting of Henrietta, wife of Charles I, giving a warmth to the dark beauty of the woman who had had such a disastrous influence on her handsome spouse. Looking at her, I reflected on the curious manner in which fate weaves its strands of history. Here she was, serene, gazing out into the very garden that King Charles had once crossed, following the path leading

* The parallel rows of magnificent elms that bordered the Fairmile were smitten with disease in 1954, and are no more. The four poplars at Pilgrim Cottage suffered a similar fate in 1970.

up through the beechwoods to reach Fawley Court. All that was nearly three hundred years ago and here was Queen Henrietta, in the flickering firelight, looking out on his path of escape.

The day closed in, the windows misted, silence engulfed me. I poked the fire. This was a good life despite the state of the world. Would the gathering storm wreck it all, I wondered.

IV

On October 24 something happened in U.S.A. that greatly perturbed me, though few in England realised its significance. The United States Congress passed the Neutrality Bill, sensitive to what was building up in Europe. It had seen China attacked by Japan in 1931. It now watched the Italian aggression in Abyssinia and the Nazi domination of Germany. There was an urgent sense that it must not be drawn again into another European war. It was determined to stop any profitable business of its citizens with belligerents. The new Bill made it illegal to export arms, munitions and articles of war from U.S.A. to a belligerent. It prohibited American citizens sailing in any vessel of a country at war. Later, the Bill went further. It prohibited all loans or credit to belligerents, and ruled that all exports bought by them must be paid for in dollars and carried in the buyers' own ships. America was still smarting from the unpaid loans of her allies in the First World War. She was determined not to be caught again. We had ceased our debt payments to U.S.A., a miserable default. Now the chicken came home to roost. There was a notable prohibition added to the Bill. It was forbidden for any belligerent country to send paid agents to conduct propaganda. America was raising its walls of isolation as high as possible. Not unreasonably. 'Uncle Shylock', as we had called him, once bitten was now twice cautious.

It was a wet November. All through these days I was much alone. A man with a house in the country discovers that his visitors are apt to be barometrical. The weather is hot—"We haven't seen you for quite a time. Could we come down for lunch?" The weather settled, the proposal might be for a weekend. But with a series of rainy days one was left alone. I was adaptable to either state. Now, the days closing in early, I was not interrupted in my work. It was often my winter habit to write in bed. My housekeeper brought up my breakfast. I stayed there, cosy, happy and industrious until noon, my desk the lid of a tea chest.

One evening, at the end of November, the telephone rang. It was my friend Fuller calling from Paris. Louis had had a lung haemorrhage and lay ill in a clinic. During his military service, sleeping out, he had contracted a chill. I was to await further news. It came two days later. The doctors reported that it was a case of rapid consumption. There was faint hope. It seemed impossible to believe that this could happen to someone so robust. Forty-eight hours later another call from Paris informed me that he was dangerously ill. I left for Paris immediately and hurried to the clinic with Fuller. Surprisingly, Louis looked almost handsome with his bright eyes and flushed cheeks. But the specialist shook his head. He gave him a month at most. "Get me out of here or I'll die," whispered Louis. Fuller and I discussed the matter with the doctor. We decided to rent a furnished flat, send for his mother from the Côte d'Or and let her nurse him until the end. We found a sunny apartment with a balcony, removed him by ambulance and installed him with his mother, a quiet little woman. Alas, I had to leave after Christmas for an American lecture tour, so I said goodbye to him now, thinking I should never see him again. "I won't die! I shall come to the cottage for Christmas," he said. "Of course!" I replied and somehow got out of the room.

I was happy about one thing; widowed mother and son were reunited. His attitude towards her had always troubled me. He had ignored her letters. It was very strange in one who had such a warm nature. Finally, I talked to him about it. I learned then that when he was a small boy his parents had closed their country home and left to run a business in Paris. They boarded Louis out with a farmer's family where he was harshly treated. He was there for seven years. When the Paris business failed, his parents returned home and collected him. Louis had conceived a hatred of them for this neglect. He soon left home and would not communicate with them. I insisted that he should write to his widowed mother. He had done so reluctantly. When I said goodbye to him in the Paris apartment the past seemed forgotten.

Two weeks later I was surprised by a letter from Louis. "I make hard fight with the microbe, who loses," he wrote. I saw him in his corduroy shorts and vest, soundly pounding the microbe in the corner of the ring. "I wish you Happy Christmas. I will think of you in front of the log fire." And since the cottage expected Louis, who helped to build the new fireplace inside the old one, and did a dozen kind things for the old house, I placed the winged chair he loved in front of the fire, and then telephoned to him in Paris. "Your chair's waiting at the fireside, the log's blazing, Ethel's brought in the coffee, and it's time you were here," I said. And Louis answered across the wintry Channel, "How nize! I can hear the log flapping, I think! Two lumps in the coffee, please, for the French boy who has been kept in bed."

My Christmas was a quiet one. Preparing for my departure for America, I had no house party. But I did not eat my Christmas dinner alone. Tony collected me to eat it with the gay Allinghams.

CHAPTER EIGHT

Florida Bound

I

In the first week of January, 1936, I sailed for New York, en route for Florida. My friends the Higbees had bought a winter home at Coconut Grove, a sub-tropical paradise south of Miami. It was embowered in palm trees, scarlet hibiscus, blue plumbago and crimson poinsettias. Red-tiled, white-walled, it stood on a corner of Leafy Way, well-named.

To cover the expenses of my journey, I had booked ten lectures, opening my tour in Florida. My boat, the *Empress of Australia*, sailed from Southampton, calling at Madeira en route to New York. The fare for this excellent passage of eleven days was £35, first-class, single cabin. On board I met Mr. Jack Waller and his wife. He was a highly successful impresario who had made a fortune with *No, No, Nanette* and other productions. A dapper little Jew, he always wore a gardenia in his lapel. He was very flattering about my *Spears Against Us*, now in its twelfth edition. Had I ever considered making a play out of it, he asked. They left the boat at Madeira where they were staying. He was so enthusiastic that when I went back to my ship, after tea with them at Reid's Hotel, I had promised to dramatise the book. The Duke of Sutherland also left the boat at Madeira. His duchess and her friend, dark-eyed Lady Abingdon, stayed on it. Throughout the voyage they kept themselves apart, sitting on deck in reversed steamer chairs so that perambulating passengers could not see their faces or get chatty. The evening before we arrived at New York we learned that King George V had died. It was bitterly cold as we went up the Hudson River. While we waited for the immigration officers, Lady Abingdon, accompanied by the Duchess wrapped in an astrakhan coat, mischievously smiled at me. "We've been reading

175

your autobiography, *Half Way*, on board, and comparing you with your text!" she said. "My dear ladies, if you hadn't been so snooty you might have found the author himself more interesting!" I replied. "Oh, forgive us," said Lady Abingdon. "We are the world's worst sailors and were too sick to talk to anyone." "We looked a dreadful pea-green," added the Duchess. We parted very friendly. I never saw the Duchess again but I was to see a great deal of beautiful Bettine Abingdon when, in 1940, she went to America to work for the British Refugees Society. She was then frequently my chairwoman.

I stayed one night only in New York and the next day took the Florida Express to Miami. Entering the dining-car that evening, I was delighted to encounter handsome Gene Tunney, ex-world heavyweight boxing champion. I had not seen him since I had guided him round Venice in 1929. He was now on his way to join his wife and family at Hobe Sound, north of Miami, where he had a winter home. After dinner we retired to his 'drawing-room' and talked until past midnight.

My host, Mr. Higbee, met me at Miami. There was sunshine, and an azure sky above the palm trees. It had not then been exploited and vulgarised and was one of the pleasantest winter resorts in America. My host had sad news. I was not going to their home. His wife was dying of cancer and they had taken a bungalow, as it was easier for nursing. I was to be boarded out near by with a friendly neighbour. My lodging was embowered in palm trees, with a large garden, pergola and swimming pool. The owners had lost their fortune in the Wall Street crash of 1929 and were now receiving paying guests. My hostess, I discovered, had an intimate knowledge of Florida, its fauna and flora. After a couple of weeks I became aware that I had rich material for a book. And so *Gone Sunwards* was born.

I breakfasted every morning in a screened sun-loggia, the blue pool shining, the scarlet flame-vine trailing over the pergola, the palm trees heavy with coconuts. It was here that I had the strange experience in this sub-tropical retreat of listening to the funeral service of King George V, on January 28, at 2 p.m., English time, in St. George's Chapel, Windsor. There was a two-minute silence while the coffin was lowered into the crypt. Beyond the loggia I was surprised to see a negro gardener standing with bowed head. When I spoke to him he said, to my great surprise, "We are all mourning for our good king." Our? When I remarked on this to my hostess she said, "Oh yes. My gardener's a Jamaican—all the Jamaicans are very proudly British!"

The circumstances in which I had heard the Windsor funeral service were so singular that I wrote an article which appeared in *The Times*. This resulted in a curious episode. The following summer, as usual, I was at Henley Regatta. One of the characters of Henley was Mrs. 'Cherry' Pitman. She was married to an Oxford 'rowing blue'. They entertained lavishly for the Regatta at their house on the river bank. Cherry's nickname came from her habit of filling the house with cherry blossoms at Eastertide. She was witty, pretty, and playfully flirtatious. Encountering her at Phyllis Court, I greeted her joyously. She walked right past me, head in air, without a word. Astonished, I went after her and asked what all this was about. "That terrible article of yours in *The Times*! There you were in Florida, breakfasting, while our king was being buried. Outrageous! Mourning and marmalade!" she cried, marching on. She was soon her old self, but ever afterwards we called her 'Mourning and marmalade'.

In Coconut Grove I spent much of my time at the Higbee bungalow down by the shore of Biscayne Bay. My tiny hostess knew she was doomed, something we all ignored. To entertain her I did a number of impersonations. My 'Queen Victoria' in a bonnet, and wrapped in a black shawl, entering in a wheel chair, gave her special delight. I built up quite a repertoire for her. "You really should have been on the stage!" she said. "I've never really been off it," I retorted, gaily, putting 'an antic disposition on'. I was moved by my host's tribute when he said, "You're our sunshine these dark days."

If not on the stage I was certainly on the local platforms. My agent had made four Florida bookings. One of these was at 'The Hundred Club'. It was a club limited to one hundred members, predominantly automobile millionaires of Detroit, wintering at Miami Beach. My engagement was at one of their dinners, atrociously prolonged, in the ball-room of a super-luxury hotel. Harvey Firestone presided. It was I a.m. when I was called on. The audience seemed moribund and had to be brought back to life. "At this late hour, inebriated as we all are—" I began. There was a moment of shock and then a roar of applause. I had their complete attention onwards.

The audience at Palm Beach, in the select Everglades Club, was wholly different. It was stiff with the addicts of luxurious living. Although it was 80° outside it took ten minutes to thaw that audience. I rather frightened them with what I thought was going to happen in the world. I was Cassandra in a palm-girt paradise, where diamonds were thicker than coconuts.

Meanwhile, I was busy collecting data for my Florida book. My landlady introduced me to an author steeped in local lore, Marjorie Stoneman Douglas, to whom I expressed a wish to see the wild life of the Everglades. This vast jungle-swamp in the heart of Florida had not yet been intersected with motor roads and made a fairground for tourists. The alligator, the crane, the ibis, a countless cohort of winged and web-footed creatures, thronged its jungle. Early dawn was the time to see this primitive life, so Marjorie collected me in darkness to motor me there. We saw the dawn come up blood-red, the sky ribboned with the flights of birds, the alligators sliding through the sinister mangrove swamps. It was a swift dawn with a sudden chorus of bird voices. For centuries the Everglades had been the haunt of the Seminole Indians whose encampments we passed, but an encroaching civilisation was destroying them. I am glad to have seen something that was doomed. A $600-million Disney World, near Orlando, now makes a new Blackpool of primitive Florida. The time came for me to leave my hosts. I was going to Orlando to stay again with the Phillips, and lecture at Winter Park, an odd name for a Florida oasis where winter never came. The parting from my hostess needed a lot of self-control. We knew we should never see each other again.

The Phillips home was as full of laughter, sunshine and birdsong as ever. We discussed the European situation. "Why don't you pull out while you can? I'll give you a house and an orange grove," said my host. "Europe's doomed. You can't stop that gangster Hitler, he'll join up with Mussolini and the Russians." I thanked him but well knew that I could not pull out—"in spite of all temptations he remained an Englishman."

In the middle of March I went north into blizzards. I spoke again at the Chicago Executives Club on 'The European Whirlpool'. They heard me, applauded vigorously, but I sensed a little reserve among some of my audience. Before I left my chairman said, "There's something you people should understand. America's not going into any war. No, sir! We've been fooled once. You must deal with your own mess over there." While in Chicago I had a new experience. I was the guest of the British Consul-General and his wife. They had a little son, Peter. They wanted to go to an evening ceremony but could not as they had been unable to find a 'baby-sitter'. I volunteered, greatly to their surprise. I undressed my charge, bathed him and tried to put him to bed, but here I failed. Peter was much too lively. Instead we had a grand romp. When my hosts returned they were astonished to find me on the floor and Peter on my back.

I fulfilled three speaking engagements in Chicago and then went on to Detroit where I had a large audience in the Cass Theatre. My subject was 'A Novelist's Workshop', but I contrived to turn it into a warning survey of what might happen in Europe soon. Henry Ford was there and solemnly shook my hand. "Well, boy," he said, slowly, "you're sure impressive but we ain't going into any whirlpool, life-saving. What's wrong with you folks over there? We employ twenty-five different nationalities and we all get on fine."

There had been a comic incident on this tour. When I went to Bryn Mawr, a large women's university situated in a sort of little Wales near Philadelphia, I was met by a hefty lass who insisted on carrying my 'grip'. She buttoned me down in the back of a convertbile Ford. There was deep snow on the ground. I was driven at a furious pace over mountain roads. When at last, somewhat scared and shaken up in the dark, my driver, releasing me, said merrily—"So you're still in. We 'lost' the last lecturer!" She ran up the steps with my bag. I was taken in hand by a staff member and shown to a study where I was to dress, and sleep that night after my lecture. It had evidently been turned over to me, for it was full of feminine things. But it was very warm, very cosy, and had a bathroom. I had to dress in tails and white-tie to dine in Hall with the Dame President and Faculty. Before dressing I took a bath. I was well-lathered when a door opened behind me and a girl walked in. There was a loud cry. I turned, to see her hastily disappearing through the door. It seems this was a communal bathroom. I had not slipped the bolt.

The dinner was very formal. I looked down the long hall and wondered where my unknown visitor sat and if she had communicated anything. In my opening remarks on the platform I said that this was my first visit to Bryn Mawr but I was not a complete stranger as one young lady had seen more of me than most people. There was an outburst from a group of girls and I knew that my adventure had been reported. The Dame President and most of the audience were quite mystified by this sudden outburst of merriment.

On March 27 I sailed home on the *Aquitania*, a lovely ship with its Tudor gallery. On board I found Lady Tredegar, Evan's wife, Lady Sackville of Knole, G. B. Stern, the novelist, Dolores del Rio the film star, and boyish Lord Carlow. We had a delightful crossing.

In the ship's library Lady Sackville had seen an English magazine which had a four-page illustrated article on Pilgrim Cottage. "That's my idea of happiness. Hundreds of rooms at Knole, and no servants. A nightmare!" she said. At Southampton Lord Sackville met his wife. They made me promise to visit them. And thus I came to know Knole, and loved its grey, vast beauty.

The fresh green loveliness of my cottage, the first snowdrops, the first swallows, the budding gold forsythia, the flowering chestnut-tree and apple blossom, a pink snowstorm! While I laboured on *Gone Sunwards*, the fruit of my Florida holiday, the renascent beauty of an English April enfolded my dwelling with flowers and birdsong. It all seemed more precious because of the discord in the outer world. Hitler had now marched into the Rhineland. France and England failed to take up the challenge. In May, Italy completed her conquest of Abyssinia. Thousands of bare-footed Ethiopian soldiers had been immobilised, the skin burnt off their legs by mustard gas. There was not a word of protest from the Pope or the King of Italy. The tiny king was promoted to Emperor. Haile Selassie had humiliated the spineless League of Nations by appearing before it, in protest. The deposed Emperor, a figure of great dignity, went into exile in Bath.

II

On the day of Ethiopia's surrender I went to Tredegar House for the weekend. As before, the company was large and festive. After all, Addis Ababa was a long way from Wales. "Poor little man. He's rather sweet, isn't he? But why did he take on the Italians?" asked a bejewelled lady at dinner. Everyone agreed he was rather sweet, and the subject lapsed with the soufflé.

My most vivid recollection of that weekend concerned some planks and a rope which I had noticed under a table in the salon. I asked Evan about them. He replied, "It's the gallows on which my ancestor David Morgan was hanged. He joined the Rebellion in 1745 in favour of the young Pretender. He was tried with other rebels and sentenced to be hanged, drawn and quartered. I'll give you a contemporary pamphlet about him." I read it in bed that night. The writer seemed hostile.

Morgan was a person of a very mean look and seldom kept company with any gentlemen of the neighbourhood. Even after he was condemned he was haughty and insolent beyond expression, and the very afternoon before his execution he grumbled to pay the cook who dressed his dinner. At the gallows he read from a book for twenty minutes to his fellow prisoners, and died very unconcerned. The morning, about six o'clock, before he went to execution, he ordered coffee to be made and bid them take care to make it very strong. He was hanged, drawn and quartered at Kennington Common, July 30, 1746.

I returned to my cottage. The apple-trees were in full blossom, as also the tulips. It was lovely and gay but sad news awaited me. There was a note from old Mrs. Harman up at Fawley, informing me that her husband, the blacksmith, had died, aged eighty-five. They were both very special friends of Louis and myself. We had visited them frequently. Walking home down through the beech woods we often sang the whole way enlivened by their home-made parsnip wine. It was sad to think that the blacksmith's death marked the end of an era. Over half a century past Mark Harman had brought his young bride to Forge Cottage. The old forge, with anvil and bellows, where the blacksmith had laboured was still intact. But no horses would come there again for shoeing; horse and blacksmith and his craft had gone forever. The old couple had been delighted when I became their landlord on the break-up of the Fawley estate.

I went to the funeral. Fittingly, the old blacksmith was carried to rest on a horse-drawn wagon along the high ridge to Fawley Church. There was a yew-tree said to be seven hundred years old and near it, for three hundred years, Harmans had been buried. At the close of the simple service Mrs. Harman stood forth, opened a small tin box and emptied its contents into the grave. Later, I asked about this.

Their only son, twenty, the last of the line, had been killed in France. When the Harmans went to visit the military cemetery they had brought back a little of the soil in which their boy lay. It was this she had emptied into the grave. Seven months later, on a wet December day, I was again at that graveside. It was opened to receive the black-smith's wife, aged eighty-one. She had not waited long to join him.

The Forge Cottage, now empty, was mine. It presented a problem. Owing to the popularity of *Pilgrim Cottage* and *Gone Rustic*, my own cottage was never free of 'fans'. They came from all over the earth, particularly from the Commonwealth, Australia, New Zealand, Canada, etc., driven by nostalgia for the homeland. I could not be churlish. I had brought it on myself and after all it was complimentary. Sometimes my lane was blocked with cars, and I had to flee to Eaton Terrace to work without interruption. Some of the visitors were delightful, some peremptory, some even rude. One day a charabanc stopped at my gate. Through it poured thirty giggling girls with cameras, led by a clergyman. "They're from my school. We've read *Gone Rustic*—you don't mind?" he said, blandly. "And now can we see inside?" he asked, after they had overrun the garden. I said "No," firmly, and again "No" when asked to pose with him in a group of his pupils.

Ethel took all this in her stride but she never quite recovered from repulsing a handsome young man accompanied by a lady. Tired with visitors that day she refused them admittance. The Adonis retreated, smiling. Reading the *Daily Mail* afterwards, from an illustration Ethel learned that the visitor was the famous Robert Taylor, making a film at Oxford. Another visitor had a warmer reception. She was a stout, blonde lady who descended from a chauffeured limousine and walked in. Learning that I was absent she said, "He won't mind, I'm sure. I've met him at Phyllis Court." It was a hot June afternoon. Under a tree she saw a swing lounge and sat on it. "Do you know what would make it perfect—tea!" So Ethel brought out the tea tray. The lady then said, "It would be just heaven if there was some music. Have you a gramophone—just something soft?" Ethel, completely captivated by this smiling blonde with a rich voice, she had been an Australian 'diva' before marrying a banker, went indoors, put on a Viennese waltz and opened the study window. As the lady entered her limousine on leaving she said, "Now do tell Mr. Roberts I've had a divine afternoon!" and put a £5 note in Ethel's hand.

I had been wondering how James Hilton was faring in Hollywood. In April there was a letter from him.

> I have been working on a script for 'Camille' for Greta Garbo. All being well I hope to return to England about May, and come out again in November, which seems a nice way of dividing up the year. The mere thought of Pilgrim Cottage makes one homesick in a place like Hollywood but I also suspect as soon as I get back to England I shall feel a definite kind of nostalgia about this place which is very exciting mentally and full of charming and interesting people.

One day, after a rather heavy week of visitors, not without some enjoyable incidents, the telephone rang. A pleasant female voice asked if she and a friend might come to see the cottage. They were Canadians touring England. I did not feel I could be churlish, tired as I was of visitors, and I said, "Yes." When I told Tony, my guest, he remonstrated. "Cecil, you are a great fool! You have much work. These people wear you out. A girl and her friend. We know what that means! One will be nice and pretty, the other awful, or they may be old ladies!"

The next morning we went to the station to collect them. Tony was all smiles when he saw them. They were indeed two beautiful girls, blonde and brunette, about twenty-six, vivacious and intelligent. They had been all round the world, Japan, India, Africa, etc., and were now ending a six months' tour. One of them told me the story of their holiday. They lived in Toronto, she a typist, her friend a schoolteacher. "When my aunt died and left me $2,000, I rang up Mabel and said, 'Come on, let's go round the world!' So we started off." "Have they kept your positions open for you?" I asked. "Oh no, we gave them up—we'll get new ones!" she replied gaily. Tony and I exchanged looks. In Europe if you lost your job you stood in a queue of unemployed. When they had left, Tony, back from the station, said, "What a lovely pair—Canadian sunshine!" "But you didn't want to have them!" I remarked. "I was an idiot," he confessed.

A month later I received a picture postcard from Toronto. On it was written, "We are both home, in better jobs. Many thanks for your memorable kindness."

To escape many of these intrusions I had thought of moving into The Forge at Fawley, but the remoteness and Louis' illness caused me to abandon this idea with much reluctance. I was now faced with another problem. Louis had not died, as I feared, during my absence in America. He was certain that if he could come back to the cottage he would live. So at the beginning of May he arrived. I took him to a specialist who wanted an x-ray. It happened that I had a neighbour, a renowned radiologist, who made an x-ray. I kept the report secret. There was little hope. The specialist warned me that there was some danger of infection. I discussed this with Ethel. She had no hesitation in facing any risk. One morning, as I was about to take Louis to the City of London Hospital for an operation, I received a cable from Miami. I knew what it said before I opened it. A merciful release had come to my hostess.

The day after Louis entered the hospital he wrote me a letter.

> Whatever might be the sentence, please, I want to know it. I hope I will again cross the threshold of this hospital on my own feet. I think I have more courage than I would have believed possible because, although perhaps I didn't show it, I was in despair at leaving the cottage, the country, the open air, in order to come here in these rather gloomy surroundings.

Two days later when I visited him, I learned it would be a two months' ordeal to be followed by three months at the King Edward VII Sanatorium at Midhurst, Sussex. "So that's that!" exclaimed Louis, looking surprisingly calm. That same evening I made a B.B.C. broadcast on my Florida visit. 'Oranges, Alligators and Coconuts'. I don't know how I got through it. I had been too near to death in Florida, and now here. At the end of June I fetched Louis from the City of London Hospital prior to taking him to Midhurst, where he awaited a bed. He was overjoyed to be back home. He walked round and round, inspecting each flower bed and kept up a false façade of cheerfulness. Each morning at breakfast, on my enquiring how he had slept, his answer was always the same—"Oh, splendidly!" But Ethel, having made his bed, reported, "The sheets are wet through again." Often I had to use forceful tact. He insisted, as before, on attending to my mail. I noticed that typing brought on coughing. I forbade him to work. He went out into the garden with tears in his eyes.

III

In the middle of June I had a visit from my friend Dr. J. W. S. Macfie, who had been in the Abyssinian War. A man of means, fifty-five years of age, very tall, lean, outwardly sardonic, he had a noble nature. He had given his services to the London School of Tropical Medicine. When I first met him in 1917 he was a member of the War Office Malaria Investigation Commission. His qualifications were impressive—M.A. (Cantab.), D.Sc. and M.B. (Edinburgh). A specialist in protozoology, he had a long experience of tropical diseases, having passed thirty years in West Africa (Lagos, Accra and the Gold Coast). Latterly, he had specialised on mosquitoes and tse-tse flies. He was very hospitable and I often dined at his London apartment. He was a great authority on ceratopogonidae, biting midges. He had a grim sense of humour. He would produce slides of midges and describe the frightful things they could do to you. "I had myself bitten by this one," he said, pointing to a midge on a slide, "I shall know the result by tomorrow." He had made his body an experimental ground through the years. Sometimes he looked ghastly.

It was a beautiful June day when he came to lunch. I induced him to tell me of his experiences in Abyssinia. When the war began he volunteered to go with a British Ambulance Service commanded by Dr. A. J. M. Melly. Macfie was second-in-command. They sailed in November, 1935. It was soon clear that their well-equipped field unit was inadequate. They established their hospital on a plateau, 8,000 feet high and dealt with over a hundred patients a day. Their skin wounds were frightful. The mustard gas ate the flesh off their bare legs. They looked as if they had been skinned alive. Thousands were disabled, all were in great agony, ambling about. "Then it is true—the Italians did use mustard gas, which they denied?" I asked. "Absolutely true," replied Macfie. "We had hundreds of cases. For many we could do nothing. They were good patients, very brave, but they showed no gratitude whatsoever. They looked on us as intruders and took everything for granted. They were flea-ridden and lousy, with dreadful suppurating wounds. I lived in daily fear of infection. Our wards were chock full. We were completely cut off from the outside world. We became increasingly worried by Italian planes. They flew over and over, swooping low at first, but they didn't bomb us. We had a Red Cross flag spread out on the ground, so they knew who we were. In February the planes came over again and dropped bombs in the vicinity, as if to cut off the wounded coming in. They destroyed three ambulances."

Macfie paused, twisting a cigarette in his fingers. I waited for him to continue. "It's a horrible story," he said slowly, in his deep voice. "The Ethiopians were stunned by the effects of mustard gas, a fiendish thing. You felt a drop of water on your cheek and brushed it off with your hand. Later the skin blistered and peeled off. On March 4 they bombed our camp, deliberately. In the middle of our group of tents we had a great Red Cross flag, forty-foot square, spread on the ground, also another on the edge of the camp. There could be no mistaking what we were. That morning the C.O. was operating, I was giving the anaesthetic. He had just made an incision of the patient's skin when a plane approached. A bomb fell near us. Even then we did not think we were being attacked. Then we heard the plane come back, very low. We threw ourselves on the ground, our patient still under the anaesthetic. This time the bomb fell very close. One side of our operating tent was blown away, our patient with it. As we scurried away two more bombs fell. The C.O. was blown into a stream. The bombing lasted half an hour—twenty high-explosive and incendiary bombs. When we went back our hospital was wrecked, the patients lying all over the place. The camp reeked of gas. We had to move and set it up again in caves—at an altitude of 9,000 feet that left one panting. Our lot was not improved by bands of *shiftas*, rebel Ethiopians intent only on pillage. I fell ill and had to go to hospital in Addis Ababa. Here our Ambassador asked us to make a sworn statement about mustard gas—there were other doctors of other medical missions who also swore that the Italians were using it. On April 4 five enemy planes came over the capital. The Emperor had made a brave last stand at Lake Ashianji, leading his massed troops. It was utterly useless, and foolish, he should have scattered them. How could they fight an army equipped with everything, armoured cars, machine-guns, planes? Obviously the war was at an end and the Italians would soon be in Addis Ababa. I had a raging fever and on April 24 I left by train. It took four days to Djibouti, the port en route for Aden. On board we learned the Emperor had fled. There was disorder in Addis Ababa, pillaging, burning, shooting. On May 3 our C.O., Dr. Melly, was shot. He had gone out in a lorry to pick up some wounded. Rioters thrust rifles in the lorry, wildly shooting. Melly was wounded in the chest. He died in hospital two days later, a few hours before Badoglio and his soldiers entered the capital. The war was over."

"Did you ever see the Emperor Hailé Selassie?" I asked. "Yes, once. He received us at Waldia, during the campaign. You know, Ethiopian names are very oddly religious. Gabre Maryan means 'Slave of the Virgin Mary', and Hailé Selassie means 'Power of the Trinity'. There sat the Power, under a tent flap, feet on a carpet, very small, frail, terribly tired. We were presented and he thanked us."

Macfie stood up, gaunt and grim. He lit his cigarette and paced under the apple-tree. "My dear fellow, it's frightful what one megalomaniac can lead a great people into. You and I have a deep love of Italy, an affection for its gifted, amiable people. They've given us the Renaissance, Dante, Raphael, Michelangelo. And here they were, massacring and torturing a helpless nation whose soil they had invaded, so that one blackguard could stand triumphant and bellow on his balcony before the delirious Romans. The human race is a horrible creation, my dear fellow. You can't trust it," exclaimed Macfie, bitterly. "Not wholly horrible," I said, interrupting. "It produces men like Dr. Melly and yourself." My friend shrugged his shoulders.

The irony of the whirligig of time! In 1970, thirty-four years after this grim story was told in my garden, and twelve years after Macfie was dead, I was living in Rome, in the Grand Hotel. In November of that year, in a suite immediately below me, the Emperor Haile Selassie lodged. I had last seen him when, in 1938, he was living in exile in Bath, dispossessed of his throne and kingdom. He was now the official guest of the President of the Italian Republic. After a brief stay in the President's palace, he had moved into the Grand Hotel. On entering Rome, from the airport, he had been escorted by the resplendent Guard of Honour, swords drawn, a mounted band playing. There had been a State banquet, a reception by the Pope. All along the streets the Emperor, a frail, dignified little man of seventy-eight, was warmly acclaimed by the crowd. The Duce who had raped

Abyssinia had been publicly hanged, upside down, after assassination; the King, who had usurped the title of Emperor, had died ignominiously, exiled in Egypt, and 'none so poor to do him reverence'. When I visited his sepulchre in Alexandria, behind the altar, the priest said, "We got him here." There was not a flower in front of the plain slab.

After the conquest, Amadeo, Duke of Aosta, was appointed Governor. He was firm but humane and did much for the ravaged country. When the Second World War broke out he commanded the Italian army in Abyssinia. Defeated, he was taken prisoner by the British. He refused to fly out, as he might have done. "A captain goes down with his ship. I remain with my soldiers," he said. An explorer, tall, handsome, cultured, he died, while a prisoner, of consumption. He lies now with his men in Abyssinian soil, revered by all.

A year after Macfie's return to England, he wrote about his medical mission in *An Ethiopian Diary*. On the flyleaf of the copy he gave me he had written, "Men are we, and we must grieve when even the shades of that which once was great is passed away."

IV

I was ill most of this summer, my condition not helped by anxiety about Louis. Also I was worried by my inability to find a satisfactory theme for a new novel. I made two false starts. Meanwhile, I had a flow of visitors, mostly literary; Phyllis Bentley with our American publisher, Valentine Williams, the thriller writer, and Archie Macdonald. One day two undergraduates came from Oxford for lunch with young Viscount Erleigh, Lord Reading's son. One of these was named Gavin Maxwell, twenty-two, of Hertford College. Three years later he served in the Scots Guards. Invalided out, he bought a small Hebridean island and started a shark fishery. He next turned professional portrait painter and author. In his cottage in the West Highlands he lived primitively as a hermit, perhaps a reaction from being the grandson of a Duke of Northumberland, Eton, Oxford, and all that. He cooked, laundered, fished, in solitary state, except for one youth as his assistant, and a pet otter. As a result of this experience he wrote *A Ring of Bright Water*, the story of his otter, which sold a million copies and made him famous. Among other books, he wrote one about a Sicilian bandit, and one about the Marsh Arabs of Southern Iraq among whom he had lived. After spending some time in Morocco he wrote an extraordinary account of the grim feud between El Glaoui and the Alouite Sultan, Mohammed V, whom the former had tried to dethrone, and before whom he had to crawl on his knees in the audience chamber for pardon. Maxwell's restless curiosity wore him out. He died aged fifty. Do I remember anything about this exceptional youth who lunched at my cottage one bright June day? Alas, very little and that somewhat ludicrous. Signing my visitors' book, he sucked the nib of his fountain pen and departed with a blue mouth and tongue.

Another visitor was the young man I had met on the *Aquitania*, Lord Carlow, only son and heir of the Earl of Portarlington. Twenty-nine, short, he had the deepest voice for a slight man I had ever known, except that of little Sir Philip Gibbs whose vocal organ was a *basso profundo*. On our Atlantic crossing Carlow and I became friends. He told me he had recently got engaged. I invited him to visit me. When Louis Golding arrived with him one day, they were Oxford friends, I was surprised to learn that Carlow had a private printing press and produced volumes that became collectors' pieces. I was to see much of him and his wife Peggy, and liked them increasingly.

That same month, Sir Burton Chadwick, the man who had taken me to London in 1917 as his assistant in the Ministry of Munitions, came to lunch and gave me a shock. A Liverpool shipowner, a man of great charm, he had gone into politics. He rose rapidly, became a Parliamentary Secretary to the Board of Trade and a baronet, but his most memorable achievement was the founding of the Honourable Company of Master Mariners, whose headquarters is H.M.S. *Wellington*, now tied up at Temple Stairs on the Thames Embankment. My friend thought it extraordinary that the merchant fleet which had gallantly fought the submarine war should have no representative body of its own, no livery company like the Mercers, Goldsmiths, etc. In Liverpool in 1921, at the Annual Shipowners' Dinner, Burton Chadwick suggested that the profession was entitled to a guild of its own. The idea took root and in 1930 the new company received its royal charter. Burton Chadwick and I enjoyed a warm friendship until he died aged eighty-one. We often playfully criticised each other. "You crazy writing fellows!" he would say. "You old barnacles!" I would retort. When he told me that he was about to leave with a House of Commons parliamentary party for Berlin, as Hitler's special guests at the Olympic Games, I was very indignant. How could they become the dupes of this dreadful creature, I asked. We had a tremendous argument. "There's nothing wrong with Hitler, he is a great patriot," said my friend. Alas, he was not alone in this view. A supine British Ambassador in Berlin endorsed it. Lloyd George, on a visit to Berchtesgaden exchanged photographs and compliments with Hitler and declared, "It is an immense advantage for Europe to have a strong man of affairs . . . the Germans are the happiest people in the world." "Thank God for Hitler!" exclaimed Frank Buchman, the Messiah of the Oxford Group. "Germany provides no threat to Europe," wrote *The Economist*. *The Times* apologising for Hitler after the 1934 Munich massacre, declared, "There is no reason to be incensed about the militaristic spirit in Germany. Hitler is genuinely trying to transform revolutionary fervour into moderate and constructive efforts, and to inspire a high standard of public service." Certainly Burton Chadwick had plenty of companions burying their heads in the sand. I told him I was deeply shocked by this proposed visit as the guest of the monster in Berlin. He laughed. "You writing fellows get so hot under the collar." I got hotter under the collar when, in August, Germany brought in two years' military service for all Germans and created the Rome-Berlin Axis.

v

In July Louis went to the King Edward VII Sanatorium at Midhurst. Despite a brave show I felt he was going downhill. I finished *Gone Sunwards*. I was still worried by my inability to conceive a new novel. I had been barren fourteen months. At the end of July I took Lucien home to Venice. It was gloriously hot and we spent our days on the Lido. I was sad to leave, to join friends in Salzburg. The musical festival craze, with its conductor fetish, was almost at its zenith, but the air was chilled by growing Nazi arrogance, visible in some of the youths of this romantic Mozartian city. It was strange how we all went Tyrolean, *Così fan Tutte* by night, *lederhosen* and *dirndls* by day. At Lanz's we fitted ourselves out in native costumes. I bought *lederhosen*, white stockings, a green hat with a feather, a cut-away jacket, with fancy brass buttons. The disguise, helped by Lido sun, must have been good. One day, when I was standing by the bridge over the grey Salzach a car drew up. A lady put her head out and began, hesitatingly, *"Bitte, mein Herr, wo ist der weg nach—"* I looked at her. She was my Henley neighbour. "Now, Mrs. Compton, try to speak English!" I replied. She gave a little shriek. What fun it all was! How young we were! We moved to music, we climbed the Gaisberg, we lunched on a terrace high up under the wall of the fairytale Hohensalzburg. In the crowded Café Basar, sitting next to an Austrian youth who mistakenly took my drink and apologised, I asked what his name was. Rudolf Braun. What English books had he read? "I have much passion for Richardson. I most wish to see his house." "Richardson? Richardson?" I repeated, bewildered. "The father of the English Novel—who wrote *Clarissa*," he explained. I started. Here was an Austrian lad who had read something I had never looked at. "And where did he live?" I asked. Very methodically, he produced a notebook. "The Grange, North End Road, Fulham, London," he read. Later, I went to find the Grange, and thus was born *And So To Bath.*

When in Salzburg earlier, in 1928, I had called on Stefan Zweig. He then lived in an old house on the Kapuzinerberg overlooking Salzburg. You approached it by a Calvary path that ended near a church. It was a little rococo eighteenth-century palace with a central tower and a terrace. It had been built by an archbishop of Salzburg for his mistress. From the terrace there was a wonderful view of the baroque town with its cathedral and the Bavarian alps beyond. At this time Zweig was living with his first wife, a woman of his own age. She had been his devoted companion for twenty years, acting as his secretary. Later I learned of the difficult life she had with this highly sensitive, neurotic and restless man of genius who enjoyed a worldwide reputation. The Zweigs seemed to live very comfortably, though faced with the continuously falling value of the currency in the difficult years following the First World War.

Salzburg in 1928 had not yet reached the great prosperity brought to it by the music festivals held towards the middle of the Thirties. It had started its successful career as a festival town more addicted to drama than music. The presiding geniuses had been Hugo von Hofmannsthal and Reinhardt. They discovered its enormous possibilities as a superb stage for their dramatic productions. In 1925 they had put on *The Miracle* with Lady Diana Cooper as the Madonna. Lady Cunard was there with the Smart Set, and Reinhardt entertained in his Schloss Leopoldskron. Then something happened. Arturo Toscanini and Bruno Walther started the cult of Mozart, the little native genius. Organised by these two gifted conductors, using the universal language of music, the cult brought a downpour of gold to Salzburg. The greatest artists of the world were drawn there. The impoverished Austrian aristocrats, living in their bare, grey castles, converted them into guest houses. Music snobbery took control. At the hour of the evening performance the bridge over the Salzach was blocked with cars of all nations. The astonished natives watched the visitors, in evening attire, flock to the Festspielhaus in which the price of a stall would have kept the whole impoverished Mozart family for a month.

In 1928 I had been received by the Zweigs with warm courtesy. An international company gathered there, the conversation running in German, English, French and Polish. I was shown the splendid collection of 4,000 autographs, and the writing-desk that had been Beethoven's. Stefan Zweig was a slightly-built man with a pallid face. His nose was long and straight. He had a thick scrub moustache, dark hair lying smoothly on his head. He seemed to me a shy man. I heard that the influx of Festival fans upset him so much that he often took refuge in his Vienna apartment.

On reaching Salzburg on this August of 1936 I learned to my surprise that Zweig no longer lived in the house on the Kapuzinerberg but was now in England. I was even more astonished to learn that he had parted from his wife Frederike, and had formed a liaison with a woman thirty-three years younger than himself. She was an Austrian refugee whom his wife had found for him in London when he needed a secretary. As I am reluctant to believe gossip, and all this came from a rather flighty Austrian lady, I decided to mount the hill and call on the Zweigs. After a stiff climb I reached the house to find the gate barred, the garden neglected and a general air of desertion. I returned to Salzburg reflecting on the mutability of human affairs. On the same evening an Austrian friend told me that what had finally driven Stefan Zweig from Salzburg had been the searching of his house in 1934 by a group of young Salzburg Nazis in league with their German colleagues in near-by Kufstein. His wife had bravely insisted on, and obtained, an apology from the local authorities for this affront. But Zweig had seen the writing on the wall. He made his new home in Bath, England, where in 1939 I was to encounter him and learn what had befallen.

VI

After Salzburg an invitation from my Hungarian friend Baron Wolfner drew me to Budapest again. He took me on the night of my arrival to a restaurant at the edge of a cliff above the Danube, the Kis Royal, overlooking the jewelled plain of Buda. Wolfner had a passion for all things English. I saw at once why I had been taken to the Kis Royal restaurant. A special table was reserved. On it stood a small statue of Edward, Prince of Wales, in a top hat. There was a plaque attached. "H.R. Highness Edward, Prince of Wales, kindly passed the evening of February 22, 1935, beside this very table."

VII

I was home at the end of September and went to my publishers to sign copies of *Gone Sunwards*, and also an agreement for *And So To Bath*. I had gone at once to the North End Road, and there, just off the Hammersmith Road I found the Grange, at the beginning of the North End Road. I feared it might have been pulled down, long ago, for it belonged to the age of Dr. Johnson, Goldsmith and Fielding. The beginning of the road now held a threat, mechanical dredgers were clearing a site for new buildings but at the end of a long hoarding masking the excavations I found a grand old house, No. 111. It carried a blue and white plaque which announced that Samuel Richardson had written *Clarissa* there. My Austrian lad had it right. I was jubilant, I had found a subject.

The Grange was a piece of eighteenth-century architecture. It stood behind massive brick piers supporting decorative urns. The house, divided into two, had a derelict air, but even so, what a lovely old-world countenance it presented to the blatant London that had swallowed it up! The plaque told me that not only had Richardson lived there, but also the artist, Sir Edward Burne-Jones. He had married the aunt of Rudyard Kipling and Stanley Baldwin, who, as boys, had stayed there and played in the great garden behind. The ruinous half of the Grange, significantly No. 113, had been made the warehouse of a house-breaker. His stock-in-trade was dumped about the front courtyard, which had once been an imposing carriage-way to the main entrance. Broken marble columns, urns, classical seats and other spoils of the Italian Grand Tour, covered the ground. A sundial was still intact on the south front. Under it was the date, 1732. It was there, it would seem when the author of *Clarissa* was living at the Grange, then called Selby Lodge, his country retreat, to which he came from his town home in Salisbury Court, London, off Fleet Street. At the back of the courtyard there was an old carriage-house, and through this one found an enormous garden with trees. It was an astonishing sight, lying there encompassed by great blocks of buildings and villas. The noise of traffic along the Hammersmith Road, the clatter of automatic shovels, the whine of cranes, penetrated this Elysian retreat where the novelist had escorted elegant ladies to the summerhouse, to read to them about the latest progress of *Clarissa*.

Why was this historic, beautiful old house almost derelict? I had fears for its future. They were well founded. In 1952 the Fulham Borough Council decided to buy and demolish the Grange. They coveted the site for a housing project. We were up in arms against this vandalism. The Fulham Grange Preservation Committee, under the chairmanship of Lord Esher, protested. An official enquiry was held. John Betjeman and I left no stone unturned. He gave evidence, I exposed the Council's vandalism in the columns of *The Spectator*. We won our case. The Ministry of Housing put a Preservation Order on the Grange, to the anger of the Fulham Borough Council. But in the end it defeated us by a wily stratagem. It put barbed wire round the house and left it to rot. In a few years, self-demolished, the Council triumphed in its vendetta. The Grange vanished forever. For some years after the publication of my book *And So To Bath*, hundreds of tourists from all over the world went to look at the Grange before its demolition. I owed to that Austrian boy in the Salzburg café the origin of my book. This house was near the road to Bath. I began to examine other houses along the route out of London and so the book was born.

Within two weeks of my return I visited the sanatorium at Mid-hurst. I found Louis, for once, depressed and suffering from isolation. Some years later I discovered there had been a rather tense love affair that had been frustrated by his illness, but of this he said no word. After a medical conference I took him back to Pilgrim Cottage. My radiologist neighbour, Dr. Cave, produced two young doctors, Taylor and England, who worked in the sanatorium at Kingswood in the Chilterns. I can never forget their kindness. As Louis went out of the gate, of Pilgrim Cottage, leaving for Kingswood, he said, "Thank God, I'm only half an hour away! I'll be back soon." I had bought him a Cashmere dressing-gown. When he put it on he said, speaking French for once, "*Je suis un enfant gâté!*" Returning to the cottage, I found Ethel in tears. "Will he ever come back?" she cried.

That month I spoke at the *Sunday Times* Book Exhibition and the following morning a miracle happened. I had called at Cook's office in Pall Mall to settle my account. The young clerk seemed somewhat agitated. "You must excuse me, sir," he said. "I've just got a son and I don't know what I'm doing." At that moment a stout foreigner interrupted us. "It is the Victoria Station, the four-thirty train?" he asked, papers in hand. "Yes, sir, you leave Victoria at four-thirty," answered the clerk. As he left, the stranger remarked, smiling sadly, "You're a fortunate young man. All my life I've wanted a son and I've never had one!" At that moment I recognised him. He was a famous Austrian conductor I had seen at Salzburg.

I lunched later at a Greek restaurant in Soho. When I paid my bill the young waiter said—rather jubilantly—'You're my last customer, sir, I'm leaving today for Athens. I'm getting married there!" I congratulated him, "Today?" I asked, "Yes, sir, soon, I leave Victoria at four-thirty." I started. "It's a famous train," I said. I tipped him well and wished him a good journey. How extraordinary! I walked to my club to the refrain of 'Victoria Four-Thirty'. At four o'clock I decided to go across to Victoria Station and see the train depart. A story had built itself up in my mind. I thought it would be interesting to follow the lives of half a dozen passengers who took that train, which, divided at Basle into two sections, ended at Athens or Constantinople. What events in their lives brought them to this train, what would be their histories after they had reached their destinations? I already knew two of the passengers, the Austrian conductor who lamented that he had never had a son, and the Greek waiter going home to Athens to be married. I also recalled the little Crown Prince Peter of Yugoslavia, aged eleven, collected from an English preparatory school, after his father's assassination, by two elderly statesmen who took him home to Belgrade. He, too, doubtless had travelled on this train. Then I remembered a strange story told me by a fellow-guest in that house in Leafy Way, Coconut Grove, last February. He was a retired employee of an American tobacco company, who had travelled in Bulgaria and Turkey, buying leaf. He had a colleague, a Turk, who lived splendidly in London with his French wife, and who also had a property in Salonika. One day, being there the American decided to call on him. He discovered that his colleague had a harem and three wives! He became the Alexander Bekir of *Victoria Four-Thirty*. Then also I had another story for my novel. Sir Philip Gibbs, with whom I had travelled across Europe in 1934, had been commissioned to write a political survey. We hired a car from Cook's in Paris. Our chauffeur was a Russian ex-naval officer. When one evening we invited him to dine with us, a little doubtfully as he was in a chauffeur's livery, he stunned the restaurant and us by appearing magnificently attired in the uniform of a Russian admiral, which he carried around with him. He appeared as Vladimir, the chauffeur in the novel.

By the time that I reached 50 Eaton Terrace, coming back from Victoria Station, my novel was born. At ten o'clock that night, I sat down and wrote the first 5,000 words. Within four days I had written 25,000 words. I finished the book ten weeks later, 120,000 words, in my cottage.

I kept in touch with Cook's clerk. He became a manager. I gave him a special copy of *Victoria Four-Thirty* when it appeared. We called his son 'The Victoria Four-Thirty baby'. He grew up to be a clergyman.

All through October and November England was shaken by the storm that blew up over King Edward's determination to marry Mrs. Simpson. Every house seemed divided by the controversy. King Edward, highly popular, was right; he was behaving disgracefully; that woman, twice divorced, would smash up the Empire—and an American! "I forbid anyone to discuss the Simpson case. I don't want my dinner party wrecked," cried my hostess one evening.

Churchill, speaking for the King, was shouted down in the Commons and for once was nonplussed. On December 10, 1936, at 4.30 p.m., Baldwin announced the King's decision to abdicate. No one could believe that such a thing could happen. On the evening of the 11th, having just signed the deed of abdication, the ex-king made his farewell speech to the nation. We were all in tears. Within a few hours he left for the Continent. Even then it didn't seem true. The sensation lasted over Christmas. Some village boys provided a Christmas carol

> Hark the herald angels sing,
> Mrs. Simpson's pinched our King.

On the last day of the old year I went to Munstead House, Lady Jekyll's guest, for her New Year's party. Howes, the butler, summed up the situation. "Very sad, sir. Very sad. His Majesty was a good lad and a bad lad, sir. Don't say a word for Mrs. Simpson. Her ladyship's got a hatchet for her."

After midnight I went up to my room. My pyjamas and slippers were laid out, a decanter of sherry stood on the bedside table with a tin of biscuits in a needlework cover. There were half a dozen new books on the round table with its flounced yellow-silk lampshade. The coal fire by which I had dressed still burned in the grate and threw a rosy glow on the walls. I crossed to the window and pulled aside the heavy curtains. The moonlight lay on the lawn below, the great Lebanon cedar stood black against the bright sky. Turning, I stood and savoured all that this room presented. Here was something, a mode, created by centuries of English tradition. It had for me the allure of a work of art, of a well-set gem. I looked at it with the eye of a connoisseur, conscious that it might soon disappear in a new era impatient of the old. I should have been sadder had I known that I was looking on all this for the last time.

CHAPTER NINE

The Finger of Fate

I

Within a month after I had left Munstead House, Lady Jekyll, who had hailed the New Year with bonhomie, died in her sleep. Timmy moved over to Munstead Wood, inherited from his famous old aunt, Gertrude Jekyll. There would be no more Jekyll house parties, no coal fires in one's bedroom. Munstead House would be for me only a kindly legend fading down the years.

I worked hard on *Victoria Four-Thirty*. While Louis was at the cottage after leaving Midhurst I had read to him each evening what I had written. To him I owed the story of the French military cadet whose illegitimate son, born on a train, was adopted by the heirless Austrian conductor. In a sense Louis had presided over the birth-throes of my novel. It was one-third written when he went to Kingswood Sanatorium. He extracted a promise that he should see the completed text, so from my typist I took the sheets twice weekly to him. His excitement was intense. One February day soon after the manuscript had gone to my publishers I showed him a letter from the chairman of the company, Percy Hodder-Williams, a dynamic character in my writing life. Publishers do not show authors their readers' reports, but this time I was shown the verdict on my novel. "My nephew Paul has just read *Victoria Four-Thirty* and I have never seen such an enthusiastic report in my life. The fellow is positively lyrical. I won't say, 'You've done it again' because you have done it as you have never done it before."

I took the letter to Louis. His hand shook as he read it. "I shall live to see its success!" he exclaimed, his face aglow. This was on the eve of an operation. Six weeks later, mending rapidly, he was back at the cottage where Ethel devotedly nursed him. After a month he left for

Paris, to work again. His considerate employers were sending him to their Bordeaux office where he would have quiet and sea air.

That spring my friend John Drinkwater died suddenly, aged fifty-four. It was another shock. My own health had deteriorated. I was too ill to attend a dinner given to Sir Edward Marsh, Winston Churchill's old secretary, the promoter of *Georgian Poetry*, and the friend and executor of Rupert Brooke. Marsh answered my letter of apology.

> I do wish you had been at my dinner which was glorious. John Drinkwater was there, so kindly and *theilnehmend* and cheerful— it is sad that we shall never see him again, though for him it was an enviable death. I hear Mrs. Drinkwater has been greatly pained by that grudging, not to say contemptuous, obituary in *The Times*, which I am surprised to see this morning called an 'appreciation' by Professor Boas.

I made a new friend that summer. I happened to be staying at Munstead Wood with Timmy. One afternoon he took me to see a garden, open to the public, at Ashford Chace, the property of the King's physician, Lord Horder. Timmy knew Lady Horder and introduced me. "Oh, my husband's hiding away up in the house. He'll never forgive me if he doesn't see you!" she said. So indoors we went and I met the fabulous Tommy, who presided over the births of royal infants and the deaths of kings. He was a dark, sharp-eyed little man. I came to know that beautiful Hampshire garden created by him on a hill-side, and the long, yellow-stuccoed house backed by beechwoods. The grounds had terraces, arcades, rock-gardens, gold-fish pools, fountains. There was even a Garden Theatre where the Steep Shakespeare Players gave performances. Horder had bought the place, with 120 acres, in 1924 for £11,000 and had transformed it into a fairyland. It was as if an eighteenth-century Cardinal-Prince had fulfilled a dream there, instead of a President of the Royal College of Surgeons and the presiding genius of St. Bartholomew's Hospital. "Wait until the crowd's gone, then I'll take you round the garden," he said. He spent two hours showing us everything. His friendliness, his humanity, his impish wit, had made him an endearing public figure until he died, aged eighty-four. Once, on arrival at Ashford Chace, I learned of another recent visitor. Sir William Nicholson had been commissioned to paint Tommy's portrait for St.

Bartholomew's Hospital Board. The artist insisted on his wearing the full regalia of a peer. So these were got out of mothballs. Sir William arrived for the weekend not only with a canvas and palette but also with a boomerang. He spent the whole of Saturday morning teaching young Mervyn Horder to throw it. In the afternoon he slept. On Sunday morning he wandered about, enchanted by the garden. On Sunday afternoon, with Tommy waiting in his robes, he said he didn't feel like painting, and went out to sketch some flowers. On Monday he departed, not having done one stroke of the portrait. "It's been a lovely weekend," he said. After Tommy's death I showed my diary note to Mervyn, who became his father's biographer in *The Little Genius*. "I myself well remember you coming here," he wrote, "and your diary entry reminds me excellently that Sir William Nicholson was one of the few men who ever led my father by the nose. I still have his boomerang."*

II

In June I was asked to propose the toast of 'Literature and Art' at the annual dinner of the London Guildhall Library. We were then at a low ebb politically. Happily, on this lovely June evening in the beautiful setting of the Guildhall Library, the guests had little foreknowledge of what lay ahead—a Guildhall bombed, in ruins. The toast I proposed was responded to by Ernest Raymond, the novelist. It was our first meeting. We had emerged together with successful first novels, his *Tell England* and my *Scissors*, which were destined to run for some fifty years, concurrently. The list of the guests was so distinguished that it almost inhibited me. To the Lord Mayor and Sheriff were added the President and the Past Presidents of the Royal Academy, the President of the Royal Society, the Dean of St. Paul's, the Duke of St. Albans, twelve R.A.s, including the sculptor Sir William Reid Dick, Sir Giles Gilbert Scott, then building Liverpool Cathedral, Sir John Murray, the publisher, and a bevy of younger

* Sir William Nicholson eventually painted Lord Horder. He also painted *Miss Jekyll Boots*, the best portrait of Max Beerbohm, and the black swans on the lake at Churchill's house, Chartwell. His daughter Nancy married Robert Graves, the poet.

guests, rising or risen, Philip Guedalla, John Betjeman and Quintin Hogg.

Soon after this a friend, Dr. Gordon Alcock, came with his mother to the cottage for tea. I was a little perturbed, as all that morning my housekeeper had complained of a headache and I wanted her to rest. She put on a cheerful face, as always, and laid tea under the apple-tree. While I talked with his mother, Gordon went into the kitchen to chat with Ethel. Presently he came out and called me. My house-keeper had suddenly collapsed and he had carried her to her room which adjoined the kitchen. He thought it was a heat collapse. Presently my guests departed. I went in to see Ethel. I was alarmed at finding her unconscious so I called our local doctor. After a brief examination he took me aside. "We must get an ambulance. She has had a stroke and I fear she will not recover." It was incredible, she was only fifty. Without regaining consciousness she died in hospital early the next morning.

After the departure of the ambulance I shut up the cottage. It was unbearable. Ethel had been its light and life. The last thing I noticed, as I left to sleep at my friend Fuller's, was a bowl of flowers on the dining-room table. She was an adept at flower arrangements. This was her last masterpiece.

III

It was out of the question to entertain for Henley Regatta on July 2. That day *Victoria Four-Thirty* was published and had a resounding success, with four reprintings in six weeks. "You have indeed 'arrived'," wrote the Poet Laureate, John Masefield. It meant little to me. A few days later I left with a friend for Bad Tölz. The little lake town was rendered unbearable by an influx of *Jugend*, frog-thighed, Hitler-heiling. We went on to Munich. Hitler had caused all the modern paintings by Jews to be collected from the German galleries and exhibited as Jewish 'modern' art. It was truly horrifying. I met Somerset Maugham there. "I must say, from what I see here, that awful man seems justified," he commented.

We went on to Salzburg. It was jammed for the Festival but the atmosphere was strained. The local Nazis were raiding the bars and cafés and beating up Austrians who were anti-Nazi. "They'd have beaten up Mozart as a musical pansy," said Timmy. Later they attacked the palace of the Archbishop who had reproved them.

In the Café Basar there was a noisy little woman, almost a hunchback, but with fine features. She presided over a gossipy group that I avoided. One day two Nazi youths came in and pushed a young couple from their table. She protested. They became threatening. "Don't you dare talk to me like that! Get out, you brainless louts, you poison the place!" she cried in fluent German. They tried to pull her from her table. Diminutive, she stood up and with her walking-stick gave one of them a sharp blow on the head. Amazed, they left. I admired her spirit but I kept away from her bohemian group. One morning, my back to her, she tapped me on the shoulder. I turned, annoyed. "I know you don't approve of me, but you're the most interesting man here and I want to talk with you," she said, in excellent English. Thus accosted, I had to reply. "If I am, how do you know?" I asked, a little frigidly. "Of course, I know—I've read your books and I've just finished *Victoria Four-Thirty*—beautiful!" she cried. "Please join us." She made a space and introduced me like an auctioneer selling something. Reluctantly I joined the table. One of her friends was a very ugly man, with curly black hair. He had an alluring smile that lit his dark face like the sun breaking through a thundercloud. He was to become a life-long friend. An Australian, from Melbourne, incongruously, his name was Guido Wertheim. We met at the crowded Café Basar several times. The lady who had thus incorporated me into her international set had an equally odd name, Giulietta Anatrella. Born American, she was a hybrid of American-German-Dutch-Spanish ancestry. The widow of an Italian, she spoke five languages fluently. She was very frail and small but dynamic. I did not see her again for two years, when she turned up in London, in flight from Austria. She was just out of prison there having been too outspoken. Her saga was to run with my own life for nearly thirty years until her death ended it.

After four days in Salzburg my friend, Duncan MacPherson, arrived and we went on to Gmunden. I had another friend there who every year rented a trout-fishing. We lodged at the Hotel Bellevue. I was given a room of such grandeur, with private balcony and a view over the lake, that I checked on the price. "We are very honoured to have you!" said the manager. Obviously I was getting V.I.P. treatment. When my fishing friend, Lawrence, called, I asked if he had been press-agenting me. He denied the charge. Duncan discovered the truth. An Englishman who had just departed had given the manager a copy of my novel, which, he told him, had made a sensation, and that Gmunden and his hotel were mentioned in it. Hence my splendour. "If it had been in England and you had written the Holy Bible, you wouldn't have had a room like this," said Duncan, sardonically. I replied, "It's bonuses like this, and not royalties, that make an author's life worth living."

Not being a fisherman I could not understand my friend Lawrence's passion. All day, often in a downpour of rain, he fished a turbulent stream. He had English colleagues. When their lines got ravelled in rocks, or the catch was obstreperous, a number of Austrian schoolboys, acting as ghillies, stripped and went into the icy water. He had employed the same boy for three seasons, Heimo Schneider, a reticent, good-looking lad of seventeen who followed my friend like a shadow, practising his English on him. His late father had been an officer in the Austrian army. His mother taught in a school. He had just won a scholarship to the Officers' Academy at Wiener Neustadt. He made vacation money as a ghillie.

My friend Lawrence owned a large Packard car. We had planned a long tour across Europe, from Budapest, our next call, via Lake Balaton, to Graz, then via the Grossglockner Pass to Davos Platz, Gletsch, Evian, Grenoble, Nîmes, Carcassonne, the Pyrenees, Pau, Bordeaux, Paris. On the day we were to leave Gmunden the car would not start. It was discovered that sugar had been put in the petrol tank. "Those bloody Nazis—they saw my number-plate," said Lawrence. I thought of that silent ghillie. "Is Heimo a Nazi?" I asked. "Don't talk rot! He's so pro-English he'd die for King George," retorted my friend.

At last we set off. In Budapest Baron Wolfner entertained us royally. One evening in a night-club someone approached and said Lady Eleanor Smith was in his party and would like to meet me. I knew her brother, Lord Birkenhead, and had dined at their London house, but I had not met Lady Eleanor, the novelist. So I went along to their box. Again it was my novel, about which she was most complimentary. With these various reactions some of the gloom that had possessed me after the tragedies at my cottage began to lift.

One day on our journey we reached St. Gaudens, at the foot of the long, snow-crowned range of the Pyrenees. It was a glorious day. We dined on a balcony with a magnificent view. The food and wine were superb. For the first time I was happy again. We found Pau empty in early September. We went to St. Jean-de-Luz, then through the forests of the Landes, and on to Bordeaux. Our arrival was a great occasion, Louis was stationed there. He was in the highest spirits. Oh yes, he was very well. "I don't like the waxen look under his eyes. Is he telling us the truth?" asked Duncan. Whatever the truth, he put up a very brave show.

Back at Pilgrim Cottage I began the quest for a housekeeper. An advertisement brought me, unbelievably, one hundred and ten replies. I weeded them down to five. Three of them lasted a week. The fourth, a respectable middle-aged widow said, on the day of arrival, "Do you expect me to sleep with you?" On my firm denial she replied, "Oh well, I wouldn't mind, really." At the end of the second week she lost hope. "You do have a lot of funny people visiting you, don't you? I don't understand what they're talking about." "Then you shouldn't listen," I replied. "Well, I don't think I'll stay the month out." I gave her every encouragement to go. A lady friend said, "You know, you men are no good at this sort of thing. Let me find you one." She found me a house-keeper, widow of a policeman, Fred, whose virtues she was always extolling. Once a month she went to visit his illegitimate son. "He looks like my Fred," she would say, sorrowfully.

I had a lot of work on hand and was at my desk at seven each morning. John Mock, the London representative of Metro-Goldwyn-Mayer Films, told me he had never written such a strong letter of recommendation as over *Victoria Four-Thirty*. The price discussed with my agent seemed astronomical. The book had already sold 45,000 copies in America. It was in its seventh printing here, all within three months. I refused to be excited. Film people are slippery fish. M.G.M. did not buy the film rights, to Mock's despair and indignation. It would need eight stars, said M.G.M., and stars would not share a picture!

Meanwhile, I met Lucien at the station, arriving from Venice, and took him to school. He was now a house prefect, captain of the swimming team, and in the school crew. He was handsome, rock-reliable. The cottage was too quiet without him. He was ceaselessly exuberant. He could be mischievous. One evening, hurrying to dress to go out to dinner, I could not get my feet through my trousers. He had sewn up the bottoms. He loved to be read to and made Louis and Tony his slaves. He grieved over Ethel, who had adored him. And now he was growing up and 'shades of the prison house began to close'. He would be seventeen next month. I bought him dress clothes for his first dance at Harry Brodie's in Eaton Square. He sat in the taxi very proud and quiet but just before we got out he flung his arms round me and kissed me. "Thank you! Thank you!" he cried. I was surprised. He was usually undemonstrative. If I sat writing he came into the room on tiptoe. There was an innate shyness also. He slipped away from company to go out into the garden. He was tongue-tied before lovely Ann Allingham and it took her a long time to thaw him into his usual merriment.

My growing apprehension about another war had some basis in my fear that Lucien, like millions of other lads, would be drawn into its vortex and destroyed. I did not want any boy to lay down his life for me; I had seen too much of the filthy traffic in young flesh in the last war. I knew that within a few years of a general slaughter those who had striven to kill one another would be attending regimental dinners given to the former enemy, and the generals would be exchanging reminiscences and compliments. There was an inbuilt flaw in human nature. Man had begun by murdering his brother and would go on doing this to the end of time. Bishops blessing battleships, the crowds singing 'Abide With Me' before an illuminated Cross, at the close of an Aldershot Tattoo, having witnessed demonstrations of new means of killing the other fellow, these blasphemies had always made me wonder about the beneficence of God, who, if all-powerful, seemed disinclined to order things better. Man, passionately driven to propagate, was passionately driven to slaughter. Was it a balancing trick? Meanwhile, as the clouds of Armageddon gathered I worked, the antidote to paralysing speculation.

My agent asked me to see a promising film producer. I found him high up in a flat on the Cromwell Road, a fat little man named Alfred Hitchcock. He outlined his idea for a story and took me to lunch at the Carlton Grill to meet his star, Nova Pilbeam. I was offered £1,000 down and £100 a week on location. But nothing came of this. I had

not the type of mind he wanted, and this was not my métier. He had a
genius of his own. Success can be a dangerous thing. All manner of
alluring diversions are paraded before one.

IV

This autumn I frequently visited Timmy Jekyll in his new home,
Munstead Wood. The rambling Lutyens house was built like a
fortress, with great oak timbers, an upper gallery like a quarterdeck
and massive walls and little windows. Timmy had an adequate income
but, a master of procrastination, his affairs were always in a muddle.
Twice I put his finances in order. I converted the large unused stables
into apartments. He thought I was a wizard, but I could not go on being a wizard, it used up my time. Once in Venice, on receiving a large
dividend, he bought a reputed Titian portrait and gave a party to
celebrate the event. Later, a visit to Coutts Bank on his behalf
revealed that it was not a large dividend but the repayment of invested capital! Repeatedly, the bank had asked about re-investment.
I found their letters unopened in his portmanteau. One could not be
angry with his unworldliness or his faith in humanity. He once
reproved me, turning the tables. "You know, my dear fellow, you can
spend so much time worrying about life that you never have time to
live." The arrow went home.

Towards the end of December there was a little postal comedy.
One morning, opening a heavy mail in Eaton Terrace, I was astonished to read a letter from the Budapest Rotary Club congratulating
me on having been awarded the Nobel Prize for Peace. On reading
the letter again I saw it was written to 'Lord Cecil Robert'. I retrieved
the envelope and found it was addressed to Lord Cecil Robert, 16
South Eaton Place, just round the corner from me. The postman's
error, with a reversed name, as is the Hungarian custom, was easy
to understand. I put the letter into a new envelope, addressed it
to Lord Robert Cecil, apologising for opening the letter, and wrote
"If, however, by any chance the Nobel Prize is mine, perhaps you
will kindly let me have it." A few days later I received a reply. "Thank
you very much. Yes, the Nobel Prize is mine. But I hear I have
written a very successful novel. Where are the royalties?"

On Christmas Day morning, to my surprise, Louis arrived from

France. He had been up all night on the Channel boat. He had to return the next evening. He looked pale and strained. I scolded him. "I would not spend Christmas Day anywhere else," he affirmed. I took him to a dinner party at Fuller's. He was riotously happy and we all forgot he was operating on one lung. He had been moved back to Paris and was living in a tiny hotel bedroom. I was increasingly alarmed. He missed Ethel, he was saddened by the sight of the empty Forge Cottage. "No more parsnip wine to make us sing going home," he commented.

V

At the beginning of 1938 I completed a small work which Lord Trent, Chairman of Boots Pure Drug Co., asked me to undertake. John was the only son of Jesse Boot, the first Lord Trent. We had known each other since boyhood. In his early years it had not been easy to work with his father, a martinet in many ways, but in the end he competently took over the reins of an ever-expanding business. As one associated with the family, he asked me to write the history of the company, to be published in commemoration of its jubilee (1888–1938). It was something outside my sphere, but I undertook the work partly from friendship and partly as a challenge. In the first week of January I delivered the book, which I called *Achievement*. It amused me, a novelist, to think that I had gone from Fripp and surgery to Boot and drugs.

After a lapse of twelve months I began to write the successor to *Victoria Four-Thirty*. My visits to Budapest had given me material for a Hungarian story. I always changed the settings of my novels. After Asia Minor, Italy, France, Texas, the Dalmatian Coast, Austria and Cuba, etc., I found a new setting in Hungary. I called the novel *They Wanted to Live* and finished it in mid-June, writing it through an enchanted spring.

In contrast to the quiet within my garden what turmoil there was in the outside world! One day my friend Lawrence called me on the telephone. He had received an urgent appeal from the young trout-stream ghillie of Gmunden, Heimo Schneider. The boy had made a desperate flight from the military academy at Wiener Neustadt near Vienna. He was now stranded in Basle, seeking to reach England.

The Nazis, triumphant in Austria since the occupation, were cleaning up. A Nazi general had been appointed commandant of the academy. One morning all the cadets were paraded. After an harangue all those unwilling to swear fealty to Hitler were ordered to step forward. About fifty cadets did so. They were stripped and interned in a gymnasium, pending their fate. Young Heimo made his escape through a transom window, got clothes from a peasant and hitch-hiked to Basle where he had an aunt in a convent. From there he wrote to Lawrence asking if he could come to England. As my friend observed, we had a certain responsibility. If we had not made the boy so pro-British and so anti-Nazi he might have gone with the herd and have become a Hitler storm-trooper. We decided we must rescue him. We arranged for Cook's to provide him with a ticket for London. After the Anschluss frontiers were closing. There seemed no time to lose. Lawrence went to Dover to facilitate our refugee's entry. The boat arrived. There was no Heimo, nor did he arrive on any boat that day. We were puzzled. Had his nerve failed him? Had the Nazis picked him up? Four days later we had a letter. The French had refused him a visa for transit through France to Calais. Cook's supplied a solution. They would issue a flight ticket from Geneva. Three days later Heimo was at Pilgrim Cottage. The problem now was what to do with him. It was my unfailing friend Harry Brodie who found the solution. He had a friend with interests in a gold-mining company in Tanganyika. Heimo could go to their Lancashire headquarters to learn assaying. Later he would be sent out to Africa. This proposal supplanted Heimo's idea of enlisting in the French Foreign Legion. He became very popular in the Lancashire town. A fine athlete, he ended up by being captain of the firm's football team. After a year it was decided to send him to the company's African mines, near Geita, Tanganyika.

He left in high spirits in April, 1939. The reports that came to us were full of praise for his work. Then Fate dealt a bad card. When the Second World War was declared he tried to enlist in the King's African Rifles but, now an enemy alien, he was rejected. He resolved, rather than be interned, to join the French Foreign Legion, which had always attracted him, having a Salzburg friend in it. Hearing that General Philippe Leclerc was gathering an army in Central Africa he made a trek of a thousand miles, on foot, to Lake Chad. He was in the famous march in 1942 with the Free French Expeditionary Army that General Leclerc made for 1,500 miles from Lake Chad through the desert to join up with Montgomery's Eighth Army in Libya. It was one of the great feats of the war and re-established the morale of the Free French after the shock of the abortive attack on their fleet at Oran. In the course of the North African fighting we learned that Heimo, wounded, was in hospital in Cairo. At the end of the war, decorated with the Croix de Guerre, he returned to his post with his mining company at Geita in Tanganyika.

In the early months of 1948 I was the guest of Mrs. Beatrice Cartwright in her villa at Palm Beach, Florida. I had a large room in the tower overlooking the swimming pool and grounds. Here in complete isolation I was able to write. One February afternoon I was interrupted by a servant bringing me the *Times Weekly Edition*, to which I subscribed. I glanced at it before resuming work and was arrested by the report of a terrible murder near Geita on January 5th. Mrs. L. Thomas, the wife of the manager of a gold-mining company at Geita, was travelling to Mwanza where she was to take the train to Dar-es-Salaam and then sail. She carried with her six ingots of gold bullion. She was driven by an African native. On the road they were ambushed and she and her chauffeur were shot. Their bodies were burnt and buried. The victims' belongings and the bullion were buried in different parts of the bush. This murder was witnessed afar by some frightened natives, who later went into Geita to report what they had seen. In due course Heimo Schneider was questioned by the police. He drew a revolver and committed suicide.

At an inquest it was reported that both victims died of fractured skulls and were shot at short range. It transpired that Heimo had prepared a grave for his intended victims a day or two before the actual murder. The coroner described the murder as 'planned with care and carried out with cold-blooded and diabolical brutality'. He also commented that 'the sending of gold bullion a distance of some sixty miles with only an unarmed chauffeur was courting disaster and it was surprising something of a similar nature had not taken place before'.

On reading this I sat in my chair paralysed with the horror of it. This, by the young Heimo whom everybody had liked! Later, I obtained some further details. He had been badly wounded fighting in North Africa and was a considerable time in hospital in Cairo. He resumed work at the mine where he was popular and highly thought of. But sometime after his return he had lost an arm in a mine explosion. One can only surmise that these physical trials had deranged his mind. There was a sad footnote to this tragedy. He had sent for his mother in Austria and she was half-way, at sea, when the murder took place. No one seemed to have made any kind of defence or explanation of Heimo's conduct, at least it never appeared at the coroner's inquest. For a long time I was haunted by this tragedy. I had only one photograph of him, taken smiling, in the garden of Pilgrim Cottage just after his flight from Nazi Austria.

CHAPTER TEN

We Look on Byron

I

Throughout the spring of 1938 I worked on my Hungarian novel as well as on the dramatisation of *Spears Against Us*, the play I had promised the impresario Jack Waller. In June I visited for a long weekend a friend, Mrs. Amy Forman, at Glenfield Frith Hall, near Leicester. There was a house party of twelve persons in a large country mansion.

After this weekend I motored to Nottingham to visit my elder brother. On arrival in the late evening of June 15 a letter awaited me, forwarded, a week old. It gave me the greatest concern. It was from Canon Barber informing me that on June 15 the Byron vault, containing the coffin of the poet, in Hucknall Church, near Nottingham, would be opened. He invited me to be present. I at once telephoned him and learned that the vault had been opened. It had not yet been sealed and if I would be there early the next morning I could see it. I said I would be there at 9 a.m.

Canon Barber, with whom I had been associated when editor of the *Nottingham Journal*, knew of my deep interest in Byron who, when a boy, had lived, neglected by his mother, in Nottingham. The Canon had long wished to learn if there was a crypt as well as a vault. He also wished to find out if Byron's body was still in the vault, as there had been rumours that it had been spirited away. He told me, when we had discussed the matter some years previously, that one day he would seek permission to open the Byron vault, and would invite me to be present. I had a slight personal connection with Hucknall Church. My paternal grandmother was née Godber. In the church there are five stained-glass windows, by Kempe, to the memory of the Godber family. They are among the finest glass in the country.

On the day of the opening of the vault, on June 15, about a dozen persons were present, a local M.P., an antiquarian, a local doctor, the Surveyor of the Diocese, two churchwardens, some members of the church council, a professional photographer, Canon Barber, and James Bettridge, the caretaker. There were also a foreman-mason and three workmen who opened the vault. Nervous of publicity, the Canon had excluded the Press. It was a pity that no eminent surgeon had been invited to be present, and no first-class journalist, to write an account of the proceedings.

The vault was covered by two large flagstones to the right of the chancel steps. These had been built in 1888 over the end of the vault and had to be removed. When the flagstones were raised it was discovered that the vault was reached by eleven steps. The first to go down was Canon Barber. The surveyor, the antiquarian and the doctor followed. It had been surmised, since members of the Byron family had been buried there for almost two centuries, that the vault would be of considerable size. It proved to be small, seven feet and a half by six, and a little over six feet deep. There were three stacks of coffins piled one on another. The left stack held the peers, the centre the ladies, and the third, the children of the family. The first object seen near the north wall was a small coffin with a chest on top of it. A brass plate bore the inscription, 'Within this Urn are deposited the heart and brain of the deceased Lord Noel Byron.' The top coffin, of oak, on the left stack, was Lord Byron's. It seemed to have suffered some damage. The coronet on it was incomplete, the pearls were missing, and also the Cap of Maintenance. There was no name-plate and some of the coffin handles were missing. It suggested vandalism at some time.

The coffins below were all in a poor state. The first under the poet's was the coffin of the 'wicked Lord Byron'. Its decayed wood disclosed part of the lead coffin. The one underneath this, the coffin of Richard, Lord Byron, also of lead, had been crushed out of shape by the weight of those above it. The central stack, of the Byron women, was in much better condition. The top coffin was that of the poet's daughter, Augusta Ada, Lady Lovelace, who had died in 1852, at the same age as her father, thirty-six. Her coronet was intact. Her interment had seen the last opening of the vault. Underneath Lady Lovelace was Byron's mother, who died in 1811. He had watched her coffin leave Newstead Abbey but had refused to accompany it to the church. The other coffins were unidentifiable. There was a great amount of decayed wood, pieces of detached lead, and a debris of about six inches. All this was seen by Canon Barber and his companions. He wrote, a year later, a book about the opening of the vault; *Byron and where he is buried*.

Later that evening the Canon returned with Bettridge to make a more leisured survey. After some members of the Canon's family and others had made a visit, Bettridge locked up the church. The vault would remain open until the workmen came the next morning to seal it.

Let us review the events that brought Byron from his death in Missolonghi to rest here with his ancestors. When the poet fell ill in Missolonghi in April, 1824, three months after his arrival to lead the Greeks in their insurrection, he was killed within ten days by incompetent doctors. Against his opposition, they bled him to death. In the room where the corpse laid, that irrepressible adventurer and romancer, Trevelyan, to get Fletcher the valet out of the room, sent him for a glass of water. He then satisfied his curiosity by lifting the shroud. "To confirm or remove any doubts as to the cause of his lameness I uncovered the Pilgrim's feet, and was answered—the great mystery was solved. Both feet were clubbed and his legs withered to the knee—the form and features of an Apollo, with the legs of a sylvan satyr." Trevelyan was the only person to assert that Byron was lame in both feet. One of his doctors also got it wrong. "We could not but admire the perfect symmetry . . . the only blemish of his body, which might otherwise have vied with Apollo himself, was the congenital malformation of his left foot and leg." We now know that it was the right foot only that was deformed.

It was in this same house that a ghastly autopsy was performed. The doctors got busy on their corpse in order to embalm him. They removed the viscera, they sawed into the skull and extracted the brain, they took out the lungs, the liver, the heart, the gall bladder and the intestines. They looked in vain for signs of syphilis. The dismembered corpse was now prepared for the voyage to England. A rough wooden chest, tin-lined, held it. The heart, brain and intestines went into an urn.* Greece was denied the body of the poet. They had

* The *Blue Guide* to Greece (1967) states that Byron's heart is in a mound near his statue at Missolonghi!

213

offered to bury him on the Parthenon. They were given only the lungs, which were put into a box and sent to the church in Missolonghi. It was lost in a revolution soon after. Greek soldiers carried the rough coffin to the church where there was a service and a long funeral oration. Then the casket was taken out to the *Florida*, accompanied by the poet's friends, Dr. Bruno, his valet, and three favourite dogs. To preserve the body holes were bored in the coffin, which was then placed in a large vat containing 180 gallons of spirits.

When the *Florida* arrived in the Thames estuary Byron's friend, Hobhouse, went on board. He found Dr. Bruno, Fletcher, who was in tears, and the dogs. The ship slowly proceeded up the Thames to London Docks where the undertaker, Woodeson, came on board. He emptied the vat of spirits and brought a new coffin. Hobhouse declined the invitation to view the body. The undertaker assured him, as did Dr. Bruno, that 'it had all the freshness and firmness of life'. But the next day when Byron lay in state at 20 George Street, Westminster, Hobhouse found courage to view his dead friend. His version contradicts that of Dr. Bruno and the undertaker. "His skin was a dull yellow parchment. So complete was the change I was not affected."

Burial in Westminster Abbey having been refused to this notorious libertine, the funeral cortège, headed by the hearse, and a coach carrying the urn with the poet's heart and brains under a velvet pall, set off for Hucknall Torkard. There was reluctance on the part of the aristocracy to follow the hearse; instead, they sent their empty carriages to accompany it to the outskirts of the city. There were fifty-seven carriages in all on that day of July 12. The streets were thronged, such was the magic of the poet's name.

On arrival at Nottingham preparations had been made for the poet's body to rest overnight at the Blackmoor's Head. All through the evening of July 14 and early the next morning a crowd converged on the inn. Twenty persons at a time were permitted to pass through the room where Byron lay in state. Among these were the Nottingham stockingers. They had good cause to remember the poet with gratitude. In 1811, their livelihood threatened by a new invention, they rioted and smashed the stocking machines. The military was called out, and in the House of Lords a Bill was proposed making frame-breaking a capital offence. Byron, in a maiden speech, denounced the Bill. "Suppose this man, and there are a thousand such, from whom you select your victim, be dragged into court, still there are two things necessary to convict and condemn him—twelve butchers for a jury and a Jeffreys for a judge." A fellow peer remarked —"The best speech by a lord since the Lord knows when!" But the Bill was passed. Remembering this, the Nottingham stockingers lined up to walk in the procession to Hucknall Church.

The *Nottingham Journal*, of which newspaper I was the editor one hundred years later, carried a two-column account of the funeral. The Mayor, Sheriff, Town Clerk and Aldermen rode in the procession. There were constables, and 'mutes' on horseback, with six black-cloaked horsemen riding in pairs. A rider on a horse richly caparisoned carried on a cushion the coronet of the deceased peer. The long procession took four hours to make the journey from Nottingham. The church was crowded. After the service conducted by the vicar, the Rev. Charles Nixon, the coffin was lowered into the vault, together with the case containing the urn with the poet's heart. Finally, Hobhouse went down into the vault. Lord Byron rested on the top of his predecessor, the 'wicked Lord Byron' who had killed his neighbour in a duel and died a misanthrope, training crickets to crawl over him. Hobhouse, having said farewell to his friend, left the vault which was not to be opened for twenty-eight years, when the poet's daughter, Augusta Ada, Lady Lovelace, would join her father. Byron's wife, who died thirty-six years after him, was buried not with her ancestors at Kirkby Mallory, Leicestershire, but alone in a grim London cemetery. In 1832 Byron's mistress, the Countess Guiccioli, came to pray at his vault. She became the wife of the Marquis de Boissy, a wealthy Frenchman, who proudly introduced her as '*La Marquise de Boissy, ma femme, ancienne maîtresse de Byron*'.

James Bettridge, the caretaker, had been with Canon Barber on the evening of June 15, 1938, when the Canon decided to make a second and closer examination of Lord Byron's coffin. The oak lid of the coffin was found to be loose, unscrewed, and on raising it they could see the leaden shell which had been cut open to reveal another wooden coffin. "After some deliberation," wrote Bettridge in an account some thirty years later, "Canon Barber very reverently raised the lid and suddenly we gazed on the face of Lord Byron. The features, with the slightly protruding lower lip and curly hair, were easily recognisable. The body had originally been covered by a shroud that time had decayed. The head was slightly raised and the colour of the body was of dark stone."

II

I arrived in Hucknall early on the morning of June 16 and from the vicarage was taken by the Canon to the church. We descended into the vault. There was, surprisingly, no dampness, but the vault was in frightful disorder with much dust and rubbish underfoot. Byron's coffin lay on top of the pile adjacent to that of his mother's. Slowly the Canon moved the lid for me and I looked on the face of the poet. The features were much as the Canon described. The eyelids were sunk so deeply that it seemed as if the eyeballs had been removed. The hands, delicate, visible where the shroud had disintegrated, were well preserved. Some hair, curly, was grey and much receded from the forehead. The neck was well-moulded. The skin of the face, taut and yellowish, gave the corpse a mummified appearance, induced probably by the long immersion in spirits during the journey home. But it was Lord Byron we looked upon in that dim light; not the Byron of the glamorous paintings by which posterity knows him, but certainly the remains of one who could have been their original. I glanced towards the feet. They were not visible under the shroud. At first I felt reproach in allowing myself to satisfy a ghoulish curiosity but this gave place to deep emotion as I stood in the presence of all that remained of one who had been young, handsome and the most famous man of genius of his age, a name throughout Europe. For a few minutes we stood in silence. My eyes turned again to the swathed feet that held the mystery of his lameness, a cause of so much controversy.

Our inspection ended, the Canon gently replaced the lid of the coffin and said a short prayer. We came up into the chancel and went out into the summer morning. The workmen were there to close the vault, perhaps never to be opened again. When I asked the holder of the title, the Rev. Lord Byron, the gentle vicar of Thrumpton-on-Trent, if he would elect to be buried in the family vault, he said, emphatically, "No! No! That's part of a legend which should rest."

I wondered, then, if he had been invited to the opening, for which he had given permission, and had refused, but I forbore to ask him. Anyhow, there would have been no room in the vault.

I have speculated very much on who desecrated and opened Byron's coffin. Certainly vandals had been at work. The Canon thought that there had been only two possible occasions, when the vault was opened in 1852 to bury Augusta Ada, and when the chancel had been lengthened in 1888.

In June, 1971, I returned to the church and was received by James Bettridge, a hale eighty-one to my seventy-nine. Exactly thirty-three years had passed since we had met at the opening of the vault. We were, probably, the only two survivors of that event. He had become a sort of historian to numerous visitors to the church, always beautifully kept. We rehearsed the details of the opening as we remembered them, still vivid to both of us.

III

The day after the Byron episode, which left me disturbed in mind, I motored home in time to go to the Regatta at Marlow-on-Thames. There I had the pleasure of seeing Lucien row in his crew against Westminster School. It was one of those days given by heaven, with the shining river between green fields, the boats, and the youthful cries of supporters running along the tow-paths. Across the river, on its wide green lawn, stood Bisham Abbey, an historic jewel in a perfect setting. It had been founded by the Knights Templars in the twelfth century and in continuous domestic occupation for six hundred years. Four earls of Salisbury had lived in it, Warwick the Kingmaker was buried there in 1471. I was often the guest of the Vansittart-Neales, the owners. There was a legend that the young Elizabeth Tudor had been confined there for three years, and a magnificent room, with a fine oriel window and dais, was called Princess Elizabeth's Council Room. My hostess Lady Vansittart-Neale's bedroom, adjoining, was once the Tapestry Room, whose tapestries now hung in the Great Hall. Certainly Elizabeth was there as the Queen and witnessed a splendid pageant in her honour on the lawn. Henry VIII had held councils there. He loved this Abbey and came frequently. As we stepped into the Great Hall, going towards a noble fireplace given by James I, we passed the empty grave of War-wick the Kingmaker. Miss Vansittart-Neale startled me by saying she had been down into it. During repairs the empty tomb was re-vealed. Who stole the body, and when, no one knows.

After the regatta I took Lucien to see the Abbey. We went up into the vast attic gallery and out on the turrets, and looked down on all the beauty of the June woods, the river, the old roofs of Marlow, the graceful suspension bridge, and the church by the weir.

IV

With July came the festivities of Henley Regatta, which meant no work could be done. I had seen the Regatta decline as a popular event. Once it had been possible to walk on punts across the river. They were rapidly disappearing. The houseboats with their flowers had been killed by the automobile. The motor launch began to appear. Henley became a day-trip and people went farther afield for their weekends. But the real destroyer of Henley Regatta was the Wimble-don World Tennis Tournament. This had become a social highmark, the stars in the centre court drawing the multitude.

The Regatta always concluded with fireworks. For this the Allinghams came over. I always called them the 'Gay Allinghams', they carried so much zest and sunshine with them. The chronicle of their lives at Pinkneys Green came to me from golden-haired Tony, with his constant refrain of 'Mummy, Dad, Ann and Pat'. "What's Mummy, Dad, Ann and Pat doing now?" I would ask. They were an intoxicating quintette, the tall serene father, the frail bird-like mother, Ann, an opening rose, Pat and Tony in blithe competition for the fruits of life. As a family they were my prize exhibit.

At the end of July I sent Lucien off to his parents in Venice. He had had his last term at the Imperial Service College. Before his return his mother left for the Riviera to nurse Robert Nichols the poet, distraught with a domestic upheaval. She stayed with him until the outbreak of war. There was now an influx of distressed Austrians whom I tried to help. When in March Hitler took over Austria and added it to the Reich, the Jews, particularly those of the intelligentsia, doctors, scientists, authors and musicians, found their country intolerable. A steady exodus began. Chamberlain had taken the road of appeasement. In July he had sent Runciman to Czechoslovakia, now under Hitler's threat to take over the Sudetenland. Runciman returned with a report in favour of the Nazi claims. We were steadily marching to humiliation, a forced march owing to our neglect of military preparation.

Somehow in that hectic July I finished my play and read it to Waller and his associates. They liked it and engaged Basil Dean to produce it—"If Hitler lets us," said one of the company, ominously. I decided to adhere to my holiday plan, visiting Lake Garda and Venice. I had a secondary reason. My companion, Harry Brodie, was going to Aix-les-Bains for a cure. He suggested I should try it. I was sceptical of these 'cures' which seemed to be more social than medical, but I was still afflicted by a mysterious skin irritation whose onset occurred every evening about six o'clock. All the doctors had failed, including Lord Horder.

Just before I departed I had disturbing news from Paris. Louis had had a haemorrhage and was in bed. I telephoned him. He was adamant that I should not postpone my holiday to come to Paris. "You know I am a cork. I always come up. It will be so again. No flowers yet. I shall hang the holly in Pilgrim Cottage at Christmas." Perturbed, I obeyed his wish.

What began as a holiday became almost a nightmare, owing to political eruptions. Just before we left London Hitler mobilised the German army, as a threat to Czechoslovakia. The news grew worse in the last week of August when we arrived at Sirmione on Lake Garda. There we found, in her villa, Naomi Jacob, the novelist. She was an odd, masculine figure with her cropped hair, monocle, tailor-made jacket and trousers. She affected a Yorkshire truculence, as a mask to her good nature. She was popular with the Italians and quite a figure in the little castellated town. In our hotel we found Mrs. Pat Campbell, also a forceful character, holding court. We made an excursion in her Rolls-Royce ("She hasn't a bean, how does she do it?" wondered Naomi) to lunch with Ivor Novello at a famous restaurant in Verona. Four days later we went on to Venice. The Hitler crisis was so menacing that my friend wanted to return home. I firmly refused. We left in September for Aix-les-Bains and for our cure. Here there was a note of comedy amid the political tension. I was told to stay in bed the next morning until the French spa doctor came. I had a beautiful room with a balcony overlooking a garden. I felt perfectly well. It was at 6 p.m. that my trouble always began. Dr. Martin, when he arrived, was a doctor straight out of a French comedy. He was neat as a blackbird in his cutaway coat and pin-stripe trousers. He had a trim beard and wore pince-nez on a thin gold chain. He greeted me, put down his small black bag, and took off his kid gloves. He was a man of about sixty, grave, precise. I explained my curious trouble. There followed the usual examination. Then he wrote down his instructions. At 7.30 a.m. I was to proceed to the baths. There I must have a hot bath of ten minutes' duration. After that I must return to bed, take breakfast, and then have *"deux heures de repos"*. At eleven I must go to the Grand Place and drink *'un verre d'Eau St. Jacques'* No pills, no medicine, no diet? No. I asked the doctor if he knew what was the matter with me. *"Oui, monsieur. Vous avez un déséquilibre du système nerveux,"* he said. With difficulty I repressed my laughter. When I met my friend who had also seen Dr. Martin, I told him what I had—a *'déséquilibre du système nerveux'*. "Do you consider I am an unbalanced person?" I asked. "Not particularly," he replied cautiously. I took my baths, I had two hours of repose. Then I dressed, walked to the Place and drank a glass of Eau St. Jacques. "You will see, it will work," said my friend, who was taking a cure for asthma. I laughed scornfully.

Certainly in the outside world there was everthing to upset one's equilibrium. The world's eyes were on Hitler. On the day we made a visit to Lamartine's Villa, Chamberlain flew to Berchtesgaden to see Hitler, who was threatening to march on Czechoslovakia. The tension was so great that my friend wanted to leave for home immediately, fearing we might be stranded by a declaration of war. I paid my doctor's bill, £3. I paid it very gratefully, for at the end of a week a miracle had happened, the evening irritation had gone. The little doctor with the beard and pince-nez had restored my equilibrium. If only he could have treated Hitler whose disequilibrium was shaking the world!

Meanwhile in this agitated September we watched Chamberlain 'the little man with the umbrella', as some Germans almost affection-ately termed him, applauding his effect to ward off war. He sacrificed his pride by going to plead with Hitler to refrain from attacking Czechoslovakia, for he was now an anxious man from a country desperately alarmed, softened up by our pro-German Ambassador in Berlin, and by other appeasers around him, and by Lord Runciman, who returned from his mission of enquiry in Czechoslovakia with a recommendation that that country should be persuaded to surrender the Sudetenland the Germans were claiming. The Munich Conference followed. At 2 a.m. on September 30, an agreement was reached. The Sudetenland was to be evacuated and handed over to Germany. The real villain of the piece was M. Bonnet, French Foreign Secretary, determined to 'rat' on France's obligation to support Czechoslovakia, which allowed Chamberlain to follow suit, with Halifax's support.

When Chamberlain returned to Heston airport after this wretched betrayal, he waved a piece of paper before the Cabinet members and the crowd assembled to meet and cheer their 'triumphant' leader. He had, immediately after the conference, persuaded Hitler to sign an agreement, drawn up by himself, in favour of applying 'mutual consultations on all questions between Germany and Britain and thus to contribute to assure the peace of Europe'. The crowd cheered wildly when he read this document. "It is peace in our time!" he cried. Later from a window in Downing Street, he waved the paper before a delirious crowd and declared they had won 'peace with honour'. Honour!

The Times, unfailingly sympathetic to Hitler, wrote, "No conqueror returning from a victory on the battlefield has come adorned with nobler laurels." And when Duff Cooper, a man of courage, resigned his post as First Lord of the Admiralty, it suppressed its Lobby correspondent's glowing report of his speech and substituted its own version, calling it 'a damp squib'.

I was home again after a holiday perturbed by these events. I wrote to my Czech publisher deploring the Munich betrayal, which I said left many of us ashamed. Years later, in New York, the gallant Jan Masaryk told me that he had read my letter in a Prague newspaper with much emotion.

V

All through a lovely October I worked, gathering data for my book *And So To Bath*. I dismissed my worry about the threat of war. There was nothing more one could do. And no one loves Cassandra. There were now several conferences on my play. Waller blew hot and cold, I had a feeling that Hitler was going to kill it. We began to cast the company.

Early in October Lucien arrived back from Venice with his father and sister. The storm clouds gathering over Italy warned them to leave. Luckily, they found a small London flat. Lucien's mother stayed on with the neurotic Robert Nichols on the French Riviera, managing his village and trying to straighten out his domestic affairs. In that same month young Lord Carlow and his wife, Peggy, visited me. They were a joyous couple and now they were the proud parents of a son and heir. They produced a photograph of a future earl, two dark eyes and a wisp of hair.

And then it was Christmas again. Louis arrived, distressingly thin but robust in spirit. I had a small house party, overflowing, a bed in the corridor, a bed in the study, a bed in the sittingroom, a bed in the summerhouse. When we dined on Christmas Eve I think the old cottage had never looked lovelier with two log fires in the great fireplaces, the table lit with a four-branched silver candelabra with gold shades. I never held a dinner party in this old cottage without ghosts of the eighteenth century being present. It had been a peasant's cottage, its inhabitants doomed to hard labour, insecurity and poverty. I imagined them now watching us.

> At the oak table in soft candlelight,
> Sit my nine dinner guests, a pleasant sight.
> Good food, good wine, I hope my table bears,
> But as we eat and talk, three hundred years
> Fade through the candlelight, and in the room
> Ten famished serfs shiver in rush-lit gloom.

We had just finished dinner when there was a stirring outside and suddenly the voices of the visiting carol singers filled the night air with the traditional, nostalgic hymn, 'Christians awake . . .' Afterwards we invited them into the cottage for drinks and they concluded with 'Good King Wenceslas'. My guest, Baron Wolfner, was enchanted. "Sheer Sir Roger de Coverley!" he exclaimed. I was astonished that he knew that famous character of Addison's sketch.*

On a golden day of December Louis, Wolfner and I, with the dogs, walked in the beechwoods above us. Wolfner paused and looked down over the valley in which lay my cottage and said, wistfully—"Do you realise how fortunate you are, famous as an author, with a lovely home, friends, security?" I agreed that I was fortunate and begged him to come and live in this England he loved. "No, no, I must go back," he said. There was a note of fatality in his voice. A Jew, he was naturally apprehensive. The newspapers were full of the anti-Semite persecutions in Germany and Austria. He could not believe that Hungary would succumb to this evil frenzy. When he left I wondered if I should see him again. I had dedicated my Hungarian novel, *They Wanted to Live*, to him. He was able to take an early copy with him.

Wolfner's words caused me to reflect on the odd phases of 'fame'. My gardener and his sister lived in a cottage across the road. She was the local postmistress and the front parlour was the post-office. Their tiny habitation was a bower of roses. My coming to the village had created for her much business. I formed a daily habit of taking my mail to her for posting and thereby collected tidbits of gossip. Had I noticed a red-haired boy at the gate? "He's too shy to ask you, so he's left his autograph album." I called him in and signed it. He had merry eyes in his freckled face. He lived in a large Georgian house down the Fairmile. "Mother says you're the local lion," confessed David Howarth, aged fifteen. One day he brought me a basket of strawberries. "Do lions eat strawberries?" he asked, grinning. In the war he became a lieutenant in the artillery. He was killed in 1945. I never eat strawberries without thinking of him. There was another boy who had observed me. I learned of this one day in Rome in 1960. I had been invited to address the seminarists of the Jesuit English College. At the close of my talk a youth arose, clad in a soutane, and proposed a vote of thanks. It gave him particular pleasure, he said. When a small boy he had lived near Pilgrim Cottage but had never had the courage to speak to me.

* Thus in 1938. In 1970, in Rome, I received a letter from the Plater family, now living in Pilgrim Cottage. "Think of us in the cottage as usual, all dressed up and looking our best. The church choir came on the evening of the 23rd to sing carols as usual. We invited the neighbours in, the choir sang in the dining-room and we spread in the other two rooms and on the stairs."

In December there was a conference with Basil Dean over my play. We seemed to be marching forward slowly. We were still looking for a leading lady. I lunched with James Hilton, returned from his American visit. He told me that he had decided to settle in Hollywood. He had had a very tempting offer to write scenarios for a famous film company. I think I startled him by saying, "Well, I warn you. You will have great success, you'll have a succession of wives, and you'll die young of exhaustion. It's a fatal place. It has no real values." He laughed. "Well, as you haven't got one wife yet, why don't you come and join us? It would be a wise move. Europe is going to blow up. You see what is happening to us. We stand on the brink of disaster again and again, we learn nothing. I just don't feel like joining the suicide club. So I'm settling in Hollywood."

On New Year's Eve I made my annual summary. It had been a remarkable year. In my youth, with never a spare penny, my mother, hearing me complain, warned me that money was the root of all evil. "My darling mother, if only I could get hold of a piece of the root you would see what a reformed character I should be!" I retorted. Money is a sweetener in the bitter brew of life. It enables you to be nice and generous and not have your character crabbed with pinching and scraping. That is what I thought then, and what I think now. In this last year I had bought my invalid elder brother, who suffered much and never complained, a house and a car. I made him an allowance that enabled him to grow roses in his garden until he died, aged eighty-three. The money bogey was dead. I could possess my soul in quiet and independence, and I had sweated no one except myself to acquire this. I had written sixteen novels, with not a dirty one, and seven miscellaneous books. At forty-six I was still productive. In the past year I had also given fifteen addresses, from Aberdeen (The English Association) to Earls Court (the *Sunday Times* Book Exhibition) and made two B.B.C. broadcasts. I had suffered illness and the death of friends. No wonder I had *déséquilibre du système nerveux*! Even so, I had enjoyed myself hugely, dispensed hospitality, and travelled. Perhaps I had touched the apex. I must now be content and husband my resources and not agitate myself over the follies of the human race. I had, of course, my inner defeats, living as one must do in the secret country of the heart.

Walking in my garden on this sharp, starry night, I heard once more the Henley bells ring in the New Year. I could not help wondering whether I should hear them next New Year's Eve. This very morning two ladies of the local air-raid defence had delivered to me a gas mask. I looked at the hideous thing and pointedly asked what it was for. "It's against gas attacks," I was told. As I signed for it I said, "My dear ladies, we shall not be gassed, we shall be obliterated by bombs." They looked at me, wide-eyed, and departed.

The bells ceased ringing. Before entering my cottage I looked at its ancient beauty. It had sat here tranquilly through over three hundred years. I hope a kind Fate would spare it for another three hundred.

CHAPTER ELEVEN

Towards the Abyss

I

In the middle of January, 1939, there were three notable events, one of them political, two personal. Chamberlain was steadily following his policy of appeasement towards Germany. He had given his blessing to an earlier visit paid by Lord Halifax as the guest of the Nazi 'fat boy', Goering. It was all on a jolly, sporting plane. He went to fox-hunt, and to shoot. It was very pleasant but the ensuing visit paid to Hitler at Berchtesgaden did not prove cordial. A High Church aristocrat and the common little ex-painter, a smouldering volcano of hate, could not even begin to measure each other. This venture into the Nazi jungle produced nothing of any value. But Chamberlain was not dismayed. Now, in January, 1939, he turned to wooing Mussolini. The Italians were still bitter over the League of Nations application of sanctions, though futile in effect. The most detested Englishman, since he was the chief figure behind sanctions, was Anthony Eden. When he left the Government, incensed by Chamberlain's conduct of foreign affairs behind his back, the latter was rid of the biggest obstacle to his overtures. He hoped to prevent the Dictator from falling into Hitler's embrace. He arrived in Rome with Lord Halifax, his new Foreign Minister. There was a photograph taken of host and guests on the balcony of the Villa Madama. The quartet composed Chamberlain, Mussolini, Halifax and Ciano. It became deadly ammunition when, seven years later, Chamberlain and Halifax were arraigned, along with Baldwin and others, as 'the guilty men' whose incompetence had led to a disastrous war.

Chamberlain and Halifax left Rome full of hope, unaware of the contempt in which they had been held by their two-faced host. "They are the tired sons of a long line of rich men," commented Mussolini.

With glee Ciano informed Ribbentrop that the visit had been a fiasco and implied that the British were cowards who would always retreat rather than fight. How far in his utter sincerity Chamberlain had been prepared to go was shown by the astonishing fact that before presenting to the House of Commons the account of his visit, he submitted through Lord Perth, our Ambassador in Rome, the text of his speech for the approval or emendation by Mussolini! Astonished by this deference, it confirmed the Dictator's poor opinion of the British. "A bad sign for them," he commented, acidly.

During that visit Mussolini double-crossed Chamberlain. The following April Italy startled Europe by invading Albania, and then by signing a 'pact of steel' with Hitler. Clio, the muse of history, must have looked at the Villa Madama photograph with a sardonic smile. Of these four figures only one survived in public life, Lord Halifax. Chamberlain died of cancer, Mussolini was assassinated by his disappointed compatriots, and Ciano was shot as a traitor by the order of his father-in-law.

It was soon after the Rome conference that I was involved in two personal events. Through Lovat Dickson, now on its staff, I was approached by Macmillan, the publishers. I was not insensible to the prestige of a firm that eventually absorbed leading English authors, and gave a classic finality to their standing. A lunch was arranged at their office where I met the director, Daniel Macmillan, with Dickson. We got as far as discussing terms, but I deferred a decision, troubled by the ghost of ingratitude. I owed much to Percy Hodder-Williams's intense enthusiasm. On my leaving Heinemann's they had published very successfully seventeen of my books. On the day of this lunch they published *They Wanted To Live*, which enjoyed an immediate success, being reprinted three times before publication, so I hesitated to change. My decision was again postponed by the outbreak of war. When in 1946 I decided to make this momentous change a personal tragedy in the life of my indefatigable backer, Mr. Percy, made my transfer utterly impossible, as will be narrated later.

The day after publication of my new novel I dined at the old Café Royal, in the large room of gilt mirrors and gold caryatids, famous throughout the Eighteen-Nineties, with Baron Wolfner, Count Sobanski, Kurt Winkler, Lord Westbury and Guevara, the artist,

a cosmopolitan gathering covering Hungary, Poland, Chile and
Germany. I took with me young Lucien who, in a Venetian sense,
could be said to represent Italy. When at coffee lovely Elise d'Har-
court arrived with her fiancé, Serge Galitzine, and joined us, they
added France and Russia. Within seven months we were all to be
scattered and shattered like a wineglass dropped on a marble floor.

This same month I received a letter from James Hilton in Hollywood. It was clear that we were going to lose him. His mood concerning events at home was somewhat akin to mine.

Metro-Goldwyn-Mayer Pictures. Culver City. Calif. Jan. 15,
1939.
Dear Cecil,

I was just about to write to you—in a somewhat nostalgic
longing for English scenes when your letter arrived and confirmed my rather sad mood about things in general. Yes, I
think England, as we know it, is fast sinking into the twilight,
in fact this is the theme of the novel I am writing now . . .
I suppose the world of the future will be exciting enough for the
youngsters who write novels about proletarians and collective
farmers, but for me—though I'm from the working classes—
I just don't know enough about these poeple to write about them,
whereas I do feel the decline of a great country, to say nothing
of a great civilisation, as something inherently tragic and, in
a sense, nobly melancholic . . . I do sincerely congratulate you
on the success of your last book, especially in America where
tastes are so capricious. I should think it almost inevitable that
you'll make a movie-killing one of these days—look at Howard
Spring, who sold his last novel to Hollywood for $50,000.
What is sad is the increasing tendency to regard England as a
museum of interesting antiquities, both human and structural—
so that we soon shall find conducted parties of American
visitors going out in charabancs to 'The Goat and Compasses'
to play self-conscious darts with professional yokels. However
it may not have got to that stage yet—also, too, I like, indeed
rather love, Americans, I am prepared to believe that the future
of civilisation lies in Oklahoma and Wyoming, and that there
is more hope for the world in these detestable American women's
clubs than in all the appeasements of Downing Street—it's a
pity but it's probably true.

All being well I might be home in February or March.
We were all packed up to go just before Christmas when Metro-
Goldwyn-Mayer dragged us back to do another job in the
typical Hollywood tradition—I mean the dragging back was

traditional, for the sight of a packed trunk seems to have an irresistible appeal to these contract-peddlers. However—once again, why should I complain? They have treated me very lusciously and all I wish for is what they cannot give—the comfort of mind I might have had in the Eighties if I'd been a Fellow of my Cambridge college, engaged in writing a nice, rosily optimistic yet thoroughly bone-dry and learned Life of Gladstone.

I hope the crisis will not occur as soon as you fear, but I admit it may. The tragedy of Europe is that we, the Allies, were strong enough to refuse these things when they were reasonably asked for by the right people, and weak enough to concede them when they were brutally enforced by the wrong people. And that, in turn, goes down to the failure of democracy to make sensible use of an overwhelming victory—so what hope can we have, even if we were to win another war, that we should make use of any second victory any better? Anyhow, democracy is the first victim of any war; you cannot fight to save it, because it is destroyed by the very act of fighting. And some of my sympathies go to Chamberlain, whose political opponents, having thwarted every attempt to give England strong armaments during the past twenty years, are now trying to push him and the country into a war with very little more than his umbrella to fight with. All of which is very depressing. I hope Alice and I will be seeing you soon and but for our own plans to return so soon, we should have sent you that cable inviting you into the land of 'stars' and sunlight.

On the last day of the month the American house of Macmillan, my publishers in the U.S.A., gave a lunch at Brown's Hotel for their English authors. The guests included Charles Morgan, St. John Ervine, Rose Macaulay, G. B. Stern, and Phyllis Bentley. We all thought we were eminent somebodies then, much envied by the less successful scribes. I have little vanity in this sense, despite 'starring' in the literary world. Between Birth, for which we have no responsibility, and Death, over which we have no control, we all strive to find an answer to the riddle of Life. Those who think they have found it are usually the most disappointed or insufferable. Harold Nicolson, after forty years of literary fame, died embittered because he failed to get a peerage—of all vanities! On leaving Brown's Hotel I saw Stanley Baldwin. He looked tired and old. He had fallen, comet-like, down the political sky, and had become the whipping boy of Press and

Public, though many of his colleagues, equally responsible for our disasters, were basking in public esteem.

In February I lunched with my friend Seddon Cripps, now Lord Parmoor, at Queen's College, Oxford, where he was Bursar. His family estate, Parmoor, was on the hills near my cottage. Seddon was a sturdy character who had not let his brother, Sir Stafford, a grim, gifted crank, overshadow him. He was very tactful about Stafford, the Labour leader who terrified his second-rate colleagues.

The next day my lunch date was nostalgic and perturbing. My old love, the entrancing Myra, had arrived from New York. We lunched at Sunningdale. It was one of those clear, sharp, sunny days that England sometimes has, interrupting her winters of rain and cold. I found she had lost none of her old allure. She was now a more mature beauty but she had the same lovely complexion and those pure, clear blue eyes that seemed to have been an inheritance, almost arctic in sharp brilliance, from her Swedish forebears. I asked about her son. He was with her mother. Though she was reticent I suspected a coolness, if not a break, with her diplomat husband. Was there any man who could hold Myra? I doubted it and felt I had had a lucky escape. It would never have worked, I was too married to my writing to make a satisfactory husband, especially to one so dominantly absorbing. She was still, turned forty, a siren. She was leaving for Paris the next day, then Rome and Luxor, then perhaps South Africa. Another mission of reform? "Not freedom for Hottentot women?" I gibed. She laughed merrily, her lovely voice a peal of bells. What made American women wish to be continually in transit, I wondered.

To my immense relief I learned the next morning that Lucien had been taken on the staff of the Anglo-Persian Oil Company. He was to start at once, at a salary of £80 a year. I had no doubt that he had a successful career in front of him. Anyone of ability 'in oil' seemed then to have entered Aladdin's cave.

On the day the Germans occupied Prague I spoke at Harrod's bookshop and made a B.B.C. broadcast. The latter is an inhuman thing for you neither see nor hear your audience, but it was soon to provide the quickest cut to 'fame' for deft performers.

I was now working hard on *And So To Bath*, inspired by that Salzburg youth who wanted to visit Samuel Richardson's home off

North End Road, where Kipling and Baldwin had spent their holidays with their uncle, the artist Burne-Jones. But the road to Bath had really started at the Knightsbridge turnpike at Hyde Park, so I began my history from there. Further along, I was dismayed to find, near Kensington Gore, that they were demolishing beautiful, splendid old houses to build apartment blocks as memorials to the Age of Concrete. Two of these houses had been the homes of the infamous Duchess of Kingston, and the glamorous Lady Blessington, in whose salon elegant Count d'Orsay was a dazzling ornament. From this house I bought enough discarded marble for £2 to lay a tessellated pavement in front of my summerhouse. Excitement mounted as I went along the road, and came to Hounslow Heath, the haunt of highwaymen, then Syon House, the Duke of Northumberland's magnificent riverside mansion. In April I attended the wedding reception held there for the young duke's sister, Lady Diana Percy, and Viscount Brackley. What history the place had witnessed!

Fortunately for me, Lord Jersey opened Osterley Park, also on the Bath Road, to the public. I was present at the ceremony in the columned courtyard. The owner's ancestor, the Earl of Westmorland, had eloped with Robert Child's heiress-daughter, and, defying pursuit, had married her at Gretna Green, thus bringing this great Elizabethan house into his family. Farther along, on the edge of Cranford, I found an old wayside pump. It had survived, one of many iron pumps on the road, placed there for keeping down the dust raised by the rumbling coaches carrying the Fashion to Bath. The Great West Road provided such incessant excitement that I feared I should never reach Bath. Day after day I motored up and down the road. I felt I was racing against the threat of world events. It was almost the end of August when I finished the book, the day of the ominous Nazi-Soviet Pact. Chamberlain warned Hitler that England would stand by Poland, but, impotent, we were to sit on the sidelines and watched her massacred.

At the beginning of April I received a lunch invitation from the incredible Rosita Forbes. She had just returned from a tour of India and would soon produce another of her twenty travel books, *India of the Princes*. The previous year she had made an arduous journey along the forbidden road from Kabul to Samarkand. It was always a rewarding time when she visited Pilgrim Cottage. In the First World War she had driven a French ambulance and was twice decorated for valour. She travelled in the Far East. She rode a camel across Arabia. She was the first woman to enter Kufra in Libya. She journeyed with the Senussi, she penetrated forbidden Taj, as a veiled Arab woman, keeping a camera hidden under her cloak, and gained the friendship of the all-powerful Sheikh el Sidi Idriss. She was an excellent linguist, speaking fluent Arabic. She blazed a new route from Taj to Egypt. On her return she was the heroine of the day and King George invited her to Buckingham Palace to hear her story. She next made a journey of a thousand miles, on horseback, camel and mule, from the Red Sea to the Blue Nile. She interviewed the notorious brigand Raisuli, who, enchanted, exclaimed, "By Allah! I can understand why Europe has left us behind if she has women such as you!" All this had been achieved before she was thirty. In herself she was very feminine, lovely and vivacious.

Rosita lived in a commodious house in Great Cumberland Place. At her luncheons one encountered the most interesting people of the day. It was here, in April, 1939, something happened that was to affect my future. One of the guests sitting opposite to me was Leslie Hore-Belisha, a middle-aged Jew who had begun as a journalist and then gone into politics. Created a Minister of Transport, he had invented safety crossings, marking them with round, yellow glass globes. They became known as Belisha Beacons. He caught Chamberlain's eye and in 1937 was made Secretary of State for War and President of the Army Council. He was now trying to modernise the War Office.

In the course of conversation I said, somewhat provocatively, "When do you think the war will start?" He looked at me coolly. "Why do you think there will be a war?" he asked. "Now, really Mr. Hore-Belisha," I replied, "you know better than to ask that question! Why have we dug air-raid shelters? Hitler will strike within a year. In one vital matter we are not prepared. There is the Neutrality Act passed by the Americans. Without their aid we shall go under." A voice down the table cried, "Oh no! Don't be so pessimistic, sir!" It belonged to a fire-faced elderly colonel with a brushed-up moustache. I began to regret having opened the subject at this genial table. "What would you have us do about America?" asked Hore-Belisha. "I would rather answer you in a letter," I replied, smiling. "Do, I shall read it with interest," he commented. Before we left I had an opportunity of speaking to him. "My letter to you will be about propaganda in America, which is forbidden by their Neutrality Act. It is a thing I understand. I know America very well," I said. At that moment a lady claimed his attention.

The next day, April 14, I wrote my letter. Since official propagandists who were financially supported by their governments were banned by the Act, there was only one way to present our case. There were English authors known to the American public who could make lecture tours. My letter was formally acknowledged. I surmised that was the end of the matter but there came a letter from Ian Hay, the author and dramatist. It was on War Office notepaper signed 'I. H. Beith, Major-General, Director of Information'. The Minister had shown him my letter. "Could you come in. I should like to talk to you about it." I went to see him. I suggested that British authors could covertly do propaganda on American lecture tours. He asked if I could give him a list of these. I produced my list. Was I going to the States myself? I told him I had already booked a tour beginning in October. I pointed out that if my idea was approved they must move quickly. These lecture tours were booked at least six months in advance. After some discussion I left. Beith said he would keep in touch with me. I heard nothing further.

Well, I had done my best. I began to realise that I was a fool bothering about the state of my own country. I paid a visit to Winston Churchill at Chartwell Manor. He was full of foreboding. Chamberlain, like Baldwin, had by-passed him and the House was hostile. He gave me a cold douche when I told him about my overture to Hore-Belisha. "There's no plan of any kind for anything. It is no good. They walk in a fog. Everything is very black, very black," he said, looking at his black swans on the lake. I wondered if they had given him the adjective. Here was the best man in Britain excluded from office.

I found myself wondering about Hore-Belisha. Beith had intimated that he was sailing stormy waters. His reign at the War Office was to end abruptly. Within eight months of our meeting at Rosita Forbes' lunch he was dismissed from office by Chamberlain.

Hore-Belisha had been responsible for introducing conscription for men over twenty, after much pressure on Chamberlain, thereby

imperilling his position with that obstinate man. The Bill had been
bitterly opposed by the Labour and Liberal parties. On the outbreak
of war the Prime Minister took him and Churchill, now back at the
Admiralty, into the War Cabinet. It would seem that the former was
soundly established but his attempt at reform antagonised the War
Office Old Guard. In their eyes he had much against him. He was a
Jew, his name was unfortunate, and to the horror of General Sir
Edmund Ironside, he wore zip fasteners on his boots! Compton
Mackenzie, in his *Octave Eight*, has thrown some light on Hore-
Belisha's dismissal from office. He had made a visit of inspection to
the army in France. He was appalled to discover a complete absence
of any 'defence in depth'. His enquiries infuriated Field-Marshal
Viscount Gort, commander of the Expeditionary Army. After Hore-
Belisha's report Chamberlain went out to France to investigate. Gort
quickly concocted a short length of 'defence in depth' and walked
the Prime Minister over it to a point of exhaustion. He returned home
convinced that his Minister was out of touch. In January, 1940, he
summarily dismissed him, offering him the Board of Trade or the
Ministry of Information as a consolation prize, which Hore-Belisha
rejected. Churchill, dismayed at this, and always generous, wrote
him a letter of condolence. "The outstanding achievement of your
tenure was the passage of conscription in time of peace. You may rest
with confidence upon this and I hope it will not be long before we are
colleagues again." Five years passed. When Churchill in May, 1945,
formed the short-lived 'caretaker Government', after the breakup
of the National Government, he made him Minister of National
Insurance.

II

Things were on the move in regard to my play *Spears Against Us*.
It looked as if Waller would go ahead. There was another conference
with Basil Dean, the best producer in London. He had found an Irish
actress for my Paula, a glamorous unknown who was filming in
Goodbye Mr. Chips, playing Chips' wife with Robert Donat. He
produced some 'stills'. She was certainly glamorous. He invited me to
lunch at the Savoy Grill to meet her. On an appointed day Waller
and I called at Miss Greer Garson's apartment in Berkeley Square to

escort her to the Savoy. A maid informed us that Miss Garson had not yet got back from the film studio. We were asked to wait. We waited, for five minutes, fifteen minutes, thirty minutes. At last she appeared, very apologetic. My annoyance evaporated at the sight of her. She dazzled one. A mop of vivid red hair, grey-green eyes, exquisite skin, mouth and features, a caressing voice, a sylph-like figure. We hurried into a taxi. At the Savoy Dean was fuming. "She's late. They're all alike!" he exclaimed fiercely, in an aside. We made a noteworthy procession between the tables.

We discussed the play. She was enthusiastic about her role. An early autumn West End production was projected. "Well?" asked Dean, after she had departed. "Very, very well!" I replied, elated. "Just right, I think. A bit of luck," said Waller.

I had taken other steps. I had sent the play to my friend William Armstrong, the genius at the Liverpool Playhouse Repertory Theatre. He had made a reputation by finding and training future stars. He informed me that he liked the play very much. Would I let him give it a preliminary run with his company? The idea pleased me and also Waller, who felt he would see what he was getting. I told Armstrong to go ahead.

In May my publishers issued a special edition, the seventeenth, of *Spears Against Us* to which I contributed a preface which foreshadowed my apprehension.

> I had never imagined that within a decade of writing this novel the world would stand in danger of losing its reason again, and plunge with unimaginable bestialities into a new carnage. I should be happy to think that this tale of mine, by its emphasis of the poignancy, heroism and futility of war, has contributed a voice, however small, to the loud protest of suffering humanity which still, marred by one war, is now herded towards another.

On the day that I wrote this, young Godfrey Winn, with his tennis tournament partner, Desmond Morris, arrived for lunch. Ten years earlier he was to have been the junior lead in my *Sagusto*, the film that had had such a farcical end. Now, out of the theatre for good, his star was rising rapidly in journalism. "I'm earning eight thousand a year from my Beaverbrook contract and that's only the beginning! Come and look at my new pale blue Renault Roadster." "It's a bit ostentatious," I remarked. "Oh, I'm so glad you think so!" he cried. He exhibited then, as always, an insatiable zest for life. "I remember vividly my visit," he recalled six months before his death, thirty-one years later. "You were writing *And So To Bath*. You told a splendid story about a foreigner who had remarked to you that the English must be a very clean race because all down the road to the West he saw signposts saying 'To Bath'."

Some found Godfrey Winn an insufferable egotist, a writer of mush but he had great courage and industry. He died leaving a quarter of a million pounds. "Thank goodness, I had the sense to save most of it. Like you, we were the sensible ones. Heaven knows what's going to happen to the majority of writers in Britain as they approach old age." Though his eye was ever on the Press cameras, he could do a nice thing. Just before his death, came a note—"I was very impressed with your speech at the Foyle's Luncheon and by the way you handled the audience. A pity the other speakers were not up to your calibre. You looked extremely elegant and spry, and I am sure you have another ten years of good writing and living in front of you."

When I took the chair at that Lunch in 1970 we had not met for over twenty years. As for his writings, I respect all industrious scribes, successful or unsuccessful. Some of us deal in ham, some in caviare. We should not give ourselves airs. He died dramatically at sixty-two on his tennis court. He had a house in Ebury Street full of French Impressionists, and a fine place in the country. He flourished, he harmed no one. There is nothing here for tears.

I lunched one day with Lady Edward Gleichen, to whom, after endless indecision, I had sold the Forge, at Fawley. She had married into a remarkable family. Her sister-in-law, Feodora, was the sculptress who made the memorial statue of King Edward VII at Windsor, the panel on the front of the National Art Gallery, and, most memorable of all, the exquisite statue of 'Diana' in Hyde Park, which had inspired my novel *David and Diana*, 'David' being the other statue across at Hyde Park Corner. Lady Gleichen's husband, Major-General Lord Gleichen, born Count Gleichen, was related to Queen Victoria. He was made an English peer and had a distinguished career as a soldier. Lady Gleichen, a god-mother of Terence Rattigan, had added a small wing to the Forge. The cottage was enchanting with its view over the Thames Valley. I agreed when she said, "I think you were mad to sell it—but how fortunate for me!" She lived there happily until she died.

I still owned cottage property. The name of the tiny hamlet in which I lived was Lower Assenden. There were about a dozen cottages in the place, and also the picturesque eighteenth-century bow-windowed inn, the Golden Ball. In front there had been a yard and stables where additional horses were kept for the steep ascent of the old Oxford Road. What I had thought was a lane passing my gate had been part of the old Roman road. At the end of the lane were two very ancient twin cottages, of the same kind as mine. They had been 'condemned' and were to be demolished when the tenants died. In an endeavour to preserve the beauty of the hamlet, I had bought them for a few pounds, on an undertaking made with the County Council that I should be permitted to restore them. In another cottage that I bought, adjacent to me, lived two brothers, wood-choppers, who had not spoken to each other for many years, having quarrelled over a girl. In one of the twin cottages at the end of the lane lived an old couple, spotless, with a beautiful garden and hedge. One of the neighbours appeared to live in a state of abject filth. Across the road, at the foot of a wood, on what was called 'King Charles's Way' was an old flint schoolhouse, now occupied by a retired gamekeeper, which I also bought. The rents from these four old cottages came to £1 a week. I spent a £100 a year patching them up. When the tenants left or died, I could restore them. I thought I was a public benefactor. Later I was grimly disillusioned. After the war the twin cottages at the lane's end fell empty and I was free to undertake the restoration. To my amazement the local authorities went back on their word. They maintained, the war having intervened, that they were still condemned and must be pulled down. I began to fight for my right to restore them. Then one day, while absent in Italy, I learned that they had arbitrarily removed all the doors and windows! Indignant, I challenged these bureaucrats. After eighteen months I won the battle. I had bought these cottages for a few hundred pounds. I employed an excellent architect and builder. I put in central heating and parquet floors, converting the cottages into a single one. We had been able to keep the skyline of beautiful red tiles, visible at the end of the lane for over three hundred years. I spent £2,500 on the conversion. The work was hardly finished when a pleasant young couple came along

and bought the cottage for £5,000. I had unwittingly made about
one hundred per cent profit but what really mattered was that I had
prevented the demolition of a characteristic seventeenth-century
cottage. Subsequently it thrice changed hands. In twenty years there
had been an astronomical rise in the price of property. I asked a
local friend what the cottage had fetched. "You make a guess," he
said. "£12,000, £15,000?" I replied. "Don't faint," he said. "Last
month it was bought for £24,000, and if the seller had hung on he
could have got £26,000."

July brought Henley Regatta again. I met many friends on the
lawn at Phyllis Court. The band played, the Grand Stand was
crowded, the river-wall blazed with roses, and youth everywhere was
triumphant. Like a proud parent I saw young Lucien stroke his boat
in the Thames Challenge Cup. His crew of the Lensbury Rowing
Club won by three lengths. But I was haunted by a presentiment
about things these days. How many of these lads would be alive for
another Regatta? My friends reproved me. But I did not allow this
foreboding to limit my activities. I held my usual lunch party. Among
my guests were cheery Lord Parmoor and young Lord Carlow with
his delightful wife. They brought with them their year-old son,
George, whom the Duke of Kent had sponsored, and who became a
page to the Queen from 1953 to 1955. I carried the infant round the
garden and tickled his chubby face with a sprig of lavender.

Our conversation at lunch could not evade the subject of the war
whose shadow overhung the Regatta. Our gaiety was a little forced. I
went to the gate after lunch to see the Carlows depart, with baby. I
little knew that I should never see Carlow again. One day after the
war I learned from his mother that he had fallen, an air-commodore,
in action over the Channel. His widow, with two sons, emigrated to
Australia. As for the baby I had carried round the garden in 1939, he
visited England in 1965, as the seventh Earl of Portarlington, having
succeeded his grandfather. He brought with him another Lord Carlow, his two-months-old son, for christening in the Chapel Royal.

III

I was now desperately trying to finish *And So To Bath*. One day,
after speaking at W. H. Smith's bookshop in Bath, which had a 'Book

Week', I was astonished to encounter Stefan Zweig. I had forgotten about him, about Salzburg and his home there, all now in the irrecoverable past. He had married his young secretary, become a British citizen and bought a house with a garden on the outskirts of Bath. He was writing, of course, but I found him despondent. Disastrous things had happened, destroying not only his career but, worse, his faith in human nature. He had written for Strauss the libretto of a new opera *The Silent Woman*. It had three highly successful performances and then Hitler banned it because Zweig was 'non-Aryan'. Strauss was forbidden to communicate with him. The composer showed neither loyalty nor courage in defending the man who had written three of his operas. Although Zweig saw his books burned in Germany and Austria, and his large royalties vanish, he was not worried financially, his other world royalties reached him, and he had succeeded in transferring some capital to England, but his spirit was bruised. I made no reference to his change of wives, which had provoked much criticism, nor to the happy Salzburg days, but he was aware of irreparable losses. "The world has gone to pieces," he said. "I make myself work—for what? But people are kind here," he added. I declined an invitation to go to his home as I had a London train to catch. I had a deep respect for him as a writer. A gifted linguist, his mind attuned to every nuance of thought, he had stood at the centre of an international world now being shattered by Hitler. I was sorry to see him so depressed. Poor man, he was the exiled intellectual Jew, a flower of the intelligentsia, wilting in a harsh world. We said goodbye to each other, unaware that within two years we should meet accidentally on Fifth Avenue, New York.

I will carry his story to its tragic end. He had decided to try the New World and with his young wife settled in a village, Ossington, outside New York. His first wife was there also and their relations were friendly, she being a woman with no malice and still devoted to him. I regret now that I did not visit him. A year later, restless, he left for Brazil where he was greatly admired and which had always been hospitable. He took a small bungalow in the country at Petropolis. He had made an error in becoming a British subject. The Treasury froze his assets and refused to let him draw his income. It even claimed that anything he earned anywhere must be remitted to England. It would decide what sum he might be allowed for living expenses. It irked Zweig that he could not put his hand in his pocket when he met someone in need. This preyed on his mind and he felt he was still in bondage. Under strain, he completed his autobiography *The World of Yesterday*, a beautiful nostalgic record of his European life. He then wrote a study of Montaigne. His wife typed the manuscript and sent it to his publisher in New York. There was no sign of any diminution of his intellect. Then one morning in February, 1942, he and his wife committed suicide. Banned from his large German public, deprived of his money, it may be the shadow of poverty fell across his lengthening years. In a letter written in his clear hand he took leave of his friends. He felt exhausted by years of homeless wandering. His spiritual home, Europe, had destroyed itself. "So I think it better to conclude in good time and in erect bearing a life in which intellectual labour meant the purest joy, and personal freedom the highest good on earth. I salute all my friends. May it be granted to them yet to see the dawn after the long night. I, all too impatient, go on before."

Brazil honoured him to the end. President Vargas attended the funeral. He was buried next to the graves of the royal Braganzas.

IV

In August the world was stunned by the Russo-German Pact of Non-Aggression. I was working in my garden when the news came through on the radio. In that peaceful setting it was like a knell of doom. I was about to depart for Liverpool to see my play in rehearsal. I hesitated about making the journey. It seemed to me that the storm might break at any moment but my friends were incredulous. It simply couldn't happen again despite Germany's bullying tone. Chamberlain warned Hitler that England would stand by Poland, having guaranteed her independence. It was a promise we could not keep. My Liverpool producer William Armstrong informed me that rehearsals had begun. So on the penultimate day of August I went by car across Oxfordshire, Worcestershire and Cheshire, over the lovely Cotswolds to Liverpool. On my arrival the rehearsals proceeded to the noise of war rumours 'heard off'. At the stage door the newsboys sold papers whose headings suggested to me that Hitler had a personal interest in preventing my play achieving its first night; but undeterred by the sudden leaving of carpenters and stage-hands called to the Reserve, Armstrong laboured on, while a nervous company made a valiant effort to concentrate on its work. On the morning of the first night the London critics cancelled their visit but, despite everything, on the evening of August 31, in a full house, the curtain rose. We were fortunate in our cast. The role of Pamela von Edelstein, for which Greer Garson was cast for the London production, was excellently played by a young unknown actress, Judy Campbell. Opposite her, in the role of the young Englishman, was a youth of twenty-one, David Dobell. They made an attractive pair. The part of the Count's illegitimate son was played by young Nicholas Bruce. Later, I discovered that he was the son, born in St. Petersburg, of Tamara Karsavina and H. J. Bruce, a Secretary of the British Embassy. I was astonished to discover that he was a son of Sir Hervey Bruce, of the old Clifton family near Nottingham, known to my boyhood. They came to see him act. Another surprise was that the part of young Anna von Edelstein was played by a newcomer to the company, Joy Frankau, the younger daughter of Gilbert Frankau.

All went well. The play had an enthusiastic reception with many curtains. Allowing for the euphoria of first nights, it was felt we had a winner. I went back to the Adelphi Hotel and slept soundly after the exhaustion that follows these ordeals of production. Waller, the London impresario, was also enthusiastic. All augured well for the London production in October. The next morning after breakfast I went across to the theatre to convey my personal congratulations to Armstrong and members of the company. I observed, on entering, that the assistant stage-manager was crying hysterically. Around me stood some members of the company, sunk in despair. I was puzzled by all this, until I learned that early that morning Germany had invaded Poland. It was probable that the theatres would be closed. The young people saw their careers in ruin. A couple of them, lovers, who had met in the company, sat on a property settee on the darkened stage, holding hands in quiet desperation. My lead, young David Dobell, fresh from Oxford, would join the Royal Air Force. He was fated to perish in 1944.

Would the curtain go up again that night, and if so would anyone be in the house? Armstrong awaited instructions. So far the Lord Chamberlain had sent no word of closure. One thing was certain, my play would not have a London production. Unhappily, it was based on the First World War. The play was dead, anyhow. The assistant stage-manager, poor fellow, was hysterical because he had long been a prisoner of the Turks in the last war.

Nevertheless, the curtain did rise that evening to a three-quarter house. A black-out descended on the city. We groped our way home that night through cavernous darkness in which the tram cars, with one little red eye, went clanging their way.

Next morning in our hotel I enquired for Waller, to discuss the situation. To my surprise I learned he had bolted for home, without leaving any word. Liverpool was a sure target. In the hotel, destined to be struck later, everyone spoke in whispers, as if Doomsday was at hand. I found a man who was sailing on the morrow for New York. He offered to take some letters for American friends, which I hastily wrote. They were never delivered. Two days later the *Athenia*, on which he sailed, was torpedoed. He was one of a hundred and twelve lost. The German Government, with perverse ingenuity, announced that the British had sunk it for public effect.

Were we going to declare war? Friday passed with no declaration. At 9 p.m., a re-addressed telegram arrived for me. It was from the War Office, London, requesting me to get in touch with a Mr. Curtis, at once. This telegram heartened me. It seemed to prove that we had gone into action, down to the smallest detail. The next morning, I took out my car for the journey southwards. It was a grey Saturday morning. I had only driven a short way when I was held up by a pathetic procession of schoolchildren led by their teachers. They were all tagged, and carried drinking mugs, gas masks and hand-baggage. So this was modern war in a progressive age, children were in it as much as the men in trenches. There was no 'front' any more. Quietly the evacuees went towards the station.

There was to be a black-out all over England that night. I hoped to reach Henley before headlights were required. It was soon demonstrated that this was a vain hope. Emerging from the Mersey Tunnel I ran into long queues of army trucks on manœuvres. I left the main highway and tried a devious route. At dusk I was in Evesham, with its church and detached bell-tower, and houses standing above the river. The inn was almost full. There was one subject in the dining-room. Surely we would declare war and not retreat again before Hitler's threats. The curtains were drawn in all the rooms. The drapery stores of England had been suddenly denuded of black cloth. We went dismally to bed.

Sunday morning broke sweet and clear in that lovely Cotswold town. I went to buy a paper, then, in a side street, I heard a voice broadcasting. It was Chamberlain's. I paused to listen. A girl-wife with a baby in her arms invited me to enter. The Prime Minister was declaring war on Germany. There were about ten of us in the little parlour. The young husband, a railway porter, sat there in his shirt-sleeves with a little girl evacuee on his knee. I was offered a seat. When the Prime Minister finished his solemn address to the British Empire the National Anthem was played. We all rose and looked gravely at each other. I caught the eye of the boy husband and he seemed to say to me, "I know this means that in a few weeks I shall be a soldier. Next year at this time my wife may be a widow and my child have no father."

The young wife turned off the radio. "Mr. Chamberlain spoke beautifully," she said, in a voice choked with tears. I thanked them and left. I was soon motoring homewards, passing through one lovely Cotswold village after another. It was a bright morning and the stone houses with mullioned windows, the spires and roofs of these tranquil villages, seemed lovelier in that golden autumn day for the threat that lay over them. The long hedgerows, the fields known to husbandmen who had strung their bows at Crécy and Agincourt, lay warm beneath the friendly sky. How peaceful my old cottage seemed when I reached it! Friends came in. We had tea under the apple-tree as of old, but everything we did had an air of finality.

The following morning I went to London to call at the War Office. My alarmed housekeeper had stitched on my coat a tag with my name and address. A bomb might blow me unconscious, she said. On my arrival at the War Office no one seemed to know who was Mr. Curtis, the sender of the telegram. After four hours, going from building to building, I finally tracked him down. Inside the new Ministry of Information workmen were moving tables and chairs. Names were pinned up on doors. It had already engaged nine hundred officials. Arrows pointed to air-raid shelters. When at last I discovered Mr. Curtis he seemed annoyed, saying he knew nothing about the War

Office telegram. He passed me on to someone who referred me to someone, who sent me to someone. This last gentleman, in the process of putting on his coat to go home, said I should see the Director of the American Division. I was glad to hear there was such a division. But the Director was away for the weekend. He would communicate with me on his return. Meanwhile I should go home.

V

I began to prepare for my journey to the U.S.A. I cabled my lecture agent. My tour was booked to open late in October in Florida.

For a whole week I waited at my cottage but no word came from the Ministry. Finally, in despair, I tracked down the Director. He was an elderly retired India Civil Servant with a distinguished career behind him. Tall, austere, he received me almost suspiciously. He had never heard of me, knew nothing of the War Office's interest, and was sceptical about the whole idea. He was not sure the Foreign Office would let me go, but that might be arranged. But he feared the American Embassy would not give me a visa. I told him I already had it. Oh! Then he thought I should find that in the suspicious state of America, they were antagonistic to any propaganda, I would not be able to book a tour. I informed him the tour was already booked. Oh! He became more interested and said he must consult the Ministry and the Foreign Office. They were very much against any form of propaganda.

"But don't you want American help?" I asked, exasperated. "Yes, of course." "And you propose to do nothing? What is this American Division supposed to be?" "Well, there are many things we can do," said the Director. "We can create goodwill." He produced a clipping. "I wrote this, it will give you some idea." It was an article for the magazine of the English-Speaking Union, on the old hands-across-the-sea theme. I pointed out that the excellent E.S.U. was largely composed of Anglophiles who needed no convincing. I asked what other steps were in mind. Well, they had not decided yet. I must wait and see. The position was difficult in view of the Neutrality Act.

I had two further interviews with him at the Ministry during the next week. He was an obscurantist and a knighted dodo. The only policy the American Division appeared to have was that nothing should be done to antagonise America. And, of course, in view of the Neutrality Act there could be no possibility of financing any propaganda. I told him I had ample funds in America. Oh! I pointed out that I was going on my own responsibility, at my own expense, and that I had special qualifications, having made several successful lecture tours, also, my books were well known there. Months ago I had informed the Secretary of State for War, at his request, and his Director of Public Relations, how propaganda could be covertly arranged. Oh! He then suggested that I might find the British Library in New York useful. It was a government agency, to further American interest in British Affairs. He would give me a letter of introduction to the Director but I must contact him in private and not in his office. He was afraid he could not secure me a passage. "I've already got it on the S.S. *Manhattan*," I replied. Oh! By this time I was at the point of cancelling the tour, tired of walking in official mush.

Three days later the Director wrote to me.

> In continuation of our discussion and correspondence may I say that I think if you can arrange to proceed to the United States as you suggest, on business connected with your books, etc., you will certainly be doing a useful service. The decision has been made here not only not to engage in covert propaganda, but to send no agents or lecturers of our own to the United States at present. I suggest you carry out your programme.

'Not only not to . . .' I had never mentioned business connected with my books. It was obvious that the Government, as represented by the American Division, had no policy at all. It was in fact going to follow a course of leaning over backwards, in fear of any accusation of making propaganda, one that would be made whatever we did or did not do, as time proved. Again, I was at the point of cancelling the whole thing. I consulted my most influential friends. Some were against my going, most were in favour. Brendan Bracken, who had spirit and a cool head, said, "Jackasses! Of course you must go and give 'em the facts!" So I decided to go but I was not happy in my state of mind. Before leaving I contracted to write for the *Daily Telegraph* a series of articles on the American scene.

In these last days in England, amid all the things I had to attend to, there were personal calls for help from those whom the outbreak of war seriously affected. The young German artist, Kurt Winkler, who had fled from the Nazis in Berlin in 1934, and who had established himself in London, called me up on the telephone, desperate. Could I do anything for him, they were going to intern him. There was nothing I could do, alas. I also received a call from Giulietta Anatrella, of the Salzburg café incident, now a refugee in England. She was not worried unduly, and had found a post as housekeeper to an old lady in Billericay. "What a name! What a place!" she exclaimed. She wanted to see me before I left. I told her I was very busy these last days, working on the proof sheets of *And So To Bath*. She would not be put off, so I invited her to come to the cottage for dinner and stay overnight. When after dinner I said I must work she volunteered to help with the proofs. I was diffident, but she proved an excellent reader, knowledgeable in four languages. We worked until they were finished at 2 a.m. The next morning a call came from Lucien. He had enlisted and would be sent to camp any day. I went at once to the Reids' apartment in London. There I found him with his parents and Bevis, who was going to enlist in the A.T.S. He was outwardly calm. I embraced him warmly. There was nothing one could say, suppressing a fear, as for every youth of his age whom the Moloch of War sought to destroy. I desperately hoped for the best yet knew that we might never meet again. As the taxi bore me away, I felt that life had become a monstrous gamble, with Death throwing the dice.

Back at my cottage that evening Tony Allingham came to say goodbye. "It's all a bad dream," he said, pausing at the gate and looking over the garden. "I'm not at all brave and I don't want to die." We held each other a wordless moment, then he got into his car. I watched it fade down the lane. There would be no more 'Mummy, Dad, Pat and Ann' days. I called Helen Stiebel. We had known each other thirty years. She had drawn my portrait when I was eighteen. She lived in a London studio attic, always happy in her work. I asked if she would go into the country. "Oh no! I'm not going to be pushed around by that dreadful Hitler. If a bomb comes, it comes, that's all!" When I took my last letters my postmistress broke down. "Oh, what shall I do without you, sir! You've brought the whole world into this room," she cried. Then there was a farewell to my neighbour's sedate Aberdeen terrier. He often came over and visited me while I wrote in bed. His legs were so short that he feared to go down my steep stairs, so when he wished to depart I had to get out of bed and carry him down.

I did not visit the Ministry again. Two days before I sailed I received a letter from the Deputy Director of the American Division. He had heard from the Passport Permit Office that I was leaving for a lecture tour in America. He would very much like to have a talk with me about this. In reply I suggested that he should have a talk with the Director and find out what was going on in their office. I delivered my finished proofs to my publishers. They had moved out of London from Warwick Square, E.C., to St. Hugh's School, at Bickley. So I went there and found Percy Hodder–Williams, as robust and jovial as ever. "Do you feel like a naughty boy visiting the headmaster in his study?" he asked as I was shown in. It was a timely move for in December, 1940, and again in May, 1941, Hodders were half-destroyed by bombs. In June, 1944, St. Hugh's School was destroyed by a flying bomb. Mr. Percy set up business again at Weald Place, Sevenoaks, his home. He returned to his half-demolished London premises in 1946. It was characteristic of him that throughout all these years, while I was in America, he never let me know of these recurrent disasters. I only discovered the truth by seeing in my American publisher's office the illustrated Annual Calendar sent out by the Oxford University Press in 1945. Their premises in Warwick Square were intact, but of their neighbour's, Hodder and Stoughton, Ltd., I could only read the sign 'Hodder and . . .' The rest of the building I knew so well had wholly disappeared. "I didn't want you bothered," he said, when I reproved him for withholding these trials from me.

VI

I had a last caller at Pilgrim Cottage, my friend Fuller, who came to say goodbye. We walked round the garden and he said, 'Well, we've had some happy years but all that's gone forever. It can never be the same again." I denied this, but my heart knew his words were true. He had been made a colonel and was off to France to direct army oil supplies.

I would have liked to spend my last night in England under the roof of my old cottage. When leaving I had never seen it more beautiful. The October sun gilded its wavy roof and touched to deep red the apples ripening on the boughs. I suppressed a fear that I might never see it again. I closed the gate sadly. I had let the cottage for a year to a neighbour who wished to move out of his large house up the hill, his servants called up. A taxi took me to the station. At the end of the Fairmile I saw a small white stone by the curb. It looked like a little tombstone, oddly placed. I stopped the taxi to read the inscription. *To Jimmy, a tiny marmoset. There isn't enough darkness in the world to quench the light of one small candle.* Years later I learned that two old ladies living in a house opposite had owned a pet marmoset. They had seen it killed by a car and had sought the permission of the Town Council to put up this memorial stone.

The S.S. *Manhattan* was sailing from Southampton on October 12. I had obtained a passage through the assistance of an American friend. On my last night in England my friends gave me a farewell dinner. After dinner we went through the pitch-black London streets to the Palladium Music Hall. At its doors there was a large crowd, and in all the darkness one felt the mass emotion that dominated us. It was the opening night, after the Lord Chamberlain had closed down all the places of entertainment for a month. My play had a run a week before this closure. William Armstrong sent me his producer's copy and a cheque for performance royalties. He wrote, "Of course it will be produced again. It is too good a play to be stopped by ill-luck." But I knew it was dead for ever, for its theme was that of one war whose emotions would be eclipsed by another.

On this opening night at the Palladium some two thousand of us had felt our way in from the darkness. Here were music and light and company. Immediately in front of me sat Hugh Walpole. When I told him I was leaving the next morning for America he wished me *bon voyage*. "You know, I've always loved it over there," he said a little wistfully. "Do you think I should go—I might help. They must come in." I was never to see him again. He was a sick man. He died during the war. There was a touch of hysteria in that audience. A sense of community lifted our spirits. We all stood on the brink of the unknown. We knew that most of us would sooner or later be scattered over the earth, some to return, if lucky, to an England that would be quite different. There were Beatrice Lillie and Ivor Novello, to sing to us. The audience took up 'The Little Dog Laughed' and 'Run, Rabbit, Run', and sang lustily in chorus. It became almost a gala evening, with cheerful faces around us and, greatest gift of all, light. For, coming out of the jet-black streets of London, from immense dark chasms formed by the high buildings, light had for us a new meaning. With Milton we might have cried, "Hail, holy light, offspring of Heav'n first-born."

Towards midnight we poured out of the theatre and furtively felt our way along Regent Street towards Piccadilly Circus. I slept that night at my club and not at Eaton Terrace. My landlady was closing the house and going to her brother's in the country. I left my diaries and letters in my writing bureau. She said she would look after my things. Within two years a bomb demolished the adjacent four houses and a corner shop. I wondered what happened to the oddly-named Dr. Quackenbos next door, and to the fascinating stationer's shop on the corner that sold almost everything. No. 50 was so badly shaken that it was boarded up. One day thieves got in and stole the furniture. The loss of my father's papers, and many of my diaries, was grievous.

I was early astir the next morning at my club. The last English newspaper, toast and marmalade, at the round table by the window overlooking the trees of Carlton House Gardens. "Will you have a kipper, sir?" Of course. When would I see a kipper again? I said goodbye to the staff, what was left of them. The young ones had all gone. At the door, when my baggage came down, I hesitated, discouraged. Should I leave or go home to my cottage and attend to my own affairs? I decided to leave. I was to learn that I had made a disastrous decision.

CHAPTER TWELVE

The Propagandists

I

There was a crowd of passengers at Waterloo. I glanced at the various trunks. They were from many countries. We were sailing, mostly Americans, from Southampton to New York, calling at Bordeaux to pick up other passengers. Officials vetted us to ensure that we were not exporting gold or valuables. The gold in the vaults of the Bank of England had already gone to Canada as a measure of precaution. At Southampton, boarding the *Manhattan*, it seemed as if all the world was leaving. The ship's lounge held dozens of cot beds. There were cots in the swimming pool. In the cabin that I was sharing with an Australian there were two cots. We attacked the purser and had them removed but one was replaced at night and its occupant proved to be Uncle Sam himself. He was tall and slim, with a goatee beard. He knew my name. He was a Chicago librarian returning from a tour of Europe. He was the first of the Isolationists I was going to encounter. We continued our argument as we went in and out of the shower in our stateroom. He was tenacious and adroit. My debating points were applauded from an upper berth occupied by the Australian. By the end of the voyage I had shaken the foundations of his faith and he wanted me to address a librarians' meeting in Chicago. From him I learned the bogey-word in the American vocabulary. It was 'propaganda', something made in England, a deadly thing to undermine the United States, and 'kill our boys again'.

In the late afternoon we slipped out of Southampton. It was a sad thing for me to see the *Aquitania*, all grey and empty at her berth. The last time I had seen her I had crossed from America with Lady Sackville, Lady Tredegar, young Lord Carlow and G. B. Stern for companions. She now had the sorry appearance of a troop ship. This was her second war. She had carried nearly a million passengers and soldiers and travelled 2,660,400 miles. Now she would sail another 487,000 miles and carry 338,700 troops in voyages to Africa, India, the Malay Straits, etc.

As we warped out, a soldier, holding rifle with fixed bayonet, stood silhouetted against a lurid sunset, a grim symbolic figure. The ship's band played 'The Washington Post'. The light began to fail. We rounded the Calshot lightship. I watched England fade on the horizon. Never had the task I had set myself seemed heavier than at the moment. I was leaving my friends and home at a time when one most wished to be with them, through whatever fate awaited us. My depression was deepened by the fiasco at the Ministry of Information.

II

I had been a few hours at sea when on the promenade deck I ran into Duff Cooper. We looked at each other with surprise, possibly the same thought in our minds. Perhaps, after all, the Government was concerned with the presentation of our case. But his story was as lamentable as mine. He was proceeding under his own steam, like myself, without any official blessing. He was going on a lecture tour more as a successful author than as a statesman, based on the *réclame* of his biography *Talleyrand*. He was out of the Government, not *bien vu* in Chamberlain's eyes since that October day in 1938 when he had resigned from the Cabinet in disgust with the Munich pact.

We adjourned to the bar. There he told me, with some irony and bitterness, of his own experience. He had consulted many of his friends about lecturing in America. Churchill, now at the Admiralty, was not encouraging. "If I went it must not be as any sort of representative of the Government but purely as an ordinary lecturer, paying my own expenses. Moreover, there might be some employment for me at home if the present Government fell. I then consulted Lord Cranborne, also Gunther and Knickerbocker, the American journalists. They were strongly in favour of my going. Lord Salisbury didn't quite know what to advise. He thought I might lose some office by leaving the country. I then went to see Chamberlain. He hummed and hawed and finally said it might be useful if I went. But only yesterday, before sailing, he sent his Parliamentary Private Secretary to see me with the request, almost the order, that I shouldn't do anything that might be considered British propaganda. I told the P.P.S. that I had no thought of doing any such thing, but that I did feel that America should repeal the Neutrality Act. Chamberlain's attitude is really ridiculous," said Duff Cooper. "When Roosevelt risked his political life by suggesting American collaboration during a crisis, he snubbed him. Well, here I am and not happy about it. What are you going to do? Has the Ministry seconded you?" "On the contrary, it has leaned over backwards. It has no policy whatever," I said. "I shall take my own line as discreetly as I can, in the role of author. There'll be plenty of prejudice and calumny to weather. The enemy will be busy—the Germans, the Irish, the Italians, the Indians, the dyed-in-the-wool Americans, the Anglophobes, and of course, the Isolationists. When I left, the Director of the American Division gave me a letter to the head of the British Library, warning me—"

"Not to go near the fellow, except by night! I've got the same letter," interrupted Duff Cooper. "The whole situation is quite ludicrous".

When, fourteen years later Duff Cooper, shortly before his death, wrote his admirable biography, *Old Men Forget*, he commented on our official attitude concerning propaganda.

> The British Government, having been informed of the exaggerated ideas entertained in the United States as to the power and dangers of propaganda, decided to abstain from it altogether—an extraordinary decision. True, it was taken on the advice of the British Ambassador at Washington. Lord Lothian was a man of singular charm, of considerable intelligence and with a wide and intimate knowledge of America. But his judgment was easily influenced and his opinions underwent great and frequent changes. Born and brought up in the Roman Catholic religion he had abandoned it for Mrs Eddy, a conversion that shook the faith of many in his intellectual discernment.

III

At 8 p.m. the next day we docked at Bordeaux. Here we waited twenty hours for a train from Paris with more passengers, a very mixed lot. We took on a cargo of champagne and Roquefort cheese.

The docks appeared peaceful, with no black-out. I tried in vain to reach Louis in Paris by telephone. I was worried about his living conditions in a menaced capital. Bordeaux showed no signs of war. Soon there would be plenty of drama, and later I was to hear, in New York, Count Sforza, a former Italian Foreign Secretary, who had quarrelled with Mussolini and gone into exile, tell the story of his escape from Bordeaux. On the day that Paris fell, June 14, the French Government with Premier Reynaud had moved from Tours to Bordeaux. Reynaud there began his battle with the defeatists led by Marshal Pétain and General Weygand. "In three weeks England will have her neck wrung like a chicken," said the latter. One evening, when Sforza was dining in a famous restaurant, he saw a man approach and whisper something to a French Civil Servant, whom Sforza knew. The official rose from the table, white-faced, paid his bill and hurriedly departed but not before he had taken Sforza aside. "Reynaud is out. Pétain is surrendering to the Germans. There's not a moment to lose! You must leave France at once!" he said. Sforza went to his hotel, collected his wife and daughter and one piece of luggage and hurried to the docks, to get a ship out. Not one was leaving. He found a small fishing yawl tied up, empty. They jumped in, cast off a rope and let the boat drift down on the receding tide out to sea, in the hope of picking up a passing vessel. They were adrift for a whole day and night before they hailed one, a Spanish boat laden with onions for England. It seemed an act of God. The Sforzas boarded her and for three days lived on onions. They landed at Plymouth, borrowed money, and took a train to London. Sforza went at once to Churchill who agreed that his best field of service to the Allies was in the United States where he had once been the Italian ambassador. He gave him money to cover necessities and procured him a passage on the next boat leaving for North America. Within a few days of his flight from Bordeaux, in the second week of June, 1940, the Germans broke through the Allied lines and entered Paris. Terror-stricken hordes, machine-gunned en route, fled to Bordeaux, to which had also fled the President, the Prime Minister and the French Government. Here the Cabinet debated whether to fight from Algiers. Reynaud was replaced by Pétain, who concluded an armistice with Germany. Pétain and Laval went over to the Germans. An unknown general, de Gaulle, landed in England.

On our third day out at sea there was a note of comedy. I discovered, travelling steerage, S. K. Ratcliffe and I. A. Richards.
Ratcliffe, an able veteran journalist, on my War Office list, was a very
popular lecturer on American platforms. He had an incisive style. A
former editor in India of *The Statesman*, he possessed a wide knowledge of Indian affairs and could counter the vicious Indian anti-
British propaganda in the United States. He was now a platform
veteran of seventy-one, tough, energetic. He introduced me to I. A.
Richards, a professor of English, who was returning to Harvard
University on a five-year Rockefeller Grant. A little bird-like man,
middle-aged, he seemed the popular caricature of a professor. I
confess I had never heard of him. The founder of a cult in literary
criticism, he had been hailed as a genius by some excited young men
at Cambridge. "Here at last was the prophet we had been waiting for,"
wrote Christopher Isherwood. "He was infinitely more than a brilliant
new literary critic; he was our guide, our evangelist, who revealed to
us, in a succession of astounding lightning flashes, the entire expanse
of the modern world." This *réclame* seemed to have been built on a
book called *The Meaning of Meaning*, written in conjunction with an
idiosyncratic genius, C. K. Ogden, who invented that gimmick Basic
English.

I found Richards amiable and quiescent. Anyone less likely to be a
formidable political propagandist one could not imagine. He had once
been a visiting professor at the Tsing Hua University, Peking, and
there he was a Director of the Orthological Institute of China, a body
that had hatched out Basic English. This invention was to provoke in
Winston Churchill one of his urgent enthusiasms, to the bewilderment of his Cabinet. When in September, 1943, he went to Harvard
University to receive an honorary degree, he touched on a rather
delicate subject in reminding the Americans that they could not
escape their responsibilities and have stayed out of the war. The world
had changed, he said. Alluding to this, he made a slip that created
great hilarity. "We have learned to fly", he said. "What prodigious
changes are involved in that new accomplishment! Man has parted
company with his trusty friend the horse and sailed into the azure
with the eagles, eagles being represented by the infernal—no, I
mean the internal—combustion engine." There was loud laughter,
ignored by the orator, who went on to speak of the gift of a common

tongue as a priceless inheritance. And then he astonished us all by embarking on a subject that now obsessed him—Basic English. He had persuaded his Cabinet, he said, to set up a Committee of Ministers to study and report upon it. With repeated cables he harassed his astonished Ministers, urging them to get on with it, an international language, the whole of it comprised in about 650 nouns and 200 verbs. It delighted him, said Churchill, to think that Harvard had done more than any other American university to promote the extension of Basic English, for was not the first work on Basic English written by two Englishmen, Ivor Richards, now of Harvard, and C. K. Ogden, of Cambridge, England, working in association?

Churchill had now got the bee of Basic English in his bonnet. As with that later bee in his bonnet, the European Parliament, after fitful enthusiasm he abandoned it. But thus powerfully endorsed Basic English started off with a flourish before declining into a moribund state. C. K. Ogden appeared before a special commission. His evidence utterly confused it. In turn he washed his hands of it. "Bedevilled by officials," he wrote in *Who's Who*. Richards was made a Companion of Honour.

Now, in 1939, meeting Professor Richards, I was deceived in believing that he could never be a propagandist. In 1942 he became involved, not in British but in American propaganda. When the U.S.A. entered the war it commissioned Walt Disney in Hollywood to make some propaganda 'shorts'. Disney enlisted Richards of Harvard University to help him with the scripts.

I asked Ratcliffe and Richards if the Ministry of Information was behind their journey to America. No. They had never had any communication with the Ministry. They were paying their own fares. I felt that Duff Cooper should be aware of two more 'British propagandists' on board, and that evening we had a conference. It was obvious that, say what we would, the Americans would assert that we were sent over by the British Government, part of a mission to pull America into the war. There was nothing we could do about it. We must face it.

To ensure that no German submarine should mistake the *Manhattan* for a British ship, we sailed at night with spotlights played on the Stars and Stripes flag at the masthead, and on the flags painted on starboard, port and stern. Lady Diana feared that the ship would by stopped by a German submarine and her husband taken off as a valuable prize. We were not comforted on learning that a number of American ships had been held up in European ports by the reluctance of crews to sail in them; recruiting had been a desperate business. There were a number of sailors of German origin in our crew. They made no secret of their pro-Nazi sympathies and were truculent. One, a typical Teutonic square-head, a pastry cook, cooling off after ascent from his galley, assured me that France was *kaputt*, next, England would be *kaputt*. And America, I asked? He knew America well, he had two brothers in Brooklyn. "We'll take care of America!" he said, grimly. One comprehended the country's problem as the melting pot of Europe.

I began to look at my fellow-passengers. A few were nerve-shaken refugees. One of my table companions, a Dutch diamond merchant, told me the war was over. The Germans had won it. The Allies would have to come to terms with Hitler. He was moving his business to New York. The lady on my left was a beautiful woman who was so obsessed with maintaining her dignity that she found it difficult to talk. A small diamond coronet on her evening bag gave me a clue. She was the youngish widow of an English peer and was returning to her homeland. Did her conscience trouble her? Despite all my genial attempts she made me feel that I was trying to break into the House of Lords. Beautiful, she had stiff competition from another American peeress. John Mock of M.G.M. had given me a note to Rafaelle, Duchess of Leinster, who would be on board. "She is very nice and lovely but unhappy," he said. I sought her out and found she was of surprising loveliness and young. It was the beginning of a long friendship. I noticed that she had recurrent moods of despondency. She confided that she had made up her mind to divorce the Duke of Leinster, being his second wife. She had a mother in New York whom she was joining. On the evening before we docked she surprised me by saying that she was returning to England. She could not bring herself to divorce Leinster at a time like this. Six months later, speaking at a Red Cross meeting in New York, I was most pleasantly surprised to find her on the platform, a fellow-worker. She had not returned to England. Later, she divorced the Duke but retained her English ties and gave delight to her friends on both sides of the Atlantic.

Ann Allingham

Anthony Allingham

At Tredegar House. The Hon. John Skeffington and Anthony Allingham

At Southampton, Long Island. Lady Ribblesdale and the author

As the *Manhattan* sailed up the Narrows all New York, cliff-like, rose up before us in the sunshine of an October morning. We were boarded by the Immigration officers and the Press. This was an old experience for me. "Your Government has sent you over?" asked a smiling reporter. "I suppose it's no use saying it hasn't!" I replied. He laughed. "Well, good luck to you! We'll wake up one day to these Nazis." I saw Duff Cooper pinned in a corner by the Press. The photo bulbs flashed. Lady Diana was always a show-shot. In a newspaper the next morning there we were, Duff Cooper, Ratcliffe and myself. 'The British Are Here To Get Us In', ran the heading. We looked like a row of criminals. There was a short biography of each of us. We sounded formidable. I posted a copy to the Director of the American Division to show him how silly all this subterfuge was.

IV

I stayed three days in New York. I was met at the dock by Jane Higbee, the daughter of my American host in Florida, with her husband. My speaking engagements in the South were not until the end of October, so it had been arranged that I should motor with them to Florida. My first New York call was on my lecture agent where I encountered a famous figure, Alexander Kerensky, the short-time Prime Minister, in 1917, of the first Russian Revolutionary Government. I lunched at the Century Club with my publisher, Brett of Macmillan's. There I was surprised and delighted to encounter Leonide Massine, my old friend of the Diaghilev Ballet of happier days. He had a singular story to tell me. After a short season at Drury Lane his company was scheduled to appear at the Metropolitan Opera House in three days' time. They were rehearsing for this in Paris when war was declared. Nearly all sailings were cancelled, following the torpedoing of the *Athenia*. In desperation Massine got a passage on the *Rotterdam* from the Hook. Thirty members of the company were compelled to take a later sailing and were due in New York in three days. As the curtain must go up they were rehearsing with a scratch company. Alas, I was not able to stay for this opening night. Massine was desperate but I heard that the thirty members of his company arrived on the morning of the opening night, went into immediate rehearsal, and the curtain rose triumphantly as scheduled on October 26. Massine told me that Dali was in New York and they were putting on a new ballet, *Bacchanale*. It was Dali at his most bizarre. He called it 'The first paranoic performance'. Death was a large black umbrella decorated with luminous skulls. There was a faun teaching its young to knit, and King Ludwig died as Lola Montez emerged from the belly of a swan. When this ballet had its first performance it created a tremendous sensation.

In the afternoon I called on the director of the British Library, to present my letter from the Ministry. The Library was situated high up in a vast monolith of steel and glass at Rockefeller Plaza Centre. I was shown into the office of Mr. Angus Fletcher. Handsome and polite, he was very scared and confessed the fact. If such obvious publicists as myself were seen coming into his office the conclusion would be drawn that they were organising propaganda. I should have telephoned him for a private meeting. I pulled out the New York newspaper with our photographs, which he had not seen. "The cat's out of the bag, anyhow," I commented. Angus Fletcher, a man of fifty-six, of Rhodesian birth, had been a lieutenant in the 1st Rhodesian Regiment, 1914–15, and in the Royal Field Artillery, 1915–19. A grave Scot, he was battling in a canoe with a typhoon. He soon lost his fear of me and we enjoyed a happy and intimate association. From the start I was appalled with what I discovered in his office. He was cramped in a few rooms, with an absurdly inadequate staff and directed, with idiotic vacillation, from London. He was so understaffed that often, late in the night, I discovered him typing letters. I did not know for some time that, a Foreign Office appointee, he was caught up in the feud between that office and the Ministry of Information.

After my call Fletcher hurried off to see Duff Cooper whom he implored not to make any propaganda. Duff Cooper very bluntly pointed out that any British subject of eminence who spoke publicly in America would inevitably be called a propagandist sent by the Government. Since we could never clear ourselves of this accusation we might just as well accept it and make our propaganda as effective as possible. This is what Duff Cooper did. He stayed four months and gave sixty-one lectures under the title of 'The Survival of Liberty'. Ratcliffe and I also pursued the same course.

On my last night in New York I went to a cinema. I had seen that it was showing a film of the Olympic Games in Berlin in 1936. This was the occasion when my friend Burton-Chadwick, with a Parliamentary party, had gone there as Hitler's guests. Anxious to see the Olympic Games film, which I had missed in England, I went to an up-town cinema. The film was excellent. It opened with a torch-bearer running from Olympia, passing through the Balkans and Hungary until a relay runner kindled the sacred flame on the tripod in the vast Berlin stadium. In presentation of the ceremonial march-past of the competitors in their national groups, a close-up was given of the official box. Under the drapings of the Nazi flags stood the hierarchs of the Reich, Hitler, Goering, Goebbels, etc. The camera 'panned' the state box and gave a special close-up of them. At this moment the quiet of the dark cinema was broken by a burst of applause. I could not believe my ears. At first I took it for a form of derision but the volume and length of the applause left me in no doubt. Then, somewhere behind me, a throaty voice cried *"Heil Hitler!"* A forest of hands shot forth and the cry was taken up. I sat in the darkness trying to assure myself that I was in a New York cinema. When the lights went up I examined the spectators and was startled to find they were predominantly German; their shaven heads and unlovely napes, with triple rolls of fat, recalled a Munich beerhall. When I told an American friend of my experience he asked the name of the cinema. I told him. "But of course! You were in Yorkville. It's part of the Reich in New York," he said. "If you care I can take you to a meeting of the *American Bund* where they drill in leather top-boots, wear swastika armbands, and *Heil* Hitler, led by the local Gauleiter." It was impossible to believe, after this experience on a night in October, 1939, when Poland lay prostrate under the Nazi terror, that a day would come, some five years later, when I should buy at a kiosk not a hundred yards from this cinema the New York *Staats-Zeitung und Herold* whose headlines proclaimed '*I Armee 26 Meilen von Köln entfernt. Russen in Sofia! Warschau beschossen. Roosevelt, Churchill einig gegen Japan.*' (First Army 26 miles from Cologne. Russians in Sofia. Warsaw bombarded. Roosevelt, Churchill united against Japan.)

V

We motored south through Maryland, Washington, Carolina and Georgia to Orlando in Florida, where I stayed once more with the Phillips. The motor journey was delightful. The gorgeous tints of autumn, the crimson of maple and sumach flowered in the woodlands as we went south. We halted one night in Washington and here I encountered the storm that was lashing the political heart of America. Congress was debating an amendment to the Neutrality Act. Here was a chicken that had come home to roost. The country was split between the pro-Allies and the Isolationists. President Roosevelt was seeking to amend the Act which prohibited any help for us. Facing a Presidential Election, he had twice assured the public that, "No American boys will ever be sent to fight in Europe" and "Our acts must be guided by a single-hearted thought—keeping America out of the war." But his subsequent actions belied his words. He had sent to Congress an amendment to the Act that would enable the Allies to purchase arms. For twenty-six days the debate in Congress raged. It saw the birth of the 'America First' organisation financed by active Isolationists. Representative Hamilton Fish, head of 'the National Committee to keep America out of foreign wars', issued appeals, on official stationery from his Congressman's office in the Capitol. He had already appeared as Germany's best friend. In August, 1939, he had arrived in Oslo from Germany in Ribbentrop's personal plane, to attend the International Parliamentary Union, where he declared Germany's cause was just. I encountered in Washington a group of women called 'The Mothers of America'. It had moved in by charabancs and was lobbying Congress. I talked with one of these women. She was not slow in showing her colours. "Why shouldn't Germany dominate Europe? The Jews? There are far too many in America, a menace. Europe is a rubbish heap and not worth one dead American boy."

But there were Anglophiles as well as Anglophobes. Before leaving New York I had called on my old friends, Thomas and Florence Lamont. This highly influential couple never hesitated to show their British sympathies. They were giving a luncheon party on November 7, Election Day, at which the Duff Coopers would be present. They invited me. I told them that I should then be in Florida. Duff Cooper has left us an account of that lunch.

At the end of the meal Mrs. Lamont arose and said, "I'm going to give you a toast which nobody need drink if they don't want to. Here's to the victory of the Allies, and to hell with neutrality." Looking round the table I saw that there were many who drank reluctantly and deplored the imprudence of their hostess. It was all the braver of Mrs. Lamont to propose the toast because her husband was a partner in the firm of Morgan, which was accused by the pro-German propagandists at the time of having played some sinister part in getting America into the previous war, for their own financial advantage.*

Soon after my arrival in Florida there was good news. The President had won his battle. In November he signed a Bill amending the Neutrality Act. It enabled the Allies, England and France, to purchase arms on a cash-and-carry basis. This marked the beginning of a campaign of calumny that pursued Roosevelt to his grave. The amendment stipulated that we had to pay cash in dollars. To do this we had to realise every dollar asset we owned. "We've got a squeeze on you," said an American banker to me, gloatingly. "You won't get any credit until you've scraped the bottom of your barrel. We're still sore about your default on the American debt. You compelled us to pass a bill blocking any loans to debtor nations. Look what it's costing you now!"

On arrival in Orlando I was most warmly received. The weather was halcyon. The poinsettias and hybiscus were in flower, the orange trees scented the town, the birds sang, the temperature was 75°, in all, an earthly paradise. But I could not enjoy it; my thoughts turned homewards. The British Expeditionary Force had been sent to France. There was an unnatural lull over England. No bombs fell, there was no sign of invasion. What became known as 'the phoney war' had set in. It was like waiting for a thunderstorm to break.

My first speaking engagement, a week after my arrival at Orlando, was at St. Augustine, on the Atlantic coast. It was the oldest city in the United States. In 1564 France had built a fort there. Then the Spaniards captured it and for 256 years made it the northmost outpost of the Spanish colonial empire. It was plundered by Sir Francis

* *Old Men Forget*, Duff Cooper (Rupert Hart-Davis, 1953).

Drake. Since 1783 it had been owned by the English and became the refuge of the Loyalists during the American Revolution. In 1821 it passed to America. It had the reputation of being conservative, with a somewhat English tradition. I was curious to experience the reactions of this my first American audience. They listened to me with courtesy but I noticed that any reference to the Allies' struggle evoked luke-warm interest. My chairman, a retired stockbroker, motored me back to the station and said, 'Mr. Roberts, we've heard you with great pleasure give us your analysis of the European situation. We have no patience with those Germans, but I think you should know we Ameri-cans have no intention of being drawn into that maelstrom. Europe is a slaughter-house. America, by the will of God, is a land where all races have learned to live in peace." I did not contest his view. As the train left he shook my hand. "Remember, sir, we have a warm regard for you Britishers, despite 1776," he said, smiling.

One morning my host's younger son threatened to commit a murder. To the isolation controversy that had broken out in a local newspaper, a man, with pro-German sympathies, had contributed a letter in which he boasted that in the last war he had acted as host to a German submarine commander and had supplied gasoline to sub-marines off the Florida coast. "I want to shoot that bastard before he does it again!" cried young Phillips.

Some English mail for me arrived at last. There were three letters from Louis in Paris. He was cheerful and well, he said. He had had to move into a small hotel which was cold. Heating was strictly rationed as also food. I wondered just how well he was. He always lied on that point. And at the end he wrote "If anything should happen to me I have left a letter for you." It struck an ominous note.

Two days later, as I came off the tennis court, there was a cable from Fuller in Paris. "Louis died today, after ten days' illness. Writing."

I put it in my pocket and went to my room. The sunshine had gone out of that glorious November morning. We had lost the long battle. He was twenty-eight, beloved by everyone. He had been an insepar-able part of Pilgrim Cottage, from my first day there. I tried to keep my grief to myself. These days young men were dying by the hundreds. I never received the letter he had left me. Some thief broke into his room and stole all its contents.

VI

At the end of November I went to the Higbees at Coconut Grove. My host was obviously failing. Jane and her husband were running the house, a haven of loveliness. I had two lectures to give in Miami. One proved stormy, with an Irish element that had joined up with an Italian one. I enjoyed the battle at question time and got an ovation. It was astonishing how many anti-British factions there were. The Irish, of course, were permanently hostile, though most of them were second and third-generation Irish who had never been in Ireland. The Italo-Americans were bitter over sanctions and Eden's 'vendetta' in the League of Nations. India had its grievances and conducted a virulent propaganda against us over independence; the Poles said we had let them down. We had. The American-Czechs accused us of betrayal at Munich, which was true. And there were the 'hundred-per-cent Americans' with prejudices imbibed from their school text books. It was all very well for us to talk about Hitler's persecution of the Jews. America had withdrawn its Ambassador in Berlin, in protest, but Prime Minister Chamberlain had signed an agreement with Hitler after Munich. We had had a pro-German Ambassador in Berlin. Chamberlain had rebuffed Roosevelt's warnings. The list arraigning us was a long one. The Hearst Press was venomously hostile, as also the *Chicago Herald*, influential in the mid-West.

I spent Christmas Eve at an hospitable house that overlooked the Bay, with Miami's towers for a skyline. On the roof of his house my host had erected an enormous model of Father Christmas driving his reindeer; elsewhere he went over the snow on his mission, here he rode above the palm trees. Indoors, a crowd of guests feasted. A cheery man, with a paper cap on his head, turned to me and said, "They'd make a mess if they dropped a bomb on us here!" "They?" I queried. "The Nazis—we're making a lot of noise here but it's only to drown our thoughts. We're bound to be in, the question is, shall we be in time—we argue so much before we decide to do anything. My boys hopped over to Canada to get into its Air Force." Many American boys hopped. Years later in a Newport home I saw a photograph of my host's grandson. He had joined the Royal Air Force and fought in the Battle of Britain. He caused some stir, for his name was John Bull. He returned home safely after thirty-five bombing missions.

At Coconut Grove we could hear the hydroplanes of the Pan-American Airline, at the aerodrome at Dinner Key, go roaring overhead on their way to South America. The landing hydroplanes were ferried into shallow water. Men then waded out and attached wheels whereupon the machines were pulled on to dry land. The aerodrome had a large restaurant and terrace. It was pleasant to go there at sunset and watch the giant clippers winging their way through a flaming sky, while the ocean turned from turquoise to crimson, mauve and indigo.

Just before Christmas I addressed, in the aerodrome restaurant, a lunch meeting of the Pan-American League. The conditions were difficult. The venetian blinds had to be lowered against the brilliant sunshine and I found myself competing with the noise of hydroplanes taking off. Some of them were on short flights to Cuba and Nassau, others went as far as Argentina and Brazil. One evening, while watching the planes I heard my name called by someone boarding the Nassau clipper. I was astonished to discover it was an old friend, Louis Paget. He was the great-grandson of Field-Marshal the Marquess of Anglesey, who, losing a leg at Waterloo, gave it a solemn funeral there. Louis' grandfather, Lord George Paget, was in The Charge of the Light Brigade at Balaclava. Louis had been an air-pilot in the First World War. Tall, elegant, monocled, he was almost a 'stage' Englishman in appearance. He had married an American widow and settled in the United States. At first he thought I had just alighted from flying the Atlantic. I asked what he was doing here with his wife, to whom he introduced me. He was visiting her mother who had a winter home in Nassau. They insisted that I should visit them. I promised to do so in a week's time, after I had filled two engagements in Miami and Palm Beach. The first was a return visit to the Committee of One Hundred, which, recalling my warning address in 1936, now regarded me as something of a prophet and gave me a cordial reception.

On the last day of the old year I found myself flying over the sea to Nassau in the Bahamas. And what a sea! The shallows of the water, with hundreds of little atolls awash, offered every colour of the rainbow to the traveller looking down into this shining submarine world. The sea was now translucently turquoise, now jade-green, purple, aquamarine, lemon-yellow and apricot-rose. Lonely little wisps of cloud floated past one like cherubs strayed out of a heavenly nursery. And then came the curving descent to Prince's Island, Nassau, shining white amid blue water and jungle-green vegetation.

Louis Paget lived across the harbour on Hog Island, in a South Sea house engulfed in palms and eucalyptus trees built around a bird-haunted patio. Hog Island was an ugly name for a strip of land that at its extremity was rightly called Paradise Beach. Below the verandah there was a bay of golden sand. A few steps and we were bathing in water of such warmth and azure blue as only tropical islands know. By day we dined in the patio, to a trilling of canaries while green lizards scuttled over a rockery. Evening was the loveliest time, with the moon upon the water, the flashing of a lighthouse, the swaying lanterns of anchored yachts, and the soft warm air of a January night. Nassau had not yet become the 'St. Helena', as she called it, of the Duke and Duchess of Windsor. It had not then been 'developed' by American and Canadian millionaires, or the Trust companies that would establish there their tax-exempt enterprises.

One day Louis insisted on my going fishing. I am not a fisherman but this was a special kind of fishing. He had a motor launch, navigated by a 'captain'. We sat in the stern with our long rods while the boat slowly 'trolled', and we cast our lines. The setting was lovely, a silky turquoise sea, off shore from our palm-tree island. Excitement took hold of me and I was taught to 'play' and bring in a plunging kingfish a yard long. We lunched on board, dozed, and 'trolled' and fished again until the great sun sank down to the horizon and we went home in a crimson glory.

Alas, I had to leave my charming hosts, a week was all too short. A clipper bore me back to Dinner Key. The next day I crossed Florida, bitten by a cold spell, to St. Petersburg on the Gulf Coast. This was a winter resort for the old. The streets were dotted with public benches so that the visitors could rest. The hall where I spoke was crowded with septuagenarians confident of becoming octogenarians. I was not surprised by an old gentleman who rose from the audience to tell me I was all wrong. What the world needed was love. The British and French should rise and open their arms to the Germans and welcome them in their homes. There could then be no wars. I asked him in that case why America did not abolish the quota-system for emigrants to America, it seemed a good opportunity to practise universal benevolence. He was vigorously assailed by indignant members of the audience who saw the fallacy of his policy.

From this oasis I went to lecture at Palm Beach. Here I found the Duff Coopers enjoying a luxurious respite between tours as the guests of Barbara Hutton. They moved almost like royalties. They had stayed at the British Embassy in Washington with our ambassador, Lord Lothian. They were guests of President Roosevelt. The wealthy elite of America rushed to entertain them for they were news and a social peak, and Lady Diana was a wonderful Press agent for Duff. But despite all this he was not happy. He found his audiences cool, the applause tepid, the Isolationists in force. In some places he had threatening letters. In Louisville, Kentucky, he was given a police guard on arrival. Quite unfairly, having once been a member of Chamberlain's Government, he was suspected of being an 'appeaser'. He had all the possible assets, perhaps too many of them; he belonged to the aristocratic set that ruled England, an Etonian, a Right Honourable, a Privy Councillor. He had a good First World War record, he had married a Duke's daughter, the most famous beauty of her day, he had written an excellent biography of Talleyrand. He had shown independence after Munich, and had resigned high office in disagreement with that betrayal. Despite all this, he was not a glamorous figure on the platform, a sturdy little man, quietly eloquent and not given to indulge in fireworks. Truculent, he made a bet not to lose his temper, and won it. He was openly honest and persuasive. His audience listened politely but remained reserved, suspicious of British subtlety.

I found him perturbed by our own blindness. Our Christian Science Ambassador, Lothian, who would soon die from his refusal to have medical attention, being surrounded at the Embassy by colleagues of the Christian Science cult, had advised the British Government to do no propaganda. When the Duff Coopers stayed with him, he gave Cooper the same advice. We were leaving the field open to all the anti-British elements in the States, German, Italian, Irish, Indian, who attacked us without restraint. I told Cooper that I thought we were at a low ebb but that there was a strong undercurrent in our favour.

By the beginning of March his tour was over and he sailed for England. He had had large audiences and good fees. He told me he had made $16,000. But British and American taxes took half, leaving him, after expenses, with a net £2,000. On his return he had not long to wait before gaining office. In May, Churchill appointed him Minister of Information. He had had two unsuccessful predecessors, Lord Macmillan and Sir John Reith. I was hopeful that the new broom would sweep out some of the incompetents and I wrote to congratulate him and wish him a happy tenure. His reply did not seem very enthusiastic, "Thank you—but God knows how I shall fare!" He had Harold Nicolson as his Parliamentary Secretary and wealthy Ronald Tree as his Personal Secretary. The Ministry had now expanded to over a thousand officials. It was clumsy and had been violently attacked. If all who had relations with it had had an experience similar to mine I could well believe the attacks were justified. It was unloved by the Press, and by the Foreign Office, which felt it had usurped its prerogative in dealing with external propaganda. At this time I was unaware of the bitter feud that was being fought with the Ministry for its control.

I was in Palm Beach to address the members of a Society that interested itself in international affairs. They were all people of considerable wealth who had their winter homes there. On this occasion the Society met in the house of one of its members, a large villa with its own beach from which one could survey the shining Atlantic ocean. In the audience was Mrs. Rose Kennedy, wife of the American Ambassador to Britain, and her young son, Robert. They came in from their villa next door. I had met Mrs. Kennedy in London. One of her boys was the doomed future President of the United States, and his brother Robert would also be assassinated, a third son, Joseph, would die in battle, a daughter in a plane crash.

I dropped a bombshell in that pleasant drawing-room with the ocean-view. America was now urging the extension of the three-mile limit to fifty, in the hope of keeping all traces of the war away. Halting in my talk, I looked out of the window at the passing ships in the inner channel and said, quietly, "Yes, though America passes a Neutrality Bill, emphasises its Monroe Doctrine, prohibits her ships sailing in dangerous zones, and seeks to protect herself by increasing the three-mile coastal limit, the war will come to you. It will come so close that one day you will see the shipping in this channel sunk by German submarines. It is not international law which protects you now, it is the British Navy, and how long we can preserve your immunity is doubtful."

Naturally my remarks provoked some opposition. A dog-fight would have followed but for the firm handling of my chairman. "You see in what a glass-house we live, and you heaved a brick," he said. "I'm afraid you're right!"

The next day I was gratified to receive a letter from Mrs. Kennedy. She wrote, "I enjoyed your lecture very much. It was a great success. I am sorry I did not have an opportunity to speak to you, but I am hoping I may do so at a later date. My husband is returning to England very soon, and I expect to join him in the spring. Do come to see us when we are there." In a letter of thanks the chairman wrote, "No one thought you were a propagandist, you were so impartial and fair."

Two years later, following America's declaration of war in December, 1941, American oil tankers traversing that channel were sunk in swift succession. In a speech in the House of Commons on April 23, 1942, during a secret session, Churchill said, "I will begin with the gravest matter, namely the enormous losses and the destruction of shipping by German U-boats off the coast of the United States. In a period of less than sixty days more tonnage was sunk in this one stretch than we have lost all over the world during the last five months before America entered the war."

My last public engagement in Florida took me to Winter Park, oddly named for a place that never knew winter. The enterprising President of Rollins College every year organised a symposium held in an open auditorium surrounded by palm trees. They called the symposium 'The Rollins Magazine' and drew speakers of eminence in many spheres to give their views on world events. The speakers this year were Carl Sandburg, a well-known poet, Countess Tolstoi, niece of the Russian author, Señorita Palencia, formerly Minister of the Spanish Republic and a member of the Cortes, Rex Beach, a popular novelist, the Editor of the *New York Times*, and myself. Countess Tolstoi, elderly, stout, had fled from Russia during the Revolution and had built for herself a considerable reputation as a speaker on Russian Affairs. The Spanish señorita looked like a glamour girl, she had a Scottish mother and a Spanish father. There was steel in her svelte figure. Sandburg, sturdy, of Scandinavian stock, surprised us all. It was the time of the political fence-sitters, who prided themselves on the virtues of American democracy, asserting that the Atlantic could keep the contamination by the Old World away from the New. This was the theme song of the Isolationists. Sandburg would have nothing of this. It was as if a little arctic wind had penetrated that sun-warmed arena. He was openly for immediate American intervention.

Winter Park was a silk cocoon. The college had something Grecian in its setting and purpose. One might have quoted Milton. It was another 'grove of Academe, Plato's retirement, where the Attic bird trills her thick-warbled notes the summer long'. Could it be that these young gods must struggle mid mud and slaughter on a European field, and the young goddesses know the stench of casualty wards? No, never, never; here in Paradise one could understand the hope of isolation from a demented Europe.

Within twenty-four hours I had stepped from scented orange groves into the snow-smitten hills of Ohio. The hospitable City Librarian of Cincinnati took me to his country home, happily named Bird Whistle. Birds sang in summer but now wintry winds struck this Tudoresque home with its great log fires. In the midst of a German colony, I was surprised by the warmth of my reception, but I was the guest-speaker of the local English-Speaking Union. This added to a doubt growing in me. I was engaged by the Anglophiles, who needed no convincing. Was one reaching the hostile Anglophobes, who would never pay to hear an Englishman? It was all very cosy and easy, but this was not what I was in America for.

Two days later I was in Chicago, in arctic weather. Here I had a heavy programme, the E.S.U.'s annual dinner, the Women's Club, the Arts League, the Rotary Club and the Executives Club. This last, a lunch club, with its large influential membership of business executives, was known ground, where I had built a reputation. This was my fifth visit. I knew I was in a hotbed of isolationism and anti-British feeling. A thousand miles from the Atlantic, two from the Pacific, what should Chicago fear from any god-damn foreign nation? Aware of what I was facing, I began my address cautiously. I told them that the defeat of England and France, twin nurseries of

democracy, was not the end of the chapter. Japan sat at the other end
of the Axis, waiting. When I finished there was long and warm
applause but I was aware of an undercurrent of hostility. Unfortunately, out of courtesy to me, the secretary had invited Bernays, the
British Consul-General, to sit at the high table. Here was proof of
the British 'plot'. A hornet-swarm of Isolationists followed us to the
secretary's office where an acrimonious debate ensued. I feared the
poor secretary might lose his job. I think the sentence that stung
the audience most was "We British once burnt your White House.
Don't let others do it a second time." "Oh boy!" I heard my chairman
murmur beside me, enjoying the scene.

However, the next morning the reaction was surprisingly good.
They were still talking about my speech, still angry, but it had been a
great entertainment. I was certain that I should never be asked again.
I was wrong. Within two years Japan had struck and isolationism sank
with the American battleships in Pearl Harbor. My return was
almost a festive occasion.

VII

In the next few weeks I became more and more aware of the spreading activity of the 'American First' organisation. It had found an
influential figurehead in young Colonel Charles Lindbergh, the hero
of the first solo flight from New York to Paris in May, 1927. It was a
mistake to call him pro-German, as some did, but he had isolationism
in his blood. His father, of Swedish birth, a representative in Congress, had opposed the entry of America into the First World War.
In 1918 his constituents, enraged, threw him out. The young
Lindbergh had met in Mexico the daughter of Dwight Morrow, the
American Ambassador there, a lawyer of great ability, a confidant of
Coolidge, a director of the J. P. Morgan banking house. At the time
of his death in 1931 *The Times* called it 'a disaster for international
affairs'. On his death his widow commissioned Harold Nicolson to be
his biographer. It was during the period that he was abroad writing
this biography that I succeeded Nicolson on the *Daily Telegraph* as
its 'star' book reviewer. The young Lindberghs suffered an appalling
experience. Their only infant son was kidnapped and murdered.
There was deep sympathy for them when they came to England, to

live there for a time in order to escape the monstrous publicity. With his special qualifications, Lindbergh, created a colonel, became a key-figure in American aviation circles and in the nineteen-thirties he made professional surveys in France, Germany, Russia. When he was the guest of the German Government Goering spared no effort to impress him with the might of her air-arm. He left convinced that it would be supreme in any contest with the Allies. Visiting London afterwards, he expressed this opinion to Nicolson who arranged a meeting with Ramsay MacDonald and Baldwin. They listened to Lindburgh and his warning, thanked him—and did nothing. From this and other experiences he wrote England off. His opinion was endorsed by Joseph Kennedy, the American Ambassador, whose reports to Washington expressed his view that France and England would suffer defeat in any contest with Germany.

Back in America Lindbergh soon found fellow-travellers. Ex-President Hoover shared his opinion. England, said Hoover, was in a decline. Lindbergh told him that the best way to prevent a war was for Britain to allow Germany to expand. Invited to join a 'Committee for Keeping America out of the War', (America First), financed from Chicago, the fortress of anti-British feeling, he met Borah, a prima donna Senator, who was quite certain about the inevitable defeat of England, and somewhat pleased by the prob-ability.* When Roosevelt began to seek the permission of Congress to amend the Neutrality Act in favour of the Allies, Hoover was thoroughly alarmed. He feared that a wave of hysteria would carry America into the war. In Lindbergh he saw a powerful standard-bearer. One day Lindbergh lunched with the J. P. Morgan directors. He told Thomas Lamont and his partners that England and France would lose the war if they attacked. He found that he was the only Isolationist in the room, and Lamont did not hesitate to express him-self as strongly pro-Ally. Borah now came out with a menacing proposition. Lindbergh should run for the Presidency against Roose-velt. 'Keep America Out of the War' seemed a winning slogan. In

* It was Bill Thompson, Mayor of Chicago 1915–31, a buffoon and hooligan, who invented the 'America First' slogan, announcing in 1927 his intention to 'bust King George on the snoot'. His crusade won votes among all the anti-British elements. Oddly enough, when he died in 1944 he had denounced the crusade of 'America First'. He declared that America's best interests lay in standing firmly shoulder to shoulder with Britain in the war.

October, Lindbergh made a radio address on 'Neutrality and the War'. He had become a very formidable figurehead of the Isolationists. He was approached by one, Truman Smith, of the White House, who said that he was acting on behalf of the Roosevelt Cabinet. If Lindbergh would desist from his radio addresses they would create for him a Secretaryship of the Air in the Cabinet. They misjudged their man. He ignored the bribe. When President Roosevelt publicly criticised him for his radio broadcasts he resigned his colonelcy. In February, 1941, he testified before the Senate Foreign Relations Committee, when the President sought further amendment to the Neutrality Act, "I do not believe England is in a position to win the war," he said. He favoured a negotiated peace and to make the best possible bargain with Hitler. "It would not be best to see Germany defeated."

Colonel Lindbergh, swept into the position of banner-bearer of the Isolationists, soon demonstrated that he had no political sense. He was reckless enough, in alluding to Canada's entry into the war, to say, "Sooner or later the United States must demand the freedom of all European possessions in the Western hemisphere as a defensive tactic." Against this Canada rose as a man.

A screaming flag-wagging mob cheered his speeches. It was a sad spectacle to see this young man who had made himself a national hero exhibit a mind without vision before an audience whose nature must have repelled any judicious person.

It was alarming to watch the swelling tide of isolationism. It was so strong that, in August 1941, only four months before Pearl Harbor, a Bill to extend Selective Service training beyond twelve months passed the House of Representatives by only a single vote, 204–203. "Britain cannot win, no matter how much aid she receives from America," declared Lindbergh, and in that same August he charged that, "There are only three groups in the country which wish America to enter the war, namely the British, the Jews and Roosevelt." This naturally was cheered by a quarter of a million Americans of German descent, and three millions of Irish.

On Sunday, December 7, 1941, the chairman, a Senator, of an 'America First' meeting in New York was interrupted during his speech by some news. He then informed the audience that the Japanese had attacked the American Fleet in Pearl Harbor that morning. "It's just what the British planned for us!" he observed. Following the Japanese attack 'America First' collapsed like a pricked balloon. But for twenty-six months prior I was made aware, as I went about speaking, of a formidable attempt to deprive us of any help. Our antagonists came from all sides, and our own past misdeeds added to the indictment. The betrayal at Munich was cited against us.

VIII

At the end of March, 1940, I was back in New York. En route I lectured in Detroit. It was there I had a disconcerting revelation. Picking up a newspaper I read that the British Government had requisitioned the funds in the U.S.A. of British subjects. Among many, the Imperial Tobacco Company was compelled to sell its leaf stock, worth several million pounds, transfer the dollars to England, and then pay enormous super-tax on the profits of the sale. In vain they pointed out that after the war they would have to buy back their leaf.

I had some seventy thousand dollars invested in America. Since no British subject could draw one penny out of England, it was this money, earned in the U.S.A. and taxed in both countries, that would enable me to give my services to the Government. I had accepted many speaking engagements without asking any fee, particularly those which I felt would serve our cause. Alarmed at this discovery, I called on the British Consul in Detroit. He did not think it could possibly mean that I should have to surrender my personal funds, but he was not sure. I then wrote my London bank who replied that I must surrender every penny I had, moreover, I must remit to England all my current dollar earnings! It would be for me to request the Treasury to remit such money as I found necessary.

Back in New York, I went to see Fletcher at the British Information office. "It's quite ridiculous! It's your own money, you're here in America doing a wonderful job!" he said. I told him I felt I must obey the law, and that I must return to England as I would be without means for I could not retain any money I possessed or earned in the U.S.A. He was quite alarmed. "How much a day do you want here?" he asked. I said I thought I could manage on twenty dollars. He begged me to stay. "You are the most valuable speaker I have, everybody wants you. I'll make a request for twenty dollars a day. There'll be no trouble about that. After all, it's from your own money. I want you to go to the Pacific Coast."

Englishmen are, or were, law-abiding creatures. It is drilled into them from birth. I found I could not sleep having some seventy thousand dollars here in America which I must hand over to the Government, now desperately pressed for dollars with which to buy American munitions. I therefore sold my stocks and sent the money to my London bank, for the Treasury. For this money I was given the sterling equivalent, which was then blocked. I had stripped myself of all my funds, relying on the twenty dollars a day that would be remitted to me. It proved to be the most foolish act of my life. I was to learn bitterly that no man should trust the promise of a Government. It has not the solidity of a soap bubble.

If I was to remain and wished to visit the Pacific Coast, I had to finance myself. I wrote to James Hilton, now one of the most highly-paid and successful scenario-writers in Hollywood. Could he get me a film commission that would finance my mission? His reply was prompt and heartening. Metro-Goldwyn-Mayer would pay me $3,000 to make a scenario of a Somerset Maugham short story. It should not take more than a month. I accepted the offer, and to Fletcher's delight left for the Coast. He was expecting a reply from the Treasury any day about my allowance. He gave me a list of sixteen meetings that he wanted me to address. I was paying my own expenses.

I had never seen Hollywood. I set off on the long train-trek across the United States. There were then magnificent pullman trains. Today they are almost extinct, for instead of a four-day journey passengers now take a five-hour flight.

On the train journey there was an amusing incident. A man, reading my luggage label, exclaimed, "But you're not the author!" On my replying that I was, he said, "For some years I was the assistant librarian at Laramie, in Wyoming. So I know all your books. We get there about noon, I am visiting old friends. Will you let me wire the Librarian that you are passing through? He would like to meet you." There would be a five-minute halt. I agreed. How very strange! I had been feeling very much alone on that train and now, here at

Laramie, seven thousand two hundred feet high in the uplands of remote Wyoming, I was known. A telegram was sent off. On stepping down on the platform at Laramie, I found fifteen persons, headed by the town's Librarian. I was introduced. I shook hands, I wrote in autograph albums. Then the whistle sounded and the cry 'All aboard!' I left, for the Great Divide, the watershed of the Rocky Mountains that separated rivers flowing east to the Atlantic and west to the Pacific.

At Los Angeles good, kind James was waiting for me. Alas, my prophecy when he had talked of settling in Hollywood was coming too true. He was enormously successful, but already he had changed wives. The new Mrs. Hilton was a beautiful, red-haired Russian. Quiet, devoted Alice had been superseded. I found that he had brought out his father, a retired schoolmaster, and his mother, and settled them near him. He had booked for me a room in a Hollywood hotel, almost opposite a cinema whose entrance had a forecourt where, in wet concrete, the famous stars had impressed their footprints. I had an ingenious bed-sitting-room with a bed that disappeared into the wall at the touch of a button. The room had been filled with flowers by my thoughtful friend. From the first day to the last of my stay he never failed in his attention. Just then he was working on a scenario of *Mrs. Miniver*, a small wartime book that had had a colossal success, and which his company had bought. "What is all the fuss about? I can't find anything in the book!" he complained. Even so, he achieved one of his big successes. The film, with Greer Garson of *Goodbye Mr. Chips* fame, as Mrs. Miniver, had a phenomenal success based on the story James concocted.

Apparently my reputation had preceded me, not as an author but as a speaker for the British cause, and James added seven engagements to my list. He had a charming home, high up above Hollywood, with a garden, from which at night one looked down on a fairyland of lights running along Sunset Boulevard to the Pacific coast. I found that the oddest object in this long highway was an oil-pumping derrick working in the very middle of the road. The following day James introduced me to the Grand Mogul of Metro-Goldwyn-Mayer, Mr. Sam Goldwyn, and I started work on the scenario. I was given an office, with a typist, and, oddly enough, it was furnished with a long couch. Was one supposed to sleep on the job? It seemed one was, in another sense, as I found later, from the indignation of other writers in the long row of offices. The names on the doors often astonished me. I thought their owners had long been dead. Certainly many of them had been forgotten, but were still here on the payroll. This was illustrated when one day, going across to the lunch canteen with one of my fellow-scribes, he suddenly pulled me back. I asked what was the matter. "Christ! There's Sam Goldwyn! If he sees me he'll know I'm still on the payroll!" Our corridor was something of a cemetery of 'has beens'.

I completed my scenario in three weeks. My colleagues were indignant. I should have made it a year's job, perhaps longer. When I worked on this scenario of Maugham's Pacific story I had a surprise. I learned from my typist that it had been handled by four quite well-known predecessors whose efforts were never heard of. This was the fate of my scenario, though they seemed pleased with it and made me a tempting offer to stay on. But I was not there for the purpose of scenario-writing. I was there to raise funds for my campaign. Moreover, there was the fear of going moribund and joining the pensioned 'has-beens'.

My first speaking engagement was at a morning meeting of a book club held in the luxurious Beverley Hills Hotel. I was there to speak as a guest-author. I listened to a very *soignée* lady reviewing a book on the Nazi subjugation of Poland. She treated it as if it had had happened on another planet to a foolish species of the human race. She ended with a panegyric of sane, civilised and safe America that was loudly applauded. The Dame President, orchid-adorned, asked me to say a few words as a distinguished British author. If an earthquake had struck the ball-room it could not have been more shaken by the time I had finished. How safe did they imagine they were? I ended with a vision of the speaker picking herself out of the rubble when the Japanese bombs had demolished the hotel. Some of the audience were indignant. Some applauded. The meeting became a debating session. The reviewer, with a very German name, was indignant but I found a strong backing, though I had destroyed a pleasant morning. If only the Director of the American Division of the Ministry of Information could have been present!

Later, I was the guest of honour at a large luncheon of film people. There were speeches touching on the war, all sounding a note of sublime detachment, although the news from Europe was terrible. The Germans were sweeping across Belgium and the Maginot Line, the British Army was almost surrounded in Flanders. Should I tell them the horrid facts and mar this love-feast? My chairman was Conrad Nagel, the film star. "Stop me if you wish," I said to him on rising, "but someone must tell you the truth." For half an hour I indulged in an apocalyptic vision of the new Assyrians (Japanese), descending on the cinema-fold in the Californian hills. When I had finished not a studio was left functioning, the inhabitants were trekking over the mountains, fleeing from the little yellow men along the coast. "My God!" exclaimed Nagel. "You make me wish our Navy was ten times the size!"

There was an echo of this occasion later, after the Japanese attack. "I was asked the other day when your name came up in conference," wrote my friend John Mock, the cinema director, "if you were that Cecil Roberts who paralysed a luncheon here with a forecast of Pearl Harbor".

In Los Angeles the next day I ran into fierce opposition. There was a large German element. It took me half an hour to get control of the meeting. Fortunately I had an able chairman, a local banker. But my suspicions were aroused. A little man with a loud voice got up and asked some very 'anti' questions. This was the third time I had seen him and obviously he was following me round. There was also a lady angry about India and our wicked repression of the Indians. She, too, kept appearing. Finally, I asked her blandly if she was referring to Indians or Red Indians, as I understood the latter had suffered much repression. The meeting roared with laughter and she vanished.

I did not always find myself battling against the tide. At a university debate where I spoke I was surprised to get a negative vote on the resolution, 'That the United States should keep out of all foreign wars'. At a large lunch at the luxurious Vista del Arroyo Hotel, Pasadena, where I shared the bill with Upton Sinclair the chairman, and two others, the applause was so loud and long that the veteran novelist of The Jungle turned to me and said, "My! You've stirred 'em! Get up and take another bow." It was heartening after so much exhaustive battling.

I felt ill in this spring of 1940. With foreboding I listened to the radio announcing the increasing darkness of the European scene. Our attack on Norway had failed. The Germans swept nearer Paris, Belgium was occupied, exposing the flank of the British Expeditionary Force. The Dutch had surrendered. I often expressed a confidence I did not feel. My financial position was precarious. I had nothing but two thousand dollars, a return ticket to New York and a fountain pen. Happily I had some good friends.

I was most hospitably entertained in Hollywood, the Hilton home was always open to me. I had weekends at the ranch home in the San Fernando Valley of Florence Ryerson and Colin Clements, a married couple, who had had a Broadway hit with their play about Harriet Beecher Stowe. They were very successful scenario-writers. Here at their home, surrounded by giant eucalyptus trees, infinite gradations of light passed across the blue foothills and flower-filled valley. One evening my hosts took me to dine at a roadhouse. The innkeeper was a Cockney who had once lived at Kingston-on-Thames. This led to my saying I lived at Henley-on-Thames. Thereupon his wife joined in the conversation. She had been on the vaudeville stage and had lived at Henley. "Have you ever read some books by Cecil Roberts about his cottage there?" she asked. Surprised, I replied that I knew those books. "I've got them all," she said. "You see, I was the housekeeper at Pilgrim Cottage." This was indeed news to me but I discovered she was speaking the truth. Some years before I acquired the cottage it had been inherited by a retired British Consul-General from New York, who died in it. She had been his housekeeper.

"You know, in *Gone Rustic*, Cecil Roberts wonders who planted the four poplar trees in the corner of the garden. I've often been of a mind to write and tell him. I planted them," she said.

"I wish you had written to me, I always wondered about them," I replied. She looked bewildered by my remark. Then my friends, unable to keep silent, revealed my identity. For a moment she stared at me, then burst into tears. There, at a roadhouse in the San Fernando Valley, in faraway California, I had brought back the past with its halo of an exile's memories.

I found other friends. There was Cecil Forester, then enjoying great success with his 'Hornblower' novels, Maurice Evans, the English actor, renowned for his Shakespeare roles, Irene Rich, the film star and broadcaster, and, first met in Chicago, beautiful Narcissa

278

Thorne. She had visited my cottage during the time that she exhibited her renowned miniature-room models in a London exhibition attended by Queen Mary. She owned a large villa in Santa Barbara and one day took me to visit neighbours, Mr. and Mrs. Stuart Chase. He was a retired stockbroker. At lunch he said he would like to show us a film he had just received from England. His daughter, Barbara, had married a young English officer in the Guards. He was in France fighting, and his wife and infant daughter were staying in a Perthshire castle belonging to her husband's family. The Scotch mist swirled in that film shown to us in the darkened library on that bright Californian April afternoon. Our host proudly showed us his daughter wheeling her baby in a perambulator across the castle's lawn. I asked the name of the young officer she had married. George Mercer Nairne. "Not of the Landsdowne family?" I queried. Startled, he said "Now, how do you know that?" I told him that I knew quite a lot about the family, that the present young Marquess was fighting in France, that in the First World War the family had suffered heavy losses; that it had French blood, the fourth Marquess's wife being a Flahaut, the daughter of Talleyrand's illegitimate son; that they owned Lansdowne House in London, which Gordon Selfridge, of Selfridge's Store, had rented, and in which he had given his famous parties; that the Lansdowne country house, Bowood, known as 'The Golden House', at Calne in Wiltshire, was a showplace, but that successive death duties had caused part of it to be demolished, and that the fifth marquess, an ex-Foreign Secretary, had been the author of the famous 'Lansdowne Letter' in the *Daily Telegraph*, in which, in 1917, he advocated a negotiated peace, sickened by the frightful bloodshed that was draining away the youth of the nations. The letter had created a tremendous sensation and a bitter controversy.

"Good heavens, are you a member of the family?" asked Mr. Chase, astonished. "No," I replied. "Just before I left England I finished a book called *And So To Bath*. Bowood is on the Bath Road. In Calne church I have seen a memorial to the late father of your son-in-law George, Lord Charles Mercer Nairne, killed fighting in 1914. George's mother married again and is now Lady Violet Astor."

My host's daughter, Barbara, left for America four months later, in August, 1940, with her daughter, the baby in the perambulator, and it was in this American home that a son and heir was born in

February, 1941. She returned to the United Kingdom in the autumn of 1943 with her two children, via Portugal. In 1944 Charles Hope, the seventh Marquess of Lansdowne, was killed fighting in North Italy. His cousin George succeeded as the eighth marquess, his wife Barbara becoming the marchioness. Their son, the young Earl of Shelburne, became a page to Queen Elizabeth in 1956.

And So To Bath, finished just before I left England, passed through six editions in the first year. It brought me a stream of letters from readers. Some must have been lost in the Atlantic crossing. Within six months of my visit to the Chases at Santa Barbara I received a letter from Lord Winterton, long a famous figure in the House of Commons.

> I have read your recent book *And So To Bath* with such pleasure and profit that I feel I must mention two interesting facts concerning Lord Lansdowne's family. Lord Lansdowne, the Foreign Minister, married my aunt. The present Lansdowne is, therefore, a first cousin, once removed, of mine. In the sixteenth century there was a miller, of yeoman stock, at Calne, of the name of Petty. He had a son who was an ambitious young man, and who eventually succeeded to his father's considerable income and business. He was not, however, content to remain a miller, and he became an 'entrepreneur' in various forms of business activities. He was knighted. His daughter married a member of the Fitzmaurice family, the direct ancestors of the present Lansdowne family.
>
> Just before the French Revolution there lived in France an old man of a very ancient family called the Comte de Flahaut, who married, a year or so before the taking of the Bastille, a young lady of considerable beauty and of good family. She was in the twenties, and he was nearly seventy. There is good reason to believe that the marriage was never consummated. About two years later the Comtesse de Flahaut had a son, whose father was undoubtedly a young priest in the neighbourhood, called Talleyrand. When the massacres of the French Revolution began Comte de Flahaut was murdered, but his wife and child mysteriously disappeared into a place of hiding which, it is believed, was provided for them by Talleyrand.
>
> Young Charles de Flahaut next appears on the scene at an inspection of the cadets of Saint Cyr by Napoleon who, seeing an intelligent and good-looking boy in the ranks, asked him what his name was. He replied, "Charles de Flahaut". Napoleon is said to have answered, "That seems to be a good name.

What do you want to do in life?" The boy replied, "To serve as near to the person of Your Majesty as possible." Napoleon was amused by the answer, and gave instructions that if the young cadet performed his first two years of service in the regiment satisfactorily, he should be put on his Personal Staff. In due course Charles became an A.D.C. to Napoleon, whom he faithfully served until the Battle of Waterloo, being among the first to return to the Emperor's side after the flight from Elba.

Flahaut became a prominent figure in Napoleonic society and was the lover of Hortense de Beauharnais, and unquestionably the father of the Duc de Morny, afterwards Napoleon III's Foreign Minister. Following Napoleon's final defeat and exile, Charles de Flahaut came to England, a bold thing for a man to do who was an émigré. Owing, however, to his charm and tact, he became very well known in London Society, and eventually married the daughter of Lord Keith of Elphinstone, an heiress some twenty years his junior. The marriage was opposed at first by Lord Keith, and was condemned in a good many circles on the ground that a middle-aged émigré who had had a *vie sentimentale* in his own country had no right to marry a young and beautiful Scottish heiress. However, the marriage proved a great success, and their daughter married Lord Lansdowne, and was thus the mother of Lord Lansdowne, the Foreign Secretary.

In his old age, during the Second Empire, de Flahaut was a frequent visitor to Paris, and the Emperor was said to rely, to a considerable extent, upon his judgment and opinion. He certainly saw a great deal of, and doubtless influenced, his own son, the Duc de Morny—Napoleon III's Foreign Minister. Fortunately he died a year or so before Sedan and the crash, being well over eighty at the time.

I once asked my uncle, Lord Lansdowne, what he thought of his grandfather, and he laughed and said that he was a most charming and dignified old gentleman, of whom his relatives and a large circle of friends were slightly afraid, since he possessed an icy French sarcasm. He also said that no one would have supposed, from his appearance and behaviour, that he had led so wild a life in French Society when he was young.

I have always thought, though as far as I know there is no scientific basis for the idea, that French blood, when mixed with that of other nations, is very potent for many generations. At any rate my young cousin, the present Lansdowne, has a distinct French look about him, and two of his first cousins, George Mercer Nairne, and Mrs. Myddleton, might be young

French people. His mother, Lady Violet Astor, always said of George that when he goes to France he talks with his hands like a Frenchman. I have always thought it very interesting, not to say amusing, that Lord Lansdowne the statesman, with his great record of public service as Viceroy of India, Governor-General of Canada and Foreign Secretary, should have been a great-grandson of Talleyrand! You will remember that Talleyrand always claimed that the interests of his country often demanded, on the part of its servants, gross, and, apparently, dishonest inconsistency. I have often wondered if the Talleyrand blood in my uncle was not one of the reasons why, with great wrong-headedness (as I think), but with complete sincerity, he suddenly, after being an enthusiastic supporter of 'war to the death' with Germany, suggested peace terms, in his famous letter.

Another letter, concerning my book, came from Elinor Glyn in London, the famous red-haired, green-eyed novelist. She had enamoured the great Marquess of Curzon, who in the end behaved rather shabbily. She was famous, or notorious, as the authoress of *Three Weeks*, a pioneer sex romance that had scandalised the Edwardians, and provoked the verses beginning 'How pleasant to sin with Elinor Glyn on a tiger-skin.' Her letter to me ran:

I want to thank a fellow author for giving me so much pleasure. I have just read *And So To Bath* and revelled in every page of it. I remember that party at Osterley Park you tell about . . . those were wonderful days of splendour and food—such food! Such gallant admirers, such divine extravagance. Indeed, 'gone with the wind'. And I am so glad that at seventy-six I can remember them all and live through the excitement again. I would like to meet and talk with you. If you are in London and ever go out in the afternoon, do ring me up and come to see me—we should have lots to say!

Alas, when I received this letter I was in New York, and she had died before I returned home. Another letter, full of reminiscences, came from the ninety-three-year-old Dowager Countess of Jersey, concerning the Bishop of Raphoe, father of an earlier Lady Jersey, who was notorious in the secondary role of a highwayman. "He induced a merchant whom he met when in ecclesiastical attire to send his goods by the Bath Road for safety. The merchant was duly attacked by a masked highwayman—but the mask fell off, disclosing the features of the Bishop. He was, I think, ultimately killed by his own dogs," she wrote, in a firm hand.

A friendly couple entertained me at their home in the foothills of Pasadena. One summer's day in 1939 they had called on me at Pilgrim Cottage. He was born English, and, settling in Chicago, had founded a successful business. Now retired in Pasadena, he was making a tour in England with his wife. They were a delightful pair. By an extraordinary coincidence I met them again on board the *Manhattan*. They now collected me from my hotel. I can never forget that first weekend, I was in Hell in their Paradise. It was the time when the British and French armies had collapsed. Each morning the newspaper had a map with a black line showing the German advance. It was a few days before Dunkirk. Thousands of Frenchmen were fleeing from Paris. We seemed naked and doomed. And here in this lovely house, with its garden going up to the foothills, my hosts tried to console me.

Distraught, I returned to my hotel on the Tuesday morning. While unpacking I noticed some of my ties were missing, also three suits. I summoned the maid and asked her about them. She knew nothing. Then I discovered that my Leica camera was missing, and Express Traveller's Cheques valued $1,200, also a box of gold studs. Obviously I had been robbed. The manager was reluctant to call the police, but I insisted. A week later someone knocked at my door. I opened it to find there a rather grim-looking man. The badge inside his coat revealed that he was a special detective. He asked to see my passport. Then he surprised me with some questions. "Are you a British propaganda agent?" "No, I am conducting propaganda in regard to the war, but I am not a paid Government agent." He made a note. "Do you communicate with the British Government?" "Yes, I write on the situation as I find it here." "Do you keep copies of your reports?" "Yes," I replied. "Can I see them?" he asked. "Certainly." I went to the lowest drawer of my dressing-table where I kept my correspondence file. To my amazement the folder, with some twenty letters to the Ministry of Information, and my correspondence with the New York office, was missing. He noticed my surprise. Then he smiled and said, "Thank you, Mr. Roberts, you have been quite truthful." He opened the wallet he held. "Here is your folder with your correspondence." He passed it to me, dumbfounded. "We have of course read it. There's nothing to which we can take exception. You may wonder how we come to possess it. While you were away in Pasadena your room was entered, without difficulty probably. The thief was in connivance with the doorman, we suspect. But he is not an ordinary thief, in fact he belongs to a rather stupid gang. On Catalina Island one of them went to a store, bought something worth $12 and presented a $100 traveller's cheque, seeking the change. As you know, you have to countersign under your own signature. The fellow countersigned but an alert girl at the cash desk detected faint pencilling, over which he had written your signature. They called the police. Now, what I am going to tell you is in confidence. He and two of his associates will come up for trial next Friday. You will have to give evidence. You will not be asked about the theft of your correspondence. We have arranged with the defending lawyer that it shall not be mentioned. It was your correspondence, not your cheques they were after, for some one whom we are watching. The stupid fellows couldn't resist your checks and some of your things—outside their assignment. We are covering a widespread secret organisation of a nature I need not define but"—here he smiled—"we wish to collect more evidence. So, please, in the witness-box confine yourself to answering the questions that will be put to you."

A week later I was in the Los Angeles Court. The men in the dock were sentenced for theft. When the detective motored me back to my hotel I asked him a question.

"Is the organisation that you are watching associated with the German Consulate in San Francisco?" He looked startled.

"I can't answer your question. Thank you for your co-operation," he said, as we shook hands on parting, then, almost as an aside he added, "I hand it to you British!" and returned to his car. Later I read in a newspaper that two agents of the German Consulate in San Francisco had hurriedly departed. One, a woman, had been arrested on a spy charge.

Meanwhile there had arrived a decision from the British Treasury regarding my application for a dollar allowance from my remitted funds to enable me to continue my work. The Director of the American Department of the Ministry of Information in London, wrote:

I am sorry to say that though we presented your case as sympathetically as possible we have received a reply from the Treasury to say, "We should look very coldly indeed upon an application of this kind. Our refusal may seem to imply that Roberts must return to this country for the summer months. There is, however, the alternative that he might pass the summer in some of the West Indian Islands where, as you know, the problem of remittance of currency does not arise. Would not this be a happy solution of his difficulties, since it would avoid the double trip across the Atlantic?"

In effect, I was to beachcomb in Nassau or Bermuda! "In any case I hope that you may be able to remain on the other side and carry out your propaganda," added the Director. So although I was working for nothing and wearing myself out they would not allow me any of the dollars I had sent home. When I forwarded this letter to Fletcher, saying I had almost decided to quit, he replied, "I am very glad you did not bolt for home because I am sure that a person as well-known as you are should, at a time like this, stay where there is a demand for his talent." I was not mollified by a further letter from the Ministry. "I agree with Fletcher's advice that, if you can do so, it would be useful for you to remain in the United States." If I could do so! I had come almost to the end of my funds but they wanted me to stay!

IX

The time had come for my return to New York. Just before I left, Alfred Hitchcock arrived at the M.G.M. studio with an unfinished film which he would now complete, half having been 'shot' in England.

I made my last visit to my friends at Pasadena. It was there, over the weekend, that I experienced my blackest hours. May had become a nightmare month. Churchill had taken over the premiership from Chamberlain. He told the House of Commons, in an immortal phrase, "I have nothing to offer but blood, toil, tears and sweat." It resounded across America like a clarion call. There followed the collapse of the French Army with the break through of the German Panzer divisions. In that lovely home in the Pasadena hills we sat by the radio while fateful news poured in. King Leopold had surrendered, without the approval of the Belgian Government. It was almost unbelievable for me to sit there and hear of the Germans overrunning Ghent, Mons, Charleroi, Tourcoing, Roubaix—all places I had known when a war-correspondent in the First World War. I had gone through them in the Allies' victorious march to the Rhine. Now the French, demoralised, faced complete defeat. The morning newspaper showed the evil black lines of the overrunning Germans on the map of France. Our army, threatened with being surrounded, kept open a line of retreat to the coast. On May 27 the saga of Dunkirk began. In the next nine days a quarter of a million soldiers were evacuated from the beaches and Dunkirk.

I left for New York. The Hiltons, solicitous to the last, drove me to the station. I had only one suit in my portmanteau, the rest stolen. They gave me a parting present of a radio. I was never to see them again. Their marriage collapsed. Fourteen years later James, in what seemed outwardly the acme of success, was dead, aged forty-five. Cancer struck him down. He had flared like a comet and disappeared.

There was a long halt in Kansas City. Again Churchill had made his lion-roar in the House. "We shall go on to the end. We shall fight in France, we shall fight on the seas and oceans . . . We shall never surrender." In Chicago I felt too ill to journey on and halted for a few days. I was having acute stomach pains, with disturbed nights. I felt that it probably arose from nervous exhaustion, to which money worries now contributed. One morning, breakfasting in the Drake Hotel, I opened a newspaper and sat stunned, my breakfast untouched. The Germans were in Paris. The French Government had fled to Bordeaux. Across a neck of water England faced the triumphant Nazi giant. Our army shattered, it was incredible that we could hold off the day of doom. I looked out over the blue lake but I saw only a nightmare world. The country lane in which I lived had not been trodden by an invader since the Norman Conquest. My cottage had lain safe in a fold of the Chiltern Hills while Spain's Armada had been broken and Malplaquet, Trafalgar, Waterloo and the Great War had been victoriously fought. As I left the dining-room a newspaper on a stand proclaimed, in heavy letters, 'ENGLAND'S INVASION CERTAIN'.

The next day I boarded the train for New York where my good friend Dr. Boehm examined me. He diagnosed a duodenal ulcer. "If you are not careful you will have a haemorrhage," he said, ordering me to bed. I asked Fletcher to get me a passage home, a thing Dr. Boehm thought sheer madness. "It's impossible to get a passage, everything's chaotic," said Fletcher, who came to see me.

I had good friends. The Louis Pagets came and took me to their summer home at Fitzwilliam in New Hampshire. For the next two months, with unwearying attention, they nursed me back to health. One day from John Mock in Hollywood came a letter. "Everyone here says you have done a magnificent job. They still talk of you. For God's sake take care of yourself." It was a ray of comfort.

There was another 'exile' in that hospitable house, a little English woman, Ann Henderson, wife of a civil servant, with two small children. He was a resident magistrate, changing posts from one remote African colony to another. Her own experiences had included living with Zulus, fighting snakes within a few feet of her childrens' cots, trekking through perilous deserts and making hazardous aeroplane flights. Henderson had just been appointed to a new post in Nigeria. He was first called to London for consultation, and then had left by boat for Africa, where his wife and children were to join him. Torpedoed, he was brought back to Liverpool, wounded, having lost all his possessions. When out of hospital he set off again. For ten harrowing weeks Ann was without any news of him. She never complained. Left without funds in the U.S.A., she nursed, washed and dressed her children.

It was from her that I got new glimpses of the man now holding England's fate in his hands. She had once been Churchill's steno-grapher-secretary at Chartwell when the politician, suffering an eclipse, turned historian. She revealed that man of genius, not *en pantoufles*, but *en chemise de nuit*. Suddenly inspired, he had a habit of ringing for her in the nocturnal hours to dictate passages from his bed or parading up and down the room, an apparition in a white night-gown, flannel cummerbund and night cap. What she loved most about the lord of Chartwell was that, on departing twenty miles distant on a mission to arouse a sluggish House of Commons to a sense of Britain's peril, he always bade farewell to the household, as if setting forth on a lengthy pilgrimage. On one occasion when Ann sought him for a telephone call she was assured by the cook that Mr. Churchill had not left for London as he had not been in to say goodbye.

At last in the month of November, 1940, Ann heard from her husband who had arrived at his post in Lagos, Nigeria. With no hesitation, taking her children, aged four and six, she set off across the submarine-infested Atlantic. I did not see her again until twenty years later when I was the guest in Nassau of Ann and her husband, now Sir Guy Henderson, Chief Justice of the Bahamas. Of such material was our Empire made.

July and August passed at Regency House. The 'phoney war' had come to a sudden end. How long could England hold out in this inferno of fire and bomb?

In September, restored to health, I returned to New York. I left that hospitable home among the New Hampshire hills all unaware that I should never again sit with Louis Paget in the little library opening on to the garden-terrace. Within a short time I was shocked by his death. One evening the butler, entering to announce dinner, found him dead in his chair. It was too early to go at forty-nine but he was of a generation that had had its youth sapped by a great war in which he was an aviator. Tall, handsome, gentle, he was the pattern of an Englishman who had endeared himself to all.

In October I spoke at twelve meetings. I found there had been a heartening change in American public opinion, it was veering towards us. Churchill's great speeches, his absolute defiance of Germany when all seemed lost, and then the great air-battle, waged through July, August and into September, aroused immeasurable admiration. He coined, in tribute to the Royal Air Force, another immortal phrase—"Never in the field of human conflict was so much owed by so many to so few." There was no longer any doubt where President Roosevelt's sympathies lay. To the point of infringing the Constitution he began to plan help, to undermine the prohibitions of the Neutrality Act. He was called a traitor by the Isolationists. Deeply hated by certain elements for his New Deal, a powerful coalition moved against him, but he was adroit, and had an infallible sense of the undersurge of public feeling. Churchill had warned Lord Lothian, the British Ambassador, not to pay too much attention to the eddies of American public opinion, but he was assiduous in his courtship of the President, and constant in subtle appeals for help. He wanted ammunition and weapons after Dunkirk. He got them. The

Sir Thomas and Lady
Beecham

Lady Emerald
Cunard

President Franklin Roosevelt

Isolationists accused Roosevelt of perilously undermining American defence, of useless aid to a beaten country, but he was undeterred. He had no doubt England would never surrender. We had now another enemy in America, the Italo-Americans. Roosevelt risked the loss of many electoral votes with his powerful broadcast when, on France's downfall, Italy declared war. "The hand that held the dagger has stuck it into the back of its neighbour."

For a considerable time before the outbreak of the war Roosevelt had been troubled by the European situation. One day in New York, in 1941, I lunched with Baron Maurice de Rothschild. A very rich man, a French Senator, in February, 1939, he was cruising in his yacht in the West Indies and went to St. Thomas, in the Antilles. There, while lunching with the Governor, a message came for him. President Roosevelt had put into St. Thomas after inspecting the U.S. Navy, on a Caribbean cruise. Hearing that Baron de Rothschild was there he sent an invitation to visit him on board his ship. Here he was received by the President who was accompanied by Admiral Leahy. In the course of three hours Roosevelt discussed with Baron de Rothschild the situation in Europe. He was worried by the fact that the outbreak of war seemed inevitable. He had received in the past few years a series of letters from his ambassador in France, Mr. Jesse Strauss, all in the same strain, namely that France was completely corrupt, that German influence and money were everywhere, that the state of the French Army and Navy was deplorable. What was worse was the situation in England. She seemed quite unwilling to believe the truth. He had again and again sent for Sir Ronald Lindsey, the British Ambassador in Washington, and produced for him information concerning the rearmament of Germany and her preparation for an early war. He had always had the same reply from the British, that Germany was bluffing. "Nothing I can say, no evidence will convince the British of their mortal danger. I except Churchill." He had the same difficulty at home. The people disliked war and would not hear of any probability that it could happen, nor would they permit the Government to take any steps to prepare for it. There was a very active anti-war, isolationist, pro-German element always at work. His own attempts to prepare met with violent threats. He had been warned that if he went to open the new World's Fair in August (1939) he might be assassinated. He would go with his wife and his mother but would be well guarded. After asking de Rothschild's opinion as a European, he concluded the long discussion with the statement that he intended to prepare the U.S.A. To do this he might have to be unconstitutional. He would ignore the Neutrality Act, he would see that the factories were equipped and ready to produce munitions and articles of war not only for England and France but also for America when the day came, as it inevitably would. He knew that the Rome-Berlin Axis had its plans complete, that Japan was to have Hong Kong, Shanghai, Burma, the Malayas, the Dutch East Indies and Australia, in return for her attack on America. German preparations for the day were very thorough, for already the country was on war rations, butter was being conserved in tins, and the German Treasury was amassing funds. Hitler at a War Council, the U.S. Ambassador in Berlin reported, had wanted to invade Holland first, before the harvest, but the War Council was opposed and the blow would probably be through Poland, after the harvest.

This conference with Baron de Rothschild took place in Roosevelt's stateroom, with only Admiral Leahy present. The President had continuously cross-questioned him about France. At that time he was a Senator, a post he held from 1930 until he fled from France in June, 1940. He had been an independent Deputy for the Hautes Alpes from 1924 to 1930. "I left the cruiser after this long talk, and the closest questioning, utterly exhausted, and amazed at the knowledge of the President," said Baron de Rothschild. When the cruiser steamed out of the harbour that evening I watched it depart. The night settled tranquilly over the hills of the island but a great apprehension had been stirred in me. We both knew that a conflict must come and we were all so terribly unprepared."

All this had happened on a hot day, February 23, 1939, at St. Thomas. Such was the man in whose hands rested the destiny of the United States and of the free world.

CHAPTER THIRTEEN

Halifax and Wendell Willkie

I

Immediately on my return to New York in September, 1940, I went to see Angus Fletcher at the British Library. He was busier than ever and the office had been greatly expanded. He gave me a warm welcome and said there was a continuous demand for me and he hoped I was quite recovered and would be able to take new engagements. There had been a shake-up in the Ministry of Information at home. Reith had gone and Duff Cooper had come in. "Dear Cecil Roberts, I am sure you will be wise to stay in America at the present time and deliver lectures stating the British case," he wrote. But there was still no news on the subject of my receiving dollars, following Fletcher's renewed appeal. His own position was curious. He had been for twenty years under the Foreign Office. Now the Ministry had taken over the British Library and he found himself in an anomalous position with two masters who were quarrelling for the command of public relations abroad.

Fletcher complained of 'endless difficulties in securing speakers of adequate standing for engagements which do not pay large fees but which are clearly good opportunities to state the urgent facts of the present situation'. Knowing I was restive, he added to a letter on the subject:

> I take this opportunity to say that the work you are doing in speaking yourself whenever opportunity occurs is valuable in meeting an urgent need. There are, alas, too many well-meaning but ineffective exponents of the Cause, and there are others who have to be paid $2,500 a time to be set in motion. I don't blame the former and cannot blame the latter, but neither meets the need as you do when you voluntarily harness your standing as an author.

I was now working for over a dozen different pro-British organisations, such as the British War Relief Society, Bundles for Britain, the British Red Cross, American Ambulances for the Allies, U.S.A. Blood Bank, Refugees of England, British Sailors' and Soldiers' Canteens and Clubs, etc.

In six months I had not earned a penny. There was now a new Director of the American Division, Douglas Williams, who wrote from the Ministry, "I read with the greatest interest the account of your doings and am delighted to see how well you are fulfilling a very important task, all the more admirably as I hear you have not been too well." There was no answer to another appeal for dollars. Destitute, I had borrowed ten thousand dollars from an American friend, aware that I had broken a Bank of England prohibition. Meanwhile, some very odd people had been sent over, well-financed. There was a coalition Government and the Labour Party had its own nominees. A stout, monocled lady doctor was sent to attend a medical conference in Hong Kong. On the way home through New York Fletcher was instructed to give a cocktail party for her. It cost the Library $280. He raised his hands in despair. He could not get a dollar for me.

I carried on, more in demand than ever, and became, not only a speaker for the cause, but an odd-job man. The British Naval Liaison Officer in New York appealed to me. There was trouble over the American custom of cutting-in at dances. "There have been occasions when our ratings have taken umbrage at having a lovely girl snatched from their brawny arms, and have taken action in a manner quite unexpected by their American hosts! Could you write something simple for our sailors? I shall be very grateful for your advice and help." So I wrote a booklet, *Now you are in the U.S.A.*, with Do's and Don'ts. When, later, three young gunners came over from the North African campaign I interviewed them and wrote their admirable story, which had a wide circulation in the American Press.

During the winter I had become aware of the tragic situation of foreign colleagues who had taken refuge from the European conflagration. I attended a symposium organised by the *Herald-Tribune*, in the great auditorium of the Waldorf Astoria Hotel. On the platform sat many persons of genius: Henri Bernstein, Leon Feuchtwanger,

'Pertinax', Emil Lengle, Maurice Maeterlinck, Thomas Mann, André Maurois, Franz Werfel, Stefan Zweig, Louis Raemakers, George Snell, Elizabeth Schumann, Geneviève Tabouis, and many others now in exile, often penuriously so.

Somerset Maugham was not among this group of exiles. He left England after having escaped from his home in Cap Ferrat on a collier that transported the former English residents from the French Riviera. Maugham arrived in New York in October, 1940, accompanied by his faithful secretary, Gerald Haxton. He had made an arrangement with the British Treasury, having handed over his dollar assets, to have an allowance of $2,500 dollars a month. Needless to say he had other dollar resources by arrangement with his American publishers, who proved very accommodating. He installed himself in a suite of three rooms at the Ritz Hotel, and here I met him.

One Sunday in November, after greeting Pamela Frankau, whom I found in a small hotel, rather miserable, I motored with a very well-known radio critic, Alexander Woollcott, to have lunch with Mr. and Mrs. Nelson Doubleday on Long Island. Woollcott, fat, debonair, bohemian, with his loose tie and broad-brimmed hat, had launched Hilton's *Goodbye Mr. Chips* with a 'rave' radio notice. Alone, my companion was charming. Later, I was to witness a chameleonic change when he had an audience to play to. On our way to the Doubledays he wished to call on Mrs. Theodore Roosevelt II. Her husband, the General, was not there but I did meet their son, Quentin. It was his twenty-first birthday. He was one of those remarkable young men who are fate-dowered from birth. Later, at Harvard, I was to renew acquaintance with Quentin Roosevelt who had my young friend Wells Stabler for a housemate. How we talked! I found that Quentin had explored remote parts of China. Within a short time how wide would be the experience of these two boys. Wells, from a desk in the State Department, would become U.S. Vice-Consul in Jerusalem in his twenty-fifth year and, thirty years later, Minister in the U.S. Embassy in Rome. Quentin, covered with battle honours in North Africa, sent home wounded, with a bullet in his chest, went forth again from hospital to take part in the invasion of France. He died there, a short time after he had greeted his father the General, who died of exhaustion in the field.

We arrived at the Doubleday mansion late, to find the luncheon guests assembled. Here was Somerset Maugham, happy to meet his lovely daughter, Mrs. Paravicini. The guests marked the tornado that had swept Europe. They included Prince Félix de Bourbon-Parme, husband of the Grand Duchess of Luxembourg, their children, and a brother, Prince René. We sat at that table on that November day aware that England, terribly bombed, stood alone in Europe against triumphant Germany. Nelson Doubleday produced some manuscripts, among them the autograph copy of Kipling's *The Light That Failed*, minutely written on foolscap sheets, with a diagonally increasing margin down the page. We stayed late, for Woollcott was pursuing his passion at the bridge table, covering his lizard-like quickness with a scintillating monologue. When we left at 1 a.m. flushed, epigrammatic, he had skinned everybody.

The following month Maugham departed for South Carolina. Nelson Doubleday had built for him a house on his plantation at Yemassee, South Carolina. Here he had four servants and a horse which his publisher had given him. Gerald Haxton, hating the loneliness, had gone to a job in Washington. In his house Maugham wrote *The Razor's Edge* in six months, for which he got an advance of $100,000, and later sold it for a film for $350,000. He had no dollar problem! *The Razor's Edge* was a concoction. He stepped into a world of which he was utterly ignorant, that of religious mysticism. For a confirmed cynic and agnostic, it might be considered a tour de force. At his request I helped him by looking up data on Indian mysticism, Buddhism and Yoga practice. The film created a sensation. I was at the opening night in New York, with all the trappings of Hollywood megalomania. At Yemassee, with his horse and a young negro groom, he spent his sixty-eighth birthday. There was a huge birthday cake and presents, "I've never anywhere had such a fuss made over me," he commented. But with *The Razor's Edge*, as with other novels, he nearly ran into libel actions. He drew acrid portraits, including one of 'The Old Bitch', who was identified as the Princess Ottoboni, a rich American woman with a villa on the French Riviera. Not approving of him, she had failed to invite him to one of her grand parties, so he took his revenge. He also drew a too-faithful portrait of another Riviera neighbour and friend, a very social American, whom he devastatingly portrayed as a fussy snob and 'queer'. Somehow

Maugham could never resist making 'copy' from his friends and acquaintances. He was always surprised when, like Hugh Walpole, devastatingly portrayed in *Cakes and Ale*, they protested.

II

In October, 1940, the British Ambassador in the U.S.A., Lord Lothian, visited England to discuss with the Prime Minister the growing dollar crisis. All the investments of British private owners had been requisitioned. These had brought in $335 million, but millions had been paid out in 'cash-and-carry' leaving only a few millions in hand. Lothian met Churchill at Ditchley, the luxurious Oxfordshire mansion Ronald Tree had placed at the Government's disposal. Churchill, fearing that Chequers might be made a special target, had transferred himself there. As a result of this meeting Churchill sent Roosevelt a long letter setting out the serious state of England's finances. It reached Roosevelt while cruising on the American warship *Tuscaloosa* in the Caribbean Sea. He returned to Washington on December 16, 1940, and proceeded to put in hand the magnanimous Lend-Lease plan that enabled Britain to get all the supplies she needed without creating a financial crisis.

On his return from England Lothian was taken seriously ill and died on December 12. A man of great experience and intelligence, with a personality that had made him very popular, he died, many thought unnecessarily, aged fifty-eight, having refused medical attention, being a Christian Scientist.

As his successor, Churchill first invited Lloyd George, as a figure of immense prestige. Not feeling physically equal to the task, though proud to have received the offer, he declined it. Churchill now turned to Lord Halifax, then Foreign Secretary, who reluctantly accepted the ambassadorship. Lady Halifax opposed the idea, and pleaded personally with Churchill not to send her husband, but he proved obdurate. It was rumoured that Churchill wished to get rid of a man branded as an appeaser, and to put his favourite, Eden, in his place. Churchill had showed his hand when, replying to Lady Halifax's plea, he said that he was conscious of certain currents of opinion against his remaining at the Foreign Office, and that he would benefit from the change. The Permanent Secretary at the Foreign Office, Sir

Alexander Cadogan, thought this a clever solution. The *Times Literary Supplement*, later, reviewing a book on the Chamberlain regime, wrote, "Halifax was equally ready to let Hitler have the German colonies, the ex-German colonies, Austria, Czechoslovakia and anything else that would appease him." It expressed a general opinion.

With this behind him, Lord Halifax's task was formidable. Alas, at this critical hour H. G. Wells had arrived in New York. His ire was aroused by the appointment. An embittered man of seventy-two, a prophet whose voice had been ignored and who was now of waning influence, he chose to contribute to a New York newspaper a fierce attack on Halifax. Coming from a fellow-countryman it was unpardonable in its place and timing. Somerset Maugham who had shown much political restraint, was, like many of us, angry at Wells's gross indiscretion. He drew a sad portrait of him in his book *The Vagrant Mood*.

> I saw H.G. for the last time during the war. It was in New York and he had come to deliver a series of lectures . . . He looked old, tired and shrivelled. He was as perky as ever but with something of an effort. His lectures were a dismal failure. He was not a good speaker—he had never been able to deliver a discourse and was obliged to read it . . . His voice was thin and squeaky and he read with his nose in the manuscript. People couldn't hear what he said and they left in droves. He was mortified to find people looked upon him as a 'has-been'.

Roosevelt, aware of the undercurrent of hostility towards Halifax went out of his way to pay an honour such as had never been shown to any other ambassador. Halifax arrived on board the newly commissioned battleship *King George V*, destined five months later to take part in the sinking of the formidable *Bismarck*. In a fog it proceeded up Chesapeake Bay as far as Annapolis. Here he found President Roosevelt, newly elected for a third term, awaiting him on the presidential yacht *Potomac*. The yacht sailed round the battleship, from which it received due honours, and then the Ambassador was taken on board to have tea with the President. The meeting was cordial, the beginning of a warm relationship. Afterwards the President motored Halifax from Annapolis to the British Embassy. A right note had been struck for the future. But Halifax found himself on foreign soil, in an atmosphere utterly alien to his own nature. An aristocrat, an ancestral landowner, innately proud, reserved, introvert, and pious almost to a degree of fanaticism, he was out of his element. He, who had held the highest offices in the Realm, had been a Viceroy of India, a Foreign Secretary, accustomed to deferential treatment from all categories, found himself plunged into the free and easy atmosphere of a powerful and exuberant democracy that had no reverence for persons and was instinctively hostile to privileges of rank. The Ambassador had to find a new manner of deportment. If in the early stages of his mission he blundered, it was pardonable. He arrived with his own chosen staff, selected from those he had known in the Foreign Office, among them the correct and amiable Charles Peake, an ardent fellow Anglo-Catholic, who wrote his early speeches.

On Halifax's arrival the atmosphere was tense with a debate, in Congress, on the Lend-Lease Bill. There was much lend and little lease in the Bill, $30 billion to $6. It aroused the bitterest antagonism of the Isolationists who were joined in their opposition by many Republicans who nourished an intense hatred of the President. At a dinner given by a group of Republican Congressmen Halifax was astonished on being told by his hosts that 'everyone of us here thinks the President is as dangerous a dictator as Hitler and Mussolini, and is taking this country to hell just as fast as he can'. The Ambassador found he was skating everywhere on thin ice. The President's friendliness only endorsed a suspicion that he was steadily leading America into the war, with Halifax assisting. It was anomalous that whereas Americans regarded the British as obtuse they also thought that in any diplomatic exchanges the British were very cunning and too sharp for them.

'Lord Holy Fox' had to be watched. He soon blundered in this perplexing new world. He visited Walter Lippmann, the foremost pro-intervention journalist. It was another British plot. One month after his arrival, when the heat engendered by the Lend-Lease Bill was at its height, he went to call on the Chairman of the Foreign Affairs Committee in the House of Representatives. It provoked a tremendous storm. How dare the British Ambassador try to tamper with the legislation of the Government! Within another month he gave Americans another shock. A passionate rider to hounds, a M.F.H., he found an invitation to hunt in Virginia irresistible. His

very attire became an offence, for he hunted dressed in khaki riding-
breeches, a pullover and a dirty raincoat, shabby in comparison with
the fashionable huntsmen of Virginia. A lord should look like a lord,
not like a lout. He was accused of bad taste. Carl Sandburg, the poet
certainly anti-Isolationist, as I had reason to know, asked indignantly how could he go hunting when his countrymen were dying in
action. Then, unwittingly, he gave offence to millions of baseball fans
by leaving half-way through a game to have tea with the British
Consul. One wondered where were the men in his suite who should
have advised him against such blunders. His speeches were lamentably
dreary, and revealed that he had no knowledge of American history.
Charles Peake and J. G. Lockhart, who wrote them, had no experience of American life, or of the way in which American emotions
could be touched. Again, his attire was often lamentable. Some
Americans who went to hear him expected to find a real lord and an
aristocrat, and would have enjoyed seeing him arrayed with orders
and medals, better still, wearing his peer's robes and coronet. With
his formless clothing, his attenuated figure, large ears, high bald
dome, and slow emotionless voice, he was a sore disappointment. "He
looks like a depressed bloodhound," said a friend with whom I went
to hear him speak. It was cruel but one saw the basis of the simile. His
stock went steadily down.

I was distressed, knowing the sound intellectual equipment,
sincerity and good will of our Ambassador. I felt there was something
wrong in the Embassy in letting him go on the platform so unrehearsed
in his role. I was not alone in this opinion. When in New York he
was entertained by our mutual friends, Mr. and Mrs. Thomas
Lamont. There I met him. I wondered if I dare take him aside and
tell him what I thought was the matter. I was in a strong position in
that I was not a paid official, stepping out of line, jeopardising
promotion and a steady climb in the honours list. I hesitated, fearing
I might be charged with abusing my host's hospitality. So the months
went on and the ambassadorial stock steadily fell.

At the close of 1940 Italy had met with disaster. In October,
the Italian Army, already in Albania, attacked Greece along her
frontiers. With Greece unprepared it looked like being an easy
victory but the Italians were repulsed and the Greeks magnificently
counter-attacked. Mussolini had sent his troops into Albania ill-

equipped and ill-officered. Their losses were heavy. An Alpini Division was wholly annihilated. Outfought, outmanoeuvred, the Italians retreated thirty miles behind the Albanian frontier, the army demoralised. This victory aroused tremendous exultation in the large Greek community in New York. They planned a public dinner to celebrate the event and asked the British Information Services, as it had now become, to send a representative to make a speech. The organising committee asked for me. I went and had a wonderful reception. My speech was published, verbatim, in Greek, in the local newspaper. Alas, this triumph was short-lived, they were to experience many bitter days. I spoke several times for The Friends of Greece and for the Dodecanesian Council in those dark days before their hopes were ultimately fulfilled with the triumph of the Allies. "Many people have spoken for the cause of Greece but I do not recall anyone who has spoken with such eloquence, erudition and personal charm," wrote the chairman of The Friends of Greece, in a letter of thanks.

III

For safety's sake there had been a movement of British children across the Atlantic, some with their mothers. There was an endless debate as to whether children should be sent out of their homeland, now under a threat of invasion. The children evacuated faced another risk. In October the *Empress of Britain* had been sunk with a loss of over three hundred lives. American hospitality was most generously offered. There was no generosity in the allowances the parents accompanying these children were able to draw from home. The whole thing became a scandal. One mother under the strain committed suicide. The English-Speaking Union organised friendly meetings for these mothers and I was frequently asked to address them. On one occasion I was the chairman of a gathering at which an official from the Treasury came to talk to them. He proceeded to admonish them. It was not patriotic for them to complain. This was too much for me and I told him his reproof was disgraceful. During his visit he was drawing expenses at the rate of forty dollars a day, and he had the effrontery to be reproving mothers who could draw only twenty dollars a month, making them appallingly dependent upon their American hosts who, in some cases, had become regretful of their early emotional offers of hospitality. It was only after a stormy debate in Parliament, for which I supplied ammunition, that an allowance of $40 per month and $12 per child was made.

There were many children without their mothers, well cared for in American homes. Those of the British aristocracy often found themselves the guests of American millionaires. Some were even sent to exclusive schools. But this was the fate of only a highly privileged few. Churchill frowned when Duff Cooper sent his small boy over. He thought English children should stay and face it. But if Hitler had won and occupied England? He had once talked of deporting all the English.

The British War Relief Society and the English-Speaking Union did noble work in trying to lessen the strain of these exiles. A few days before Christmas they arranged for a number of children to have a trans-Atlantic talk with their parents in England. I was asked to monitor the talks. It was a frightful ordeal and would have broken down the toughest person. I knew that, thousands of miles across the sea, in complete darkness, under a terrible threat of bombs, anxious parents stood by the microphone while in a room off Broadway, little Jimmie, Johnnie and Mary, for a few seconds, holding back their tears, forced a note of cheerfulness into their voices. They assured their unseen parents they were well, they were happy, and there really was nothing to worry about. One little girl of ten, with tears streaming down her face in grief at the sound of a loved voice, repeated desperately, "I'm very happy, Mummy darling. You mustn't worry. I'm very happy here." I confess I resorted to a handkerchief at moments. One little chap of eleven stood in a trance when he heard his mother's voice. I explained he was microphone-shy, and turned to the next child on our list but he pushed his way back to the table and desperately said, "I'm not! I'm not!" But again he could utter no word while his mother pleaded across the Atlantic. Sometimes a child was distressingly self-possessed. One fond parent asking, "Do you want to come home, darling?" received a firm, "No—never! You've no idea what it's like here." This from a grim young lady of twelve, whose frightful candour I could not check in time. "Darling!" came an agonised cry from England.

Christmas approached. I hope never again to see one like it. Alone, unwell, for I had not got back my strength, living in a small back bedroom of a second-class hotel, without money, the New York shops, bright and crammed with luxuries at a time when the fate of my country was hanging in the balance, were a mocking contrast. Every shop was crowded with customers buying in the first flush of war-time prosperity. I descended from my bedroom to speak at meetings and banquets with an assurance that was whipped up for the moment. Then, out of the skies, came deliverance. Someone I scarcely knew spoke to someone I did not know at all, who went out of her way to draw me into the Christmas cheer of a beautiful home. I found myself installed in a house overlooking the Long Island Sound. A log fire crackled in an immense grate, the light of candles shone on silver and linen at a long table. Gay, lovely daughters with their swains filled the rooms with laughter. There was a fine library and the services of a richly and perfectly ordered house. Outside the woods were powdered with snow. I did not know of the heavy shadow that lay on this house where no master now sat in the study with its row of silver sporting trophies. My hostess, beautiful and still young, gathered her children around her in this first widowed Christmas. Later I learned of a recent tragedy, of a suicide. I remember standing in darkness on the landing while moonlight streamed through long windows on the portrait of the man who would no more mount the wide stairs. On Christmas Day I met some English children. We made visits and in the house of Henry Morgan, we found a Christmas tea-party in full swing. Mr. Pierpont Morgan II had come with his contingent of British youngsters. There were present young Lord Primrose, the Earl of Rosebery's heir, and Francis Rennell Rodd's children, some twenty in all. They unloaded the immense Christmas tree with cries of delight. Watching their merriment I was glad to know that it was not only in the house of millionaires these juvenile representatives of England were having Christmas cheer. The English-Speaking Union had given a large party for the young exiles.

My first engagement in the New Year was at a Bundles for Britain meeting. This was an astonishing organisation of mushroom growth that had sprung out of the brain of Mrs. Natalie Wales, a slender, pretty, young woman, mother of two girls, with a genius for organ-isation. The task was to collect and send to England all the things, clothes, food, footwear, etc., that would give relief to a severely-rationed nation. I became one of her constant helpers. Energetic, punctilious, she had a quick eye for details. I never spoke for her without having the following morning a letter of thanks.

Bundles for Britain grew and grew. No one was more entitled to the C.B.E. awarded her at the close of the war. Later she made a further tie with England. In 1957 she married Lord Malcolm Douglas Hamilton, a son of the 13th Duke of Hamilton. Seven years after the marriage he was missing in West Africa during a flight in a private plane.

The Bundles for Britain meeting at which I was scheduled to act as Master of Ceremonies, proved a momentous occasion, personally, for it brought me into touch with the Roosevelts. The meeting was held in the 'Starlight Room' of the Waldorf Astoria Hotel. The most notable person present was Mrs. Sara Delano Roosevelt, an imperious old lady, the mother of the President. I was introduced to her at the close of the meeting. Through the mother I met the President's wife, Mrs. Roosevelt, a controversial figure in American life. She was very adversely criticised and the most scurrilous things were said about her, all wholly false. She was a dynamic person. She syndicated in the Press her diary 'My Day'. Many thought it very undignified for a President's wife, who should be dumb. It was she who invited a negro singer, who was snubbed elsewhere, to sing at the White House, and thereby raised a storm. Much of the venom poured upon the President spilt over on to her. They even suggested that he had no control over her. The caricaturists were merciless, and gave her a mouth overloaded with teeth. All this in no way affected her prodigious activities.

When I met her I discovered a woman of much charm, endowed with a beautiful speaking voice, vivid in conversation and widely informed, *une grande dame*. She invited me when next in Washington to call on her. In February I went to Washington. Sir Angus Fletcher, as he now was, having been knighted in January, had written to the Embassy asking for my official services, but, this apart, I went to call on Charles Peake, Halifax's intimate and right-hand man. Very able, he had been Halifax's Private Secretary at the Foreign Office. In the beginning he wrote Halifax's speeches, though he had no experience of America. I saw Angus Malcolm, also on the staff. I asked whether something could not be done over this preposterous dollar business. I was shown much good will, and passed on to a Treasury representative who was about to leave for England. He would bring up my case there. The result was nil. I received, in due course, the enlightening information from the Treasury that any application for dollars should be presented by the Ministry of Information. As this had been done thrice, without result, we were back to starting point.

After visiting the British Embassy I went to the White House in response to an invitation from Mrs. Roosevelt. I was asked for six o'clock, the cocktail hour, I presumed. This was my second visit to the White House, but on the former occasion I had been received by President Coolidge in his office-annex. This time I was in the House itself. When I was shown in there was a company of about ten in the drawing-room. Mrs. Roosevelt took me round introducing me. The white-jacketed servants served drinks. In about half an hour, to my delight, the President entered in his invalid's chair. I had seen him on several public occasions but now I had a closer view. He had a magnificent head, and features of great strength. The upper half of him was that of a man of much vigour. His voice was clear, his eye penetrating. In turn I was introduced. He must have been primed regarding the guests for he asked me how I found American audiences. In the few minutes' talk I spoke of my former visit to the White House and that President Coolidge had given me a signed photograph of himself, which I much treasured. I said this somewhat artfully. He was much amused when I told him that I had met Woodrow Wilson, then President of Princeton University, when I was a boy in the Lake District and had taken him to see Wordsworth's Dove Cottage at Grasmere. After about half an hour, during which he had a few words with everyone, he was wheeled out of the room. On my leaving Mrs. Roosevelt asked me if I was speaking anywhere in Washington. I told her I was appearing at the English-Speaking Union and elsewhere.

The following afternoon when I returned to my host's house, I was the guest of Mr. and Mrs. Eliot Wadsworth, I found a large envelope awaiting me. I opened it with the liveliest anticipation. My hint had not gone unheeded. Inside was a generously autographed portrait of the President.

IV

That winter my circle of acquaintances expanded rapidly. I was fortunate in meeting Mrs. Murray Crane. She was a born hostess with a beautiful apartment on Fifth Avenue that overlooked the trees of Central Park and the amusing little zoo with seal-pond and terrace restaurant. Mrs. Crane's long drawing-room was no creation of an interior decorator. Though a staid, matronly figure, she was artistically and intellectually adventurous. You found in her collection of pictures, a Carracci, a Moreau, an Augustus John, a Salvador Dali. Her quick eye having examined the world from Moscow to Mexico, she collected beautiful and interesting objects. There were some who said our hostess was a bluestocking but it was a quite incorrect definition of Josephine, as all her friends affectionately called her. I owed this rewarding friendship, which was to become lifelong, to young Philip Steegman, the English artist. He was a gifted, bright lad who had painted maharajahs in India, from which experience he wrote a most delightful book, *Indian Ink*. One day he said to me, "Look! I'll take you to Mrs. Murray Crane's. She has a weekly class of intellectual ladies, who subscribe to have lectures by the brightest minds in America. I think we come into that category! The real point is that Mrs. Crane pays you $50 for an hour's lecture, and afterwards has a jolly tea-party. Always on Sundays, at five, she receives." So he took me along. We arrived with Salvador Dali and his pointed moustaches, and André Maurois. Our hostess sat on a settee with Carracci's *Apollo flaying Marsyas* behind her, and a resplendent tea service on the low table before her, the company disposed in a semi-circle. She was a gentle but firm ringmaster. She had not the whip-crack of another ringmaster I much admired, Lady Cunard. Josephine tickled the flanks of her team with a seemingly artless question. In turn we were all drawn in to make a contribution to the lively symposium. In addition to her lecture classes and afternoons she had 'evenings'. These were preceded by a dinner for about twelve guests after which a general company of some forty persons would assemble for the evening entertainment. It is impossible to recall all the singular persons who knew these happy occasions. It was a mélange from which emerged surprising enchantments. It was there I encountered the encyclopaedic, smiling Professor Wind, of Berlin, Vienna, the Warburg Library in Hamburg, and the Pierpont Morgan Library in New York, who lifted a necromancer's wand and left us spellbound by his exposition of Raphael's *School of Athens* or *Pagan Mysteries in the Renaissance*. Eventually, he went to Trinity College, as a Professor of Art in the University of Oxford. I was not at all surprised to learn that his lectures there created a furore, and students who could not get into the packed hall listened in through the windows.

Mrs. Crane's guests were drawn from two continents. They had various talents, so that one met at tea or at dinner a bearded Spaniard with a famous art collection in Madrid, a former *chef-de-cabinet* of the Daladier Government, a Greek Minister, a Polish ambassador's widow, a Chinese ambassador's wife, a descendant of Madame de Staël and sister of the scientist, the Duc de Broglie, a State Department official, a director of the Metropolitan Museum, or of Washington's National Gallery, or of the Museum of Modern Art, a Czech pianist, and a member of the French Academy. One could not start any subject without the possibility of extending one's knowledge. Any topic provided a scent for a *chasse intellectuelle*. It seemed as if Mrs. Crane had combed all Europe and the American continents. There might have been collisions but our hostess, like a benevolent aunt, diverted antagonists, such as Vichy and de Gaulle supporters, with an artful innocence. Firmly Anglophile, it never diminished her sturdy Americanism. Her love of the English scene once inspired a wish that she fulfilled. "I wanted to be buried in Westminster Abbey when I was a girl—and a bit of me was." Seeing my surprise, she added, "I was travelling with my father and had been to a dentist in London to have a tooth pulled. I took it to the Abbey, scratched a hole between the flagstones and buried there that bit of my bones." The daughter of a former Senator, and the widow of one, she had lived in Washington and had met everybody. One day, among her parents' guests were Mr. and Mrs. Rudyard Kipling. "My mother gave me the task of entertaining Mrs. Kipling while she looked after the lion. We all wanted to hear Kipling but Mrs. Kipling, an American, held the stage and wouldn't allow him to say a word. Oh, how we American women talk!" said my hostess.

I never got to the bottom of her fund of knowledge. I arrived one day and mentioned my fruitless efforts to trace a copy of the Thorwaldsen bust of Byron, made in Rome and brought to America by young Mr. Coolidge, who had called on Byron. "I've seen it, I know who has it," said Josephine. "I saw it many years ago in the house of Thomas Jefferson Coolidge at Boston. He was a great-grandson of Thomas Jefferson, and was at my wedding. He was our Minister to France and a great collector. You can see the bust now in the Athenaeum Club at Boston. I think he was the son of Byron's visitor." I found she was correct.

One day I called on her with a young British naval officer who had come to New York to take delivery of a Landing Ship Tank. He had shown me over the new empty ship at the dockyard. At the tea-table he said he wanted to pick up a few pictures for the wardroom. Thereupon Josephine took the embarrassed young officer to her cupboards and commanded him to make a choice of pictures. To this she added a chest of tea. A month later that Crane-decorated wardroom was in the assault on Sicily.

Every time I went to see Josephine she had acquired some fresh object. There had been a big art sale. Arriving one Sunday, after absence on a speaking tour, I looked around. "What are you seeking?" she asked. "Your new loot!" I replied. "It's over there. What do you think of it?" The newcomer was a delightful genre picture by Squadrone, a worthy addition, standing cheek by jowl with a study by Gérôme of Rachel in *Phèdre*, not far distant from an Augustus John portrait of James Joyce, Whistler's original sketch of his famous study of Carlyle, and, cheekily, Salvador Dali's enigmatic painting of a melted watch, hanging on the branch of a withered tree in a vast desert, called *Shadow of the Future*, which she had bought for $100 in a side street in Paris, thirty years earlier. One day she acquired a fine portrait of Haydn, painted by Fuseli when the composer was in London. She gave a dinner-party, hired a string quartet to play some Haydn music, and made me read a poem I had specially written for this occasion.

V

At one of the meetings of the English-Speaking Union an American lady, Mrs. Elizabeth Stabler, an ardent Anglophile, took the chair for me. This was a beginning of a warm friendship, and when one day she discovered I was suffering agonies from stomach troubles she insisted on my becoming a guest in her home, where I was dieted and wonderfully looked after. She was a most remarkable, energetic woman. Her husband had been an American diplomat, and she found herself left with two sons to bring up. She sent them to Harvard University. Warwick, the elder entered the Army, the younger, Wells Stabler, went into the Diplomatic Service.

Mrs. Stabler loved entertaining and every Sunday she gave a lunch for about a dozen persons. All my friends were welcome, and thus it came that, when they visited New York, I took there representatives of literary England—Ian Hay, Sir Norman Angell, Sir Charles Webster, Cecil S. Forester, Valentine Williams, Louis Golding, Sir Philip Gibbs, Ann Bridge, Mrs. Charles Morgan and Phyllis Bentley.

It was there that I met Austin Strong, a little man with a ruddy complexion. He became one of my most devoted American friends. His history was remarkable. He was born in San Francisco. An aunt, fitting a dress on his destined mother, discovered his advent. "You're fitting it too close!" had cried the niece. A short time after, on the wall of her husband's studio she took a piece of chalk and wrote *Austin Strong*. She thought it looked well. Later she saw it outside San Francisco's leading theatre which announced a new play *The Drums of Oudh*, by Austin Strong. He was twenty when he wrote it, a one-act drama that has been played round the world ever since. It was chosen to fill in a bill with two one-act dramas written by James Barrie. It ran away with the house, playing in London for two years. Austin Strong visited Barrie to apologise for this overshadowing. Later, he wrote *The Exile* for Sir John Martin Harvey and *The Toymaker of Nuremberg* for Cyril Maude. Then came a resounding success on stage and screen, *Seventh Heaven*, which had a two-year's run in New York. His grandmother, living, had taken his mother, Isobel, and her two sons, Lloyd and Harvey Osbourne, to Nevada where Austin's grandfather had bought a gold-mine. Itinerant, they moved to Paris and Grez, to join a colony of artists. To this village came young Robert Louis Stevenson, who married Mrs. Osbourne. Her daughter, Isobel, had her own romance and ran off with a young artist Joe Strong, Austin's father. They settled in San Francisco, to which the Stevensons had moved. The next move of the Stevenson-Osbourne family was to Honolulu, where Joe Strong had a commission to paint scenes for a shipowner's office. The little boy, Austin, was caught one day taking goldfish from the pool of King Kalakawa, who had received a present of double-tailed goldfish from the Emperor of Japan. They proved irresistible to the little boy. Caught, he did not go to prison. The King sent him home in his carriage, bearing a grant authorising him to fish in the royal park. In Honolulu R.L.S. finished *The Master of Ballantrae* and worked with his stepson, Lloyd Osbourne, on *The Wrong Box*. Then one day R.L.S. bought a house on a South Sea Island, which he called Vailima. So the little Austin Strong now lived with his step-grandfather. On Stevenson's death the South Sea home was broken up. A heavy-hearted boy was sent to school in New Zealand. He arrived at Wellington College strangely attired for there were no school outfitters in Samoa. He wore German trousers, a striped straw hat and one of R.L.S.'s velvet jackets cut down. He had for a friend at the school a young husky who won all the swimming prizes, good training for the famous swim by night to a Gallipoli beach that brought the future Colonel Freyberg, V.C., to fame, and, later, the Governor-Generalship of his native place. In the city of Auckland there is a memorial park that was designed by a young landscape gardener, Austin Strong, but destiny took him to the writing desk. Such was the history of my new friend.

In March, 1941, Congress passed the Lend-Lease Bill. With this, in Roosevelt's words, America had become 'the arsenal of democracy', and Churchill, announcing it in the House of Commons, described it as 'the most unsordid act in the history of any nation'. On the day after it was passed, I lunched with Madame Geneviève Tabouis, a very remarkable Frenchwoman. We often found ourselves fellow-speakers at various meetings in aid of Allied activities. A journalist, the niece of Jules Cambon who had been French Ambassador in England, she was widely known under the pseudonym of 'Cassandra'. It was strange to find that the pregnant prophecies of Europe's doom, of France's corruption, had come from a body as unsubstantial as thistledown. She had a pinched white face, piercing eyes, a high-pitched voice. She was a formidable person. *Travaille tout le temps, même le dimanche, ne connais pas le week-end*, she said. All this energy came from a tiny woman with one lung who seemed

308

to exist on a cup of coffee and a lettuce leaf. She went all over the United States, commuting between Washington and New York. She founded a French newspaper in New York, *Pour La Victoire*, and was the enemy of the Vichy Government. The United States showed a perverse loyalty to Pétain to the very end of the war and regarded de Gaulle with displeasure.

In the course of time Mme. Tabouis and I became very friendly. We had known days of despair, dark days when it appeared that Europe would be overwhelmed by the Nazi terror. She had a sick daughter in France and a mother living in a Normandy château, their fate unknown. With her pen and lectures she financed her campaign from two tiny rooms in a small hotel by the East River. After the events of June, 1940, she was fiercely anti-Pétain. At my instigation my friends, Dr. and Mrs. Boehm, gave a small dinner party to which Mme. Tabouis and her colleague, M. de Kérillis, a former French deputy, were invited in order to meet my friend Commander Alec Lacy, then *en poste* in Washington. He had been at one time British Naval Liaison Officer with General de Gaulle. I had thought this would be a happy gathering of pro-de Gaullists. Imagine my surprise when Mme. Tabouis launched a terrific attack against the General. For some reason she, and de Kérillis, one of de Gaulle's former aides, had deserted him. When later we emerged into the cool night air and I apologised for this contretemps, my friend surprised me by saying, quietly, "Although I wasn't going to tell her, I agree with much of their opinion of de Gaulle."

But in March, 1941, at the time of our lunch, she was very anti-Pétain and at war with the American State Department for its odd backing of the traitorous Marshal. After lunch, stimulated as always by her spirit, I went to the University Club, of which I had been made an honorary member. It had a splendid library most useful to my work. On my way I saw a newspaper headline—'Nazi Invasion Soon. Churchill Defiant.' Thinking of him, some lines came into my head and when I reached the Club I wrote them down.

A man arose, in England sired,
And suckled by the young, free West,
Of lineage proud, of blood inspired,
That long gave England of its best.

309

That same week, coming from a club run for the British Merchant Navy, on whose behalf I had spoken, ten more lines came into my head. At 1 a.m. that night I woke with the lines still ringing in my head. I got up. By 6.30 a.m. I had written the whole of *A Man Arose*, some two hundred lines.

I lunched that day, Sunday, at Mrs. Stabler's. When all the guests had gone save Austin and Mary Strong, I read *A Man Arose* to them. Austin Strong from that moment had only one idea. It must be heard throughout America. A few days later he took me to see his friend, Wendell Willkie. A great national figure, Willkie had recently returned from a visit to England where he had met Churchill. Willkie's rise to fame had been phenomenal. He had been nominated for President by the Republican Convention. In the resulting election he had polled 22,305,198 votes to Roosevelt's 27,244,160. This he had achieved despite his firmly backing the President's war policy, on which many Republicans dragged their feet. He was forty-eight years of age, a huge black-curly-haired boyish sort of fellow, with an enthusiastic following. "We might call it charm," said one of the leaders of his Party, "but let's not, because the word for that abstraction has been worn out on Mr. Roosevelt's great undoubted quality. Franklin could charm a canary out of a tree to sit at a tomcat's dinner. The difference is that Mr. Roosevelt has to turn his on for the occasion. Mr. Willkie's seems to be effortlessly working all the time".

When he went to England he took the Londoners by storm, wearing his white tin hat, going into the Underground, talking to everybody. Lady Diana Cooper gave a dinner for him at the Dorchester. She wrote in her diary, "Willkie was treated like a king and film-star rolled into one. The newspapers told us what he ate for breakfast and what size boots he wore. Now he has gone. I waved him Goodbye last night, and I pray God he will give a good account of us when he comes to testify to the Senate." He did, indeed, give a good report of us, everywhere and at all times.

The idea in my friend Austin Strong's head was that Willkie should hear the poem and then arrange for the National Broadcasting Company of America to broadcast it. So I was taken to see him in his office. He rose to greet me, the whole six-foot-one of him. He was one of a family of six children from a small town in Indiana, who had proved a successful lawyer, working for the Firestone Rubber

Corporation. He turned down an increase of $10,000 a year to go to another firm. This annoyed Firestone. "Young man, I like you but I don't think you'll ever amount to a great deal," he said when they parted. Four years later he was earning $75,000 a year. He later turned down a post worth $250,000 a year. He declined a 'golden handshake' when giving up his position on nomination for the Presidential Election. Within a year of his defeat he was supporting the President, believing in his war policy. It cost him a nomination by his Party for the 1944 election.

One could not fail to like this genial smooth-faced man with blue eyes and a mass of untidy dark, curly hair. "Austin Strong tells me you've written a fine poem about Churchill. Will you let me see it, or read it to me?" he said. "I should be glad to read it but it will take some twenty minutes," I replied. "As long as you like. Do you mind if I smoke?" he asked. He seated himself in a chair before his desk, throwing one leg over its arm and lighting a cigarette. I began to read. All the time I was apprehensive that it might bore him. It seemed terribly long. I purposely did not look at him, keeping my eyes on the manuscript. When I finished there was an ominous silence. I looked at him and was moved to see that he had tears in his eyes. "Beautiful! It's worthy of a very great man," he remarked, solemnly. Austin Strong said there was a proposal that he should read it over the N.B.C. network. "Me read it, Austin? Oh no! He's the poet. He must read it. But I'd be happy to introduce him over the air, if that would help." We accepted the offer at once. The N.B.C. had to proceed warily. It was nervous of the pressure that the Isolationists could bring to bear. Finally, to absolve itself from any charge of playing politics, it was arranged that the broadcast should be made under the sponsorship of the British War Relief Society.

The time chosen could not have been better. The hook-up would cover America and Canada, South America and India. There had been a purpose in choosing 3 p.m. on a Sunday afternoon. Wendell Willkie was anxious, in introducing me, that England should hear his own tribute to Churchill and its people. It was his first opportunity after his return to America. The N.B.C. had offered to transmit the programme on short wave, so that England could hear it. We had the co-operation of the B.B.C.'s representative in New York. To make sure there was no hitch in the acceptance of this courtesy I cabled, a week ahead, Brendan Bracken, then the Prime Minister's secretary. Just before Willkie began to broadcast he turned to the N.B.C. President and the Chief Engineer and asked what was the hook-up. The Chief Engineer rolled off the stations it would reach, and the pick-up on short-wave. England was not mentioned. "And England?" asked Willkie. "For some reason England isn't taking it," was the answer. There was a look of surprise and disappointment on Willkie's face. "That's a pity," he said. "I hoped England would hear."

Later we made enquiries. Bracken acted promptly on my cable and replied at once. He would communicate with the Director-General of the B.B.C., F. G. H. Ogilvie. A little later Bracken sent me the Director General's reply. "I have enquired into this and unhappily reception conditions are likely to be so bad that it would be inadvisable to make this commitment." I could not help wondering how, on March 25, they knew the conditions would be bad on the 30th. Actually they were not. They were very good. The reception was so clear that a young friend, James Pepper, in his camp at Swindon, recognised my voice. He cabled, "Very good reception. No static or interference." The N.B.C. sent Churchill two discs, in a special case. "They were played over on the gramophone and Mr. Churchill asks me to convey his thanks and appreciation," wrote Mrs. Hill, his Private Secretary, from 10 Downing Street. The broadcast reached over four hundred million people. Among them was President Roosevelt who told a friend, Congressman Colonel Wainwright, who had introduced me to President Coolidge in 1924, that it was 'a splendid, moving tribute to Churchill and his nation'.

There was a pleasant sequel. The Librarian of the Library of Congress wrote asking if I would present the manuscript to the Library. I readily did this. It was exhibited with a very distinguished companion. Churchill had concluded one of his famous broadcasts by quoting Arthur Hugh Clough's poem, 'Say not the struggle nought availeth'. Messrs. Scribners, the publishers, presented the manuscript of the poem to Churchill, who sent it to the Library of Congress.

The next broadcast of *A Man Arose* was on behalf of 'Refugees of England', whose American headquarters were in charge of the Countess of Abingdon. Refugees of England was an organisation that looked after foreign refugee children in England. Lady Abingdon toured the United States raising funds. She enlisted my aid from time to time. I had described her in *Gone Sunwards* as, 'Slender, with a high complexion, dark long-lashed eyes and black hair. She might have been an Andalusian beauty.' She obtained 'time' on the N.B.C. network, an evening service, relayed to England the next morning. As soon as the irascible Toscanini had finished a rehearsal in the Rockefeller building (I once saw him hit an elevator boy over the head with a role of music because he had taken him past his floor), we began our broadcast, Lady Abingdon introducing me. Again it was perfectly heard in England. I repeated the broadcast four times in the next three months. The poem was published in England and the U.S.A. It sold a hundred thousand copies, bringing some income to the Royal Air Force Benevolent Fund, to whom I gave the copyright.

For the next twelve months I gave readings of the poem all over America. Once I committed a *faux pas*. I spoke at Gary, Indiana, and at Winnetka, on the shore of Lake Michigan, just out of Chicago. There was a request that I should read the poem at Gary. In error, I did not read it there but at Winnetka. To my surprise it had a very cool reception. The chairman motoring me to the station explained. "Most of the audience is of German origin and sympathy." America was not yet in the war. This was then a strong Isolationist patch. I could not have read the poem to a more hostile public. And I disappointed Gary by not reading it.

When later my English publishers issued a special edition of the poem, including Willkie's introduction, I sent a copy to Winston Churchill. "It will have an honoured place on my bookshelf," he wrote. One reward of this poem was that it brought me the friendship of a remarkable and warm-hearted man. "I shall never forget your poem. It was a joy to come to know you," wrote Willkie after the broadcast, "and I hope in the coming years we may all be joined in the same cause to bring about a better world after this mess is over. As a matter of fact, we must, or else there will be no world at all except chaos." Fate hid from us that our meetings were to be few. On October 8, 1944, the world was stunned to hear of his death, aged fifty-two.

One day Lady Abingdon telephoned me, asking if I could call on her at five o'clock, there was something she would like me to do. When I arrived at her hotel there was a young Frenchman with her, named

Hervé Alphand. He was an attaché at the French Embassy in Washington. Wholly out of sympathy with its Vichy connection, he was taking the grave step of resigning, it being his intention to go over to de Gaulle. He had written a letter to the Press stating his reason for resigning. Lady Abingdon had called me in to 'vet' his English. Actually, it required very little alteration. I looked on Alphand with admiration, as a man of principle. Like many young Frenchmen he was faced with a cruel dilemma and was jeopardising his future. It proved to be a right decision. His career went full circle. Some twenty years later he returned to Washington as the French Ambassador, in which post he had much success. Subsequently, he reached the peak of his profession as Permanent Under-Secretary at the Quai d'Orsay.

VI

The dollar quest went on. I got more and more restive. In February, 1941, Fletcher, ever helpful, had replied to my outburst.

I am very sorry that we have not been able, so far, to carry through the proposal we had in mind. As I have told you more than once, we receive nothing but the most enthusiastic reports of your contribution as a speaker, and we should be extremely sorry to see you leave the United States at this moment. We have good reason to thank you for the great personal efforts you have made to undertake engagements which were significant to the British cause . . . I still hope that some means may be found to enable you to stay here, not only because of your reputation as a speaker, but also because of your exceptional knowledge of the United States and your wide and representative contacts among Americans. Nobody knows better than we do the value of these personal relationships. I therefore very much hope that a way will be found to retain your services on this side of the Atlantic.

How much was done to retain my services? A month later Fletcher had some news for me.

We have now a cable stating that the Ministry has officially decided against the arrangement we suggested for dollar exchange. They seem to hope that you will be able to return to Great Britain for a brief stay, as they consider it would greatly enhance the value of your lectures on your return.

This letter contradicted all those which had preceded it. The idea that I should mark time beachcombing in Nassau or Bermuda had now gone overboard. My immediate response was to ask Fletcher to obtain a passage home at once, but it should be understood that I had no intention of returning. Nothing happened. No passage was forthcoming despite our efforts. Two months later the wind veered again. Douglas Williams wrote from the Ministry:

> As to the question of arranging a return trip by bomber transport or clipper, this matter has been referred by cable to Sir Gerald Campbell, our Minister in Washington. While he sympathises with your wish to return on a brief visit here, and thinks that the war background you would thus acquire would enhance your lecturing value, the time element now presents difficulties. I fear you might find yourself stuck here when you should be on the lecture platform in America.

The intransigence of this correspondence is emphasised by the fact that within a year the Ministry contrived to send over by clipper and bomber sixteen persons, with expense allowances.

I will not weary my readers with further details of this farce. My doctor would have banned a bomber-passage in any case. "At this time such a flight may lead to a serious internal haemorrhage and possibly jeopardise your life. You need a long rest," he wrote.

In July I went to Bermuda to take a rest. The visit also served another purpose. I was able to live on my sterling money and to renew my shabby and depleted wardrobe. While there I addressed the English-Speaking Union and those employed there at the censorship base. I was most generously entertained by the Governor, downwards. There was an occasion when I was asked to accompany the Colonial Secretary to meet ex-King Carol and his red-haired mistress, Madame Lupescu, flying through to Mexico. There was a protocol difficulty. She could not be received by the Governor, so he sent us, with a handsome young kilted A.D.C., to detach the lady and take her to lunch while he entertained King Carol. I found the heat and the humidity unbearable and was kept awake by the croaking at night of tree-frogs. After three weeks I returned to New York. I had bought five suits and fitted myself out, with my sterling money. It was an odd experience to have money to spend.

About this time there was a change in the New York office. The name of the British Library became the British Information Services. A Lecture Bureau was created, and by some wire-pulling, Granville-Barker was put in charge of it. These days he was a pathetic figure. In middle-age he broke his marriage with Lillah McCarthy and married a rich American woman. Helen Huntington was the wife of her wealthy cousin, Archer Huntington, whom she divorced, to his grief. She got from him a yearly income of fifty thousand gold dollars for life. Bernard Berenson wrote in his *Last Diaries*:

> She was a *femme inassouvie*, and eager for fame as a novelist and as a woman of high society. Cold as a fish. When she married Granville-Barker she took him off the stage, and tried to establish him as a country gentleman in England. It did not work and she moved over to the Place des Etats Unis, Paris. I knew her as Archer's wife, and as I was with one toe in Parisian society, she invited me repeatedly to meals attended by French generals, second-class society people and a very few Anglo-Saxons. On me Barker made the impression of a gifted but weak creature, who had never grown up and was afraid of the future.

As she did not think theatrical people respectable, she cut her husband off from them, including Bernard Shaw, who accused her of practising witchcraft on him. He had to propose a vote of thanks to Granville-Barker at a public lecture. Shaw openly said in his remarks that Barker's desertion of the stage was a public scandal. Mrs. Granville-Barker sat behind him, her body and face tense with hate.

> The moment I got up to leave the platform I felt that my spine has been converted into a bar of rusty iron which grated on the base of my skull. The pain at the top and bottom of my spine was so frightful that I could not even bend down to get into a taxi. Somehow I reached home on foot, and when my wife arrived I was lying flat and helpless on my bed. The doctors could make nothing of it.

Shaw was quite certain she had bewitched him.

On the outbreak of war the Granville-Barkers went to New York. I used to meet her at Lady Cunard's soirées. She showed an acid disposition towards the writers she met there who did not accept her pretensions. Granville-Barker proved a failure at the Lecture Bureau and was frequently absent. He would stop a conversation, the perspiration breaking out on his brow, and say, "I must go. Helen is waiting for me below." S. K. Ratcliffe wrote to me, "Hamish Hamilton is here from the Ministry, looking at things. There is the difficulty of G–B. Pleasant and distinguished though he is, he is not attending to the work of the Speakers' section." On his wife's urging Granville-Barker tried to by-pass me. It riled them that I was in continuous demand. The Bureau collapsed. He died in August, 1946, aged sixty-nine. It was a sad end for a gifted playwright, actor-manager and Shakespearean scholar.

In 1944, hearing I wished to go home, I received a letter from Mrs. Stillwell, of the Speakers' Bureau of the British War Relief Society, after I had spoken at the Anzac Club.

I hope you are remaining in America. Personally I feel it is vital. You have done more for the cause than you know, it comes back to me from far and wide. The British Information Services here have fallen down on their job. If you could see the comparative figures in the two Speakers' Bureaux—the B.W.R.S. has done twice and sometimes thrice the work and gone into fields that the B.I.S. have not ever bothered about. My great difficulty was that I dare not step out of the narrow form contained in our Charter—do propaganda in any form. You did it most skilfully.

In the spring of 1941 I had edited and published a volume of letters that had been written to me since the outbreak of the war by a soldier of twenty-one, James Pepper. He had been stationed in Paris from which he had escaped on the downfall of France, and succeeded in reaching a rescue ship at St. Nazaire. Later, he joined the Special Air Services, was dropped behind the German lines in North Italy, was wounded, and gained a M.C. His letters from France were remarkable in style and matter, and on showing them to Macmillan's they suggested publication under the title of *Letters From Jim*. This resulted in a letter from Somerset Maugham in California.

Dear Cecil,
I found a volume of *Letters* from your friend Jim at somebody's house the other day and read as much as I had time to. It was a very good book to publish. I found the letters singularly moving. They reminded me that since I arrived here I have wanted to write to you. I see in the papers that Gerald Campbell has been put in full charge of propaganda and publicity in this country. I hope that some arrangement will be made to enable you to stay here. The work you did all through last winter was very

valuable and I am convinced that it would be a very good thing if you could go around the country again next season. In all the places I went to I heard the same thing about you which was that your addresses were moving and amusing. There are too few people who have come here from England and can hold and interest an audience. For my part I am sure that you can be very much more useful here than ever you could be in England.

In July Duff Cooper left the Ministry of Information, after little more than a year in office. He had always disliked the post. He had been virulently attacked by the Press, Beaverbrook vowing he would get him out of office. "When I appealed to the Prime Minister, I got little support. He was not interested in the subject of propaganda, he knew it was not going to win the war," said Duff Cooper. Exhausted and unhappy, feeling impotent and frustrated, Cooper asked to leave. Churchill appointed Brendan Bracken. I had had little support from Duff Cooper, and I did not expect much from Brendan Bracken, although I knew them both. By now I, too, felt unhappy and frustrated.

Then a bombshell hit us. Angus Fletcher, who had been knighted in January, was dismissed in July. 'Retired' was the word used. He was given a totally inadequate pension on which he could not live. He had a wife and three sons, two of them at American colleges. He was compelled to retreat to a tiny flat and to take a job hawking books for an English publishing firm. His dismissal created the greatest resentment in many circles. Everyone respected him. He was efficient and devoted in his work. He maintained a dignified silence.

Fletcher's successor was Professor Charles Webster, well known as an historian. He was also an authority at Chatham House and did work for the Foreign Office for which he was a consultant. His chief title to fame was as an historian of the Congress of Vienna. He was a heavy, growly man. He said to me when I called on him, "I don't know why they've sent me here. I know nothing and care nothing about propaganda or about America, which I dislike." I told him that I was disgusted with the treatment accorded to Fletcher and to myself, and I wanted to go home. He exclaimed, "For God's sake don't go! I'm told you are our best man here. What would you do if you went home? They need only soldiers and factory workers."

I did not raise the question, unknown to him of my means of

support. We got on well together. He had no social graces, was a lamentable speaker, and avoided public engagements. He burbled and growled all the time. I got Mrs. Stabler to give a lunch for him, collecting notable Americans. I dragged him to Mrs. Vanderbilt's. "I don't know how you keep going at all these love-feasts," he said. "I know it's valuable but I'm not an Aubusson carpet performer." Despite his churlish manner he got on well with the staff, which was sore at the loss of Fletcher.

My threat to leave seems to have created a stir. Letters poured in on Sir Gerald Campbell from sixteen organisations who had called on my services, from Dr. Butler, President of Columbia University, from Thomas Lamont of Pierpont Morgan, from the Chairman of the British War Relief Society, etc. "I think he is one of the very best ambassadors-at-large that England has in the United States today," wrote the President of Macmillans. "Can't you persuade him that he is serving his country well by staying right here. I have asked him what earthly good he can do England by returning there. He can think of no adequate answer, nor can I. He is doing a magnificent job here." A cable came from the Ministry of Information. "We do very much hope you will stay." I cabled back. "I do very much hope you will let me have some of the seventy thousand dollars I sent you, on which to exist. It is as simple as that." Nothing happened.

CHAPTER FOURTEEN

Mrs. Vanderbilt, Lady Ribblesdale, Lady Cunard

I

Let us turn to something more pleasant. I was most generously entertained and met with great kindness from my American friends. One morning I was surprised to receive an invitation to dinner from Mrs. Cornelius Vanderbilt. Some rumour of me must have reached her. Her invitations were almost in the nature of a 'royal command'. She was still the foremost figure in New York Society although the once-exclusive Four Hundred had disappeared. She still lived in a large brownstone mansion at the corner of Fifth Avenue and Fifty-First Street, now dwarfed by the skyscrapers of Rockefeller Centre, and squeezed in between massive office buildings. Through the mansion's portals during nearly half a century had passed names which composed the contemporary history of Europe and America. Here Mrs. Grace Vanderbilt, or 'Her Grace' as she was nicknamed, had held court. She still received everybody who was anybody, from emperors, kings, princes, ambassadors, down. It was said she was a snob. She was. She would recall repeatedly what the Czar of Russia had said to her when the Vanderbilt yacht went to St. Petersburg, what Queen Mary, her friend, had said, when she was a guest at Buckingham Palace. On her table she kept open the signed copy of the *Life of Marlborough* which Winston Churchill had given her when staying there. She gave her snobbery an enjoyable quality; it was a peephole into history. She loved entertaining. She had lunch and dinner parties of twenty and thirty. The house had become slightly shabby with time and her failing eyesight, but the food was still superb. It was characteristic that her butler was a tall, handsome English ex-guardsman. The house was a French palace. It had cost four million dollars. In this palace the Vanderbilts had reigned. The

Emperor Wilhelm, Queen Marie of Rumania, King Albert of Belgium, the Queen of Spain, the King of Greece, the Prince of Wales, Marshal Foch, President Theodore Roosevelt, Lord Balfour, the Duke of Kent, Paderewski, Toscanini, Field-Marshals and divas, all had mounted the steps of 640 Fifth Avenue.

In the early days there was a line of Vanderbilt houses stretching up to Central Park. All but this mansion had disappeared, giving place to expensive shops. Time stood still with 'Her Grace'. She was recognised by the bandeau she always wore. She received her guests in the Library that looked on Fifth Avenue, a high beautiful room with French Regency furniture and gilt, inlaid oak panelling. In winter a log fire blazed. On the marble mantelpiece, on either side of a great Louis Seize clock, two candles ceremoniously burned before the long mirror. On a small side table, near our hostess's chair, there were always four single red roses in four silver vases. The four roses and the two candles, like her head bandeau, were part of the formality of the house. Once, on the settee, I found a brilliant cape, crimson and black, embroidered with gold lace. In its folds rows of minute emeralds and rubies, worked in an elaborate pattern, scintillated under the shaded lights on the side tables. I picked it up, lost in wonder. Had it belonged to a King, a Spanish grandee, a cardinal? "No, but it's Spanish," said my hostess. "Once, when we were visiting Madrid, King Alfonso took me to a bullfight. I was in the Royal box. Following a custom, the leading matador came and threw his cape up to me. He was the greatest matador of the day and afterwards he inscribed it. Look!" She reversed the cape revealing a lining of yellow silk. Under the collar, written in ink, was an inscription with the name of the donor, Ignacio Sanchez Mejias. I stood dumb. The previous evening I had been the guest of the Marqués de Cuevas, who had given a Spanish entertainment. There was guitar-playing by Segovia. On a special floor La Argentina danced for us. I had the good fortune to be her companion at dinner. She informed me that Spain's great contemporary poet, Garcia Lorca, shot by a Falangist squad in Granada, had written a poem, *Llanto por Ignacio Sanchez Mejias*, on the death in the Mexican arena of Spain's greatest matador, her husband. She lent me a copy. And now at Mrs. Vanderbilt's the following evening I handled his cape.

I was fortunate in being treated by Mrs. Vanderbilt in terms of warm friendship, a frequent guest at her table and in her parterre box, No. 3, at the Metropolitan Opera House, with its side-view of the stage, and 'The Diamond Horseshoe', a scene as yet untouched by the war ravaging Europe or the oncoming death of the old regime.

While dispensing her lavish hospitality, Mrs. Vanderbilt was ever aware of the raging war across the Atlantic. I took young officers there who had been in the fighting. She was staunchly pro-British and always gave them a warm welcome.

On May 27, 1941, there was a lunch party with thirty-two guests. Just before entering the library where the guests were assembling, two of us had received news of a naval battle off Crete, under air-attack, in which British destroyers had been sunk, among them H.M.S. *Kelly*, commanded by Lord Louis Mountbatten. It was obvious our hostess did not know the news, although it would particularly affect her, for she had given asylum to the two Mountbatten daughters. We decided that she should be informed. At any moment the newspapers and the radio might announce the sinking of the *Kelly* and the presumed loss of its commander. His young daughters were at their day-school, from which they were to be collected by their governess, who was to take them to a cinema. Obviously, they must be guarded from learning of their father's death so abruptly; it might be only an unconfirmed report. Drawing our hostess aside, we informed her. She took it magnificently and most of the guests throughout lunch had no idea of the tragedy threatening the house. The governess was despatched to bring the girls directly home from their school. Precautions were taken that on their return neither broadcasts nor newspapers should reach them. That afternoon some papers printed an obituary notice of Lord Louis Mountbatten. Meanwhile we communicated with the British Embassy but it had no news. Not until very late in the evening did we learn that Mountbatten's proverbial luck had held, and he had survived the sinking of his ship and been rescued from the sea by the destroyer *Kipling*. The next morning the two girls, on waking, heard the whole story. A few months later their father was a guest in the house, before assuming command of H.M.S. *Illustrious*.

It happened that I was to be a witness of the end of an era in this great house. New buildings, like adamant bulldozers, encroached.

The servant question, and a diminishing fortune, made a forty-four-roomed mansion too difficult to maintain. One day in October, 1944, after lunch, while we were taking coffee in the library, the butler came in and said Mr. X was in the morning-room. "He's come," said Mrs. Vanderbilt. "I shall have to go in and see him." "Who?" I asked. "Mr. X, from my lawyers. He's brought the lease of the new house for me to sign." To the very end this moment had been deferred. We rose. At the door we paused. Beyond, inexorable Fate, in striped trousers and polka-dot bow, was waiting. I said goodbye and watched my hostess go to greet him, well aware of the tumult in her heart. But her head was high.

There was a Hollywood touch at the sale of the fittings. An agent of the Paramount Film Corporation flew in from California and bought the panelling of the dining-room, ball-room and library, for $5,800, to his great astonishment. These interiors would be used over and over for de luxe French settings. Mrs. Vanderbilt retained her Turner landscapes, her tapestries, and Madrazo's portrait of a beautiful young woman with a petite head of fair curls, holding a strand of roses, young Grace Vanderbilt of the Nineties. When I saw her in the new home, higher up Fifth Avenue, she was standing under this portrait and with her, among two hundred guests, were the Duke and Duchess of Windsor. He looked incredibly boyish at fifty-one, newly released from the torrid 'St. Helena' of the Bahamas Governorship. Uprooted, assailed, my hostess was carrying on as before. When she died a few years later, aged eighty-three, people were astonished to learn that the twenty-million-pound estate had shrunk to little more than half a million. She had always been a generous benefactor.

II

It was at one of Mrs. Murray Crane's dinner parties, with company coming in afterwards for Professor Wind's enthralling lecture, that I first met two very remarkable women with whom I formed a warm friendship for the rest of their lives. Some fifty guests assembled in the long salon overlooking Central Park. There appeared Sir Thomas Beecham, accompanied by Lady (Emerald) Cunard, and Lady Ribblesdale. The last, born Ave Willing, whose first husband was John Jacob Astor, later married Lord Ribblesdale, the tall *grand seigneur* whose portrait in hunting attire by Sargent was the sensation of its year. It now hangs in the Tate Gallery, to which he gave it in memory of his two sons. It was dubbed 'The Ancestor'.

In appearance Ribblesdale was the acme of nobility. After Harrow he had lived in France until his father committed suicide. He married, first, Charlotte Tennant, sister of Margot Asquith, the Prime Minister's unpredictable wife. The marriage was an idyll. A man of culture, well-read in French and English classics, a lord-in-waiting to Queen Victoria, a Master of Hounds, he rode in the opening procession of Ascot races. He had had three daughters and two sons, one being Charles Lister, handsome, clever, a friend of Rupert Brooke, who died, like him, in the Aegean in the First World War. Ribblesdale was unfortunate. His elder son was killed in India. Eventually he married the ex-wife of John Jacob Astor, of great beauty and riches. At her house, Hanover Lodge, in Regent's Park, she became one of the great Edwardian hostesses, renowned for her tennis parties, and her entertainments. For one of these she engaged Pavlova to dance. On the outbreak of the Second World War, she re-established herself, being a widow, in a luxurious apartment on Park Avenue, New York. Here she entertained almost every distinguished person who visited the city.

When she walked into the Crane drawing-room I could only think of a swan in superb and calm movement. She had a striking head of white curls, wonderfully poised on a superb neck and bosom. Her eyes were dark and lively, her figure, beautifully gowned, was slim and svelte. I learned to my amazement that she was in her seventies. She was a very well-read woman, rich in reminiscence.

By her first marriage she had a son, Vincent Astor, and a daughter, Alice, who gave her much trouble. Alice ran through a series of husbands. She married first, Prince Obolensky, descended from the Grand Dukes of Kiev since A.D. 862, a handsome, remarkable and enterprising man. In the Second World War he became a colonel in the American Air Force and at fifty, a paratroop leader, was dropped in Sardinia and then in France. The little Mayor of Châteauroux, into which he dropped, gave him a great welcome, and was shot for this, two days later, by the retreating Germans.

By Obolensky, Alice Astor, of great wealth, had a son, Ivan, born at Hanover Lodge in 1925. She divorced Obolensky and married

Hugo von Hofmannsthal, the son of Richard Strauss's librettist, and after another divorce, Philip Harding, and then, divorced again, David Pleydell Bouverie. "I had a great shock and sorrow over my Alice's last marriage," Lady Ribblesdale wrote to me, in 1946. "He is quite a nice man, I think, but all this humbug about 'marriage' seems to me like mocking God. She has a blind spot and is an idiot idealist. I pleaded on my knees but she was adamant."

As a result of these various matrimonial tangles there was utter bewilderment when, at the beginning of the war, Lady Ribblesdale went over to Ireland, en route to the U.S.A., with all her grandchildren. The customs official simply could not understand the passports in the name of Astor, Ribblesdale, Obolensky, Hofmannsthal, all in the same family.

I met Alice Astor-Obolensky-Hofmannsthal-Harding–Pleydell Bouverie, in her mother's apartment in New York in 1945, just before her last marriage. She was a vague, pretty woman of about forty-eight. She had dreamy eyes, a sleepy voice and was somehow *simpatica*. She was one of the four persons present when the tomb of Tutankhamen was opened.

At the close of the war there was a trek to America and at lunches at Lady Ribblesdale's I met among many Cyril Connolly, the critic, Sir John Maxwell-Scott, the descendant of Scott the novelist, who lived at historic Abbotsford with his two half-American daughters; thus it was that I had a special welcome from them, 'fans' of mine, when I visited Abbotsford. Other visitors included Victor Cazalet, M.P., and the two Sitwells, Osbert and his sister Edith, with her setter's long nose and gothic face. I could never read her verses nor accept her pretensions, but she matched her venom for some fellow-scribes with much kindness to others. Lady Ribblesdale lived in a large apartment on the fifteenth floor. Her long drawing-room was filled with beautiful Louis Seize furniture and Aubusson carpets. Her chef was superlative. One had a continuous surprise in conversation with her. You never could tell with what facet she would shine. I learned one day that, a famous sportswoman, she had been the first woman to do the Cresta run at St. Moritz. I alluded to the fabulous Duchess of Plaisance. She was the widow of one of Napoleon's statesmen. As a girl she was captured by a famous Greek brigand. When the money for her ransom arrived she refused to leave him and they lived together until it was spent. In her old age she lived in a palace built of green marble at the foot of Mount Pentelicon. Eccentric, the Duchess preserved her dead daughter and also her favourite dog on each side of her fireplace. One day the palace caught fire. It was impossible to rescue these relics as they were preserved in spirits. Watching from afar, the Duchess suddenly saw a great flame shoot up, and exclaimed, "There go my dog and my daughter!" To my amazement Lady Ribblesdale said she knew a great deal about the Duchess, who was born Sophie de Barbe-Marbois, in Philadelphia in 1785. "She was my great-great-aunt," said Lady Ribblesdale.

III

The second lady at the Crane reception was Lady Cunard, who arrived with her *ami*, Sir Thomas Beecham. She was, I think, the most astonishing among many astonishing women I have known. For thirty years she had been the most talked-of hostess in London. I had never met her but one heard of her exploits continuously. She had been an *eminence grise* behind the Diaghilev Ballet, and the Beecham opera seasons at Covent Garden. The table at her town house was crowded with celebrities from all walks of life. The handsome young Prince David of Wales and his set frequented it. Prime Ministers, Cabinet Ministers, conductors, divas, the Bright Young Things, headed by Lady Diana Cooper, were in and out of her house. It was a triumphant achievement for little Miss Maud Burke of California. She was sixty-eight when I met her. She had seven more years to live. But you could never think of her in terms of years, she was so vital, so piquant in style, so alert in mind.

She was born in San Francisco, in 1872, a city that has always produced remarkable women. Her mother was half-French. Her father died in her teens. At eighteen, her mother married again. She travelled with her in France, where she acquired her passionate love of French literature. It was commonly believed that she was the daughter of William O'Brien, a big man of the Comstock Lode, one of the greatest of all silver-mines. Herbert Agar, his grand-nephew, believed he left her a large sum of money. In London this bright, pretty girl met George Moore, whose work she greatly admired. Finding herself a fellow-guest at a Savoy lunch party in 1894, she changed the place-cards in order to sit next to him. This ravishing young girl with her intellect enchanted him. He never ceased to love her and embarrassingly showed it. Back in the U.S.A. she met the glamorous young Prince Poniatowski, grandson of a King of Poland. He went back to Europe, and kept up a correspondence with her. On hearing of his return to San Francisco she persuaded herself it was to marry her and indiscreetly told some friends. It appeared in the local Press. Instead, he married a Miss Sperry, daughter of the leader of local society, who looked on the Burkes as upstarts. It was a heavy blow and Maud Burke left at once for New York. There, on the rebound, she married in 1895 Sir Bache Cunard, grandson of the founder of the shipping line. He was forty-three to her twenty-three. He took her to his beautiful property, Nevill Holt in Leicestershire. Walking one day with my father in the woods there, then aged fourteen, I saw Lady Cunard, her daughter Nancy, and George Moore, but did not know who they were. And now some thirty-four years later I met her again, a famous hostess who had reigned at Nevill Holt and Carlton House Terrace.

The marriage was not happy. He loved horses, she hated them. The conversation of her intellectual friends bewildered him, George Moore particularly, a cuckoo in the nest. Sir Bache's passion was ironwork. He made a gate on which he wrought 'Come into the garden, Maud'. But Maud ignored the invitation. There were disagreements. She rebelled against formality. He reproved her when she addressed a footman instead of the butler. She told me that once, wishing to see Sir Bache, who had gone to his club, she went down St. James's Street, looking in the windows, not sure which was his. She hailed him in White's. He saw her and was horrified. "How dare you go down St. James's Street looking in club windows! Only whores do that! Go down on your knees and ask God's forgiveness," he said, on arriving home. "And I went down on my knees. Dear me! No, it didn't work." There was a scene in 1914. Against his liking, George Moore was a constant visitor to Nevill Holt. A break came when Moore talked of 'the obscene state of marriage', told risqué stories, and scoffed at Holy Communion, saying, "You can't change God into a biscuit." The unhappy pair separated. He kept the Fernie Hounds, and she kept her salon in London. He died a lonely man in a country inn, an amateur blacksmith. They had one child, Nancy, brilliant, wayward, who was found drunk in a Paris gutter. Unconscious, she could not remember her name and died alone in a French hospital. She carried on a long feud against her mother, wrote a scurrilous pamphlet about her, and lived with a negro pianist.

Lady Cunard spent large sums supporting opera, and she and Beecham saved Covent Garden when it was floundering. In 1939 she went to Mexico with Sir Thomas, to investigate her inherited silver-mine, which proved worthless. She was at the Ritz-Carlton Hotel in New York when the war broke out and remained there. It was at this time that I met her at Mrs. Crane's. She invited me to call and I became one of her circle. Emerald rapidly established a little salon. She was *petite*, with a birdlike face, quick, sharp-eyed. She was not only a marvellous conversationalist of the widest intelligence—she read until dawn every day and could cap any quotation—but she was a wonderful ringmaster, bringing you into the ensemble with a flick of her tongue. Her circle included Sir Thomas Beecham, Somerset Maugham, Virgil Thomson, the music critic, Frederick Prokosch, the young novelist, conductors and composers. But the war had shattered her world. An intimate friend of the Prince of Wales, she had not been *bien vue* at Buckingham Palace. The Mrs. Simpson imbroglio and the abdication crashed all hopes of passing through its gates one day.

In association with Sir Thomas Beecham she had been behind many of the musical achievements of the past quarter of a century. Her circle embraced Mayfair and Bohemia, the smart young things, the 'knowing' old ones. Rising young politicians, others in full phase, some setting, had frequented her dinners. The intimate of George Moore, Winston Churchill, George Curzon, the first Earl of Birkenhead, to name only stars in her constellation, she always commanded a circle of dazzled friends. I had conceived her to be an elderly dominating dowager. Instead, she seemed incredibly young and dainty. Light as thistledown, her blue eyes looked out of a head belonging to a Nymphenburg shepherdess. There were often moments when I had to shake myself out of an illusion that I had been put into satin knee-breeches in a landscape of floral swings and garden urns, and was sitting at the feet of a Fragonard creation—until the lady spoke. It is impossible to imagine that any of Fragonard's ladies ever possessed such intelligence and wit.

I saw from the first moment the cause of her celebrity in London.

Always chic and delicate to behold, her mind never flagged. She had a prodigious memory regarding music, literature, painting and politics. One evening after a performance of amazing virtuosity, four of us, men of letters, gathered at the bar downstairs and held an enquiry into how it was possible for one small head to hold so much. Her reading was wide and thorough. She could quote Baudelaire, Paul Fort, Schiller and Rainer Maria Rilke. If the conversation veered to Euripides, Dante, Leopardi, she kept up and was in at the kill. In the field of music she had the knowledge and resources born of a life-devotion. Sometimes the talk would be illustrated by Sir Thomas Beecham at the piano in her sitting-room. I recall a magic afternoon when he was rehearsing a lecture he had to give on Mozart. There was a running comment from Emerald, Somerset Maugham and others, with Sir Thomas making a Mozartian embroidery at the piano in illustration of some point in the argument. It was in odd contrast to the state of the world at that moment. There we were, in an oasis of Mozartian harmony, on the tenth floor of a New York hotel, snatching an hour of respite from disaster, for Europe lay at the feet of the Nazi monster, and England, like an exhausted bird in the tempest, beat her brave wings through the darkness.

Sometimes a royalty or two arrived, sad and courteous, a little like animals driven from their zoo into the harsh world. Feminine beauty contributed its leavening grace to that circle. One recalls Mona Harrison Williams, Betty Lawson-Johnstone, the Duchess of Grammont. It was a circle ever revolving, with visiting British and American colonels and commanders, the Windsors, Duff Cooper, Ronald Tree, young attachés, etc. Air-clippers, warships and liners brought transients, en route to Washington, so that there was always the latest news 'not for publication'.

The talk was not always political or intellectual. Gaiety of spirit never quite deserted that Fragonard head. Sometimes I felt we perched around her like the parakeets in a fortune-teller's cage. She tapped us deftly with her wand, we flew off the perch obediently and delivered our contribution, rewarded with a smile if our turn was well done. At the worst the pace of the performance was never slow, sometimes it was breathless and hilarious. Any name was apt to provoke some astonishing footnote from Emerald. While one never thought of her in terms of age her experience touched points almost in antiquity. She had talked with Verlaine in a Paris café, with Delius in a French garden. She had been a frequent visitor to George Moore, the oracle of Ebury Street, appearing in those *Conversations*, so often concocted but real in her case.

One day I mentioned a letter from Noël Coward, and the discussion turned at once to his new play *Blithe Spirit*, whose première I had just attended in Boston. "Oh," said Emerald, "that reminds me of his first venture *The Vortex*, which Michael Arlen financed. I took Lord Curzon to see it at a repertory theatre in Hampstead. It was a play about an undergraduate whose friend was in love with his mother. Lord Curzon went behind afterwards and was very complimentary." The next day I checked the story with Michael Arlen, who was sitting, possum-like, in the bar of the St. Regis Hotel. "Quite right," he said. I met Noël one evening in the Embassy Club. He told me he wanted to produce a play. We had a drink or two and just then I was on the top of the world, having published *The Green Hat*. So I wrote him a cheque for two hundred pounds, not caring if I lost it. Well, I didn't and you've seen what happened to that lad."

Emerald had once invited Ezra Pound to the opera. Hearing that he had no dress clothes, she got a spare suit from a friend, furtively mounted the stairs, terrified of offending the poet, and dumped the parcel outside his door. He appeared in evening dress in her box. One day Eddie Marsh, the purveyor of poets to Mayfair, came to ask her help for a person who was ill. His name meant nothing to her but she opened her purse. Some years later the recipient called on her. He was James Joyce.

Kind, responsive, yes, but under the silk there was iron. Sometimes she reminded me of the Virgin Queen, castigating a courtier. "Imagine! The insolence!" she exclaimed. "That Mrs. Dash asked me to lunch. When I got there she had twenty women, not a single man! I asked her how she dared, and came home." Her wit could be devastating, and acid. One evening, when Somerset Maugham wished to retire early, she protested. He said, "I have to keep my youth." "Why don't you bring him with you? I should be delighted to meet him," was her parting shot. But these moments were rare. Grace and light characterised the entertainment she gave.

In the winter, 1940–41, Sir Thomas Beecham, who occupied a suite at the Ritz adjoining Emerald's, was conducting at the Metropolitan Opera House. Here one day in the Artists' Room he introduced me to a boy of twenty-one named Leonard Bernstein. He had just been acting as locum-tenens for Bruno Walter, with much success. Modest, dark, in 1958 he would be the first American to become musical director of the New York Philharmonic. One day there was an astonishing incident. Sir Thomas Beecham called me into his room. "My boy, what is this? I'm told about your having money difficulties? I hear you are doing marvellous work. Don't they pay you enough?" I explained that I never had asked for payment, that I had sent home all my dollars on which I had thought to support myself and that, so far, they would not make me any allowance. "The bastards!" he said. "Would $5,000 dollars help you?" Astonished, I looked at him. "But Tom, you can't give it to me. We are compelled to remit all our earnings to the Bank of England. Also, I could not repay you. We are not allowed to do so. It is illegal to exchange pounds for dollars." "So they say, and what the devil do those bloodless Moghuls care if you die here in the gutter! My boy, what I earn here I spend here, and they can whistle for it!" He opened a drawer in the writing-table, and wrote me a cheque for $5,000. "There you are, my boy. Get on with the good work," he said, handing it to me. I was quite speechless. "Come along," he said, and marched me into Emerald's room.

All that evening I was in a state of uncertainty. The next morning I went to cash the cheque. I had doubts, having heard about Sir Thomas's easy way with money. The teller took the cheque, looked at it front and back, then walked away. "It's going to bounce," I told myself. After a few minutes he asked me to follow him. I was taken to the manager's room. He received me politely, the cheque in hand. "Isn't it good?" I asked. He looked a little embarrassed. "Well, I won't say it's bad but—unfortunately—just now Sir Thomas's account has not a balance to meet it."

I thanked him, and took back the cheque. I did not see Sir Thomas. He had gone off on tour. I locked the cheque away.

Soon after this Lady Cunard became greatly perturbed. She was left much alone. The rumour went round that Tommy was travelling with Betty Humby, a pianist who appeared with him. She was a clergyman's wife, with a young son. It was said he was in love with her and intended to marry her. She would get a divorce, and he also, in Reno, from his wife Utica, with whom he had not lived for some time. The rumours grew and Emerald began to question us. Was it true Tommy was with the Humby woman? He never wrote. "We must keep our mouths shut," said Somerset Maugham. For a time we pretended we knew nothing. Poor Emerald approached the verge of hysteria. One night at 2 a.m. she rang me up. Time meant nothing to her, she read all night. "Tom can't behave like this! You must speak to him!" she cried. I had to tell her that one man cannot interfere in the love affair of another. I should be told to mind my own business. Her agitation brought on a severe attack of shingles. Then the bomb fell. At a lunch Leonora Corbett, the beautiful actress who had made a great hit in Noël Coward's *Blithe Spirit*, said, "I hear that my old schoolfriend, Betty Humby, now with Beecham in Seattle, is going to marry him." Emerald, present, heard this. It confirmed her fears. "I want to die!" she cried. Thus ended a life-long infatuation with the errant Tommy. She made arrangements to leave for England and at the close of 1942 crossed the Atlantic on a Portuguese ship. One vessel in the convoy was torpedoed. She flew on to London from Lisbon. Her house in Grosvenor Square had been demolished, so she moved into the Dorchester Hotel.

When, in New York, the train faded down the platform taking her to the port of departure, I was sadly conscious that some of the light had gone out of our lives; but I reflected that dark and bombed London would know her dauntless spirit, and around her again, as once in Grosvenor Square, she would gather her friends and lighten the shadows.

IV

In my gallery of delightful ladies I must hang the portrait of Countess Mercati. She was an American, a patron of art and music, a doctor's widow who had married Count Alexander Mercati, former grand-marshal of the royal court of Greece. Though well in the seventies, small, frail, she was a dynamo of energy and delight. She lived in a suite, all green, in the St. Regis Hotel, the most prominent ornament, spot-lighted, being a Dali painting. In the First World War she had been awarded the Cross of the Legion of Honour, the Queen Elizabeth Medal by Belgium and the silver medal of the

Italian Red Cross. By her Greek marriage she was the stepmother-in-law of Michael Arlen. Everyone seemed to come to her apartment. It was there that I met the man who, if he had had his rights, would have been the heir to the French throne. Jerome Bonaparte Patterson, related by marriage to Countess Mercati, was the great-grandson of Prince Jerome Bonaparte and Betsy Patterson. They had been married in the Roman Catholic Cathedral by the Bishop of Baltimore. Napoleon would never acknowledge this marriage, had it revoked, and forbade his brother and wife to set foot in France. Finally, the weak Prince Jerome, under pressure, deserted his wife, and, created King of Westphalia, married a German princess. The little man who sat on Marie Mercati's couch died childless. One evening in 1945 he took his dog for a walk in Central Park, tripped over its lead, and died, aged sixty-seven. This ended the Bonaparte-Patterson line.

Salvador Dali would come in and out of the apartment, with his rapier moustache and wild ideas. One morning, on calling on the Countess I was surprised to see a table elaborately set for about a dozen persons. When I remarked on this, she laughed and said, "I'll let you into a secret. It's a wedding breakfast for the Fritz Kreislers!" I remarked that I thought they had been happily married for forty years. "Yes, but it's like this," said Marie. "When they were married in 1902 Fritz was a Catholic and Harriet wasn't. Recently she's become a convert and she's got the idea that for forty years she's been living in sin with Fritz! So this morning in an obscure Roman Catholic church on Long Island, to avoid publicity, they're being married, and I'm giving the wedding breakfast." The 'newly-weds' lived happily for almost another twenty years, Harriet surviving to the age of ninety-three, a year after Fritz's death.

I saw Michael Arlen frequently. The man who had shaken London with *The Green Hat* was an extinct volcano. Armenian-born, he married Atalanta Mercati, Count Mercati's daughter, who had great charm and elegance. It was a completely happy union. He lunched every day at the St. Regis. Arlen always carried himself with an air and never moaned. His last novel, *Christine*, published in 1938, showed that the flame had gone out. He came back from failure in Hollywood with no bitterness. He sat in the bar, his hands folded over a malacca cane, always well-groomed, polite. Just before he died in 1964 I sent him a message through Alec Waugh, a close friend.

When in New York, public engagements permitting, I never lacked opera, ballet, music. Boxes and stalls were given me most liberally. My friend, Mrs. Boehm, an ardent music-lover, always had two seats for everything, so I was frequently at Carnegie Hall. There, one day, I heard Rachmaninoff in a superb performance of the Concerto No. 3. A few weeks later he was sitting in the stall just in front of me. Having trouble putting on his coat, I helped him. It was the beginning of a friendship. He always looked as if he had just come out of prison, pale, worried, close-cropped. He taught in the Julliard School of Music. He had lost a large estate in Russia at the Revolution. "I was so nervous when I first came to America that I dared not go out to tea. I spilt it over everyone who talked to me," he said.

In September I solved a dollar crisis by getting an advance of $2,000 from my American publisher for a novel as yet unwritten. I kept it and used it for my work. It was ironical that I could have got £3,000 from my English publisher but that money would have been blocked in England. I had the novel all clear in my head. That small monument on the roadside at Henley, which I had seen on leaving England, gave me the theme. I would call the novel *One Small Candle*. It would open in Henley, go to Venice and then to Poland where I had been in the autumn of 1929, and which now lay devastated under the murderous rule of the Nazis. That autumn my friend, Mrs. Stabler, had rented a little house situated on an estuary at York Harbor, just over the Maine border. She would be there for a month, and invited me to be her guest. In utter seclusion in that lovely haunt I wrote my novel. The whole family was interested in its progress, including the coloured cook and maid. One evening in the first week of October, just before our return to New York, the novel was finished. Mrs. Stabler opened a bottle of champagne to celebrate. Seeking a typist, I was in luck. In that little village I found one. Had she ever typed a novel, I asked. Oh yes, she had typed *The Keys of the Kingdom* for Dr. A. J. Cronin, who had once rented a house on the Point. So the job was beautifully done.

One day, playing tennis at a neighbour's, on enquiring I learnt that my partner was a British naval officer, the second in command of the submarine *Pandora*, which had put in at Portsmouth near by. He made the right kind of remark for an author—"I've been enjoying your last book, sir." He told me that he had been reading it while challenging death fathoms deep in the ocean, the most singular of circulating libraries that I ever penetrated. This was almost matched by the dozens of letters that somehow reached me from prisoner-of-war camps in Europe.

One evening, in response to a request, I made a public appearance on behalf of the local Red Cross, winding up with *A Man Arose*. The next day a controversy shook the village. Had I read my lecture or learnt it by heart? The dispute was settled by the discovery of the local reporter, who asked for my notes, and to whom I confessed that none existed since I was always an extempore speaker.

I returned to New York and sent the novel to both my publishers. My opening engagement there was singular. I never declined any invitation, anywhere, small or large. This time I found myself sent to Public School No. 37, in Manhattan, East 87th Street. I went on behalf of the British War Relief Society. The subject asked for was 'The British Empire', one of a series an enterprising schoolmistress had organised, with speakers from various European nations. When I arrived I discovered it was a mixed school for children with 'behaviour difficulties'. Their ages were from nine to sixteen, three hundred, of all nationalities, sixty per cent coloured. We opened by saluting the flag and singing 'The Star-Spangled Banner'. Then to my astonishment a small boy played 'Land of Hope and Glory' on his accordion. The whole school sang it lustily, every word of it. They listened with close attention to me for three-quarters of an hour. There followed fifteen minutes of questions. They were intelligent and pertinent. One little black boy of fourteen, rolling the whites of his eyes at me, wanted to know what method, other than decapitation, we had for disposing of objectionable kings and queens. Another asked, if we were a democracy, why we went on creating lords and knights. I said that perhaps it was to supply titles for rich American girls who liked marrying them. That went down very well. And of course we came to the Duke and Duchess of Windsor. If the Duchess had not been born an American would she have become . . . The chairman steered them away from that one. Finally, they asked me to undergo a test. The school choir would sing two American songs. Could I name them? I did, correctly. 'The Battle Hymn of The Republic' and 'Anchors Away'. Loud cheers, then a vote of thanks, the tapping of a drum, and a guard of honour escorted me back to the headmistress's room. My reward was a request that on Graduation Day I would make the Address and distribute the prizes. Alas, an engagement a thousand miles away denied me the pleasure.

The homeland of isolationism was in the Middle West. So I made a tour taking me as far as Chicago and down to Kentucky. These lectures were paid for, and covered expenses. I used them for missionary work; on the side I took other engagements. This entailed a battle with the lecture agent who demanded that my appearances should be confined to paying societies. "We can't sell you if you aren't exclusive. The condition is that you do not appear twice in the same town." I would not agree to this. I told him that if I was not free to speak anywhere I would not make the tour. I won my point though I realised he had reason in his demand. In all, I fulfilled fifteen paid engagements, and sixteen unpaid. One of the latter was at the Boston Book Fair, held in the vast Boston Garden.

After Louisville I went to Lexington and found myself in an atmosphere of horses and hounds. My host was the M.F.H. of the Iroquois Hunt. He lived in a vast house appropriately called Harkaway. Twenty sat down for dinner. In the library it was hard to believe I was not back in Market Harborough in the Jorrocks country. The shelves held volumes of Bailey's *Hunting Almanac* and well-bound stud books. I was taken to see that marvellous horse, Man o' War. It was here, in Lexington, that I found a friend. Less than a year before there had come to one of Mrs. Stabler's lunches a young widow with a baby a few months old. On the day that he was born, May 25, 1940, his father, a naval officer, was killed. This tragedy made the baby the 7th Baronet, Sir Marmaduke Adrian Francis Blennerhassett. I now renewed my friendship with Lady Blennerhassett and this alluring infant. His mother was another of those penniless English refugees. Happily, generous friends at Lexington had installed her in a little house, with a coloured maid. That poor girl could not get these strange English names right, and she transposed Sir Adrian into Satan and Lady Blennerhassett into Ladybirdhasit.

v

From Lexington I went to Toledo, Ohio, for two speaking

engagements, then on to Chicago, with four. The day before I was due to leave Chicago there was a railway strike and I was marooned. Luckily there were six days before my next engagement in New York. I had time on my hands and took the opportunity to explore Chicago, in which I had always been a transient. I was warned not to go into 'The Loop', a part of the city encircled by its overhead railway, as it was a haunt of gangsters and hoodlums. It had a lurid night-life. One evening I decided to explore it. It was garish, vulgar, full of saloons. I was soon satiated and went into a café to get something to eat. It was an 'automat', where you put coins in a slot and drew out a prepared dish. I took my dish to a table. The place was crowded but I found a place next to a young giant in an open-necked, diced shirt. I learned he was a lad of Polish-Lithuanian stock, born in America. Blue-eyed, blond, massive, he drove a truck for a Chicago meat-packing company and travelled all over the country. He was very interested in my accent, nationality and profession. He invited me to go with him to a bowling alley in the next street. I received a lesson in the art. When he learned I was stranded in Chicago and wished to get to New York his face lit up. "Hey, now! You come with me! I'll drive you there. I'm going to New York." It would take four days. Realising I should see the country as I had never seen it, I hesitated but he overcame my reluctance. "Hey, now!" George cried, giving me a slap on the back with a great hand that knocked the breath out of me, "That's great, kid." I asked when he was leaving and was astonished when he said that night, at ten, and that he drove all night and slept all day. I wanted to withdraw but he would not hear of it. "Hey now, you'll be all right, sure you will!" He asked where I was staying, and was a bit startled when I said at the Drake Hotel. "Fine, I'll pick you up there."

The manner of my leaving the fashionable Drake Hotel touched my sense of the ridiculous. It stunned the 'bell-hop' when he took my bag out and saw me climb into the cab of a great truck rimmed with lights. We went off down Michigan Avenue. The previous night I had been driven in the opposite direction in a chauffeured Rolls-Royce, sitting between two dowagers who had given me a lift from a dinner party. After a time George saw me shivering, it was four below freezing and the cab was cold. "Hey, now, Kyril!" he cried, pulling up. He could not pronounce Cecil and for the rest of the journey I was Kyril. He took off his heavy greatcoat and leather gloves and insisted on my wearing them. He had nothing on but a heavy flannel lumberjack's diced shirt open at his massive throat. He tucked a rug round my knees. I might have been a baby in a perambulator. While he drove he questioned me about the London blitz. "Sure, now, that's wicked! And they've blown down the churches, hey?" I learned his own history. His father came from Cracow, his mother from Memel. He was one of nine children. They lived in four rooms and worked in a stockyard. "Not me—I live out—and get out. Better, hey?" I agreed it was. "But I like dames, sure. One day I'll have kids. But I want 'em learned." "Learned?" I queried. He grinned with healthy animal teeth. "Sure, like you. You're learned. I like to hear you talk, funny though. I always wanted education, but was working at fourteen, and I'm dumb, anyhow. Hey, but I don't worry. 'Still to ourselves in every place consigned, our own felicity we make or find,'" he repeated, adding, "Goldsmith." In the next four days I was to hear a stream of quotations. Puzzled, I found the source when, among a pile of delivery invoices, a little diary fell out. It was entitled *A Thought For Each Day* and was filled with quotations of the uplift variety.

About 3 a.m. we drew up beside a line of trucks. There was a roadhouse, streaming with light. He led the way in. There were some twenty tough-looking fellows inside, and some girls, all talking above the noise of a juke box. George hailed Mike behind the bar. We ordered hamburgers and coffee. Then George went over to a group in a corner shooting craps. They were all truck drivers, going north, south, east and west. While he played I talked to a red-haired girl whose line was very obvious. In about half an hour the game ended, with an exchange of dollars. We went out into the cold night and took to the road again. At seven o'clock we drew into Grand Rapids. I had lectured there twenty years ago, the visit memorable because I had slept there for the first time in a wooden house, which was quite luxurious. George made three deliveries, then we breakfasted in a drugstore with a policeman and a billsticker. George talked Polish to the policeman and the bar attendant. They spoke of Annie. "That's a skirt I knew. She's married a marine. Hey, what do you know, they get picked up these days. That's the third I've lost on this route," commented George.

We were now bound for Detroit, which we reached before noon.

338

There were more deliveries, then the truck was left in a yard. We ate in a drugstore. I could hardly keep my eyes open. We then went across to a barber's shop but not into it. Over a narrow stairway there was a sign 'Beds 75c'. We went up. It was kept by another Pole. We were given a room with two beds. George drew the blinds to keep out the daylight. He took off all his clothes in the hot room and lit a cigarette. It was odd to see Hercules, naked, smoking. He watched me putting on my silk pyjamas. "What's this?" he cried, derisively, picking up the jacket. "Hey, now, only dames wear silk!" He shook with laughter. Then he opened a Coca-Cola bottle. He lay on the floor and placed the glass he had filled just behind his head. "Hey, now, watch me, kid." He raised his legs over his head, lifted the glass between his feet, bent his legs over again and put it on the floor. Then he leaned forward until his mouth touched the glass, picked it up with his teeth and drank its contents. He sprang up grinning triumphantly. He revelled in my astonishment. "Hey, now, I ought to be in a circus!" he exclaimed, getting into bed. My own bed was clean and comfortable. When I woke up it was 7 p.m., the room dark. George took me along a passage to a shower and almost scalded me. I gave a yell and leapt out. Later we went in a bus into the centre of the city. I insisted on taking him to a restaurant I knew. He was horrified by the bill I paid. He thought seventy-five cents was quite enough for a meal though he would cheerfully lose ten dollars in a crap game. Afterwards, we happened to pass the Cass Theatre as people were leaving. I told George that I had lectured there. He immediately wanted to look inside. We went in. He stared across the empty stalls. "Hey, now, you stood on that stage?" he asked, awe-struck. He said no more until we were in the street. "That's what learning'll do. Boy, you could be President of the United States!" Later, we went to a bar-pool-room. He seemed to know everyone there, mostly truckers. This was a continental brotherhood whose tentacles reached into every state, city and small town. There was a political argument, on the basis that whoever won any war the capitalists came out on top because they could shift their money around. It was a fact that explained everything in a cock-eyed world.

At midnight we were on the road again bound for Toledo, Sandusky and Cleveland. It was bitterly cold. An icy wind blew off Lake Erie. We were in Cleveland at dawn, made four deliveries, and pushed on to Youngstown. After deliveries we went to a house in a dreary street where we had a warm welcome. It was a Polish household, relations of George's father. There was a pretty daughter obviously in love with George. He treated her cavalierly. "She's a soft-egg," he commented. I asked if he liked them 'hard-boiled'. "Hey, no, but I don't want 'em raw". Poor girl, she sat and watched him eat as if Apollo had come to breakfast. I never found out who was who in that Polish warren in Youngstown. There were numerous children, a grandmother, a blind aunt, two daughters and four or five youths. Father I never saw, he cooked in a restaurant. The whole household talked Polish, except the youngsters. George, a great favourite, was festooned with grand-children to whom he gave 'quarters'. There seemed plenty of money. Youngstown, like Cleveland and Detroit, was reeling with prosperity from war contracts although then, in March, 1941, America was not in the war, but the great furnaces were flaring day and night.

We started from Youngstown before midnight, having gone to a cinema with three girls and a youth. Later we ate in a 'joint', with a small dancing floor in the centre. It was jammed. They were all young, amorous, with that half-casual, half-purposeful manner that repressed eroticism indulges in. George perspired with good behaviour, holding his partner as if she were a glass of water. A black-eyed little Polish girl provoked him all the evening. In the taxi she began again. George suddenly put out his big hand and seized her by the nape of her neck, holding her as if she was a rabbit, then, amid squawks, pressed his mouth on hers in calm possession until she lapsed in acquiescence. Then he released her. "Hey, now, that'll keep you quiet!" he said, pushing her back, ruthless. "George, you behave!" said one of the girls. We parted with a correctness that was ambassadorial. George's hair was damp on his forehead with strain. "Marie's nuts on you," observed Alex, our companion. "Hey, she's wasting her time," retorted George. But somehow I didn't think Marie was.

Out of Youngstown, on the way to Pittsburgh, George suddenly said, "Would you have kids if you couldn't give 'em a chance? Some girls never seem bothered about that. Guess I'm cracked on learning." We discussed whether it was wise to educate children to a point where they were embarrassed by their parents. One of his brothers had worked his way through Northwestern University. "Now Fred's married a dame who's high-hat. You'd think we all had measles. Boy, I'd rather sleep in a Frigidaire than in his bed!" Nevertheless, he would like to give his kids a chance to go to college. "But it takes some doing on forty bucks a week." "And crap games," I added. "Aw, I'd lay off that," answered George.

We were in Pittsburgh at 1 a.m. The sky was bright with furnaces. At 2 a.m. we stopped at a roadhouse on our way to Harrisburg. Beyond the bar-restaurant, in a dark saloon, about a hundred persons were dancing to a jazz band. Again there was a Polish contingent. A fat young woman seized me and insisted on dancing. She reeked of beer and hamburgers. There was a special gambling room. After twenty minutes of this little hell we got out into the cold night air. George was apologetic. "I thought you'd like to see it. I could show you a dozen joints like that." "One's enough. I wonder the police don't close it." "Oh, they keep raiding it, but it opens up again, they milk it. Two years ago it was a shack, now it's a gold-mine."

We drove all night over the Allegheny Mountains. It was a long cold drive. We ate in Harrisburg where he had two deliveries, and pushed on to Scranton. It was a straggling place in the Lackawanna Valley. I was told that a third of the population was foreign-born, drawn from Poland, Italy, Wales, Ireland and Germany. Outside a chapel a placard announced a performance of Handel's *Messiah* by a Welsh choir. These Welsh were from South Wales, miners who had emigrated, following strikes in the Welsh coalfields. After two deliveries and a quick meal at a snack-counter we went to a private house, not relations this time but again Poles. We shared a brass bed in a room decorated with Polish religious texts. A frightful china Virgin and Holy Infant looked down on us, and there was a mantel-piece with wax effigies of saints with tin aureoles, pathetic expressions of peasant piety. We were soon asleep. We had to rise at 7 p.m. We were going to a Polish festival dance with 'the loveliest girls you ever saw'. I was so exhausted I would have forgone Helen of Troy for an extra hour in bed. George woke me and with towels round our waists we went to a bathroom. We must have been seen. Cries came from the landing above. George looked up hopefully. "Hey, come down and look at a man!" he called. He was answered by mirthful screams. I let him go first under the shower but my caution was unnecessary, the

341

water was tepid. I left the bathroom first, conscious of many eyes watching from the landing above.

When George came in he opened a bag he had brought from the van. I watched him with eyes agog as he began to dress. He pulled on bright blue riding-breeches with a yellow seam-stripe, then a pale-cream silk shirt, embroidered at the neckband and at each wrist. I admired the flowered embroidery, in blue, red and gold silks. "My mother did it," he said, proudly. Then he put on some high leather black boots and a magenta cummerbund. Finally, he stuck on his head a red cap with a blue peak, and a yellow flower embroidered on the crown. He looked magnificent, a giant who might have been in a king's bodyguard. His hair was golden under the red cap, and his eyes, bright with excitement, were as blue as his breeches. He made a jump and a turn, slapping his boots. "Hey, now, what do you know!" he cried. I felt like a shabby sparrow beside this cardinal bird. "Now we'll go and collect 'em." "Collect who?" I asked as he pushed me through the door. "Dames! Boy, you wait!" he cried jubilantly. We entered a room crammed with people and blazing with light. There were eight girls and four youths, with three old women and a stout white-haired man. All the young people were in gorgeous costumes. I was introduced. To my dismay the whole company was talking Polish. I could not imagine how they could dance in this room but a youth, with silver hair and long limbs clad in white skin-tight breeches and Cossack boots, told me, in English, that the dance was at a hall in the town. Two of the youths wore frogged dragoon jackets, one sleeve loose. Most of the girls were amazingly pretty. I knew George's girl at once; she was at his side, her eyes shining as he towered over her. We were there for half an hour until the dressing was completed. Finally, there was a tremendous shouting up and down the stairs and we all went down. A large truck with two benches inside was our transport. We arrived at a hall festooned with flags and coloured paper decorations. At one end there was a buffet, at the other a dais with a band. Its members wore frogged hussar coats and hats with a peacock feather, a Cracovian costume which I recalled, having seen it in Cracow. It was a string orchestra and played joyously. There must have been two hundred people dancing. There was some jazz but folk dances predominated, and old-fashioned waltzes and polkas. I was not allowed to stay out. George somewhere procured what looked like a Paisley shawl, in which they draped me, completing the costume with a yellow curtain rope tied round my waist and an American sailor's cap that had been dyed red. Thus attired I was bounced through Polish national dances. Sometimes, in the great swinging rondos, my feet were off the ground. I sailed, uplifted, through the air. The dancing grew faster, the music louder. And then, like an old friend, I knew the music. We were dancing to one of Chopin's mazurkas!

We were not all Polish; there were some Russians, Lithuanians, Czechs, Germans and Belgians. Here they were, all dancing happily together. If they had been across the Atlantic they would all have been fighting each other. I noticed that in the dance hall nearly everyone spoke English, but often when in groups they lapsed into their native tongues.

At one o'clock the whole company stood still while the band played the Polish National anthem, and 'The Star-Spangled Banner'. The truck took us back to the house. At two o'clock we left, with much embracing. I had learned Polish for 'Thank you very much', and 'I hope we shall meet again'. What good kind souls they were! We left Scranton asleep in the moonlight, heading for New Jersey and New York. After some deliveries at Bethlehem we arrived in Newark at breakfast time. We stopped at a roadhouse used by truckers.

And so we came to New York, the end of our journey. Looking back, certain facts stood out. I had never been really uncomfortable. Our beds were clean, the toilet facilities adequate. I had met all sorts and conditions of people. My outstanding impression was one of admiration for these cheerful, hardworking folk. Their surroundings were often drab but nothing seemed to lessen their pleasure in a vigorous life. I had really been in 'The Melting Pot', as Zangwill had called America.

It was hard to part from George, for whom I had conceived an affection. He was so gay, gentle and considerate, with a delicate soul peering out of the cage of that huge body, a soul somewhat wistful and puzzled by the human scene. I saw him in New York three times again. His appearances were always unpredictable. Then came a long gap and I wondered if he had forgotten me but in February, 1945, a silence of almost three years was broken. He was in the Marines and had been in the desperate fighting at Okinawa, but so far he was safe.

Then another silence and in 1946 a wedding card. "You remember Marie," he wrote. I replied, with a present, expressing a wish that she would make him a good wife, and his children would get 'learning'.

VI

I arrived back in New York to find that my old friends Philip Gibbs and Ian Hay had come over. The latter was a sad man. He was reluctant to talk about what had happened at the War Office. "I was thrown out with Hore-Belisha. Chamberlain capitulated to the War Office barnacles." His experience in America was not happy. His name was little known, and he found few engagements. Reserved, a great gentleman, he returned home after a few months. Gibbs' experience was no happier. He gave a few talks and then retired to a village in Massachusetts, to write and earn dollars. His son and wife and their two small children were there, refugees, desperate, as others. "I am in the position of having earned quite a bit of money over here but not being able to hand it over to my kith and kin, even if they are starving, or to spend it myself. I have already broken every rule and regulation by using the royalties on my books for that purpose but I dare not do so any more. Consequently we are very near to the edge of the precipice with no more bread for the babies. I really feel like a rat in a trap," he wrote. On reaching home the authorities threatened to prosecute him, this to a man who had paid over half a million dollars in British taxes on his American earnings!

On December 7 Michael Arlen, C. S. Forester and I lunched with some friends. When we came away we were told that early that morning Japan had bombed Pearl Harbor and caused enormous casualties. All America was in a furore. It was a bad business. On the previous evening a spy in Honolulu had sent off a cable to the attackers, reporting nine battleships, seven light cruisers, and nineteen destroyers in harbour. "No reconnaissance is being conducted by the fleet air-arm," said the spy. The message intercepted, was thought to have no priority and was not decoded until too late. The timing of the Japanese was clever, early on Sunday morning, when the crews in Pearl Harbor were somnolent under a Saturday night 'hangover'. Yet there had been plenty of warnings. On November 27 one of our

British agents reported, "Japanese negotiations in Washington off. Services expect action within two weeks." The Foreign Secretary asked Halifax if he knew anything about this. Our Ambassador was away hunting in Virginia. (The Germans had called him 'Tally-holifax' when he visited Hitler in 1938.) He returned home and cabled that he knew nothing about any action. Two days later the U.S. Secretary of State informed him, "The diplomatic part of our relations with Japan is virtually over. The matter will now go to the Army and Navy."

When the news of Pearl Harbor reached London, Churchill ordered champagne, and declared that the war was won. But if America's eyes were now not on Europe, Europe's eyes, in the following months, were not on America. A decisive American naval victory in the Pacific went almost unnoticed in England.

So America was now at war, and isolationism was dead. I went to see Webster at the British Library of Information and said I felt I could now go home. "Don't you realise that we have a bigger job than ever?" he said. "America won't have any interest in the European war, all her enthusiasm will be for the Pacific zone. We shall have to insist that the war will be won or lost in Europe. What can you do when you get home? I want you here."

Three days later we heard of the sinking of H.M.S. *Prince of Wales* and the *Repulse* off Malaya. Two magnificent ships and over a thousand lives were lost. On February 15 Singapore surrendered. It was a disgraceful business. The Japanese, in a minority, were astonished at the ease of their victory. Its fall followed a long period of mismanagement for which Churchill, Duff Cooper, Air Chief Marshal Brooke-Popham, General Perceval, and Sir Thomas Shenton must take the blame. We had spent millions on defence, installing great guns that could not be turned landwards over the peninsula down which the Japs poured in.

VII

In the New Year, 1942, I was touring in the Middle West again. In Chicago I spoke at the Executives Club, where I had fallen into disgrace two years earlier by warning them of the Japanese threat. I now returned, an honoured prophet. The Grand Ball-room of the Sherman Hotel was packed. I said (from a verbatim report):

> I really wonder why you have me here again. On my other five visits I have made you uncomfortable by saying what I thought was going to happen to you. I warned you about the myth of isolationism, I prophesied what would happen in the Pacific. I beg of you not to make another error. The bastions of resistance in the Pacific are seven or eight thousand miles away, those of Europe three or four thousand. Any sound strategist will tell you that we should act along the lines of the shortest communication, thereby conserving effort and transport. Our chances of knocking out Germany are infinitely greater, quicker and less costly. So I hope we shall not be diverted into what would be disastrous strategy. The collapse in Germany will be total and not long delayed. There will be no immediate collapse of Japan.

Bernays, the British Consul-General, almost danced with delight. "That's the line! That's the line!" he cried. I kept to that line in all my talks.

I arrived in New York with a septic throat and was operated upon in hospital by my good friend Dr. Boehm, whose repeated warnings I had ignored. I said goodbye to Philip Gibbs who was going home. "They didn't put me on a bomber after all," he wrote. "They said the bomber crossing was too severe an ordeal for a man of my age. They go enormously high and one has to take oxygen and suffer other unpleasant things. So they will put me on a flying boat in two weeks' time." I was glad to learn this. Professor Mowat and another colleague had died in that bomber crossing.

That month in Washington Mr. Stopford, a Treasury representative, had asked me to write him a letter about my dollar needs. "What, again!" I said. But I wrote it. A month later the Treasury surpassed itself. It could not sanction the remittance of any dollars as 'you are not under the aegis of the Ministry of Information'. I should apply to the Bank of England!

Meanwhile I had watched the public figure of Lord Halifax with growing alarm. "The Ambassador reached his nadir in 1941 when it was said of him that his popularity had risen from zero to freezing point," wrote Lord Birkenhead in his biography of Halifax.

In March, S. K. Ratcliffe, who travelled all over the States lectur-

346

ing, and had to take the smallest fees and distant engagements, to keep afloat, wrote to me, "I hardly ever get into talk with an American about England, etc., without his saying something bitter about Halifax. 'Why don't you get him sent home? He stands for everything that the normal American can't abide!'"

I decided to take action and wrote to Lord Halifax to say that I should be in Washington and would like to see him. I got an immediate reply, "Would May 5th suit you to come here and lunch with me?" I arrived in Washington the previous afternoon. The next morning I called on Field-Marshal Sir John Dill, who showed me great courtesy, as he did to everyone, which caused him to be much liked. He invited me to lunch but I had my engagement with Lord Halifax. I would not see him again for he died in harness two years later. The Americans paid him the singular tribute of an equestrian memorial in the National Cemetery at Arlington. I next called on Sir Ronald Campbell, our Minister. Like Dill, he asked me about my American tours. Then I saw Charles Peake, who said he would have another try with the Treasury for me. I heard this with more incredulity than gratitude!

Shortly before 1 p.m. I was escorted up the Grand Staircase to the Ambassador's sitting-room. On my way I passed Allan Ramsay's large portrait of George III, impressive in state robes. I recalled Lord Lothian's quip. When visiting Senators asked who it was, he replied, "The Founder of the American Republic—not George Washington but George III." On the mantelpiece of the small sitting-room I was curious about a clock inscribed 'To Rastie Roustie'. Lord Halifax came into the room and greeted me. As we walked to the dining-room I learned that the inscription was from some hunting friends who had given him the clock in India. I was relieved to discover that we were alone in the large dining-room, with its red chairs bearing the royal arms. This made my task easier. Perhaps he had an intuition that I would prefer it so. I remarked on the beauty of the room. "Yes," he agreed, "but as in New Delhi, Lutyens has shown an architect's indifference to domestic details. The kitchen is too far off. Worse, this dining-room is too small. It won't seat all the ambassadors. Some have to eat in another room, which creates a problem in precedence."

During lunch he asked me about my experiences, and when coffee came the atmosphere was cordial enough for me to observe that I was sorry to see that his speeches had not been too well received. His reaction gave me some relief. "I am only too well aware of the fact," he replied, gravely. "I don't seem to make contact." I told him I thought I knew the reason. His speeches did not reveal any knowledge of American life and history, they lacked an intimate touch. If he cared to tell me where he was going to speak, and what was the occasion, I should be glad to supply him with appropriate data. "It is most kind of you. I know you have a long and wide experience of America. I should be most grateful for your help," he replied. He would send me an advance list of his engagements. He was due to speak at Wesleyan University in Ohio on May 13, and at Syracuse on June 8. "But perhaps that does not give you time?" I said that he should have the data for both places.

It was a quarter to three when we left the table. He escorted me out, saying he would always be glad to see me. I was to let him know whenever I came to Washington. When the Embassy car took me to the Metropolitan Club I felt like Ulysses who had passed the Narrows of Scylla and Charybdis. But I realised I had given myself a tremendous lot of work.

In the course of over three years I supplied him with material for forty-two speeches. Lord Halifax seemed grateful. "My dear Roberts," he wrote in September of that year, "Once more I have to thank you for some admirable and useful notes. I am really most grateful to you for the research and trouble you have taken." And again, in June, the following year, "I cannot think how you managed to acquire such a lot of information about such a wide stretch of country." He wrote in 1944, "The notes you have sent are of the greatest assistance," and, again in 1945, "What you have sent me has always been most useful. I am deeply indebted to you."

I covered his tours from the Atlantic to the Pacific and Caribbean shores. I also gave him pointers. When he went to a distant state, I wrote, "The Senator is anti-British. His wife is a canary-fancier. If you have a chance, talk birds to her." I sent him three sheets about roller-canaries, from a bird magazine.

In Washington I discovered that Halifax was not popular with his staff. He was too aloof. He seldom entered the Chancery or walked in the gardens. The fortnightly conference with his staff bored him.

He was very 'pi'. He and Charles Peake ignored the Embassy church, it was too Low and went down the road to the Mission Church of St. Agnes, very High Church—"Just what we like with incense and little boys in scarlet cassocks." There, at 9.30, with Father Dubois, they heard mass and made confession. Sir Ronald Campbell found him too aloof, William Hayter, too reserved, Sir Gerald Campbell, a cold fish.

In the next three years I saw and lunched with Halifax several times. He was always extremely courteous, grave, a good listener. But a natural gloom seemed to envelope his long lugubrious face and domed head. I never saw him laugh, I was never able to feel any kind of human warmth or intimacy. I think as an ambassador he suffered from the new era of communications, with radio and telephone. Churchill in his close personal relations with President Roosevelt often by-passed him, and he had to make efforts to catch up with what was happening in those talks between the two giants.

After a few months I had a request from Sir Gerald Campbell who asked if I could supply him with notes for his public engagements. I continued to do this for him, but the strain was heavy and I had to employ a typist at fifty dollars a week.

There was a note of comedy on one occasion. Sir Gerald was asked to represent England at a celebration of the centenary of the Webster-Ashburton Treaty. In 1842 England and America nearly went to war in a dispute between Canada and the State of Maine over territory claimed by both parties. An inebriated Canadian boasted that he had raided and fired an American boat that was engaged in gun-running on behalf of men raising a rebellion in Canada. The boat was set on fire and sent over the Niagara Falls and an American was killed. Three years later this Canadian, in a bar on American soil, boasted of his deed, claiming also that he had killed the American. He was arrested and held for trial. Palmerston said that if the man was hanged it would be a *causa belli*. The case collapsed when, during trial, it emerged that the man was lying and he proved an alibi. The public excitement was so great that President Tyler and his Secretary of State, Daniel Webster, asked the British Prime Minister to send a representative to negotiate a territorial treaty. The British Government sent Lord Ashburton, of the Baring banking family. The result was a treaty that established an unarmed frontier between the United States and Canada that has existed ever since.

Compiling this speech entailed much research and a journey to Washington, where the Library produced the actual Treaty. When the carton was opened there fell out the gold pen with which the two statesmen signed it.

Sir Gerald's speech was a great success, too much so, for Senator Claude Pepper, present at the dinner, suggested that it should be printed in *The Congressional Record*, the official journal of Congress. It occupied seven columns of close print. Sir Gerald was embarrassed. "I could hardly tell the Senator that the speech wasn't mine though I had made it," he wrote, sending me a copy. I replied that a ghost-writer had no body and could not put in a claim.

It was a pleasure to do this work for Halifax and Campbell. Some three years later I received from S. K. Ratcliffe a letter that made me feel my efforts had not been wasted. He wrote:

> On my last tour I had a talk with our Consul in Buffalo. You may be interested in what I have to report. He was talking about Halifax and what a failure he had been at the beginning of his term in U.S.A. "Very odd," said the Consul, "suddenly, almost like magic, Halifax picked up and astonished everybody with his extraordinary insight into American affairs. He surprised his audiences with how much he knew about them and their history." He wondered who was behind all that, and why he didn't have someone like that behind him from the beginning.
>
> I enlightened him and told him that you had taken Halifax's speeches in hand, and given him background data. "So that's the answer. Well, Roberts did a magnificent job on him, the whole picture changed, we were all amazed."

As part of the price of the National Government, a coalition, the Ministry had sent Socialist M.P.s to speak in America. Their indiscretions had raised a protest there, and a storm blew up in the House of Commons. Bracken, to save his skin, had thrown us all overboard in his apology. "They do much more harm than any possible good and I think they should stay home." This was cheered. American papers reported it gleefully. I exploded at this betrayal in a letter to Bracken. He replied, "I am sorry you were upset about the way in which my remarks in the House were headlined by the American papers. You are a special case. Everyone tells me that your

350

lectures have done an immense amount of good and I realise how much you have put into them." But he had bloodied our heads, to the delight of the anti-British. Gallant old S. K. Ratcliffe was deeply wounded. But we had some American defenders. A letter appeared in *The Times*, written by the Chairman of the Committee of Speakers, from the University Club, which provided one of the most distinguished platforms in America, on which I had been honoured to speak. He wrote:

> Mr. Bracken's statement does a grave injustice to many British lecturers who have splendidly served the British and, later, the allied cause. There are many of us here who would pay tributes to the work done by Mr. Bracken's fellow-countrymen. . . . Two of these gentlemen, Mr. S. K. Ratcliffe and Mr. Cecil Roberts, have been highly popular on American platforms for a quarter of a century. They have been here since the outbreak of war, throughout those deadly months when this country was bitterly divided. Mr. Ratcliffe's splendid interpretation of Indian problems, and Mr. Roberts's brilliant platform gifts and unfailing tact have created for their country an admirable impression. There are others. . . . If no more are to come many of us will feel the poorer.

At this depressing time I had good news, personally. *One Small Candle* had appeared in the United States and England. Hodders sent me a cable saying that over forty thousand copies had been subscribed. Within five months it ran into four editions, but this did not benefit me since my earnings were blocked. Anyhow, I was not forgotten at home; and in America I had earned the $2,000 advance, which went to my 'Propaganda Fund'. The novel brought me a letter from Somerset Maugham, "You have put as much into it as many novelists would have thought sufficient for half a dozen novels."

I was now living very frugally but comfortably in a bed-sitting-room in East 79th Street. Two windows faced south, it had an open fireplace, good heating, a cupboard-kitchen with a refrigerator, a box room, a bathroom, and a lift to my fifth floor. For all this, including cleaning and linen, I paid $200 a month. I was a few yards from the Metropolitan Museum and Central Park, and opposite the excellent New York Society's Library, which had a large sitting-room where I could read while my own room was cleaned. I did my own cooking (with the help of a delicatessen shop open day and night round the corner) and laundry. I had a Harris Tweed overcoat which had become dirty. I decided to wash it but it was so heavy in the bath that I got in also, put it on, soaped it down and rinsed it under the shower. It took a week to dry but I saved $30. I went out to lunch in it at Mrs. Vanderbilt's. As her tall, English butler took my coat he said, "Ah, sir, there's nothing like a bit of Harris Tweed!" "I think so, too," said someone behind me. It was the Duke of Windsor, a fellow guest, who had just arrived. If they had known what I'd done to it!

In July the news from England was disconcerting. Owing to an accumulation of disasters, Singapore, Tobruk, etc., Churchill was under attack. He had to make a secret speech in the House of Commons answering his critics. The speech was not released until January, 1946. The weakness of the attack lay in the fact that there was not a single man in England who could replace him. Churchill knew this and was truculent in action, though he always displayed a façade of unfailing courtesy to the members of the House. He weathered the storm.

VIII

My contacts with the various agencies catering for the army and navy men who passed through New York kept me in constant and close touch with the battle fronts. One day the British Information Service asked me to interview two young officers, Captains Bullen and Marsh, just arrived from Libya. I wrote their vivid story which was circulated in the American and Canadian Press. Later I had two camera men from the North African front. The cool courage of all these boys, newly out of an inferno and dazzled by the ease and luxury of life on this side of the Atlantic!

To the infinite variety of the societies for which I spoke I now added the 'British Blood for American Forces'. The national chairman was Gertrude Lawrence, the actress. Its purpose was to collect blood for the American forces from British people born in America. Miss Lawrence told me that donors included Welsh miners, Scotch dockworkers, English stevedores, the veterans of Scotch and Canadian 'Legions', as well as celebrities of stage and screen. "Have you collected from Noël Coward?" I asked, mischievously, knowing their close friendship. "I shall, when Noël arrives," she replied. At the

Mrs. Grace Vanderbilt and the author at a Beecham concert, New York Stadium

Estella, Palm Beach, Florida

Baroness Eugene de Rothschild (Kitty). By de Lázlo

meeting she read cables from Mr. and Mrs. Churchill, Lord and Lady Halifax, Merle Oberon and Gladys Cooper. The day after, Miss Lawrence wrote thanking me. "You spoke delightfully as usual and it was the greatest pleasure to hear you again. Your listeners were thrilled." Well, she thrilled New York audiences with *Lady In The Dark* and I was happy to give some words and some blood to her bank. In exchange she kissed me on the platform, duly illustrated in the Press.

The variety of my work was endless. I became a sort of odd-job man. Somerset Maugham wrote, "The Office of Facts and Figures has turned to me for 400 words on what books should be read to know England today. I know you are much better acquainted with contemporary writing in England than I am, and I am asking if you can give me a few titles to help me." I gave him a few titles. "How prompt you are! Your list has proved most useful," he replied. I began to feel with all these various requests that I was the Office of Facts and Figures. Maugham wrote again. "Can you tell me who was the famous politician who, on his deathbed, said, 'I think I could eat one of Bellamy's veal pies'?" I told him. Pitt. When a speaker fell ill I was often sent for in an emergency. "You are our Fire Brigade. You arrive and save us." There was one who always put me last on the list of speakers. I protested saying, "I inherit a moribund audience." "Yes, dear Mr. Roberts. You are our corpse-reviver. When the other speakers have slain my audience, I turn you on." But all this added to the wear and tear.

My thoughts often turned to England, wondering how young Lucien was faring. In July he was still training there. He wrote:

> I passed through Henley the other day in convoy and managed to break away for a few minutes just to go and have a look at some of the old haunts where I have known so much happiness. Pilgrim Cottage was looking as lovely as ever but something seemed to be missing, I don't know what. It may have been my imagination. I felt it as soon as I opened the little green gate. Everything was just as it always had been but there was something cold and lacking; perhaps it was the warmth and welcome of its master's greeting.

He gave me news of Bevis, his sister, a lieutenant in the A.T.S. "She is expecting to be given an adjutant's job which will mean a

captaincy for her, and greater responsibilities. I am still a lieutenant
but expect a change soon."

IX

In July and part of August I was on tour again. Happily there were
few air-services in those days, and you got a complete rest from hostesses, committee secretaries, the Press and telephone, immured in
those long trains that covered the great continent. They had at the
tail an observation parlour-car. Here you could talk to everybody and
get a wonderful cross-section of humanity. Americans liked you to
talk. There were no frozen faces in divided compartments, but long
parlour-cars with swivel armchairs, so that you could chat with your
neighbour. The horror was the upper-berth sleeper where you had to
undress with the skill of a gymnast in the confined space to which you
ascended by an attendant's step-ladder. As the heating in winter was
controlled by the negro attendant the atmosphere was sub-tropical.
But I enjoyed the rest on these journeys before the flurry started again
on the platform with its 'receiving delegation'.

I arrived back home exhausted, the gastric ulcer having given me
frightful nights. I was just in time for a farewell soirée given by Lady
Cunard who was packing for departure to England. I found there
Princess Marguerite, Prince René de Bourbon-Parme and his brother,
last seen at the Doubledays', on Long Island, some politicians, some
scribes. Emerald threw a wide net and I would miss her galaxy.

At the end of August I left for the island of Nantucket, the guest of
Austin Strong, who had there an enchanting little house. What a
fairy-tale town it was, preserved against the inroads of fashion and
time! It is an outpost in the Atlantic. The *Mayflower* just missed it.
The Nantuckers are admirable curators. They know they have a
lovely thing and they show care and taste in preserving it. It was 97°
in New York. Here there were cool zephyrs. A hundred and fifty years
ago its prosperity was founded on whaling. The lovely houses one
sees were built by the owners and captains of whaling ships. Some of
them have roof-promenades built between chimney stacks at each
end. They are called 'The Widow's Walk'. Anxious wives went up to
look out when the whalers were overdue. Old sailors called Nantucket
'The Little Grey Lady'. As my steamer rounded the point bringing

354

me from Woods Hole, where I had stayed en route at Mrs. Murray Crane's, I saw how apt was the name. It was a wooden town, Quaker grey, undulating and marked with steeples and cupolas of churches, with a great golden dome gleaming in the afternoon sun, and a harbour full of boats, riggings, and the coloured sails of what they called 'The Rainbow Fleet', for so it seemed when they tacked in the sun.

Austin and Mary Strong lived in a clematis-bowered house in Quince Street. Quince Street, Gay Street, Pearl Street, Mulberry Street, Lily Street, Milk Street, the names were a symphony. We know of the reign of William and Mary, here it was the reign of Austin and Mary. The house had Stevenson relics. Here was the Stevenson family clock. It had travelled from Vailima in Samoa. It formerly had counted the hours in Stevenson's home in Edinburgh. Since 1927 it had ticked in the library of this house in Quince Street.

The gilded dome that flashed in the sun belonged to the Unitarian church in Orange Street. In the tower hung a bell brought by a sea captain from Lisbon, around 1810. Its six chimes made sweet the hours. It was in this church that I was to have one of the most singular audiences I have ever faced. For the entertainment of summer visitors from all over the States they had a 'Neighbours' Night'. I was asked to address a packed assembly, some eight hundred, over which Austin Strong presided. I chose the title of my lecture with deliberate duplicity. 'A Novelist Looks at His World'. Quite reasonably they expected a literary lecture; actually they were given a two-hour address on India. It was Mary Strong who had suggested the subject.

India was much in the air, and we were greatly maligned. Stafford Cripps's mission to India having failed, Gandhi had just started Civil Disobedience. The India Congress League was busy all over America spreading its anti-British propaganda. I had met one of its agents several times. He was a very handsome, brilliant young Indian, an Oxford graduate. He wore a turban with a jewel, was sleek, perfectly dressed, eloquent, and moved over difficult ground with the litheness of a python. He always insisted on speaking last, so that one could not answer back. I was once invited to debate with him at a public dinner in Pittsburgh. I stipulated that this time I should speak after him. This was agreed upon, but during the dinner an agitated secretary came up and said that my opponent insisted on speaking last, and if this was not granted he would not speak. Would I concede? Though annoyed by his intransigence, I agreed. By this time I knew his speech off by heart. So when I stood up I said, "My distinguished Indian friend will tell you that . . ." and I made his speech with my additions. It spiked his gun, he floundered desperately.

This Unitarian church was the most beautiful place I have ever spoken in. It was snow-white, the ceiling, the walls, the pews. It had long plain-glass windows. My audience was admirable. It was not until later that I discovered it was a most diverse one. I spoke for an hour and three-quarters. I explained in detail the Indian problem. My speech was reported in *The Nantucket Inquirer*, which had a history as remarkable as its size. Its pages were two-foot square, with nine columns on a page. It circulated throughout the United States. It carried a verbatim report of my address in ten columns.

Reprints were run off to satisfy the demand. It brought letters from California, Oregon, Kansas, Georgia, Minnesota, Pennsylvania and Nebraska, a striking illustration of the potentialities of an audience gathered in an island holiday resort.

I sent copies of this address to Lord Halifax and Brendan Bracken. Halifax wrote, "I have read with the greatest interest and admiration your clear and forceful exposition of the India problem," and Bracken, "We think it a masterly performance. It is of immense service to us."

On arrival back from Nantucket after three weeks, I was met by a singular request. The Director of the U.S. War Bond Drive wrote to me from the Treasury, Washington, asking if I would speak for them. As I was in an independent position I could do so. My first engagement was at Boston in the Symphony Hall. I was one of three speakers. It was a large beautiful hall and I recalled how, a year ago, I had been disgruntled at finding myself speaking in the small, old-fashioned Tremont Temple there, until, looking down at the reading desk, I saw a brass plaque which said, "Here on Monday, April 6, 1868, Mr. Charles Dickens gave a reading."

On my return from Boston the next morning two letters awaited me, from England. One informed me that Tony Allingham had died. One night, while fire-watching over his father's business premises, during an air-raid, his nose began to bleed. It would not stop and he was taken to hospital and detained. A month later, to a friend who visited him, he said, "Jack, I'm not dying, am I?" He was assured he was not but he never got up again. Two months later he died of leukaemia in the London Clinic. He was only twenty-nine. I found it impossible to believe the news. Never was there a person so full of the joy of life, of such zest and physical beauty, with his golden head, his rosy complexion, his constant laughter. 'Mummy, Dad, Ann and Pat'—no more would I hear that happy refrain of Pilgrim Cottage days, the gate opening to reveal him rushing down the path with his lovely sister or his younger brother. I lay down on my bed, sunk in grief. Then I remembered that I was due to speak that evening at the Anzac Club, which catered largely for Australian and New Zealand soldiers, en route home. My first impulse was to cancel the engagement. Then I thought it would be better for me to go and somehow get through it rather than be here in grief. So I went, I spoke somehow. When I came back I opened the second letter which I had forgotten. It was from Philip Gibbs, informing me that his brother, Cosmo Hamilton, had died in the English village to which he had retired, his success flown, his marriage a wreck. I recalled his great kindness to me when I had made my first lecture tour in America in 1920.

On November 3 I heard that Lord Halifax had lost his son, Peter, in action in Egypt, aged twenty-six. On the 30th I learned that Lady Gleichen had died in her sleep in the Forge Cottage at Fawley, the Harmans' old home that I had sold to her. She was godmother to Terence Rattigan and I was told that she had left the place to him. He would be a nice neighbour. But the news of this legacy was incorrect, Terry wrote. That month Professor Webster, who had never liked his job, went back to the Foreign Office. His successor was Aubrey Morgan, to whom I talked. Afterwards he wrote to me, "I was extremely glad to have that talk with you and should like to put on paper my keen appreciation of the valuable work you are doing. We are very conscious of it here and most grateful for your co-operation." How conscious? They were starving me of dollars and my situation was often desperate. That same day I lunched with Madame Balzan, formerly Duchess of Marlborough. Very tall, very thin, very deaf, she was a gracious hostess. I walked the whole way there from the B.I.S. office in a snowstorm because I could not afford taxis. At Christmas I was in bed with gastric trouble.

I lived near to the Myron Taylors. The President of the United

357

Steel Corporation, a multi-millionaire, he was home after a term as a special presidential envoy to the Vatican. His home was like a Renaissance palace; one seemed still in Italy, with its large salon, Italian masterpieces, marbles and tapestries. The Taylors were most hospitable to me and it was there that I often heard Artur Rubinstein play. On January 9, in the New Year, 1943, I was invited by the Taylors to lunch. The Halifaxes were to be guests also. That morning the telephone rang. The lunch was called off. The Halifaxes had just heard that their third son Richard, on the North African front, had been severely wounded on December 30 and had lost both legs. After a time he was brought home to Washington and fitted with artificial ones. He showed the utmost courage and, when he was able to walk, went to the American military hospital to show soldiers who had lost their legs how to walk and cope with life. As I was writing this page in London, in July, 1971, a doctor friend, Alistair Thomson, called on me. I mentioned what I had just written. He said, "I can tell you all about that. I was the doctor who attended him. He was lucky in a way. A bomb fell on him but it did not explode, however, the weight of it cut off his legs. I saw him this week. He is happily married, and has children." Poor Lord and Lady Halifax. Was there a hoodoo on the family, I wondered. He had succeeded to the title because three elder brothers, aged twenty, eleven and seven had died. He himself had been born with a withered arm and now this tragedy.

Soon after, I was invited by an Austrian exile, Prince Windischgraetz, who was making a living by doing book covers and illustrations, to dine and meet the Archduke Otto of Hapsburg, the heir to the Austrian throne. He proved to be a grave, extremely intelligent young man of thirty with a grasp of European affairs. He had been one of that sad group, mother, brothers and sisters, who had seen their father die, exiled and impoverished, in an isolated house on a mountain slope in Madeira. I had met the exiled family. A mutual friend, Calvin Bullock, a New York stockbroker, had lent them his country house on a lake near to the Pagets, with whom I had stayed. We went over to see the royal exiles, and found them rowing a boat, the Empress Zita, the young archdukes and archduchesses. Otto cherished no vain hope, unlike his unhappy father. He did not think he would get back his throne, nor did he desire to. Later, he re-nounced all claims, took a degree at Louvain University, married, wrote a number of books, and went to live quietly near Munich.

I heard with much regret, next month, of the death of Sergei Rachmaninoff. We should no more take tea in the Russian café near Carnegie Hall, where he stipulated that the laid-on music should be switched off if it played his Prelude in C Minor, which he had come to hate. At his funeral service Josef Holbrook played Chopin's 'Marche Funèbre'.

I now received a letter from young Lucien, written the previous month. He was with the 1st Army in North Africa. He described the voyage out. He had left England last December. His ship was torpedoed on the voyage out but not sunk. Passing the Straits of Gibraltar he saw the snow mantling the Sierra Nevada range. Then, a postcard, received on March 25, revealed that he was near Algiers. I found what he wrote rather perturbing. "Just a line to let you know that I am well and happy despite one or two godless moments. This is some of that beautiful, majestic and barren country that I have passed through—part of the Atlas Chain." One or two godless moments. Just what did the boy mean? He had a naturally sunny nature. In the middle of March came another postcard, with native figures in the desert, at sunset.

> Here is another one of those most heavenly sunsets lighting up the whole sky with splashes of red, yellow and green, and all their wonderfully varying intermediate shades of colour. The hills are showing up a deep purple against its brilliancy— it is very godlike, such a contrast to that which lies below. In great haste but with much love, Lucien.

In April, there was a performance at the Metropolitan Opera House organised by the American Friends' Fund for Starving Children of the World. I was asked to write a poem for the Souvenir Programme. Bach's Passion Music was played, Stokowski conducted.

> I heard the voice of millions of children
> Crying in the darkness, calling through the night—
> "We are the lost and famished generation
> When we are perished for whom do you fight?
> You will bring back the fire to the hearthstone,
> You will see Freedom sitting on her throne,

But nowhere again will there sound young laughter,
We cried for bread and you gave us a stone."

I arose and said, remembering the children,
And One who sat on a mountain high,
"If these are of the Kingdom of Heaven, O Saviour,
What gains the whole world if we let them die?"
A voice from the mountain, above the low thunder,
Reviving as rain to the sun-scorched flower,
Answered—"Succour them, the storm will pass over,
Of these are the Kingdom and the Glory and the Power."

There was another cause for which my services were enlisted. This was about the time when the 8th Army had made its great march in North Africa, defeating Rommel. I spoke for the American Red Cross Drive at a great cinema in New York. The following appeared in the *Daily Mail*, from its New York correspondent:

The best story I heard this week was about Cecil Roberts. He was addressing a tough crowd in the Bronx district the other night in impeccable English. The audience became restless and began to gibe. Suddenly Roberts stopped dead. The crowd grew quiet. Roberts said very softly, "I know what you have been laughing about. It's my English accent, the way I talk. May I remind you, ladies and gentlemen, that the men of the British 8th Army talk the way I do?" The audience gaped and then they cheered. There were no more interruptions. He got a great ovation.

One day I had a telephone call from Sir Thomas Beecham, who had returned to New York from a tour. He invited me to lunch with him at the Savoy-Plaza. When I arrived we were alone, Lady Beecham being upstairs with a cold. It was an excellent lunch, then, when coffee came, Tom said, "I hope you won't mind my mentioning it, my boy, but I'm in rather a fix for money just now. Would it bother you to let me have some of those five thousand dollars I lent you?" I told him that I had never had any of those dollars, his cheque had bounced. "Good God! You don't owe me any money? Then you can't help!" he exclaimed. He turned and called the waiter, "Another bottle of champagne"! A new bottle was opened.

On May 18th Mrs. Crane gave a birthday party for me. Among the guests was André Maurois, the biographer and Academician. We often met on platforms. He was an excellent speaker in both French and English. At the beginning of the war he was attached to G.H.Q. as French eyewitness. He was so gloomy as to seem defeatist. He proceeded to the U.S.A., where his attitude was so ambivalent that he lost many of his English friends. He had been knighted by us. He had now come off the fence and was about to leave for North Africa, where he had offered his services to the French military authorities. I admired his writing and our friendship was to last until his death in 1967.

When I returned home from my birthday party there was a cable waiting for me. I opened it and read, "Lucien killed on active service, Algeria. Reid family very brave. Fuller." I was dazed with grief. The light had gone out of the day and of my life. It was impossible to believe that a boy of twenty-two years, of such singular charm, physical beauty and staunchness of character, could be no more. Everyone loved him.

After a sleepless night, frozen with sorrow, I somehow spoke for the Greek Relief Fund at Madison Square Garden. I came off the platform not knowing what I had said. It was a week before I could find the courage and the words to write to Lucien's parents. I thanked them for letting me share their son with them. Later I had news from them. His beloved sister Bevis had arrived in Algiers, from Palestine, only five days after Lucien's death, not knowing what had happened. Theirs had been a particularly close association, their childhood spent together rowing and swimming in the Venetian lagoons. She would live on to have her triumphs. Within five years she would be the British women's champion at shot-putting, discus- and javelin-throwing. In 1948 she would represent Great Britain at the Olympic Games.

Lucien had not been killed fighting. On May 2, while practising with grenades attached to rifles, one had exploded blowing his head off. A letter came from Fuller. He had seen Lucien in Algiers only a short time before. He found him not very happy about his set-up so he had spoken to General Browning, who had got Lucien posted to the Roughriders and had accepted him for the Airborne Division, to his great delight. Mrs. Reid, in her letter to me, enclosed an extra-ordinary one she had received from Robert Nichols, the poet, in Cambridge.

No, I had not heard that the brave and beautiful Lucien had been killed. This is the most daunting personal news that has come to me either in this war or the last. It is daunting not because Lucien has laid down his young and promising life in a good cause but because this sacrifice has been required of you and your husband, and of you particularly, since I cannot believe, however deep a man's feelings for his only son, it can equal in poignance those of a mother. I write in tears, not for Lucien but for you. He has gone the way of the true and brave, fighting that which the honour of man's soul dictates must be fought if there is to be any purpose for youth upon the earth, any kindliness, any honour, and freedom to live the private life.

I wish I could say that I believe there is another world in which all we have suffered will be made up to us, and all we have lost restored, or, better still, that we shall return to this one and live the life and know the happiness and enjoy the fulfilment which has not been ours. But I cannot. All we can hope for, as I see it, is darkness and silence in which our sufferings will be healed and our griefs annulled forever, and even the shadowiest memory of them wholly forgotten.

Lucien's face was as serious as it was beautiful. In it shone health, integrity, lively intelligence, courage and most manly virtue. If there was one fine quality more than another which shone out of him it was staunchness. It is a quality I envy but little possess. And I know the reason why I do not possess it: I had no mother whose hand could steady me when I was tottering, no hand to be lifted at just the right moment in just the right way when I stood upon my feet and looked about me with a confidence her care might have given. It is a loss that nothing in this world can make up for and I think Lucien understood, and understood a great deal better than most boys, what you had been to him and to his sister and what the cost to you had been and how much brains as well as devotion you put into your handiwork. Ponder this, my dear, it is the very perfume of your flower and neither time nor accident can deprive you of it.

CHAPTER FIFTEEN

The Rothschild Saga

I

At the end of May, 1943, the U.S. Treasury asked if I would do a War Bond Drive tour with Ilka Chase, a well-known radio and film star, and Colonel Romolo, a very gallant Philippino who had made a spectacular escape from the Philippine Islands when the Japanese occupied them. He had a wonderful story to tell. When after the war he returned home he became president of the university there, a national figure. Ilka Chase was pretty and quick-witted. I had good competitors. One of our halts was at New Bedford. We spoke first in a large school auditorium, and then from a whaling boat in front of the Town Hall. Before going on the platform in the auditorium the Mayor greeted us in a classroom. While my colleagues were talking to him I observed a blackboard, turned away. It listed the names of children who had sold War Bonds, with the amounts. Many of the names were foreign. I memorised them. When I came to speak I congratulated them by name, stating the amounts they had sold. The audience was utterly astonished. For a long time I did not let my colleagues learn the secret of my information.

After the tour the Director of the Campaign wrote to me from the Treasury. "I want to express my thanks to you for your effective support of the Drive. We raised over twenty-nine million dollars, more than double our target. I shall never forget the brilliant and polished talk you gave at New Bedford."

In the next two years I made twenty appeals for them and received a Treasury citation for my services, something I never had from my own Government. Then came another letter sent on from the R.K.O. Cinema Corporation, for whom I had spoken in the Bronx. "We want

Sir Cecil Roberts for our War Bond Drive. He has been such an overwhelming success here that the public is clamouring for his compelling presence again." I was exhausted, but I went. "You will kill yourself," warned Dr. Boehm, after another gastric attack. Vanity, the fascination of handling a big audience, a sense of duty? Perhaps a little of all three. The manager of the cinema wrote afterwards to the President of the Corporation. "In my time I have heard many speakers but none of them can compare with Sir Cecil Roberts who appeared on our stage. His talk and appeal was so splendidly done that the audience applauded vociferously and responded generously to the solicitation of funds."

Americans are puzzled by our complex titles. I was 'knighted' again and again and finally gave up protesting. There was an occasion in Detroit when my chairman got hopelessly muddled and introduced me to the audience as Lord Cecil Roberts who had received the Nobel Prize for his work for peace! There was loud applause. I could not humiliate him by correcting him in front of his own townspeople. Someone later would tell him. So I ignored the error and went straight into my address. In a week or two they would not remember whom they had heard. It was not the first time I had been confused with Lord Robert Cecil, the famous champion of the League of Nations.

II

My Australian friend, Guido Wertheim, had a genius for finding cheap apartments. He suggested a summer at Southampton, on Long Island, with its glorious sandy beach. He found in a small house on a lawn, fronting the fashionable Irving Hotel, two rooms and a bath for $18 a week. We took them for two months. The day before I left I lunched with Somerset Maugham. In the evening I dined with Dr. and Mrs. Boehm in their Park Avenue apartment. It was 97° in the shade, New York was an oven.

Our summer retreat was delightful. I had for neighbours, in the hotel opposite, Countess Mercati and Lady Ribblesdale. Also in near-by villas dwelt Dr. Nicholas Murray Butler, President of Columbia University, and Mr. Charles Mitchell, President of the

National City Bank. Mrs. Mitchell was musical, which meant a procession of eminent musicians as guests. And near to me, Elizabeth Arden had a villa. Her guest was the Duchess de Grammont, by her first marriage, Mrs. Victor Hugo by her second. She had a delightful little boy of ten who was Victor Hugo IV, with whom I played on the lawn. I had only been there four days when I was stunned by the news that Dr. Boehm had died suddenly of a heart attack. His wife asked me to make the funeral address, so I was back in their apartment only ten days after I had dined there. It was an irreparable loss. We had been friends for ten years, since our meeting at Ottagono on the Venetian lagoon. His warm hospitality apart, he had been ceaseless in his medical care of me.

When I returned to Southampton I began to write a novel I had in my mind. The dollar situation was again serious and I sold my next novel, outright, to Doubledays for $10,000, less commission and tax. It was to be about Crete. I had never seen the island, but I had followed closely Freyberg's desperate battle against the German airborne invaders. I had some news through Timmy Jekyll, his brother-in-law, and the Mountbatten incident last summer at Mrs. Vanderbilt's had increased my interest in Crete. I interviewed in the Anzac Club, the British Army and the Merchant Navy Clubs, soldiers and sailors who had been in the Crete campaign. I was lucky in meeting Captain Melas of the Greek Resistance, and the Greek family in whose house we lodged was from that island.

I wrote the book lying on a chaise-lounge on Countess Mercati's loggia, where I read it to her, or, under a large elm, to Lady Ribblesdale, who moved across the adjacent lawn like a figure in *Swan Lake*. I was in luck for I discovered that Mr. Francis Rundell, in our Consular Shipping Department in New York, had been British Consul in Crete before the war. He kindly read my proofs and could not believe I had not lived there. Doubledays did not like my title, *So Immortal a Flower*. I kept it for the English edition and changed it to *The Labyrinth* for the American. I had two months' anxiety waiting to hear the manuscript had arrived safely in England. An American friend, Mrs. Natalie Spencer, who had a large ball-room at the top of her house in East 62nd Street, gave a party for a hundred on its publication. There was a large cake made in the form of a book, with the title in white cream. The book carried a dedication.

To L.B.R. Lieut. R.A. 1920–1943.
It may be again that life will mould a young face
To break a heart with, in some new day unseen,
But never again, for me, can return the grace
That was yours, dear Lucien, beyond Fate's malice, serene.

His mother wrote, "I was greatly touched by your lovely lines.
How glad I am his beauty was not marred by having caused anyone
to be wounded or taking anyone's life."

Several years later, Brigadier Sir Bernard Fergusson, later General
Sir Bernard Fergusson commanding the 1st Bn. Black Watch,
B.A.O.R., wrote, "I would like to tell you how much I enjoyed
So Immortal a Flower, after a visit to the battlefields of Crete a couple
of years ago." I received from Bombay a letter from Brigadier B. H.
Chappel.

I have just read with great personal interest your novel, *So
Immortal a Flower*. Crete and the Cretans were very attractive
to me despite my relatively short stay on the island. I was
particularly interested in the lay-out of the operations carried
out by your heroine in the latter part of the book. Those operations were very like others suggested to me in outline by Captain
Pendlebury. He too, like your hero, was an archaeologist at
Knossos and had been under my command at Herakleion,
during the German invasion, until he was unfortunately killed.
The coincidences, and the great knowledge of the island shown,
have prompted this letter. I hope I shall not seem presumptuous
in writing to ask whether in fact he was in any way concerned.
Actually this, despite the coincidences, appears unlikely as he
was reputed to have been killed before we evacuated.

Later, I had a letter from Malcolm MacDonald.

Brigadier, now General, Chappel and I were lunching together
recently and talking over old times in the Cretan campaign.
We were agreed that in your admirable novel, which I have read
with great pleasure at least thrice, you might have been an eyewitness of the events that actually took place. I cannot believe
that you have not at some time taken the road from Herakleion
to the Labyrinth.

I confessed, of course, that at the time of writing the novel I had
never been on the island. When at last I visited it in 1952, on an
Hellenic Club cruise, a lady in the party came up to me and said,
very emotionally, "I'm visiting Captain Pendlebury's grave. From

your novel I know that you knew him well and was with him in the Crete campaign. Do please tell me just how he died." When I said I had never been in that campaign, nor in Crete, and had never met Captain Pendlebury, she looked at me in amazement.

I felt I had very luckily escaped exposure. The immediate value of the book for me was that it brought me in dollars when I was in great need. It also earned money in England but as this was blocked it availed me nothing for my purpose.

III

In Southampton I met Mrs. Aubrey Cartwright, an American, who was to become a friend for life. She was an extraordinary woman of considerable wealth, being the grand-daughter of H. H. Rogers who had been a partner of Rockefeller, the oil tycoon, reputed the richest man in the world. She was a tall, beautiful woman who entertained lavishly. She had rented a house for the season. When the war broke out she was caught in France, in her pine-tree shaded villa, Casa Estella, whose terraces ran down to a cove and the blanched rocks at Cap d'Antibes. It had been, in the Nineteen-Twenties, a much smaller house belonging to Lloyd Osbourne, the stepson and collaborator of Robert Louis Stevenson. Literary friends visited him, among them George Bernard Shaw, who swam off the rocks.

In those days no one stayed on the Riviera in the summer. The skin-broiling fashion had not started. Mrs. Cartwright bought her villa in 1932 and slowly added to it. Then the war came. Thirteen hundred British subjects, among them Somerset Maugham, were crammed into two coal freighters and made a nightmare journey to England. "A coal ship, even with Willie Maugham, would never have done for my mother, who had no intention of abandoning her customary panoply of travel," records her elder son, Dallas Pratt. She had recently married her fourth husband and continued the honeymoon until September, 1940, under the Pétain regime. Then the guns came too near and she travelled by train, with immense piles of baggage and a faithful maid, to Lisbon, and thence by an American ship to New York and her home on Fifth Avenue, with its white drawing-room overlooking Central Park. She had also a villa, with a large swimming pool, at Palm Beach, Florida, where I was to become a frequent guest. By a former husband, Captain Cartwright,

R.N., whose name she retained, she had a son, Aubrey. Cartwright, doing intelligence work in Holland, was murdered by the Nazis. Alarmed by his wife's extravagant and hectic life, he had made the boy a ward in Chancery. This was a great grief to her, for he was kept in England until the end of the war.

Before my return to New York I paid a visit to Lady Fletcher and her three boys, who were living near by in a little country home they owned. Sir Angus was absent in New York. He had written to me about my Nantucket Address. "How clear it seems to us over here that people like yourself are worth a wilderness of press-release merchants. I put in three days a week in New York on a part-time job— but 'the heart knoweth its own bitterness'."

On my return to New York in October I had somehow let myself be heavily booked. There was a conference with two bright young men on the B.B.C. staff, Stephen Fry, and Alistair Cooke who would make a name for himself with his letter from America, also a broadcast for British Merchant Sailors, a Friends of Greece banquet, a Master of Ceremonies engagement for a British War Relief show at Madison Square Garden, and a lecture at the Free Library, Baltimore. Between all this I sat for my portrait to Baron Kurt Pantz, a very clever Austrian artist. Kurt was tall. He had a brother who was short, so they were dubbed 'Long Pantz' and 'Short Pantz'. After the war they returned to Austria and became figures in Salzburg, and proprietors of an ancient castle at Mittersill, which they turned into a very deluxe hotel where Americans paid large sums to live like and mix with arch-dukes.

The portrait finished, I left for Washington, with five engagements. My typist said, 'You'll crack. It's insane," but I always, somehow, came off a platform exhilarated. In Washington I visited a remarkable couple, Mr. and Mrs. Robert Woods Bliss. He had been Ambassador in Argentina, Minister to Sweden, and had served in diplomatic posts for more than thirty years, and was consultant to the Secretary of State. He was not only very experienced but rich and generous. The Blisses gave the nation their Dumbarton Oaks estate. They moved a short distance, from R to Q, in an alphabetically designated section of Washington. Mrs. Bliss was frail, time-defying and very modern. I wanted to talk politics but she would talk about the French Symbolist poets. She quoted Cocteau, against a background of Titian, Velazquez, El Greco and Renoir paintings on the walls. In the evening we went to Dumbarton Oaks where they entertained for a concert of eighteenth-century music in a great Renaissance salon. It had a painted beamed ceiling from the Château de Chimerey, and a seventeenth-century polychrome mantelpiece. And here, before five hundred guests, Wanda Landowska, the greatest living exponent of the harpsichord, gave us Couperin, Rameau and Scarlatti. What music that room had heard! Here, in 1938, Stravinsky had played his 'Dumbarton Oaks Concerto' in honour of the siver wedding anniversary of the Blisses. Here Paderewski had sent Chopin's polonaises ringing beneath the great ceiling. Next summer Dumbarton Oaks would give its name to a conference of the United States, Great Britain, Russia and China, that drew up the plan for the United Nations, its deliberations resulting in the San Francisco Conference of April, 1945, where a new covenant and charter would be promulgated. Here was planned the atomic bomb that was dropped on Japan.

Our Minister, Sir Gerald Campbell, gave a lunch for me at his house. The guests included Admiral Sir Percy Noble, Fourth Sea Lord and head of the British Naval Delegation, the Hon. David Bowes-Lyon, Mr. Cecil King, and the Embassy Information Minister, H. Butler, Sir Percy Noble was handsome, well-groomed, debonair and so great a social success that he had been dubbed 'The Lend-Lease Lover'. After lunch I asked Sir Gerald whether he was the consul in Venice during the time of that scurrilous mountebank-genius, Baron Corvo (Fr. Rolfe.) He said he was. He was in Venice in the days of Lady Layard and Lady Radnor, powerful social leaders known as 'Thou Shalt' and 'Thou Shalt Not'. It was the time of Horatio Brown and Mrs. Eden of 'The Garden of Eden', now owned by Princess Aspasia of Greece. He said that during the funeral of Lady Layard the author of *Hadrian VII* came up to the English church in a boat with his three Ganymedes, screaming abuse of the dead woman. He was dressed as a cardinal, all in scarlet, and rowed around during the whole of the service, knowing it would scandalise the friends of Lady Layard, who was very anti-Catholic. Sir Gerald said that when Corvo died he had the task of dealing with his affairs. He turned over his papers to a very respectable brother who came out to Venice. The Italian authorities insisted on seeing these, and were struck with horror. The diaries were scurrilous and pornographic. Sir Gerald bought his library but when he came to look at the books he found that Corvo had written notes in them of such a nature that he put them in a bag and dumped them in the Grand Canal.

That same evening I was the guest of Mrs. Truxton Beale at Decatur House, a red-brick building with a Georgian front. It was built in 1818 by Commodore Decatur, with prize money he had gained subduing the Barbary pirates. There was a wing of the house, with an enclosed garden that, as late as 1844, was a slave market. Decatur House was the second to be built on Lafayette Square, the first being the White House. It was reputed to be haunted by Decatur's ghost. Of a bellicose nature, he fought a duel with Commodore Barron, whom he blamed for the surrender of the *Chesapeake* to the British. Decatur was mortally wounded and brought back to die in his home. It was in the room where he had died that my hostess greeted me. Public-spirited, she devoted her last years to raising money for the repair of St. Mark's at Venice. She is commemorated by a plaque in it.

In the next few days I lunched with the Director of the National Gallery of Art, Washington, and met Orville Wright, the pioneer aviator. A dinner was given for me to meet the Chief Justice, Harlan Stone and the Swiss Ambassador, by Miss Boardman, national President of the American Red Cross. I was also the guest for three days of my good friend Mrs. Stabler, now working in the State Department.

I lunched before leaving with Lord Halifax at the Embassy. He unbent a little and faintly smiled when I told him I had seen a member of the North Carolina Assembly nurse a page-boy on his knee, both chewing gum until reproved by the Speaker. I came away with a list of places he would visit. The next evening my friends, Señor and Señora de Cardenas, gave a dinner for me at the Spanish Embassy. He was the doyen of the ambassadors. His beautiful Rumanian wife, Lucienne, owned a famous huge white poodle, Timmy, but back in Madrid, three years later, he fell into disgrace for he proved to be a lady and gave birth to three puppies. While in Washington I had spoken for the British War Relief Society, Bundles for Britain and a Conference of the Colonial Dames of America. My negro chauffeur, after seeing me with a group of these ladies, amused me by saying, "Sure, sah, you can't deflate dem dames. Dey has it!"

I was back in New York for Mrs. Vanderbilt's Christmas Day party.

A great tree was lit in the art gallery. All the rooms were thrown open, an orchestra played in the small ball-room, log fires blazed in the great fireplaces. Chandeliers and lustres threw their light on damasks, tapestries and gilded panelling. On the long table in the dining-room, decorated with great bowls of roses, a buffet high tea was spread. Some three hundred guests greeted the hostess but on this Christmas Day, 1943, we were all somewhat sad despite the gaiety of the scene, for we were saying farewell to the house, soon to be demolished, with all its rich memories.

I had breakfasted with my near neighbours, Thomas and Betty Beecham, going with them later to the Opera House where he conducted a matinée performance of *Mignon*. After calls at Mrs. Crane's and Mrs. Vanderbilt's, I went to the Beechams' apartment for my Christmas dinner. The other guests were Lauritz Melchior and his wife, and Virgil Thomson, the critic-composer. Melchior told me how much he had owed to Hugh Walpole, who had sponsored him when young and struggling. Afterwards in the Tudoresque study Sir Thomas's twelve-year-old stepson, Jeremy, gave us a clever caricature of certain musicians at the piano. After this entertainment I had to dash off to bid Godspeed to some fifty young American nurses leaving for an unnamed war destination.

At midnight when I passed the Vanderbilt mansion I saw before the door the square-topped old Rolls-Royce that probably had just brought its owner home. It rode like a Gothic chair through New York's streets, a period piece. It now looked forlorn. If engines had hearts, I thought it might be weeping.

I saw the New Year in at a supper party given by the Marqués de Cuevas. He had married Rockefeller's grand-daughter, had joined two houses together and gave bohemian entertainments. He had founded a ballet company that would tour Europe later. There were eighty guests, among them lovely Lucienne de Cardenas with Timmy the poodle, whom I took for exercise. I walked home at 2 a.m. on a cold starlit night. I was too wide awake to go to bed. I lit my fire and reviewed the past year. I certainly had been generously entertained but how I had worked! I had given sixty-four addresses in twenty-two cities, I had travelled eight thousand miles, produced fourteen lots of notes for Halifax and Campbell, and sent monthly reports to Bracken in London. I had written five articles of interviews with soldiers from the battlefields and, to support myself, had written a novel requiring much research. I realised the pace was too hot. I was menaced by gastric pain. I resolved to go slower in the New Year. 1943 had been a sad one for me, overshadowed by the deaths of Lucien, Dr. Boehm, Louis Paget and Tony Allingham.

IV

In America a great institution in the New Year is the Egg-Nog party. I attended the one given by the University Club. It was a crowded occasion, the only one on which I met ex-President Hoover, a somewhat lugubrious character who had never really recovered from being in office during the Wall Street crash. He was not so much anti-British, though he had been an Isolationist supporting Lindbergh, as anti-European, yet he had given noble service after the First World War, organising famine relief on the continent. I had a few words with him. He paid a tribute to the courage of the British people which both surprised and pleased me. My next introduction was to the new British Consul-General, Sir Francis Evans, who astonished me by saying, "Yours is a famous and honoured name." It was a drop of appreciation in a pond of despair.

That month I was back again at the R.K.O. cinema on 59th Street, speaking for the American War Bond Drive. I looked into a black amphitheatre holding a huge audience. I had been preceded by a barn-storming Senator and the audience was restive. It was there to see a film, not to listen to war speeches. So I stood still at the microphone, fiddling with a bunch of keys. This aroused curiosity. Was I crazy? I then said, quietly, "We are all creatures of habit. When you leave here you will go home, almost automatically, catch a bus or take the Subway, then walk up to your home, pull out a key, go in, and go to bed. Here is the key of my home in London, but there's no doorlock to fit it in. The house was bombed. And one doesn't get a good night's rest, in bed, one dosses in a basement or an air-raid shelter. Aren't *ony* lucky?" They were all attention, and responsive after that. I got $16,000 subscribed in twenty minutes.

The next day I lunched in an astonishing house on Fifth Avenue belonging to Dr. Hamilton Rice. Among the twenty guests were Señora de Cardenas and the lovely Leonora Corbett, the ghostly wife

372

in Noël Coward's *Blithe Spirit*. We lunched in style, with wonderful food and wines, no semblance of a war within sound or sight. The whole place was in excellent taste. Its owner, Dr. Hamilton Rice, a man of seventy, was handsome and cultivated. He never wore an overcoat outdoors, even when the temperature was 20° below. Alas, I could not eat anything and had to toy with my plate. Two weeks earlier, suffering pain that caused me restless nights, I had seen a doctor, my kind Dr. Boehm being no more. After an X-ray he told me I had chronic gastric dyspepsia and must diet carefully and avoid nervous strain. That evening after Dr. Rice's, I went to one of Mrs. Vanderbilt's dinner parties. I asked the butler to let me have a glass of milk, not an easy thing to procure in that house.

After midnight I walked home. At 3 a.m. I was awakened by a feeling of wet stickiness. I turned on the light and found I was lying in a pool of blood. I was alone. I waited until 8 a.m. and then called my doctor. An hour later I was in New York Hospital, with a haemorrhage from a duodenal ulcer. How very odd, that, only a few months previously, I had been taken over this great hospital by the President, Mr. Marvin, and the Matron. He had asked me if I would address their annual meeting. He felt that as the biographer of Sir Alfred Fripp, the eminent surgeon, I had a special qualification! I did so, and afterwards met the nurses and toured the hospital.

The doctors hoped to avoid an operation. As I lay there I thought how fortunate it was that the day before this attack I had got off the data for Lord Halifax and Sir Gerald Campbell. I was in hospital for a month. There was a touch of irony in a message that came from the British Consulate to say that I was not to worry about money as I should be allowed to have dollars for medical expenses. So, sick and useless, I could at last have dollars! The fact that, well, I had not been able to get them, had contributed, by the worry entailed, to this illness, largely nervous in origin.

The amount of flowers that arrived became embarrassing. My room could not hold them all, and when I was convalescent there was a stream of visitors. I had never felt so important in my life. Among my callers were Sir Thomas and Lady Beecham. When the time came for me to leave they would not hear of my returning to my own apartment, without attention. So Betty Beecham fetched me in their car and took me to their apartment. I was to stay there until I was quite well. What unwearying kindness they showed! At last I went home, and began the rounds again, with some caution. I spoke at the Junior League Club with the British Consul-General in the Chair, at the Brooklyn Institute of Arts and Sciences, etc. I thought I was cured. I did not foresee that this monstrous thing would afflict me for the rest of my life, causing me frightful pain and knocking me out twice or thrice each year.

v

One April Sunday morning my friend Commander Alec Lacy, R.N., with our Naval Mission in Washington, called on me. He had with him Lieutenant Stuart Chant of the Gordon Highlanders. He was a handsome young man of about twenty-five, dark-haired, with a neat figure and a pleasant speaking-voice. He wore a Gordon tartan kilt, light green stockings and bonnet, and a khaki coat with a Sam Browne belt. Altogether he was a vivid and dashing personality. He had come to America under the auspices of the British Information Services to lecture on his experiences as a commando leader. Gradually I drew out his story, told with great modesty. He had been on several commando raids and was chosen for the raid upon the dock gates at St. Nazaire, in March, 1942. Earlier, on June 17, 1940, St. Nazaire had been the scene of a terrible tragedy. On the downfall of France many thousands of British soldiers had made their way there. Several English vessels waited to rescue them. The 20,000 ton *Lancastria* took 5,000 men on board. Just as she was about to leave the estuary she was bombed and set on fire. A mass of flaming oil spread round the ship and 2,800 men perished. This news was so dreadful that Churchill forbade publication, feeling that the British just then had as much as they could take. Some seven years elapsed before the full story became known. But I had known of it almost at once, for my young protégé, who had written *Letters from Jim*, was on a companion ship and saw the whole disaster, later being landed in Devon. From his letter to me, discreet in view of the censorship, I was able to locate the scene at St. Nazaire. It was here, in March, 1942, that Lieutenant Chant was in a commando raid, a desperate enterprise. At St. Nazaire there was the second largest dry dock in Europe. It was to this dock that the maimed *Bismarck*, under attack,

374

had attempted to make its way. It was decided it must be put out of use. Among the commandos was Chant, on board H.M.S. *Campbeltown*. He lay flat on the main deck when the ship charged the gates under a devastating fire. Many were killed but Chant got ashore with his company and set about destroying the dock installations. It had been a submarine base. The destruction cut off their retreat and they began to fight their way through the town, the hope being that they might eventually get to Spain. Chant was badly wounded and lay on the dockside, tended by one of his men. Presently three Nazis came along crying *Heraus*! "My man stood up, holding his hands high in token of surrender. They deliberately drilled the poor fellow through the stomach," said Chant, "and then turned to deal with me, but I could not rise and, bending over me, they saw I was an officer, and the German reverence for rank stopped them killing me."

Chant was kept a prisoner in France for six months and was then sent to camps in Germany and in Poland. After nineteen months he was sent home to England as an exchange prisoner, the Germans believing he would never walk again, quite erroneously. Chant told me that nothing regarding the brutality of the Germans was exaggerated. They had a hard, iron spirit in act and manifestation. Hundreds of St. Nazaire citizens were rounded up and shot, following the panic in the town. He was well treated in the French hospital. In prison the Germans tormented the men by long rollcalls, standing them for hours in exposed prison yards, many men dying of pneumonia. There were also deaths from bad food, ulcerated stomachs, particularly among those over thirty years old.

I took Chant to see Sir Thomas Beecham, to tea at Mrs. Crane's, and to Mrs. Vanderbilt's. She had a dinner party of twenty-eight that evening. She insisted on his staying and she placed him at her right hand at the long table, the guest of honour.

Twenty years elapsed before I saw Chant again. In the interim he had been liaison officer to General Eisenhower, had married the Baroness Sempill, and was the father of two sons.

I was still unwell and had to cancel two meetings. I was able to utilise the time in bed. Sir Thomas had written a book of memoirs which he had called *A Mingled Chime*. I read the proofs for him. It is a tedious business and very rarely does one come out unscathed. One must read first for enjoyment and again for detection. I returned the corrected proofs of the English edition of Beecham's book on the eve of his sixty-fourth birthday. He made me stay to supper. They were leaving soon. I had been amused to read that his American publisher had advertised the book as *A Mingled Crime*. I gave him the clipping, with my verses attached.

'Tis nice to learn in this sweet clime
You have achieved a mingled crime.
Let others boast, the U.S.A.
Do things in a much better way:
One thing is clear, it takes a Beecham
In this stupendous land to teach 'em
How to become, long versed in law,
A criminal at sixty-four.

One day I was called up by Somerset Maugham who asked me to lunch with him at the Ritz-Carlton. There he told me that his life-long friend and secretary, Gerald Haxton, was dying of consumption. When Maugham had gone down to live in Carolina Haxton had worked for two years in Washington. After an attack of pleurisy there, tuberculosis had developed. Maugham took him to a sanatorium in the Adirondack mountains. Then in November, I heard that Haxton had died, after an operation, in Doctors' Hospital in New York, aged fifty-two. I called Maugham, saying I would come and see him. "I don't want to see you! I don't want to see anyone! I want to die!" he cried in a distressed voice, and put down the telphone. Nevertheless, I went along to the Ritz and up to his room. He opened the door, very haggard in appearance. I walked in and talked to him firmly. It was noon. He said, "Let's go down and lunch." We lunched in the little Japanese garden beside the artificial running stream. When I left he was in a normal mood. "You are a good friend, Cecil," he said, holding both my hands. Later, he went down to his Carolina retreat, where his nephew, Robin, joined him.

VI

About this time I met at a lunch the Baroness 'Kitty' Rothschild, the wife of Baron Eugene de Rothschild, now living in America. Her great beauty had been a legend in Europe, and although now a woman of about sixty she was still strikingly beautiful, very slim and *soignée*.

The Rothschilds were living at Glen Cove, Long Island. She invited me to visit them. One weekend in May I went there. Still House was set amid wooded hills, with not another dwelling in sight. It was a large double-winged mansion with extensive grounds. The entrance front was in the Regency style. The house had been designed by Delanty, then a favourite architect. The property had belonged originally to Mr. Paul Cravath, a corporation lawyer. When he died the property was sold to meet estate duties. It had cost Cravath $1,000,000 and the Rothschilds had bought it for $112,000. The house had two wings joined by a large salon. In the west wing was the white drawing-room. Over this there was a large bedroom with a wide balcony that commanded a view of the gardens and woods. This room I occupied. The long salon had eight French windows and led to the library. This was an immense room, the height of two storeys, with a gallery giving access to the upper tiers of shelves. It was full of expensive editions in de luxe bindings. The collection covered classical as well as modern literature, in Greek, Latin and French texts. There was no sign that the books had ever been read. The library seemed to be an interior decorator's idea of the intellectual life. Still House was known to Sir William Orpen, who had spent a hot summer here painting Cravath's portrait, for a fee of £10,000.

When I arrived there was a house party. Our host, Baron Eugene, was tall and blond, a simple, kind man who adored Kitty. When I left on the Monday morning the Baroness invited me to come again. She saw I was pale and thin. "I will watch your diet," she said with a smile, "and here you can rest. No more meetings!"

Great things were happening in Europe. We began to see light at the end of the tunnel, although England was being ruthlessly bombed. The flying bomb was now harassing London. The German Army had surrendered in Tunisia, Mussolini had fallen, we had invaded Italy. Our landing at Salerno was followed by Italy's surrender. It had been thought safe to let Oswald Mosley out of prison where he had been since 1940. Monte Cassino had been taken, and the great monastery, on the assumption that it was used by the Germans, had been reduced to rubble, a gross act of vandalism that had served no purpose. The Allies had broken through the German Line and had occupied Italy. We had invaded Normandy.

Back in New York I saw Lady Blennerhassett. She was leaving for

England, with her baby, Sir Adrian. I went to Philadelphia to speak at the Art Alliance and to Pittsburgh for a War Bond Drive. I worked on more notes for the Ambassador and Sir Gerald but I had not the stamina of old. Towards the end of the month I left for Still House, keeping my promise to return. I found the woods in magnificent bloom, the whole hill-side covered with masses of white and pink dogwood, a blossom almost unknown in England. These, together with the azaleas and dark cypress trees, constituted a paradise under a bright blue sky. I was made to breakfast in my room.

Little by little I learned the histories of my host and hostess. Baron Eugene had been for a short time with the Rothschild bank in London, later he became an officer in a crack Austrian cavalry regiment. He gave much time to managing his large estates, hunting, and breeding race horses. He lost his fortune with the Nazi occupation and would have been destitute now but in 1938 the Baroness visited America, aware of the growing storm, and before returning to Paris and Vienna, left behind some jewellery. They had owned a house in Paris, another in Vienna and the medieval Schloss Enzesfeld. This castle had played a part in recent British history.

When in the autumn of 1936 King Edward, together with Mrs. Simpson and some friends, went on an Adriatic yachting cruise in the S.Y. *Nahlin*, they returned overland via Prinkipo and Vienna. They visited the Rothschilds at Schloss Enzesfeld and there the King suffered from a bad cold. One evening in December, 1936, the Baroness was rung up by Lord Brownlow, who had been one of the visiting party in 1936. He asked if he might come and bring with him his young brother David, the one who had had a bad cold on the last visit. They knew then who the 'brother' really was but it hoodwinked the telephone-tappers and the journalists tracking the ex-King. When the car from Vienna drew up in the courtyard, Edward, twenty-four hours previously King of England, stepped out with Lord Brownlow. The new Duke of Windsor stayed at Enzesfeld until the following April. The luxurious *schloss*, with a private golf course, was well-enclosed but the harassment of over four hundred journalists was overwhelming and the Duke finally conceded an interview. He held it in the courtyard. "It was a terrible ordeal," said the Baroness, "but he faced it wonderfully. When he came back into the house he was rather pale but the nightmare was over."

He left when arrangements had been made for his marriage to Mrs. Simpson at the Château de Candé in France. The Baroness told me that during his stay the Duke had behaved quite well, contrary to rumours that said he had left large debts behind for telephones, etc. Every evening he talked with Mrs. Simpson in Cannes. One of his customs the Baroness found trying, his habit of sitting up until three in the morning. She insisted on retiring at her usual hour. Later, she was invited to the Château de Candé, the property of M. Bedaux, a French-American with a suspect history that ended in his suicide in Miami when threatened with arrest. At the Bedaux château the Baroness attended a dinner party on the eve of a wedding performed by an imported English clergyman who afterwards, trafficking in the notoriety, became a considerable nuisance.

I came to learn a little of the personal history of my hostess. When she first appeared in Paris she was one of the most celebrated beauties of Europe. De Lázlo painted her portrait in 1922 and it created a sensation. She was at this time the wife of Count Schönborn Buckheim, of a family of art patrons comparable with the Medici. He had a famous palace in Vienna, was a Royal Chamberlain, and a captain of cavalry in the Imperial Army. In Paris he was Secretary of the Legation. His family, of a *maison princière*, had *les droits d'egalité de naissance souveraine*, the equal rights of royal birth. The result was that when Kitty married him in Paris it was a marriage *non-égal de naissance*. She was born in Philadelphia, the daughter of Dr. and Mrs. Wolff, who were German immigrants. In her late teens she had married a Mr. Spotswood, by whom she had a son that died. She obtained a divorce in 1910 and married Schönborn. This marriage, in turn, was dissolved and she married in 1924 the Count's fellow-officer, Baron Eugene de Rothschild. He was madly in love with her.

There is a small room in the Hotel Sacher, in Vienna, lined with portraits of the reigning beauties in the closing years of the reign of the Hapsburgs. Kitty Rothschild is among these. Their house in Paris was famous for its pictures and furniture. She owned one-third of the famous diamond necklace of Marie Antoinette.

When Paris fell in June, 1940, my hostess escaped via Biarritz. She carried with her a pendant of this famous necklace. With the Baron, her maid and chauffeur, and Stefan, their Hungarian major-domo, they motored to Biarritz and crossed the frontier at Irun. They went on to Madrid, out of which they hurried as soon as possible. It was packed with refugees. They flew by clipper from Lisbon via the Azores, coming down at Bermuda for a customs check. There was a terrible moment when the Baroness, sitting in the plane, saw a negro porter cross on a plank over the water, to the plane, with a wheelbarrow loaded with baggage. Her jewel case was precariously balanced on the top of the swaying pile. "Part of the Queen's necklace was in that case and if I had not been able to take it across the Atlantic we should not be sitting here, for I bought and furnished this house with the money it fetched," said Kitty.

The guests at Still House touched the European tragedy at many points. I talked with Prince Edward Lobkowicz, a captain who had fought with a Czech brigade in the British Army in Syria and the Western Desert, and with a Polish brigade in the British 8th Army in North Africa. He was in the siege and relief of Tobruk, and had received for his gallant services, having enlisted at the age of forty, the Military Cross. For six months from May to October, 1943, he went on a secret mission in the Balkans and Hungary, disguised as a French journalist. Also, staying overnight, came 'Chips' Channon, a great gossip. Chicago-born, rich, naturalised, he married into the Guinness millions, became an M.P. and was knighted. He entertained lavishly in his Belgrave Square mansion. His ambition was to know everybody, which he fulfilled. A social butterfly, his *Diary*, published in 1970, recorded his thrust into society and politics. It had an entry, "I belong definitely to the order of those who *have*—and through no effort of my own, which is such a joy." A lightweight with brains, he wrote two novels and an excellent book *The Ludwigs of Bavaria*. I had reviewed this favourably, as he reminded me when we met at Still House. Since our rooms adjoined, we breakfasted together the next morning. He astonished me with his gossip, much of which I discounted. He was certainly an entertaining fellow, who reminded me of Wordsworth's lines—'The world is too much with us; late and soon, getting and spending we lay waste our powers.'

The next day the Duke and Duchess of Windsor arrived for tea. They often played truant from Nassau which they regarded as a sort of St. Helena to which he had been banished. They were now visiting in the neighbourhood. About this time the Kodachrome, a colour film, had just been put on the market and I had developed a passion for colour photography. The dogwood and azaleas at Still House were magnificent subjects. Kitty asked me to show my photos. The Duke said he had never been able to take colour photos successfully, so I gave him a lesson, as to exposure, etc. He was like a young boy in his eagerness and delighted with a viewing magnascope I gave him.

VII

On my return to New York in the heat of June, to fulfil three speaking engagements I found that my friend Lawrence, he of the Gmunden trout-fishing and the Heimo Schneider tragedy, had arrived from England. He was now a King's Messenger, en route to Washington and Buenos Aires. He would fly to South America from Miami, the hydroplane airport I knew. The Foreign Office had rented a small apartment there so that the King's Messengers had no trouble about a lodging before they took off from Dinner Key. He would be there in the New Year. Why would I not go down and be his guest there ? He thought I looked very thin and worn. "What have you been doing to yourself?" he asked. I promised that I would visit him, perhaps after Christmas if he was in Miami then. I kept my speaking dates, and one evening escorted Mrs. Vanderbilt to the New York Stadium open-air concert, at which Beecham was conducting. I should have enjoyed it but I was ill.

The heat and my engagements proved too much for me. I was in bed for a week. To escape the heat I spent July and August with my friend Wertheim in our old quarters at Southampton, Long Island. Here I worked on *And So To America*, and received the cheering news from my publisher that *So Immortal a Flower* had subscribed 50,000 copies and was selling well. In October I was shocked by the news of the death of Wendell Willkie. He was only fifty-two, a robust man who seemed to have a great future. Our association over the broadcasting of *A Man Arose* had been most happy. On November 7, after dining with Madame Balzan, we sat up to get the result of the Presidential election. Thank God Roosevelt was elected for the fourth time, defeating Dewey, to the great anger of the anti-Roosevelts who said, "We've got another Hitler in the White House. We'll never get rid of that fellow!" They thought a fourth term endangered the Constitution.

In December I was asked by Lowell Thomas if I would speak at a Soldiers' Rehabilitation Centre, located in the small town of Pawling, where he lived. Thomas was the foremost radio commentator in the United States. His sponsors paid him $400,000 a year for his news commentaries. In the First World War, reporting on the Palestine campaign and the Arab revolution, he had met the young Colonel Lawrence, then unknown to the outside world. Lowell Thomas wrote a book about him called, *Lawrence of Arabia*, and, coming to London, his illustrated lecture at the Albert Hall drew packed audiences for a month. From this the legend of 'Lawrence of Arabia" grew. Lowell Thomas was assisted by Lawrence's penchant for dressing-up in costume and being photographed. The legend was enlarged by his curious character. Undeniably a great man, he had a gift for 'backing into the limelight', as Guedalla put it. Then came all the ballyhoo of his book, *Revolt in the Desert*. A special edition was sold at a fabulous price.

Thomas did his broadcasting from a large studio at his home in Pawling. I watched him make his famous news broadcast. I was his guest for the night. For some reason all that night I was sleepless and searching for what I could say to the soldiers the next morning. For once in my life I simply could not find a theme. It eluded me until I stood on the platform facing some three hundred young men. Everything was against me, I was tired, my gift of extempore speech deserted me. The young soldiers were restless. I learnt later that at noon they had weekend leave to go to their families. Many of them were suffering from war hysteria, some were on the verge of break-down. I utterly failed to hold their attention, and floundered about. Poor Lowell Thomas, he had had such glowing accounts of me and had sponsored a flop. Something had gone wrong with me. I cancelled two public engagements and spent Christmas at Still House.

Guests came there, among them Eugene's brother, Baron Louis. I heard the story of his ordeal, sitting in that large library before a blazing log fire. He had been seized by the Nazis when they marched into Vienna. He was two months in the city gaol, being considered too rich to 'liquidate'. He was then taken to the Hotel Metropole and confined to an attic bedroom, a guard living with him night and day. He was kept there for a year, being repeatedly interrogated by a judge. Then through the British Ambassador in Berlin, Henderson, a friend of Kitty's, wires were pulled with Goering and Himmler. He was released. In May, 1939, he reached Paris, with only one portmanteau. "If war had broken out while I was in that attic I should never have come out alive," he said. Almost a year after his arrival in Paris he was a fugitive again, fleeing to America, and thus came to be sitting this Christmastide in the library while Germany faced defeat and misery.

I left Still House at the end of December to stay with my friend Lawrence, who had arrived back in Miami. So closed the year 1944. I looked back on it, a year of illness and loss, with little pleasure.

CHAPTER SIXTEEN

Churchill in Florida

I

I arrived in Miami from New York on New Year's Day, 1945, eight hours late owing to a snow blizzard. My friend Lawrence met me and took me to his apartment. It was just over the Miami River Bridge, in a new apartment block on Brickell Avenue. The position was delightful. The apartment overlooked a neighbour's large garden. The owner had four gardeners and one had nothing to do but admire their work. This garden had a very long lawn, bordered with Royal Poinciana palms that went down to the shore of the Biscayne Bay. We had a small balcony from which to enjoy the garden, ablaze with 'unimaginable flowers', as Flecker wrote. Here I worked happily in sunshine on speeches for Halifax, visiting Tallahassee in Florida and Providence, Rhode Island. I was fortunate in finding an excellent library in Miami for reference. Moreover, I was familiar with Tallahassee, the capital of Florida, a few miles from the Gulf coast. Its name came from an Indian word meaning 'sun-town' which was appropriate, for, slightly north of the Gulf of Mexico, it was baked in sunshine.

In his old age Lafayette re-visited the United States. He had a triumphal progress and Congress voted him $200,000, the township of Tallahassee, and an estate of 23,000 acres. The Florida Council hoped he would come to live there but he did not come, and the estate was ultimately sold for $150,000, which went to his heirs. But another distinguished Frenchman did come. This was Prince Achille Murat, son of Napoleon's Marshal, the executed King of Naples. Impoverished, Prince Achille Murat, Duke of Cleves, emigrated at twenty-eight. He acquired a small estate near Tallahassee, married a grand-niece of Washington, and tried to earn a living as a farmer, a

Winston Churchill at
the Parrot Reservation,
Florida

Winston Churchill sitting for Douglas Chandor, Miami Beach,
Florida, 1946

The author at Baron de Rothschild's, Long Island, New York

cotton planter, and then a lawyer. Charming, he had no success. All that he inherited when his mother Caroline, ex-Queen of Naples, died were curtains, bedsheets and one hundred cooks' aprons. Out of the curtains his wife made dresses. The Prince was eccentric, he chewed tobacco and he once served buzzard soup to his guests. To provide him with a small income they made him the town's postmaster. One evening, dining at Madame Balzan's, I found myself placed next to a Princess Murat and we talked of Tallahassee. Madame Balzan surprised us by saying, "My great-aunt was the Kate Willis who married Prince Murat. She inherited, via the ex-Queen of Naples, her mother-in-law, a Capo di Monte table service. I, in turn, inherited this, took it with me to Blenheim when I married the Duke of Marlborough, and then brought it here. We are dining off it." So I had plenty of data for Lord Halifax.

I was Lawrence's guest for only ten days. To his chagrin he was called to Washington and then sent to London, ending his role of King's Messenger. He suggested I should take over the remaining tenancy of the apartment. So I took the place at the absurd rental of $800 a year, sharing it with my friend Wertheim. That same day I spoke at the Miami Booklovers' Dinner, and sent off my notes to the Ambassador. A few days later he asked for notes for visits to Oklahoma City, Tulsa, and Fayetteville. Soon after I had acquired the apartment I went to visit Mrs. Cartwright at her villa *Estella* in Palm Beach. It was a splendid property with a large swimming pool. Surprisingly, the house was filled with paintings of horses by Stubbs, Herring, etc., bought by her third, English, husband, Captain Cartwright, R.N. They had to be kept in cold storage during the summer. I occupied a room in the tower, with a panorama of Palm Beach, the river, the sea, the jungle, from its three windows. The sunsets were magnificent. Here I continued to work on *And So To America*.

One day I was invited to the Graduation Day at the R.A.F. training base at Clewiston. It was no longer a secret American training base for our airmen before the U.S.A. came into the war. I watched these lads, drilled by a tall, trim cadet. He had come a long way for this, Cedric Henderson of Linares, Chile, so strong the call of the blood. The Commandant asked if I would give them a lecture, so a few days later I addressed over three hundred cadets packed into a lecture hall. With this lecture I was coming to the end of a long trial. For more than five years, from the Canadian border to the Mexican Gulf, from the Atlantic to the Pacific, I had faced countless audiences. This R.A.F. audience consisted of my own countrymen, of boys drawn from all over the British Empire. Their presence here seemed to fulfil the dream to which some of us had dedicated our efforts, the union of the English-speaking people.

Here in a hamlet on the edge of the vast Lake of Okeechobee was an outpost of Britain, created before America had entered the war. I asked the Commandant if they had a record of the fate of the boys who left here. "Yes," he said quietly. "I fear fifty per cent of them were casualties." The people of Palm Beach and around delighted in showing these boys hospitality at weekends. Mrs. Cartwright placed at their disposal the long swimming pool, which echoed with youthful cries and was noisy with slim, brown bodies splashing in the azure water.

On the evening of April 12 I was driving to a dinner party given by a neighbour in Palm Beach. The chauffeur driving us said "Well, it's sad news, isn't it?" I asked what was sad news. He was astonished we had not heard. That afternoon President Roosevelt had died very suddenly. All the morning he had worked on papers and letters. The speech he was to make the next day, Jefferson Day, was written. He had been quite happy at luncheon. The war news was good, the end was in sight, the Allies were only twenty miles from Berlin. After lunch he gave a sitting to an artist. Suddenly he collapsed in his chair. He never recovered consciousness and died an hour and a half later from cerebral haemorrhage.

I was surprised that the dinner party had not been cancelled. When we arrived I was shocked by the remarks of some of the guests. One of the greatest men in American history, and of the world, who had taken America into the war and seen it triumphant, lay dead. I felt that everything should have stopped, blinds be drawn and a deep silence prevail. "Well, the Dictator's gone," said a wealthy stockbroker, to an approving chorus. The champagne flowed, the spirit was festive. I wanted to leave. There was scarcely an approving sentence about a great President, an ailing man with a lion's courage. I had to remain, smothering my disgust, for I had come and must leave in my hostess's car, and I could not offer an affront to my amicable hosts.

I was in New York eighteen days later when the news came that Germany had surrendered. There was some hysteria, with the ticker tapes deluging the city from its skyscrapers. The next day Hitler was dead, a suicide. Then, a week later, came news of the official end of the war in Europe. I was a guest again at Still House, of a famous Jewish family, the Rothschilds, of a race that had been hideously persecuted. There was no jubilance, no champagne. A dark cloud had passed, a foul tyranny lay in the dust. Baron Eugene made one remark at dinner, touching on this great event. "It is sad the President didn't live a little longer to see this day."

On July 26 news of a different kind stunned us. The unbelievable had happened. The Conservative Government had been swept out of office. Attlee took over from Churchill. To many of us it was inscrutable, and an act of base ingratitude to the man who had saved us. "I suppose your people are punch-drunk from victory," said an American. "Given a chance, we'd have done the same to Roosevelt." And then, on August 14, while driving with Mrs. Cartwright at Newport where I was her guest, we heard that Japan had surrendered, knocked out by the atomic bombs on Hiroshima and Nagasaki. Was Truman right, was Truman wrong, to have done this? Had he saved a million soldiers' lives by massacring a multitude of civilians? The debate went on and on. The argument had no sense since there is no sense in war, anyhow. The slopes of history are slippery with blood.

In September, in a beautiful house in Newport, which my hostess had rented, hung with works of the French Impressionists, I worked ten hours a day on *And So To America*, nearing the end. On fashionable Bailey's Beach I met Madame Balzan and her grand-daughter, Lady Sarah Russell, and the second husband of Barbara Hutton, Count Reventlow. He showed me over a mansion he had acquired, Hopedene. He had bought it at auction for $28,000! It had cost $500,000, an example of perfect French workmanship. It comprised six acres of grounds with garages etc. He sold at once three paintings for $15,000. But perhaps his greatest achievement was a small son, now the only link between him and Barbara the fickle.

Mrs. Vanderbilt also had a vast house, The Breakers, that had become a nightmare. It was shut up. Servants had been a war casualty. Thirty years earlier she had given a party at which eight hundred guests had dined and danced until dawn, when the orchestra, brought from New York, had played 'Auld Lang Syne'. She was now content, at a smaller villa, to give a dinner for thirty. At one of my hostess's lunch parties a guest was Lord Camoys, a Pilgrim Cottage neighbour, at Stonor Park. Everyone with American ties was crossing the Atlantic. How crazy it all seemed. Three thousand miles away in Europe, eight thousand miles away in China, they were cold, ragged, homeless and dying of hunger. I had a letter from England. "It is worse than ever here. Everybody and everything is worn out. My sheets came back from the laundry held together with adhesive tape. I have been in four chemists' shops in search of a cake of soap." My letter was from a woman who had never complained during five years of war. "We have thrown out Churchill. I hope that that dear, good, brave man can now take the rest he deserves."

In that month young Aubrey Cartwright, a tall, frail boy at Eton, arrived on a visit to his mother. She was very happy after a separation of six years. They were shy of each other and this reunion was touching. His appearance in her Fifth Avenue drawing-room provoked me to exclaim, seeing his fair English complexion and blond hair, in the words of Pope Gregory, *Non Angli sed angeli.*

In October, again at the Rothschilds, where the woods still glowed with the gold of the Indian summer, a slim English youth arrived, an ex-Guardsman, Peter Daubeny. He had survived the landing in Salerno, losing an arm. I discovered that he had once been with the Liverpool Repertory Theatre. In future years he would win renown by importing foreign players to give London a World Theatre. He flung his net wide. He even brought a company from Samarkand.

At the close of the year I was still working hard on my book. One evening in New York I dined with Elizabeth Arden in her Fifth Avenue home and was glad to meet again the Duchesse de Grammont (Mrs. Victor Hugo III). Little Victor Hugo IV, my Southampton playmate, was now at school. This evening she told me a little of her history. She had been born Princess Ruspoli. When a girl she had lived in the vast, gloomy family castle perched above Lake Nemi. It seemed bewitched. One brother was murdered, one committed suicide, one was drowned in the lake. Aged seventeen, in Paris, she was proposed to twice by the old Duc de Grammont and had married him as a way of escape from the gloom and tragedy of her home. She would never go back there again, perhaps she would return to France. She had young Victor to educate.

I could not return home yet. I had let Pilgrim Cottage until next March, my lodging in London was bombed. I should be another mouth to feed in a strictly-rationed England. I could do my work writing anywhere. I decided to remain in New York for a time. I had sent my last notes to Lord Halifax, who would soon be retiring from his ambassadorship. Sir Gerald Campbell was also retiring, My health was not yet normal, I suffered from what I called 'my Treasury ulcer'.

In this month I had a terrible shock. My friend, Dr. Alcock, whose brother, with wife and child, had been so completely obliterated by a bomb in their Chelsea house that not one iota of them could be found, sent me a newspaper clipping. I read it and was frozen with horror.

Young Tony Allingham's lovely sister, Ann, of that 'Mummy, Dad, Ann and Pat' refrain, had gone out as a lieutenant in the Red Cross to Indonesia. On December 5, in Sumatra, she had made an excursion on the south-west coast with a young Army major. While swimming they had been ambushed. After a week their mutilated bodies had been found in the village of Padang. Almost the entire village was implicated and those responsible were rounded up and the ringleaders shot. With her companion she was buried in the Padang European Cemetery. She had been helping with the refugee and rehabilitation problems after the surrender of Japan.

So never again would lovely young Ann come down the path at Pilgrim Cottage, as radiant with life as was her adored brother. There were now only Mummy, Dad and Pat of that joyous family which had so often brightened my life.

II

By the end of the month of January, 1946, I had finished *And So To America*. It was 250,000 words, the longest book I had ever written. I went south to my small apartment in Miami. Pilgrim Cottage would be free in the Spring when I planned to return. When I arrived at Miami I learned that Winston Churchill, with his wife and daughter, Mrs. Vic Oliver, were staying on Miami Beach. They were the guests of Colonel Frank Clarke, of Quebec, who had a winter home there.

Churchill had just received the O.M. His doctor had ordered him to take a rest in a warm climate, so Florida had been chosen. They made an excursion to Havana for a week and were back at Miami Beach on February 10. I wrote to Churchill inviting him and Mrs. Churchill to tea. They came a few days later and I had only my friend Guido Wertheim, who was staying with me, present. Winston was in very good humour, looking well, and 'Clemmie', as ever, was as charming as she was beautiful. When I told him how I got the apartment, "What a nest for a King's Messenger, but those poor devils have always to be on the move!" he commented. He wanted to know the name of the giant palm trees that lined the garden I overlooked.

They stayed an hour and I learned that an artist friend of mine, Douglas Chandor, who lived in Texas and was renowned as a portrait painter, had just arrived to paint Winston. The portrait was to be part of a triptych. He had already painted the President, and after Winston he would go to Russia to paint Stalin. It was commissioned for the National Gallery in Washington. At tea I told Winston about a wonderful parrot jungle, south of Miami. It was a reserved territory in which hundreds of them were in a wild state among the trees. Knowing his love of the bizarre, I suggested a visit. He said he would be delighted to go. It could be arranged for the 'Jungle' to be closed to the public during his visit. Later we fixed a date and he and Clemmie, with a small party, visited the reservation. Winston was delighted. He had parrots all over him, on his arms, shoulders, and knees. They were quite undeterred by his cigar. He left after a joyful hour.

I learned from Chandor that he was painting the portrait in a special room in the Miami Beach Surf Club. Winston posed in the uniform of a marshal of the Royal Air Force. He was a good sitter and talked easily but he would not sit for more than an hour. He discussed painting technicalities with Chandor, and wanted details of how he laid out his palette. He smoked all the time.

Chandor said, playfully, that, as Winston was in uniform, he could not paint his cigar. "All you artists object to my cigar," he replied. "Do you know that Breughel's peasants do pee-pee in a corner of his pictures?" "Oh, I wouldn't ask you to do that, sir," replied Chandor.

The portrait was not wholly finished when Winston left. Chandor was doomed to disappointment over his triptych. Stalin refused to sit, so it was never completed.

While Winston was in Miami he received an Hon. LL.D. degree from Miami University. I was invited to the ceremony on February, 26. It was held in the vast Orange Bowl, the football stadium, filled to overflowing with 18,000 spectators. It was a wonderful sight in the bright sunshine. I found myself sitting near Hore-Belisha. He had come from a visit to South America with his wife. He was now having a belated honeymoon. When the band ceased playing there was a great hush. Everyone's eyes were turned to a small footballers' entrance half-way down the long stadium. Thousands of field-glasses were trained on it. Presently two black-gowned figures emerged, after them two more, and two more, and two more, until the figures grew into a long black snake creeping up to the platform at the end of the stadium. "Where's Churchill? Which is Churchill?" everyone asked, searching down the long processional line. But there was no Churchill. It seemed as if all the professors of the United States were in that gowned crocodile. And then, at last, out of the distant little hole he came, wearing the vivid scarlet gown and velvet cap of an Oxford doctorate. The stadium went mad as he slowly walked down it, ceremoniously doffing his cap to the multitude. After the degree-conferring he made an address. I had suggested that he might mention the hospitality shown to our R.A.F. cadets. He did it nobly, giving deep satisfaction.

> I take the opportunity to thank you for the training of some one thousand two hundred cadets before this country became belligerent. They flew five and a half million miles, I am told, over Florida upon instructional courses, and the majority, indeed the very large majority, gave their lives shortly afterwards to their country in our common cause. It is a consolation to learn that they left so many pleasant memories behind them among the two thousand Miami households who received them with true American hospitality and afterwards followed their fortunes and their fate almost as if they were sons of the soil.

Before the end I left the platform in order to take some coloured photographs of the scene. When later I presented a set of them to Winston he was delighted. "They will go into my archives," he said. Dr. Moran, his physician, had sent him abroad for a rest in a warm climate. There was not much rest about it. A photograph taken of him in the parrot reserve showed a white cockatoo perched on his shoulder and looking most inquisitively at his head, as if wondering what would come out of it. Something did, which made history. At this time he was working on the speech he would deliver in the Westminster College gymnasium at Fulton, Missouri, President Truman's home State. Five days after the Miami ceremony he was in Washington, conferring with Truman on the subject of his forthcoming speech. He left Washington two days later with the President for Fulton and on March 5, made the historic speech which gave the world a warning about Russia. "From Stettin in the Baltic, to Trieste in the Adriatic, an iron curtain has descended across the Continent." After this momentous utterance he received, on the way home, an honorary degree from Columbia University in New York. He went out to Hyde Park, the late President's country estate on the Hudson, to lay a wreath on his grave. In the journey northward he had visited historic Williamsburg in Virginia, and on the day he sailed he dined with Madame Balzan, his cousin by marriage. Rest? In a visit of nine weeks he had had four weeks' repose in Miami. Much of the time was consumed in journeys and speeches.

Hore-Belisha, still in Miami, invited me to have a cocktail with him and his wife. He lived off Collins Avenue, Miami Beach, in what was called 'Gulf Stream Apartments'. I could not help wondering how he got sufficient dollars out of the Treasury to go wandering about in South and North America with his wife. He was very cordial, but when I sought to learn something about the shabby treatment meted out to him at the War Office by Chamberlain, I found him reluctant to talk. I admired his restraint in the matter. But he did tell me that Chamberlain could give him no reason for his dismissal. "He was both an obstinate and a weak man. He hadn't the courage to stand up to the War Office *embusqués*. You remember that even Curzon lost to Kitchener over India. I was perhaps perversely gratified when the whole lot of them had to serve under Eisenhower, an American with no military experience in the field—a good man, however."

Five days later I was the guest speaker of the Pan-American Society. It was my last public appearance. It was singular that I should end my six years of propaganda lecturing, in Florida, where I had begun in 1939. Then I left for New York, on the first stage of the journey home. I had an amusing episode. I broke my journey in Washington, and a lady who knew that my books were translated into Spanish took me to a meeting of the United Nations Club where there was a dinner sing-song held by members of a Spanish class. They ate and sang, learning line by line the words and music of popular *canciones*. It was all very jolly. The lady on my right was Mrs. Eisenhower. Her husband also was there, learning his lines. "He's quite a good pupil!" she said. "Well," I replied, "there's one thing the General will never be able to learn—how much my countrymen love him." Her face lit up. "Why, that's the nicest thing I've ever heard of him—you must tell him yourself!" she cried. I demurred. It's not easy to pay compliments to a man's face and not sound fulsome. But Mrs. Eisenhower leaned back and touched her husband. "I want Mr. Roberts to repeat what he has just said about you." So I repeated the words to the man who, on being given the Freedom of the City of London at the Mansion House, had gone out on to the portico and said to the crowd, "Whether you know it or not I am now a Londoner myself. I have as much right to be down yelling in the crowd as you have." His face shone with genuine pleasure and later we had a long talk. It was the beginning of a friendship.

On my arrival in New York in April I bade farewell to my friends. Sir Francis Evans, the British Consul-General, gave me lunch, Countess Mercati gathered for a farewell tea Lady Ribblesdale, Mrs. Vanderbilt, Mrs. Murray Crane, the Marchesa Sommi-Picenardi, Mrs. Harrison Williams and others.

I sailed on the *Queen Mary*. The boat was in great disorder for she had recently been a troop ship. I had friends on board, Sir Thomas and Lady Beecham, young Jeremy, Mr. and Mrs. Schnabel, Sir John Dashwood, my neighbour at High Wycombe, and the pretty, widowed Marchioness of Hartington, the Joseph Kennedys' daughter, whom I had met at Palm Beach. There seemed to be a doom upon the Kennedy family. The young Marquess of Hartington had fallen madly in love with her. He defied his father, the Duke of Devonshire, anti-Catholic, and she defied her father, strongly Catholic. Their marriage in 1942 was an idyll. Her brother Joseph was best man at the wedding. Then in 1944 Hartington was killed in France and her brother killed on a flying mission. When we met on board

Fate had not done with her. The handsome, rich, Lord Fitzwilliam fell in love with her. They were a glamorous pair but, a Roman Catholic, she would not agree to his divorcing his wife to marry her. In 1948, flying together, they were killed in an air crash.

On board, Sir Thomas had a birthday party. There was a large cake. A piano was moved into the state-room and both Schnabel and he played. We also had on board a number of war *embusqués*, young 'Oxford Groupers', returning from California, nervous of a demonstration when they landed.

On a perfect spring morning, at 7 a.m. we approached Southampton. As we rounded the Isle of Wight and Carisbrooke Castle I could hardly see for tears. My friend Duncan Macpherson met me with his car. Thus, on a day of spring's perfection I came home. We left for my cottage at Henley through bomb-scarred Southampton and the lush, green countryside. England in her springtide blossom and leafiness enchanted me until that great moment when I stood before the gate of Pilgrim Cottage. Isled on its emerald lawn, it smiled as if to say, "Look, I have survived it all!" Above the garden well the russet tree was a snow-storm of blossom whose petals, wind stirred, fell on me like a benediction.

Alas, I began to find the cottage inexpressibly sad. There were too many ghosts of lost happiness; young Pat Southby, beautiful Nadja Malacrida, smiling Ethel, gallant Louis, my Lucien, gay Tony and his lovely sister, Ann. They were in the house and the garden, woven into the tapestry of my life.

III

I found the cottage in a disastrous state. I had let it to a neighbour who wished to leave his large unworkable house on the outbreak of the war. Something had gone wrong with him. His wife went off with his chauffeur, he frightened the woman who came in to do for him with talk of suicide. He smashed a beautiful Copenhagen china tiger I had been given in Denmark. He went off for long periods, leaving the cottage unheated through the winter, so that many pictures and dozens of books were mildewed. When he turned on the heating the frozen radiators cracked. A current of water from upstairs fiendishly trickled along the bookshelves downstairs. Many of the books were art volumes. Their pages stuck together, they had to be destroyed. But who was I to complain? Others had lost their treasures and homes and lives with the bombing.

My new housekeeper arrived, my Salzburg acquaintance, Giulietta Anatrella, a name meaning 'the duckling'. She was the most extraordinary woman. Born in New York, she had one sister who felt superior because she had been born in London and had a British passport. Giulietta was almost a hunchback, with a voice like a corncrake's. She had mysterious seizures which I suspected were epileptic. On these occasions she locked herself in her bedroom. When she appeared the next morning and I asked if she was better she would say, "Better? What do you mean? I've never been ill!" She had the courage of a lion and was a dynamo of energy. She was extremely well-read, but a romanticist, so that I never knew when she was speaking the truth. She suggested using my car to do her shopping in Henley. When I asked her if she could drive she said she had driven a Daimler for years, belonging to a friend in Florence. Her sister, who 'lived in sin' with a lawyer, in a sixteenth-century house at Arcetri, reputed to have the ghost of Galileo, taught English in the most exclusive college for girls, in Florence. When I asked her how good Giulietta was at driving a car, she said, "She's never driven a car in her life. She would be a menace!"

Her husband had been a bank manager in Paris after Florence. She told me that they had befriended Modigliani the artist. He had made a drawing of her. She found it so awful that she gave it to the Uffizi Gallery. This proved true. There was much talk of her son, tall, handsome. It was a mystery how anyone with so warped a body could have given birth to a child. Her son, she said, had disappeared in Russia, where he was taken prisoner, fighting in the Italian army. I never believed in that son, but at the end of her life he turned up, with a German wife. He had been living in Hamburg after a Polish and a Russian gaol. It was a triumphant ending for Giulietta. He bought her clothes and made her an allowance. She talked much of a teashop she had once run with a friend in Florence and rattled off the names of various royalties she knew who had been customers. She knew the ex-Queen of Rumania very well, and the parents of Prince Philip. One day, meeting Queen Helen at lunch, I hesitantly mentioned Giulietta's name and was astonished when the Queen, her face smiling, said,

"Oh, have you news of Giulietta? Do tell me about her. What a character!"So that was true.

She fell passionately in love with Pilgrim Cottage and I sometimes wondered if I or she owned it. The same thing happened when I bought a villa in Italy. But she developed a tiresome complex. When she was in the cottage she longed for the villa, when she was in the villa she longed for the cottage. Fluent in languages, a born *raconteuse*, she would sometimes take charge of the conversation with my foreign guests whose language she spoke. After ten years I had to part with her. I gave her a small pension. She was a cork, and in a hundred extremities that had marked her life she always floated to the surface. I was not at all surprised when I discovered her, later, running for a lady an apartment in Eaton Square, of whom and of which she had taken complete charge. When, away in Florida one year, my Christmas cheque was delayed in the mail, she wrote me an angry letter from a hospital bed. "You don't really care what happens to your poor Giulietta, who has wasted her life on you!" A month later she had received the cheque. "You are an angel, your old Giulietta knows you will never fail her." I failed her at the end. Abroad, I could not get to her deathbed in hospital at Bognor Regis, and missed the funeral her son came over from Germany to give her. Such was the housekeeper who ran my cottage.

After a week Lady Cunard telephoned, inviting me to dinner. She occupied a suite on the seventh floor of the Dorchester Hotel, to which she had gone on her arrival from New York. During the bombing she had refused to go with others down to the air-raid shelter or to sleep there. She went about fearlessly. Her apartment had a long room overlooking Hyde Park. She dined at one end of this salon which was filled with the furniture she had retrieved from her bombed house on the corner of Grosvenor Square. It was an amazing room, with French commodes, Buhl cabinets, Louis Seize chairs, Sèvres vases, busts and bibelots. All the trappings of a wealth she no longer had were displayed here. For, financially pressed, she had sold her jewellery. The emeralds were now paste. She soon had a coterie, mostly of smart young men. With her was her faithful Scotch maid, Gordon. I had a dinner appointment that evening, so I went in about ten o'clock and found half a dozen friends, Lord Kemsley, Mrs. Keppel, etc., sitting at her dining-table. We greeted one another joyously. The conversation rippled as always in her vivacious presence. About eleven o'clock a tall, thin man came in, Sir Archibald Clark Kerr. He had just been created Lord Inverchapel. A man in the sixties, a diplomat, he had served in Chile, Stockholm, China and Moscow. He had now been appointed Halifax's successor in Washington. That morning he had received his credentials from the King. He was sailing the next day for America. Emerald pointed to me. "There's the man you should take with you. He did wonderful work for Lord Halifax. He knows America inside out." I protested. "After the way I have been treated, never again, Emerald!" I said. "It is your duty Don't be peevish!" she retorted.

Inverchapel stayed only a few minutes. He had much to do. As he rose to leave, Emerald said to us, "Now go and have a talk and arrange matters." There was a small hall, and I followed Inverchapel out. We were both a little overwhelmed by Emerald's insistence. We knew nothing of each other. Moreover, I had no desire to engage myself in another frustrating business. I was returning to the U.S.A., next winter, but I wanted to have a rest among friends there and to write in peace in Florida. We had a hurried conversation. He asked me if I would be able to help him, and foolishly I said I would. With that he left. I said I would write to him. Later I wrote to say I would place my services at his disposal for a trial period of six months, but I must make one firm stipulation, that I should be allowed by the Treasury at least forty dollars a day, of my own money. My services would be wholly honorary, as before. He replied that he quite understood my position.

When next I lunched with Emerald I did not mention that I had dined with Sir Thomas Beecham. Her deep wound had not healed. I told her she had pushed me into something I did not like, with Inverchapel. She lectured me severely. It was my duty to go. At lunch she exhibited her old form. Her company was varied and eclectic, Peter Quennell, the author, Lady Abdy, Lord Winster, Lady Carrington, Mrs. Daisy Fellowes, Lady Diana Duff Cooper, eight of us, all told.

The next day I had an ordeal in front of me. I was lunching at the Carlton Grill with my ebullient publisher, Percy Hodder-Williams of Hodder and Stoughton. Their premises had been bombed three times. They had never once reported this to me. I had gone to lunch with the purpose of breaking the news that I was going over to Macmillans, the publishers. I rather dreaded the ordeal. Mr. Percy had been a wonderful force behind me. At coffee, before I could summon the opening sentence, he won the first round. He took out a cheque and gave it to me. It was an advance of £2,000 on *And So To America*, to be published in the autumn. "Now you're back you'll be wanting money. I wish you'd draw your accumulated royalties, about £10,000," he said. It had been taxed at source. The last thing I wanted just then was blocked money. I thanked him and put the cheque in my wallet. I tried a new opening. I said how sorry I was to learn of their repeated bombings. I hoped the business had not suffered. "No, but I must now replan its future," he said, quietly. Then seeing the query on my face he added, "My boy was killed. He would have succeeded me." I found words somehow, but not the words I had come to say. They could never be said. It was the end of the Macmillan business. He would remain my publisher until after his death, and his brother Ralph's death.

We went out into the busy street. I thanked him for the lunch. He took a taxi. Poor man. He retired next year and died soon after. Replying to my letter of condolence to his brother who was taking his place, Ralph wrote, "You know you were his favourite author. He was always excited and confident about you and, business apart, he had both pride in and affection for you."

CHAPTER SEVENTEEN

The British Treasury

I

Dear reader, this chapter can be skipped. It is a story of intransigence, frustration and arrogant bureaucracy. A man with a grievance is apt to be a bore, looking for a sympathetic audience; the grit in his shoe lames him for life. I have shaken the grit out of mine but I feel that the record should be made. You need not read it. You can pass from this dreary story to the final chapter called 'Sunshine'.

I decided to approach the Treasury and try to get some settlement over the money that should have been transmitted to me. I had only requested, throughout my work in America, twenty dollars a day from my own funds. The estimate was too low, my expenses became nearer fifty dollars a day. A dollar remittance had repeatedly been requested, by various officials who wished to retain my services. It was repeatedly refused, although I discovered that quite a number of persons had been receiving forty dollars a day. I expressed surprise when Valentine Williams, the novelist of 'Clubfoot' fame, told me that he and his wife had been drawing this sum. He remarked, "Ah, my boy, you don't go about it the right way. You must know the right people."

Having tabulated some facts and figures, with a mass of correspondence that had accumulated on the subject between me and the Ministry and Treasury officials, fifty-nine letters in all, I called on June 18 at the Treasury and asked to see someone who could deal with my case. A young woman interviewed me, cool, precise, probably a Girton graduate. After I had outlined my case she said, talking to me like a typist under notice (in days when a man dared give notice to his typist), "Have you anyone, official, who could say what you had done in America?" I was dumb for a few moments and then replied. "You have only to ask the Ministry of Information, who must have a

399

hundred reports and letters from me." With an icy smile she said, "The Ministry of Information doesn't now exist. You have mentioned Lord Halifax, Mr. Brendan Bracken, and a Minister, Sir Gerald Campbell. It would help if they would write letters to us, endorsing your claim." I said I thought it extraordinary that I should have to bother these gentlemen. There must be plenty of documents on the Treasury files. I had seen half a dozen of their representatives in Washington, and got nowhere. Nevertheless, I agreed to send in a statement and to get letters endorsing my claim.

It took me six weeks to write the statement, with documentation. It occupied fourteen pages. Lord Halifax wrote:

> Most gladly will I bear testimony to the value of the work you did in U.S. for the cause of better understanding, and in a variety of ways of the British cause and viewpoint.
>
> I had plenty of occasions to appreciate the worth of your contribution to Anglo-American relations, and of course the British cause reaped benefit from it. I should certainly hope that with the endorsement of your work which can most rightly be given, the Treasury would feel able to place you in a position of clearing these difficult financial questions away.

Good, but there was no mention of the service I had rendered him personally. Sir Gerald Campbell, Minister in Washington, replied at some length.

> I am sorry to learn that you are still striving to obtain the allowance which you consider due to you for the years you worked in the U.S.A. I have never known exactly why you did not receive this, but I know that during the years of the war you spent money and time explaining the issues of the war to Americans for I heard from various admirers in different parts of the country that they had listened to you with interest and profit. That this sort of work needed doing was never in doubt, and the number of those who could do it without offending American susceptibilities was pitifully small. So I have no hesitation in writing you up as an asset.
>
> I am also grateful to you for the kind and generous way in which you responded from time to time to my appeals for information which would help to make my addresses more acceptable to American audiences through the introduction of items of local or national interest. I know you had to undertake research in order to supply me with such details.

Brendan Bracken was even more forthcoming:

Here is the letter. I must say I think you have been very badly treated. When I was at the Ministry of Information I had the best of reasons for knowing that few men worked more effectively for Britain in the United States than you.

If Mr. Churchill's Government had been re-elected we should certainly have tried to persuade you to accept some recognition.

The letter he wrote for me ran:

Mr. Cecil Roberts had enjoyed for many years in the United States a wide audience for his books and lectures. When the war broke out he was encouraged by the British authorities to remain in America, for it was generally felt that by so doing he could render great help to our cause.

British propaganda or publicity in the United States was a delicate and difficult matter in those days. As Mr. Roberts was already a familiar and well-accepted figure there, he escaped the reproach of being an imported British propagandist. He had his audiences ready-made, and he could speak for England without seeming to be a British agent. There were, indeed, few Britons on the spot who combined his talents for the task with his freedom from official handicaps. His writings and speeches undoubtedly contributed to that marked rallying of sympathy and support which was of priceless benefit to our cause during the blackest days.

A spontaneous propagandist such as Mr. Roberts, who drew no funds from His Majesty's Government but paid his own way, and provided dividends of friendship for us by his exertions, possesses a value to Government which surely is not exhausted by the ending of the war.

I added a letter from Robin Cruikshank, soon to be editor of the *News Chronicle*, a former Assistant Director at the Ministry.

It was a great asset to have someone there like yourself with your combination of literary gifts and command of the platform, to champion the ideals of our country. You were free from the sad limitations of an official person and had that privilege and authority of expression which is denied to mere propagandists.

On July 29 I sent in these letters to the Treasury, accompanied by a list of the repeated applications officially made on my behalf and repeatedly refused. I appended a financial statement of my expenses, living, secretarial, travel, etc., for six years and a half. I had borrowed from an American friend, without interest, $50,000 which I now sought to repay. I had sent to England from the sale of my American securities, $52,000, plus some $20,000 cash. Had I been allowed to draw from my blocked English money the equivalent of $40 a day, the 'business man's allowance', given to others, I should have received $94,000. I had given the British Government, free, six and a half years' service, paying all my expenses. Had I attended to my own business as an author I should have earned in that period at least $200,000. I now requested from the Treasury the release of my blocked sterling to the equivalent of $72,000.

In the course of my time in America, I had made 500 speeches in some forty-four States. I had also worked for the U.S. Treasury in their War Bonds Campaign, for which I had received their official thanks. I had worked for more than twenty organisations devoted to British interests, with the result that I had a dossier of over two hundred letters of thanks. I had written eighty reports to the Ministry of Information, and for four years had supplied American data for the British Ambassador's and the British Minister's speeches.

This was my case. I made no claim for physical wear and tear, and official harassment which had resulted in a breakdown that was to afflict me for the rest of my life. I sent in my statement, requesting the Treasury to give it early attention as I was returning to the United States, to attend to business, in October next. I made no mention of the Inverchapel proposal, as this had arisen later.

II

Through June and July I enjoyed once more the delights of an English summer. I gardened, I walked through the beechwoods, I gossiped 'on the lawn of Phyllis Court during the Regatta, which I found a little sad, so many faces had vanished since the last Regatta of 1939. There were fireworks on Saturday night, as formerly, but no Allinghams. Seddon Cripps, now Lord Parmoor, stayed with me, as in the old days. He was as jovial and full of good sense as ever. During the war he had let Parmoor to King Zog, who, with his beautiful Queen and entourage, departed when King Farouk of Egypt offered him hospitality. Seddon found the house and estate too large to manage; also he had to live mostly at Oxford, being the Bursar of Queen's College, so he sold Parmoor.

At the end of July I went to Knole to spend the weekend with Lord and Lady Sackville. A bomb had shattered four hundred windows of this noble pile. Now there was servant trouble. "We are living in four rooms," said my hostess. Knole covered four acres, had seven court-yards, one for each day of the week, fifty-two staircases, one for each week of the year, and three hundred-and-sixty-five bedrooms, one for each day of the year. I trembled to think what would become of this magnificent place. The son and heir was settling in Ireland. My host was a handsome man of seventy-six. In the course of conversa-tion there was a singular link with Kitty Rothschild. Our talk turned to the Duchess of Sutherland, who had just left. She owned a part of the famous diamond necklace ordered by Cardinal Rohan for Marie Antoinette. Lady Sackville owned another part, Baroness Rothschild a third part. One evening in Paris the three ladies dined together so that they were able to have a complete necklace and to wear it in turn. Lord Sackville's share was now part of her peeress's coronet.

The next weekend William Armstrong of the Liverpool Repertory, who had produced my ill-fated play, *Spears Against Us*, stayed with me. Then the garden gate opened and young John Smyth came down the path. A passionate gardener, no flower bed had been safe from his marauding hands in the pre-war years. Since then, a pro-fessional soldier, he had come safely through service in France, the Norway invasion, campaigns in Iran and Egypt and was now joining our occupying army in Trieste.

And so came September, the time drawing nigh for my departure. Since I had sent in my statement to the Treasury on July 29 there had been silence. On September 17, in answer to a letter of mine pressing for a decision, they had rung up my cottage to say I should shortly hear from them. I heard nothing, so I wrote on September 24 to say I would call on the 27th at 11 a.m. as I was leaving for America shortly. It seems they had answered on the 25th but their letter just missed me, I being in town. It said, "No useful purpose would be served by your calling. We shall not fail to notify you when a decision has been reached." But eight weeks had gone and I was sailing soon. So I called at the Treasury and sent in my card to Mr. T., who was dealing with the matter. In a few minutes an office boy came back to the enquiry desk to say Mr. T. could not see me. Yes, he was in, but could not see me. I could hardly believe my ears. I told the youth to go back again and tell Mr. T. that, as I was in the office, I would like to see him. He went back and returned saying, "You can't see Mr. T."

Once or twice in one's lifetime there are things happen so incredible that you cannot believe them. This was one of them. All over the world I had been courteously received by presidents, ambassadors, governors, admirals and generals, and here was a Treasury clerk refusing to see me, by the voice of an office boy. I walked to my club for lunch, humiliated by this underling dressed in a little brief authority.

But I had not yet touched the nadir of this business. In August I had asked my bank, Lloyds, to obtain for me from the Bank of England a dollar allowance for my coming visit to U.S.A. My bank replied, "They are not at the moment in a position to discuss with you your future requirements for Foreign Exchange as your case is being investigated by the Treasury, following your recent approach to them." I knew that the Bank of England was the minion of the Treasury, but my case with the latter had nothing whatever to do with my request to the Bank for a business man's quota of dollars. I told my bank manager that this simply would not do. I must insist on seeing the Bank of England in the matter. So an appointment was made for me, on this same day of my visit to the Treasury. "Mr. Y, of the Foreign Currency Control, will be pleased to see you," reported Lloyds.

I lunched, still not quite myself. On arrival at the Bank I was shown into an empty room. Presently two gentlemen came in, one with a dossier in his hand. I explained that my request for dollars had nothing whatever to do with my transaction with the Treasury. I was sailing to the United States in October to settle business with my publishers and attend to my affairs. I was therefore applying for what I understood was the allowance of forty dollars a day for business men.

Mr. Y, who had an unpleasant resemblance to Mr. Molotov of U.S.S.R., *Nyet! Nyet!* fame, did all the talking. His companion seemed slightly ashamed of him. He began to question me about my

404

time in America. What had I earned there, and had I transmitted it to the United Kingdom? I said that I had not transmitted any earnings, like others I had used them to avoid starvation. I was not an emigrant mother with a child, being kept by generous Americans, I was an unpaid agent of the British Government. Anyhow, this was not the business on which I had come. I wanted a dollar allowance for my forthcoming journey. "You have broken the law in not transmitting your earnings," said Mr. Y. "In that case," I retorted, "you should prosecute me. I will very willingly go into court."

Mr. Y. changed his tactics. He did not consider that an author had the status of a business man and the allowance of dollars did not apply. "Then I seem for many years to have been paying tax and super-tax on an illegitimate business!" I observed. At this point the silent colleague emitted a few soothing words. They would consider my application and let me know. I got up and said, "I hope your decision will be favourable, and quick. Let me repeat, my case with the Treasury has nothing to do with this transaction. And, if I had known I was going to be cross-examined by two of you I should have brought with me my solicitor." "We will write to you," reiterated Mr. Y. They never wrote. I sailed without a dollar.

I returned to my cottage and from the worry of all this had a nervous collapse and was in bed three days. I had learned from my old friend Sir Norman Birkett that he and 'Billy', his adorable wife, were sailing to America, the guest of the American Bar, in the great new Cunard liner, *Queen Elizabeth*. She was making her maiden trip as a 'civilian', hoping to recapture the Blue Riband of the Atlantic. There was a tremendous Press build-up. "Why don't you sail with us?" asked Norman. I discovered that every berth had been taken. I went to see the official at the Foreign Office who controlled sailing priorities to ask if he could do anything for me. He received me with courtesy. Later he wrote, "I find that the priority position has changed recently and that we are no longer able to intervene but I am furnishing you with a letter showing that we are interested in your journey. I am afraid this is all we can do to help you." The letter enclosed ran—"The Foreign Office is interested in Mr. Roberts's journey and would wish every proper facility to be given to him in obtaining a passage on the *Queen Elizabeth* on October 16." Cunard informed me that the best they could do at this late date was to give me a berth in a two-berth cabin, second class, in which to sleep, and I could eat in and use the first class accommodation. I accepted this.

In my last ten days in England I had two public engagements. I went to Southport to give a lecture in a 'Celebrity Lectures' series, and I took the chair at a Foyle's Lunch to introduce the speaker, Lord Tredegar. He was *méchant*, as so often. He changed his announced subject and bored the audience by reading a lecture he had given elsewhere, on Donne the poet. I took Lady Cunard with me. "What a dreary bore Evan was—and he can be so bright!" was her comment. I scolded him for his behaviour. We could not know that he would die within three years of lung cancer, at the age of fifty-five. It was a loss; he was a vivid, bizarre personality.

Before I sailed I received a cable from Baron Eugene de Rothschild. His beloved Kitty had died very suddenly of a cerebral haemorrhage while sitting by the library fire. I remembered all her kindness to me, her beauty, her thoughtfulness during my convalescence. Still House had lost its radiance. My return to America had been full of the hope of seeing her again and staying in that lovely home where, after losses in Vienna and Paris, she had conjured up a new enchantment of hospitality.

On my penultimate day at Pilgrim Cottage, which I loaned to a friend for the winter, in Giulietta's charge, Lady Abingdon came to lunch, as beautiful as ever. We went over old times in our New York work. I motored to Southampton. We sailed at 2 p.m. I found Norman and 'Billy' Birkett on board, and also another eminent lawyer, Sir Hartley Shawcross, the Attorney-General, leading a deputation to a meeting in New York of the U.N. Assembly. They had been together at the International Military Tribunal which sat at Nuremberg in 1945 and 1946. In the next three days I heard from them the inside story of the trial. There was also on board a most agreeable young couple, Lord and Lady Birkenhead, whom I knew. There was one sinister figure, the grim Mr. Molotov, also proceeding to the U.N. meeting in order to say *Nyet ! Nyet !* and put a spoke in the wheel. He hardly ever appeared. The corridor in which his cabin was situated was guarded at each end by Russian soldiers armed with pistols.

On the second day out I gave Norman a copy of my Treasury statement to read. I had sailed without receiving any answer to it. The next morning he returned the statement to me. "It is one of the most disgraceful stories I think I have ever read. If I had still been a counsel instead of a judge I would have had a field day in court with this!" We discussed it in detail. He thought I had understated the record. "Surely one of those fellows at the top, Halifax, Bracken, Duff Cooper, Gerald Campbell, Alex Cadogan, who entertained you, should have taken your case in hand and settled it in a few days. All this duplicity and subterfuge over a few thousand dollars that would cost them nothing. And the insolent behaviour of that Treasury official!" He asked me to show the document to Shawcross. We all dined together that evening in the Observation Grill. The next morning I discussed my case with Shawcross, sitting in adjacent deck-chairs. Lady Birkett, a skilled photographer, took a photo of us and wrote on it, 'Conference between plaintiff and his counsel'. Shawcross said he was willing to raise the matter in the House of Commons. I had two objections to this course. In the first place I had not yet had an answer from the Treasury. Secondly, what I had done for Halifax and Campbell had been under a self-imposed seal of secrecy. I did not feel it right that this should be publicised, it being a very personal service on my part. He agreed. "But if you get no justice in the matter I feel you are entitled to take action, since they seem to have done nothing to put this mean business straight," he said. He would act whenever I wished. I thanked him. I remember his offer with gratitude.

III

On arrival in New York I went back to my old room, which I had sublet during my absence. The next morning with my mail came a letter from the Treasury, forwarded from my cottage.

Sir,
  I have laid before the Lord Commissioners of His Majesty's Treasury the memorandum contained in your letter of July 29 last, regarding the expenses of your stay in the U.S.A. during the war. In reply I am to state that, after full consideration, My Lords are unable to allow your request to transfer $72,633 to the U.S.A. . . .
  I am to add that emigrants to places outside the sterling area are, subject to certain conditions, allowed to transfer a certain

amount of their capital in instalments, over a number of years, after which they may be designated as resident outside the United Kingdom and allowed to receive the income of the balance of their capital remaining in the United Kingdom . . .

So rather than meet a moral obligation and return to me my dollars to enable me to discharge my debt, and admit their past delinquency, My Lords of The Treasury suggested I should emigrate! They had probably never seen my memorandum but the bureaucrats who operated behind this high-sounding façade, in the spirit of the official who had refused to see me, were not going to concede anything. I already knew the emigration terms. You received £5,000 of your capital in four annual payments of £1,250, after which you could receive the interest only of your blocked invested capital. I found the proposition as mean as it was insolent. My first impulse was to call on Sir Hartley Shawcross, show him the letter and ask him to go ahead. But by this time I was exhausted and sick of the whole wretched business. I had to preserve such tranquility of mind as I could and get on with my creative work. My generous American friend to whom I owed $50,000 told me not to worry, I could settle my debt when the Exchange Control was taken off and one was free to use one's capital. I did not answer the Treasury letter. I wanted nothing to do with them, but there was one thing more. In 1940 the Chancellor of the Exchequer had invited the public to make free loans to the Government for the duration of the war. I lent £9,000. The war was over and I did not feel disposed to continue my loan, so I instructed my bank to ask for repayment. This was made, without one word of thanks.

I wrote to Lord Inverchapel in Washington, saying that in view of the Treasury's reply I must withdraw my offer to him. The following March, when I lunched with him at the British Embassy, he said that he regretted it had not been possible to carry out our proposal. I had no regrets and was glad to be rid of any obligation.

IV

Before leaving for Palm Beach, to stay with Mrs. Beatrice Cartwright, I saw my American publisher and visited my friends. I lunched with Alec Waugh, who lived at the Algonquin Hotel, and had cocktails with the Birkenheads at the Plaza. They both gave me

surprising news. Alec was drawing the 'business man's' allowance of
$40 a day, and Lord Rothermere maintained a suite of six rooms in
the Plaza! It was the most expensive hotel in New York. Later
Lady Scarsdale, swimming in my hostess's pool, informed me that
on the prompting of Lord Horder, her doctor, she had been given
£5,000 for exchange. As Williams had remarked, I had not gone the
right way about it.

I lunched with Sir Francis Evans, our Consul-General, and booked
a return passage to England for next April. I spoke at the Dutch
Treat Club, said goodbye to the Birkenheads, and went down to
Still House to see Baron de Rothschild, very shaken by Kitty's
death. He took me to her grave, which he visited every day. He talked
of turning the house into a memorial convent, which would please
Kitty, who had died a devout Catholic. I dined with the Duke and
Duchess of Windsor in their suite at the Waldorf Astoria Hotel. My
typist, Miss Joy, brought me some script. Wasn't I going to write
another novel? It was three years since I had published one. I told
her I had started, had written twenty pages in Pilgrim Cottage, then
had stopped, but I hoped to write in Palm Beach. Then one day,
picking up a newspaper, I read paralysing news. The British Government was making Exchange Control permanent! In fighting for
liberty we had lost it. An Englishman's money was never to be his
own, to use as he wished. He was freer in the time of George III than
George VI. It marked the triumph of bureaucracy. I faced a grave
problem. The prospect of paying off my debt had vanished, since all
foreign income had to be transmitted to the Bank of England.
Emigration now seemed the only way out of the trap. If I emigrated
the Treasury would have no claim to my foreign earnings. I could then
pay off my debt with my American royalties, but it would take time.

I was in no mood to make a decision. On my last day in New York
I lunched at Mrs. Crane's, took tea with Mrs. Vanderbilt, and dined
with Mrs. Boehm. What hospitable friends they had been. Then, on
December 22, I caught the night train to Palm Beach. I had not
written a line of my new novel in three months. I felt I was going to
pieces. I vowed to work at Palm Beach and return to England in
April with the novel written. No one realises how a writer, a man
without office hours, has to discipline himself.

Let me finish, anticipating the calendar, the Treasury affair and then return to a pleasanter subject. When I informed Brendan Bracken of the result of my application, he replied:

I am disappointed by your news about the Treasury's response to your legitimate request. If you were an inhabitant of the Balkans, under Communist patronage, you would certainly have got more than sixty thousand dollars out of the Songster in the Treasury!

In England, I showed the Treasury letter to my solicitor. He said, "You know what Lord Justice Goddard has written about bureaucratic tyranny? He has told us that freedom is dead. Take them at their word—get out! You are a fortunate fellow in that you can earn your living anywhere. There are plenty of authors who have got out— Somerset Maugham, Max Beerbohm, Aldous Huxley, Francis Brett Young, Nevil Shute, James Hilton, Cronin, Noël Coward. They breathe a freer air, while no less British in sentiment. Shelley, Byron, Gibbon, Keats, Landor, Browning, were never troubled by Exchange Control."

Commenting on the requisition of British subjects' dollar holdings, *The Economist* observed, "It is an act of injustice towards one section of the public. When national needs demand the requisition of a subject's assets the refund of these should be the first charge upon the national exchequer when the war ends."

The Government had made a mess of it. They had sold millions of dollars of securities before it occurred to them that they could place these holdings as a collateral and borrow on them, without sacrificing them at knockdown prices. The pounds I had received in exchange were blocked, and twice devalued.

There were a few souls who challenged the Treasury. Some were frightened by its threats. Anyone who signed a cheque for £5, to enable him to have an extra day's holiday abroad, was hauled into court and fined, despite the fact that he was spending his own money. Noël Coward, who must have earned and been taxed on a million dollars, was fined for leaving a few dollars in his American account. Yet his film, *In Which We Serve*, did as much for British prestige in U.S.A. as ever Churchill achieved with one of his great broadcasts. It took thirty years for him to be sufficiently redeemed to get a knighthood at seventy. Sir Thomas Beecham would not be browbeaten. "They can go to Hell. I'll spend my money where I earn it."

They left him alone. One day a friend of mine, Sir Wilfrid Greene, the Master of the Rolls, arrived in New York. He had been invited to address the American Bar Association. I called on him at his hotel. I mentioned my difficulties. "You don't surprise me at all," he said. "My dear fellow, you can't imagine what petty tyrants those Treasury nabobs are! Just before I left I asked them for a modest thousand dollars for my expenses here. What do you think they said? No, I must get the Americans to entertain me. I was to sponge on them! I sent my clerk round to say that if he did not come back with a chit for a thousand dollars I would cancel the visit. I got the dollars. Some little jack-in-office thinks he's the nation's watch-dog. And how good are they at it? When the war broke out they put an embargo on the export of shares and money, but they were too late. When they shut the stable doors the horses had gone. The wise boys knew all about it, and millions had left the country."

I had been a dollar-earner for twenty years. I had paid heavy British income-tax as well as American. When a ballet company earned a few thousand dollars it got a congratulatory telegram from the Chancellor of the Exchequer on arriving home. I know of no dollar-earning author who ever had such a telegram.

In 1949 there was a tragi-comedy created by the British Treasury. There was an old lady of ninety, Mrs. Maitland-Tennant, who had in her New York pre-war bank account the sum of $117,000, then about £30,000. She declined to surrender her dollars. She lived near Edinburgh, behind barbed-wire fences and padlocked gates. She refused to see anybody. They could not serve a writ on her. All mail had to be left at the lodge. 'The Black Lady', as she was known, was inaccessible. She went out in a carriage with drawn blinds. The Treasury did not relish dragging into court an old lady of ninety, and sending her to prison. All they need have done was to wait, and soon at death the money would have fallen into their hands, dutiable at that. The Treasury decided to sue her American bank, the Bankers Trust Company, to make them give up their client's money. In case Mrs. Maitland-Tennant sued her bank for handing over her deposit, the Treasury offered an indemnity to the bank against any such action! This high-handed proceeding set the American banking community up in arms. A New York banker observed to me, "Who do they think we are? Let them try it on with a Swiss bank and see where they get! Their action undermines the whole probity of banking in this country."

Some of us have spent our lives in promoting Anglo-American unity. For a paltry $117,000, owned by an old lady of ninety, the Treasury was prepared to arouse intense opposition from Americans, who regarded the whole business as a piece of British arrogance.

Will all this be repeated, at infinite cost, in a new crisis? Mr. Nicholas Davenport, financial editor of the *Spectator*, observed in 1956, "The Treasury can always borrow as a last resort on the dollar securities held by U.K. residents. Please note that I say 'borrow'; there is no need to repeat the grossly unfair sequestration of dollar securities of the last war." And Mr. Graham Hutton, another financial authority, in the same paper, drew attention to a fallacy. "The French buy bar gold. The British and others set up companies abroad, or shunt goods, or other assets, about in the sterling area, eventually finding a loophole. The whole trading world prefers dollars, German marks, or Swiss or Belgian francs, or gold or equity shares in companies in these lands, to being confined and controlled and probably devaluated or expropriated in their home currency." Have we learnt a lesson, or shall we still pursue old ladies of ninety, or drive one, who gives his services, freely to his country, into a hospital with a duodenal ulcer, or to emigrate?

v

In the summer of 1957 I went to spend the weekend with my friend, Sir Norman Birkett. I found him fuming. "Have you read this book?" he asked. He passed me a copy of Lord Halifax's autobiography, *Fulness of Days*, just published. I had not read it. "He hands out bouquets to his friend Peake who, he says, wrote his early speeches, and to others who helped, mostly the Foreign Office coterie he surrounded himself with, but there's not a single mention of what you did. You're not even in the index. What base ingratitude!" I read the book that evening. It was a smooth performance, a little *de haut en bas*, very short, full of squirarchal activities, with a few anecdotes. One of these was his famous retort when an Isolationist threw some eggs at him. "They are lucky to have eggs to throw around when in England we get only one a month." This was much relished, but he did not say it. It was an invention of the Press Office. Wisely he accepted paternity. When he sailed home in May, 1946, the feeling about him was warmer. A son had been killed in North Africa and another had had his legs blown off. He sustained these blows with admirable fortitude, and his later speeches had won favour.

In 1954 I was the guest of Dr. A. L. Rowse at All Souls College, for the *Encaenia*. I saw Lord Halifax go in procession, gowned as the Chancellor of Oxford University. In the afternoon there was a garden-party at Trinity College. We greeted each other on the lawn. I wondered if he would ask whether I had had a satisfactory settlement with the Treasury, but he made no mention of this, and I passed on.

In 1965 Lord Birkenhead published his biography of Halifax. When I learned he was engaged on this I wrote saying I would be happy to place at his disposal my dossier in connection with the work I had done for the Ambassador. We had a correspondence. "I must thank you for further details," he wrote. But when the *Life* appeared there was not a single mention of me, and, again, my name did not appear in the index. "He disliked to compose his speeches, which were done by Charles Peake, and afterwards by his secretaries, Angus Malcolm and J. G. Lockhart," observed Lord Birkenhead. "Oh these speeches, they exhaust me in preparation and bore me in delivering!" moaned Halifax. Four of his entourage received knighthoods as well as pensions.

The *Life* was a very full work, skilfully written, with a masterly treatment of the intricate Indian period, but a *Times* reviewer spotted its weakness. He called it an 'amiable biography'. It was written in 'Edward and Dorothy' terms and dedicated to the latter. I felt that despite its compass it had veered too much to the home wind.

VI

Had I been a great fool to exhaust myself and neglect my career? I sometimes felt so, but perhaps the person concerned cannot assess his work. At the end of it all a gratifying verdict was pronounced from an independent source. In May, 1954, an American friend wrote to me saying that he had heard on the New York television a discussion, by four leading journalists, of the shortcomings of the

American Information and Propaganda Services. He obtained a
transcript of the broadcast and sent it to me—

Mr. Garrity (*New York Times*) said, "The best propaganda in the
world is the British, and the most efficient expression we witnessed
were the lectures held all over the U.S.A. by the noted author, Cecil
Roberts. These lectures had never the flavour of propaganda but
brought more goodwill towards Britain than anything else."

CHAPTER EIGHTEEN

Sunshine

A few days before Christmas I left New York for Palm Beach to stay with Mrs. Cartwright. I arrived on a morning of blazing sunshine and was met at the station by Leslie, the chauffeur, with the old, up-holstered cabriolet that smelt of the camphor in which it had been stored through the summer. In fifteen minutes I was at Estella, a house in Banyan Road which lay between the ocean and an inland watercourse. I was given my former room in the tower with its superb view of the woods, ocean, lake and the swimming pool in the grounds. It was completely isolated, ideal for work. I rose early, breakfasted, and laboured for four hours with the greatest difficulty, for I was mentally tired and out of mood, but work kept my mind off the Treasury fiasco. I fought despondency and the ominous signs of the duodenal ulcer. I am a naturally happy and friendly person. A guest, I felt I had to be bright and companionable.

I had settled down to my proposed novel, *Eight for Eternity*, telling the story of eight soldiers who had died at Monte Cassino and been resurrected through meeting St. Benedict, the monastery's founder-abbot. After work I made my appearance at noon by the swimming pool. The water of this long pool, pumped from the Gulf Stream near by (70°), was of a bright emerald colour, so translucent that it seemed as if sunlight had been dissolved in it. There were dressing-rooms, with an al-fresco bar where the guests gathered for cocktails. The house party was small but it grew after Christmas. Could this be December? Here at night the fireflies flitted, a warm wind blew off the ocean, the scent of jasmine and tuberoses was overpowering. Brilliant in the sunshine, soft in the moonlight, it was an enchanted land. I found it impossible to believe that I had just come from a New York lashed with an arctic blizzard. My hostess loved parties so that I was not surprised to learn that this Christmas Eve, 1946, there was to be a dinner-dance for sixty guests. Estella was floodlit, as also the pool. There was a buffet-supper in the patio and we danced to a small orchestra into the small hours of the morning. A full moon shone, and the tall palms lifted their black, wavy plumes against the bright sky. After the dance the younger guests swam in the pool.

The day after Christmas I had a great surprise, and a great piece of luck. "A Catholic neighbour is coming for lunch and bringing two of her guests, a Monsignor and a Father," said Mrs. Cartwright. At a round table seating twelve I found myself talking to the priest. He was of Maltese birth. I asked him what he was doing here in Florida. He was the ex-librarian of the shattered monastery of Monte Cassino, and he was collecting funds for the rebuilding! Here was a mine of information that I quarried mercilessly. He told me an astonishing story about the Keats and Shelley relics that had been housed in the Keats-Shelley Museum on the Spanish Steps, in Rome. For safety's sake they had been sent to the monastery. Then, when the monastery seemed threatened with bombardment, though, he assured me, there had never been a German soldier in it, he thought it wise to take the two portmanteaux of relics back to Rome. He smiled and said, "What was amusing was that I begged a ride from the monastery into Rome in a German Staff car! If only they had known!" In Rome he took his precious material to a monastery and placed it in the charge of the Prior. When the Allies entered Rome, the curator of the Keats-Shelley Museum, Signora Vera Cacciatore, went to the monastery and retrieved the portmanteaux, which the Prior had hidden under his bed.

"You look very happy," said Mrs. Cartwright, when the guests had gone. "Happy!" I exclaimed, "Fate has brought Monte Cassino to Estella!"

On New Year's Eve I read to the family a new chapter I had written about Father Sebastian, an Englishman who had been a monk at the monastery, and then, when war broke out, had exchanged his habit for an English uniform, and died on the slopes of the Mountain.

Towards midnight a bottle of champagne was opened. This was a private, domestic celebration. We were Mrs. Cartwright, her son, Dr. Dallas Pratt, his English friend John Judkyn, our hostess's nurse, and her maid, Jeanne. After various toasts Beatrice Cartwright raised her glass again and said, "To Aubrey, in England." So we drank to her son at Eton.

I went out alone into the garden after midnight. Not a leaf in the scented air moved, the moonlit pool was a mirror. I stood looking back at the illuminated windows of the long, white villa, like sheets of gold. The palm trees seemed gigantic, the silence was absolute. I stood there in the warm night, my body in Florida but my mind in England, in that corner of the Chilterns which held my cottage. And in my mind on this New Year's Eve of 1947 I heard the bells of Henley Church ring out the Old and ring in the New, as often before, bringing memories of those I had 'loved long since and lost awhile'.

The End of the Fourth Volume of this Autobiography.

Index

Index